Ultimate .NET MAUI Projects

Design and Deploy Cross-Platform Applications with .NET MAUI Using C#, XAML, MVVM Architecture and SQLite

Raúl Pimienta

Pedro López

www.orangeava.com

First Published: August 2025

Published By: Orange Education Pvt Ltd, AVA®

Address: 9, Daryaganj, Delhi, 110002, India

275 New North Road Islington Suite 1314 London,
N1 7AA, United Kingdom

ISBN (PBK): 978-93-49888-87-6
ISBN (E-BOOK): 978-93-49888-06-7

Scan the QR code to explore our entire catalogue

www.orangeava.com

Dedicated To

My Wife, Alexa, My Cat, Tofu

And

My Beloved Parents:
Raúl
Claudia

- Raúl Pimienta

My Beloved Wife, Laura Belén

My Dear Brothers:

José de Jesús

Alondra Guadalupe,

And to My Beloved Parents:

J. Jesus

Ana Rosa

- Pedro López

About the Authors

Raúl Daniel Pimienta Ramos was born in Hermosillo, Sonora, Mexico, on June 12, 1995. He holds a degree in Information Systems Engineering from the University of Sonora.

His passion for programming began during his college days. While taking his first programming course, Raul made the decision to switch his major from Industrial and Systems Engineering to Information Systems Engineering, aligning his studies with what would become his true calling.

During his academic journey, he was fortunate to land his first job as a programmer, thanks to a professor's recommendation. In this role, he worked on an ERP system, where he was responsible for creating and maintaining pages, using Visual Basic. It was during this time that he discovered Xamarin. Forms—the tool that sparked his passion for mobile application development.

Today, Raul works with .NET MAUI, the evolution of Xamarin.Forms, and the focus of this book. He has accumulated approximately seven years of experience in the software development field, primarily using Xamarin.Forms, .NET MAUI, C#, SQL Server, the Azure platform, and Blazor for building web applications.

Throughout his career, he has worked for several internationally recognized companies, and has also contributed to various freelance projects.

Pedro Luis López Gaitan was born in Ayotlan, Jalisco Mexico on July 21, 1996. He is a computer engineer, graduated from the University Center of La Ciénega, part of the University of Guadalajara. A passionate advocate for technology and innovation, he has more than five years of experience in software development.

Pedro's passion for video games got him into the world of software development. That same enthusiasm inspired him to pursue a degree in computer engineering. Over the years, he has worked on different projects, with various technologies, such as PHP, JAVA, WEB technologies, C#, Unity. His experience spans developing web, desktop, and mobile applications—as well as video games. Pedro has worked as a full-stack developer on various applications, such as CMS, ERP, SST, and so on.

Currently, working as a semi-senior developer in .NET Framework, he has played a pivotal role in the orientation of the development of multiplatform applications, using MAUI, Blazor WebAssembly, webapi, Azure and C#.

About the Technical Reviewer

Vladyslav Yefymochkyn has a vast experience of about 9 years in mobile application development, specializing in building cross-platform solutions, using Xamarin.Native, Xamarin.Forms, .NET MAUI, and Flutter. With a Master's degree in Computer Science, Vladyslav has been passionate about creating high-performance, and maintainable mobile applications from the early days of his career.

Throughout his professional journey, Vladyslav has worked across various mobile technologies, helping companies deliver reliable and scalable mobile products. His expertise spans, both native and cross-platform development, with a strong focus on modern frameworks, such as .NET MAUI and Flutter.

Presently, Vladyslav works as a Senior/Lead Mobile Developer, where he drives technical excellence and architectural decisions in mobile projects, using .NET MAUI and Flutter. He is passionate about mobile technology, building efficient development processes, and mentoring teams to deliver high-quality, user-centric applications.

Acknowledgements

There are a few people, I want to thank for the continued and ongoing support, they have given me during the writing of this book. First and foremost, I'm deeply grateful to **my wife, Alexa**, whose unwavering support and encouragement made this book possible. Thanks also to my cat, Tofu, for the comfort and companionship during countless writing hours. Special thanks to **my parents, Raúl and Claudia**, for their unwavering support and belief in my work. I'm truly grateful to **my friend and co-author, Pedro López**, for his insights and dedication throughout this journey. Thanks to the .NET MAUI and Xamarin.Forms communities for their invaluable resources that shaped much of the content in this book. I appreciate the **technical reviewer** for his thoughtful feedback, which greatly improved the book's quality. Above all, this book was driven by my desire to share the knowledge I've gained over my career and to guide others in mastering .NET MAUI.

- Raúl Pimienta

One of my dreams has always been to write a book, and today, finally, it has become a reality. However, I did not achieve this feat alone; it was only possible–thanks to the love, support, and patience of those around me. I am truly thankful to **my wife, Laura Belén**, for her unconditional love, steady encouragement, and for taking on added responsibilities that allowed me to devote myself fully to this project. To **my parents, J. Jesus and Ana Rosa**–their love and example have been my greatest inspiration. This book wouldn't exist without them. To **my siblings, Jose de Jesus and Alondra Guadalupe**–thanks for the laughter and relief during stressful times. To **my friend and co-author, Raúl Pimienta**–his dedication made this journey unforgettable. And to Gabriel, Luis, and Eduardo–their support during tough times meant the world. To **my teachers and the institutions** that shaped me–especially the University of Guadalajara and University Center of La Ciénega–thank you for guiding my path and helping me discover my passion for software development. To the .NET MAUI community–their collective knowledge and generosity were instrumental in making this book possible. This book is for you, with all my gratitude. To the **technical reviewer**–his thoughtful feedback greatly enhanced this book's quality and clarity. Above all, this book comes from my desire to share what I've learned. .NET MAUI is complex but rewarding, and I hope it serves as a helpful companion on your journey.

- Pedro López

Preface

In this book, we will show the best practices of programming with C#, learn about XAML, explore the MVVM design pattern, review the main concepts and basics of .NET MAUI, set up test environment with emulators, or why not with real mobile devices, make requests to API'S, and much more. Hence, this book will present the best practices in the creation of cross-platform applications with .NET MAUI.

Chapter 1: Here, you will learn what .NET MAUI is, its predecessor, Xamarin. Forms, and how to properly migrate from Xamarin.Forms to .NET MAUI.

Chapter 2: In this chapter, we will see why .NET MAUI is a very good option for cross-platform application development, and the reader will be able to understand the advantages and disadvantages, as well as its architecture.

Chapter 3: This chapter explains the basic concepts of .NET MAUI that will give a better understanding of the possibilities, which we will have, when developing with this technology.

Chapter 4: Here, we will explore in detail the design patterns, more specifically MVVM, which is recommended for the app to have a correct architecture, and will also explain how to implement it in a simple and effective way.

Chapter 5: In this chapter, we will learn a little about how to use Blazor in our applications, as this will help the reuse of components between a web application made with Blazor, and a mobile application made with .NET MAUI.

Chapter 6: This chapter deals with how SQL Lite works, and how to connect to an API which is very useful in any application that you want to create. This is because a large percentage of these have to connect to an API, either to obtain or store information, the reader will have the best tips and practices to do in the most correct way.

Chapter 7: This will see you through several tips and best practices, regarding libraries, c#, improve the performance of an application, and learn more in detail, the best components offered by .NET MAUI.

Chapters 8 to 11: These will dive into creating applications in specific areas, such as E-Commerce in which we will incorporate in detail the purchase flow, an ERP that will have modules, such as sales, purchasing, customers and suppliers, as well as a social media, with instant messaging service, and an educational application in which you will see how to run a modern course-based online learning application.

Get a Free eBook

We hope you are enjoying your recently purchased book! Your feedback is incredibly valuable to us, and to all other readers looking for great books.

If you found this book helpful or enjoyable, we would truly appreciate it, if you could take a moment to leave a short review with a 5 star rating on Amazon. It helps us grow, and lets other readers discover our books.

As a thank you, we would love to send you a free digital copy of this book, and a **30%** discount code on your next cart value on our official websites:

www.orangeava.com

www.orangeava.in (For Indian Subcontinent)

☑ **Here's how:**

Leave a review for the book on Amazon.

Take a screenshot of your review, and send an email to **info@orangeava.com** (it can be just the confirmation screen).

Once, we receive your screenshot, we will send you the digital file, within 24 hours.

Thank you so much for your support – it means a lot to us!

Downloading the code bundles and colored images

Please follow the links or scan the QR codes to download the ***Code Bundles and Images*** of the book:

https://github.com/OrangeAVA/Ultimate-.NET-MAUI-Projects

The code bundles and images of the book are also hosted on ***https://rebrand.ly/qe0wzax***

In case there's an update to the code, it will be updated on the existing GitHub repository.

Errata

We take immense pride in our work at **Orange Education Pvt Ltd,** and follow best practices to ensure the accuracy of our content to provide an indulging reading experience to our subscribers. Our readers are our mirrors, and we use their inputs to reflect and improve upon human errors, if any, that may have occurred during the publishing processes involved. To let us maintain the quality and help us reach out to any readers who might be having difficulties due to any unforeseen errors, please write to us at :

errata@orangeava.com

Your support, suggestions, and feedback are highly appreciated.

DID YOU KNOW

Did you know that Orange Education Pvt Ltd offers eBook versions of every book published, with PDF and ePub files available? You can upgrade to the eBook version at **www.orangeava.com** and as a print book customer, you are entitled to a discount on the eBook copy. Get in touch with us at: **info@orangeava.com** for more details.

At **www.orangeava.com**, you can also read a collection of free technical articles, sign up for a range of free newsletters, and receive exclusive discounts and offers on Print Books and eBooks.

PIRACY

If you come across any illegal copies of our works in any form on the internet, we would be grateful if you would provide us with the location address or website name. Please contact us at **info@orangeava.com** with a link to the material.

ARE YOU INTERESTED IN AUTHORING WITH US?

If there is a topic that you have expertise in, and you are interested in either writing or contributing to a book, please write to us at **business@orangeava.com**. We are on a journey to help developers and tech professionals to gain insights on the present technological advancements and innovations happening across the globe and build a community that believes Knowledge is best acquired by sharing and learning with others. Please reach out to us to learn what our audience demands and how you can be part of this educational reform. We also welcome ideas from tech experts and help them build learning and development content for their domains.

REVIEWS

Please leave a review. Once you have read and used this book, why not leave a review on the site that you purchased it from? Potential readers can then see and use your unbiased opinion to make purchase decisions. We at Orange Education would love to know what you think about our products, and our authors can learn from your feedback. Thank you!

For more information about Orange Education, please visit **www.orangeava.com**.

Table of Contents

CHAPTER 1

Getting to know .NET MAUI

Introduction

In this chapter, we will learn about the .NET platform, its origin, and the evolution of each of its variants, such as .NET Framework, .NET Core, and .Net, resolving the possible confusion that may arise, when we hear about .NET. We will also learn about what cross-platform applications are because in recent years they have become popular, what type of technologies, frameworks, or libraries exist for the development of these types of applications, and why .NET MAUI is an excellent option. We will learn about the history of MAUI and explore the environment of this framework. We will also get to know its predecessor, Xamarin.Forms, and finally show you how to migrate our project created in Xamarin to .NET MAUI.

Structure

In this chapter, we will discuss the following topics:

- Understanding .Net
- Multiplatform Application
- Cross-platform Application Frameworks
- History of MAUI
    - Xamarin.Forms: The Beginning
    - The Start of .NET MAUI
    - Key Features and Benefits
- Working of MAUI
- Migrating from Xamarin.Forms to MAUI
    - Step 1: Introduction
    - Step 2: Creating the Project in .NET MAUI

- Step 3: Code Migration
- Step 4: Testing and Debugging
- Step 5: Deployment and Distribution

Understanding .Net

When we start in the world of software development, specifically in the development of mobile applications, we find different types of technologies and frameworks that provide a set of tools, frameworks, and structures that help direct our projects to solve different defined objectives. To be honest, we feel that listing the large number of frameworks would be complicated because every day new technologies are developed that are introduced to the market, and solve different needs. But among this large number of frameworks is an application development environment called .NET Multi-platform APP User Interface (MAUI), which was designed and developed to run on the .NET platform.

When we talk about .NET, it may cause confusion because over time different variants have come to market, such as .NET framework, .NET CORE, and .NET, and it may even cause confusion with .NET Standard, C#, Xamarin, Visual Basic, .NET MAUI, and so on.

.NET is a platform developed by Microsoft with a modular architecture for the development of modern software such as mobile, web, desktop, cloud, gaming, AI, and machine learning applications, compatible with different operating systems such as Windows, Linux (available for different distributions such as Ubuntu, Red Hat, Fedora, Debian, and more), Apple, and Android, offering different types of programming languages such as C#, a highly typed, high-performance cross-platform language that is popular among the community; F#, an elegant language that allows you to write code in an orderly, understandable, and effective manner; and Visual Basic, which is a historical object-oriented language.

.Net includes tools such as CLI infrastructure language, NuGet for administration, creation, and publication of packages, Visual Studio, the best IDE for developing in .NET, and Visual Studio Code, one of the best code editors available at the moment, mainly for web development.

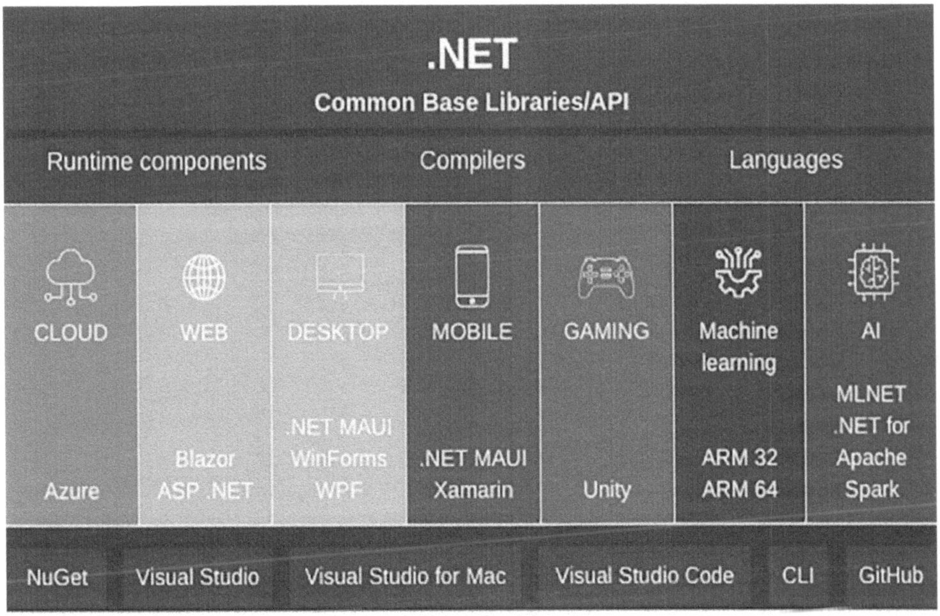

Figure 1.1: *.NET Ecosystem*

The .NET Framework is the first variant of .NET, also known as the Original .NET, released in 2002. The peculiarity of this version is that it is not cross-platform because it was intended and designed to run only within Windows environments. This version allows you to develop desktop applications with WinForms, allowing you to program in multiple programming languages such as C#, VB.NET, and F# to create applications, sites, and web services with the ASP.NET framework.

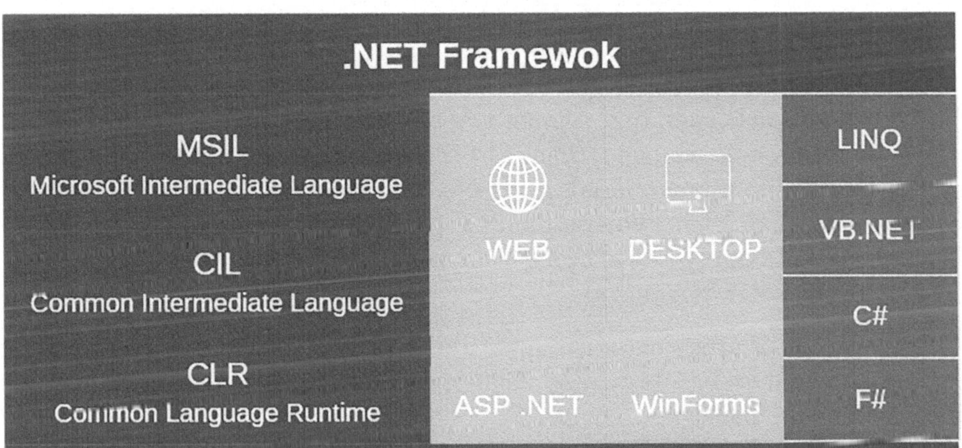

Figure 1.2: *.NET Framework Ecosystem*

.NET Core is an open-source platform with a modular architecture launched in 2014 for the development of modern, high-performance, cross-platform software without the need for dependency on the Windows operating system. In .NET Core, you can create applications of all types, from web, desktop, mobile, cloud, gaming, IoT, and AI. But applications developed with .NET Core do not have interoperability with those written with .NET Framework, which is why in 2017 Microsoft launched .NET Standard with the aim of standardizing and offering uniformity in the .NET ecosystem through a formal API specification.

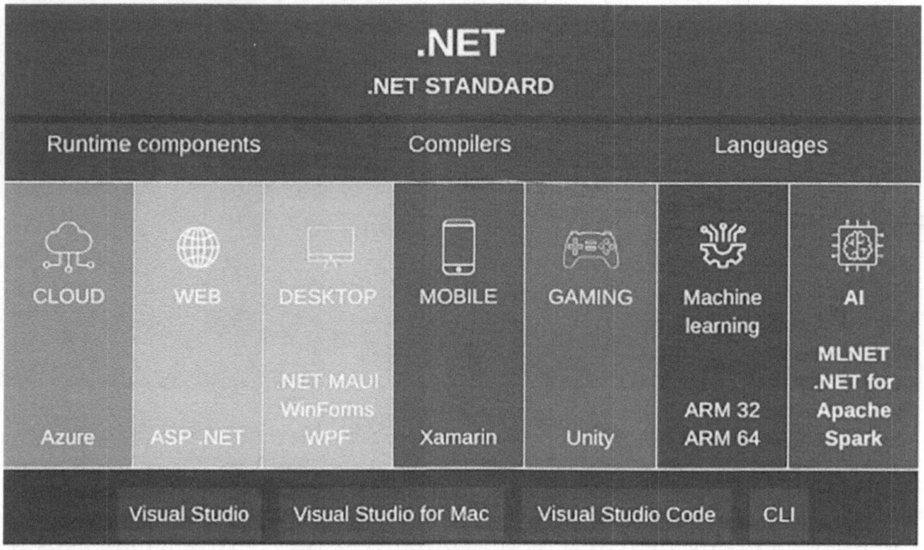

Figure 1.3: *.NET Core Ecosystem*

Multiplatform Application

In the past, developing an application that could run in different environments was very complicated, so it was necessary to write the same application in different technologies for each operating system where you wanted to deploy the software. But over the years, this changed, thanks to cross-platform application development: write once and run on any operating system. This refers to being able to share the same code base of an application on multiple completely different operating systems; an example of this would be developing a single application and compiling it to run on Android and iOS.

The development of cross-platform applications is possible, thanks to the fact that each operating system has its own Application Programming Interface known, as API, which contains the package of instructions on how the software iteration should be carried out with the operating system itself; an example would be .NET MAUI because it contains an API that unifies different platforms such as iOS, Android, macOS, and Windows, as shown in *Figure 1.4*.

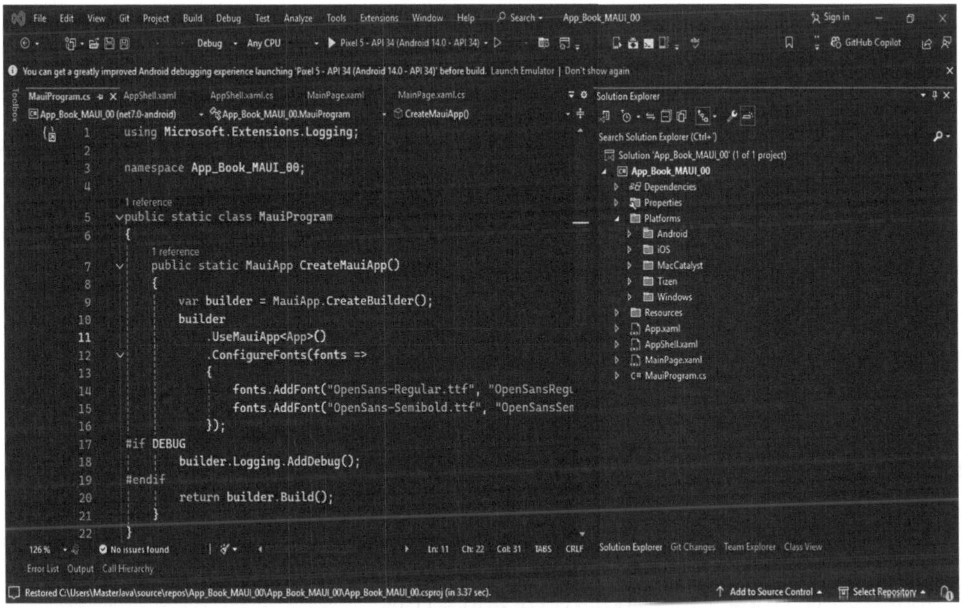

Figure 1.4: .NET MAUI *will load the APIs of different platforms into the Platforms folder*

It is worth mentioning that there is also another way to develop a cross-platform application through web technologies such as HTML, CSS, and JS by developing a type of application called a Progressive Web Application (PWA) that runs through a browser. Although it is true that PWAs are revolutionary, they bring certain limitations, such as limited access to different functionalities and characteristics of the devices where they will be executed, limitations in the ability to offer offline services, that they are not as complete and depend on web browsers, and other features that could affect the development of an application.

It is for this reason that when programming cross-platform apps, they could be implemented in a better way through tools and frameworks that generate native codes through the use of the APIs of each operating system, such as .NET MAUI, React Native, or Flutter, providing a better experience to the user and the programmers.

One of the main advantages offered by cross-platform apps that have been mentioned above is the ability to run on different platforms without the need to write codes in different technologies, improving development costs and production times. It does not need to depend on a browser like web applications, with the ability to take advantage of most of the device's features, offering great performance that is quite close to native applications.

Although there are a large number of advantages, there are also some negative points that can cause difficulties in development such as less access to native features and a limitation in performance. But there is a large number of libraries and plugins that will help solve certain difficulties.

In a few words, developing an application that can run on Android, iOS, Windows, and Mac could not have been easier.

Cross-Platform Application Frameworks

There is a list of frameworks that facilitate the creation of cross-platform applications, allowing programming in different languages, and providing tools, libraries, and components that significantly improve the development of new projects. However, of all these frameworks, we will provide you with some of the best.

.NET MAUI is a cross-platform framework that allows you to develop native mobile and desktop applications using the Extensible Application Markup Language (XAML) and C# language. It has the ability to use a code base, which is shared to run on Android, iOS, Windows, and macOS, as shown in *Figure* 1.5. .NET MAUI is the evolution and improvement of Xamarin.Forms. Although they share similarities and features with each other, MAUI has major differences, such as improved performance, using a single project for different platforms, thin rendering, an API for graphics, support for the Model-View-Update design pattern, and so on.

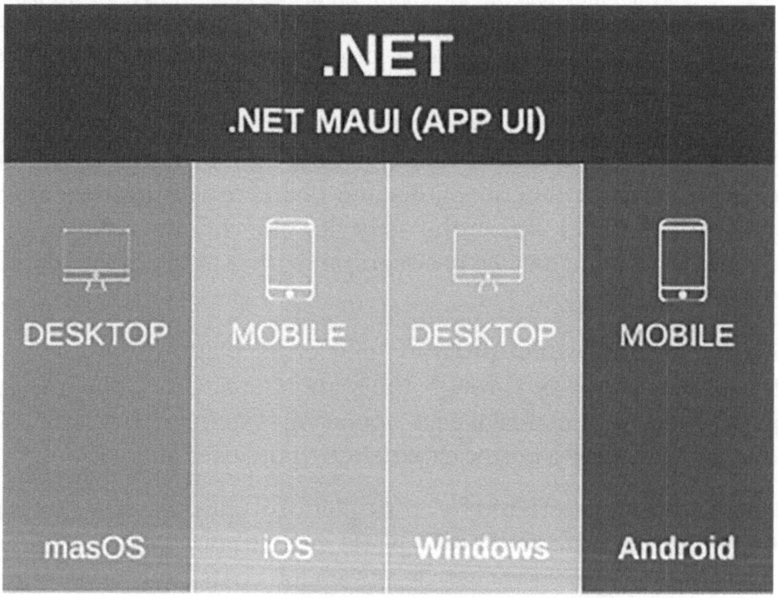

Figure 1.5: .NET MAUI

.NET MAUI works by unifying the different APIs by providing native aspects of each platform. Where .NET provides specific frameworks for creating .NET for Android, .NET for iOS, and .NET for macOS and WinUI 3 applications which have access to the base class library (BCL). Although each platform defines its own models to interact between the components of a user interface, .NET MAUI offers a single framework for creating interfaces for both desktop and mobile.

.NET MAUI provides a collection of controls that provide user interaction, from displaying information to selecting and launching actions that can trigger events, using canvas, displaying data collections, and offering the ability to create controllers, along with APIs that allow access to native features such as GPS, network, camera, accelerometer, and so on. It is becoming one of the best options for the development of cross-platform applications.

In conclusion, .NET MAUI is an excellent development framework that allows the creation of complex applications with excellent performance. It has a large ecosystem of libraries, components, and the ease of developing a single project for all environments, saving time and development costs, and is constantly updated. In addition to the large number of ecosystems and tools that .NET provides to facilitate the development, maintenance, and sustenance of an application.

React Native is an open-source framework launched by Facebook and published in 2015 for the development of cross-platform native mobile applications for iOS and Android based on JavaScript and ReactJS. Unlike PWAs and WEB applications, React Native does not need a browser for its full operation; on the contrary, this framework has the ability to run on platforms offering almost native functionality.

An application created in React Native uses the JavaScript Core VM which is a virtual machine in charge of executing the code written in JavaScript. But this code needs to communicate with the native APIs of the platforms and the native code that the project may contain. To carry out this action, React Native Bridge is used, which will be the communication bridge between JS executed in the VM, the native code, and the APIs.

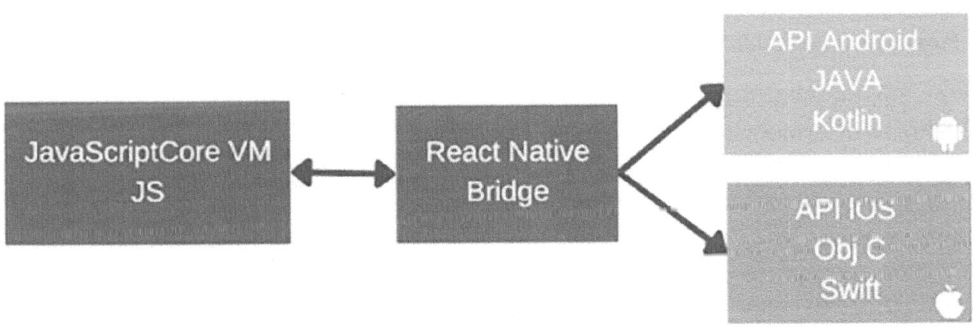

Figure 1.6: *Representation of communication through RN Bridge with VM and the native model*

In conclusion, React Native is an excellent framework for developing applications. It has the ability to write in one of the most popular programming languages today, such as JavaScript, making it a very good alternative for those programmers who have experience in web development. Although it has limitations, since it may be necessary to have fundamentals of native mobile development, its memory management, which is not very efficient, can affect the performance of an application.

Flutter is an SDK that allows the development of cross-platform native applications, launched by Google in 2017, using the same code base written in the Dart programming language that is specialized in the development of interfaces. It also provides two types of compilation: Ahead-of-Time (AOT) compilation that allows complete compilation of the project and Just-in-Time (JIT) compilation in parts according to the time of execution. This enables the Hot Reload feature, which is useful when developing and testing, as well as the ability to compile for different architectures and operating systems such as iOS, Android, Linux, macOS, and Windows.

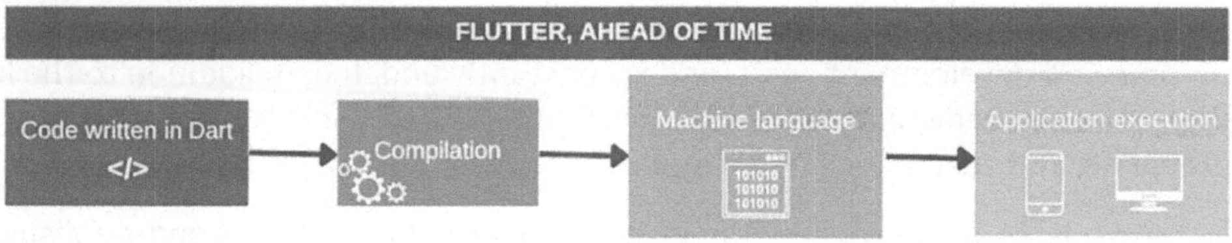

Figure 1.7: *Representation of the Dart compilation process for executing an APP using AOT*

The Just-In-Time compiler has the ability to allow source code modification while the application continues to run, thus eliminating the need to stop the program and go through the compilation process again. *Figure* 1.8 represents this process.

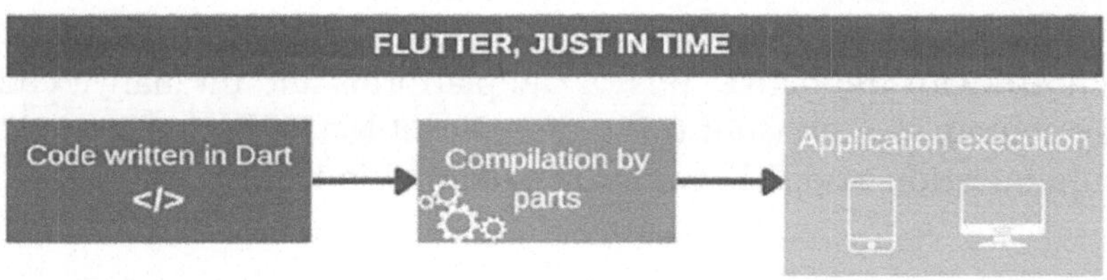

Figure 1.8: *Representation of the Dart compilation process for executing an APP using JIT*

Flutter has its own SKIA rendering engine with the ability to control the pixels that make up an interface, improving the performance of an application when making fluid animations without generating lags. It also has a library of widgets that are components: interface, input, buttons, text, and so on. It includes native styles for each operating system. Among the great virtues of Flutter, there are some limitations that must be taken into account as well. One of the disadvantages is limited documentation and libraries that can cause difficulties in the development process, as well as limited native APIs, so Flutter is more dependent on its own widgets and API. Another important point is the size of the application, since they usually weigh a little more than their counterparts.

In conclusion, Flutter is a sophisticated framework that allows the creation of powerful applications with good performance and amenities in the developmental phase, such as Hot Reload, but it is necessary to take into account the limited ecosystem of libraries and the size of the application because it can cause significant challenges or problems depending on the type of project.

History of MAUI

The road to the creation of .NET MAUI began with the evolution of Microsoft's development frameworks and the changing landscape of cross-platform application development. It was a time when developers were looking for easier ways to create applications that could run seamlessly across multiple devices and platforms without having a deeper understanding of various technologies to do so.

In the early 2000s, Microsoft introduced the .NET Framework, a powerful platform for creating web and desktop applications. As technology advanced, the demand for mobile applications increased, which led Microsoft to buy Xamarin, an environment that allowed developers to write cross-platform mobile applications using C#. Xamarin gained a lot of popularity for its ability to share codes between iOS, Android, and Windows platforms, but it still struggled to deliver a unified development experience.

Xamarin.Forms: The Beginning

Recognizing the need to have a more cohesive approach, Xamarin introduced Xamarin.Forms in 2014. Xamarin.Forms was intended to simplify cross-platform app development by providing a single code base for creating user interfaces that could run on multiple platforms seamlessly. While Xamarin.Forms improved developer productivity, it was not without its limitations and problems. Developers still faced platform-specific nuances and lacked access to certain native features. Like any tool, it was still being updated to provide the best performance for developers.

The Start of .NET MAUI

The .NET MAUI journey began in May 2019 at Microsoft's Build conference, where the company announced its plans to unify Xamarin, Xamarin.Forms, and other cross-platform frameworks into a single framework called .NET 5. This ambitious initiative aimed to streamline application development across mobile, desktop, and web platforms. As part of this effort, Microsoft introduced .NET MAUI at Build 2020.

NET MAUI promised to solve the various problems developers were facing with Xamarin.Forms. Leveraging the power of .NET 5, it aimed to provide a unified UI framework for building cross-platform applications with native-like performance and experience. Building on the foundation of Xamarin.Forms, which would help those already familiar with this tool to have an easier adaptation, .NET MAUI aimed to offer enhanced features, improved performance, and a more intuitive development model.

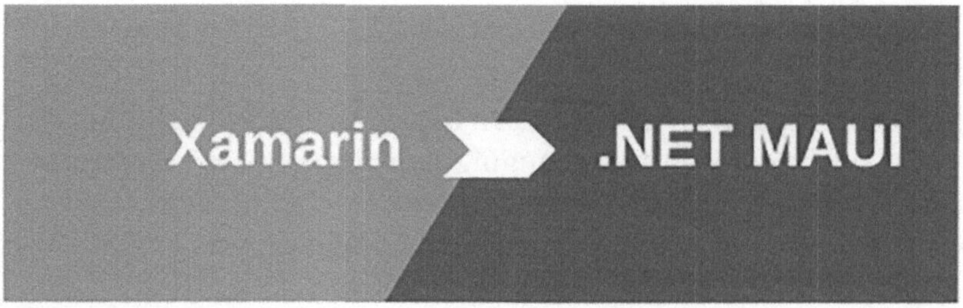

Figure 1.9: *Represents the evolution of Xamarin to what is now known as .NET MAUI*

Key Features and Benefits

One of the most significant features of .NET MAUI was its compatibility with a wide number of platforms, including iOS, Android, macOS, Windows, and others. Developers could leverage a single code base to create applications that seamlessly adapted to different screen sizes and form factors. In addition, .NET MAUI offered better tooling support, a more robust ecosystem, and improved performance optimizations, thanks to its integration with .NET 5.

As .NET MAUI continued to evolve, Microsoft remained committed to providing developers with a unified, modern framework for building cross-platform applications. With each release, new features and enhancements were introduced to further simplify development and improve the end-user experience to make it much simpler and more comfortable. .NET MAUI represented an important milestone in Microsoft's journey to provide developers with the tools and technologies they needed to succeed in the ever-changing and increasingly competitive application development landscape.

Working of MAUI

.NET MAUI works internally through a robust, modular architecture designed to provide an efficient development experience and optimal performance across multiple platforms. Some key aspects are:

- **Single Code Base:** .NET MAUI allows developers to write a single code base in C# for the user interface and application logic. This is achieved by using modern design patterns and shared libraries that abstract the differences between all platforms used.
- **Modular Framework:** It is built primarily based on Xamarin.Forms but has evolved significantly to improve modularity and extensibility, which it has achieved 100%. It uses a project structure that clearly separates application logic, visual resources, and platform-specific components.
- **Renderers and Handlers:** To adapt to the native features and behaviors of each platform (iOS, Android, Windows, and macOS), .NET MAUI uses renderers

and handlers. Renderers are responsible for translating the definition of the application controls to native visual elements, while handlers manage the interaction and behavior specific to each platform.

- **Services and APIs:** Provides access to common services and platform-specific APIs through a unified layer. This allows developers to use features or functions such as cameras, sensors, geolocation, push notifications, and so on, consistently across all supported platforms.
- **Execution and Performance:** .NET MAUI benefits from the performance optimizations inherent to the .NET platform, JIT and AOT compilation as needed. This ensures that applications developed with .NET MAUI are as fast and resource-efficient as possible.
- **Compatibility and Evolution:** Microsoft updates and improves .NET MAUI regularly, adding new features and performance improvements from time to time. Microsoft works hard to polish its products to keep users happy. Compatibility with the latest versions of mobile and desktop platforms is a top priority, ensuring that developers can take advantage of new capabilities quickly and seamlessly.

In short, .NET MAUI operates internally with a flexible and efficient architecture that optimizes cross-platform application development. By abstracting away the complexities of cross-platform differences and offering a unified development experience, which is ideal when creating such cross-platform applications, .NET MAUI is positioned as a powerful tool for creating modern and consistent applications on iOS, Android, Windows, and macOS.

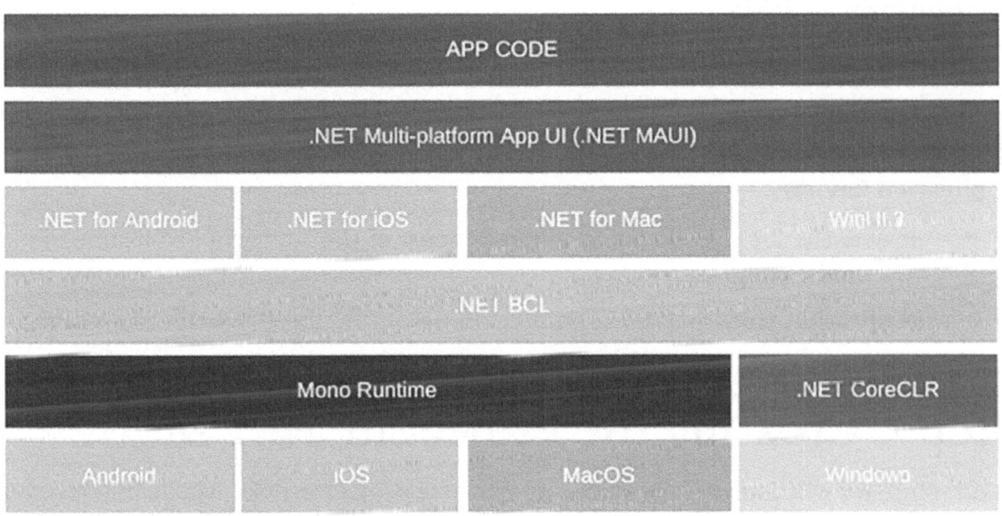

Figure 1.10: *Represents the inner workings of .NET MAUI*

Migrating from Xamarin.Forms to MAUI

Migrating an application from Xamarin.Forms to .NET MAUI can be a very rewarding and beneficial process due to the significant improvements and standardization of the platform. The following is a basic guide to get you started with the migration process:

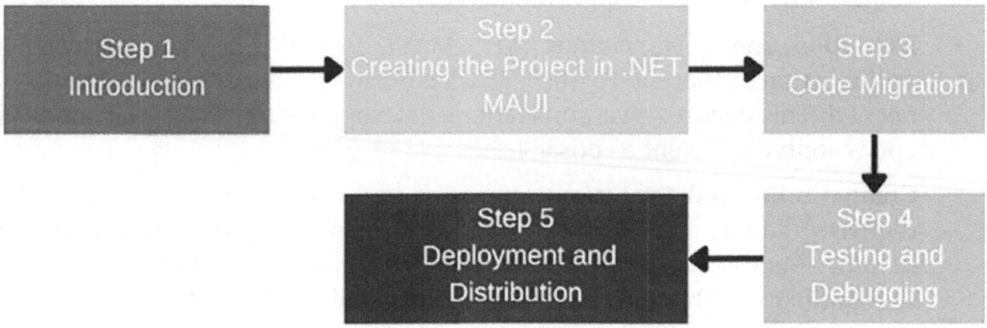

Figure 1.11: *Represents the steps to be undertaken to migrate from Xamarin.Forms to .NET MAUI*

Step 1: Introduction

In this step, we will explain what you need to have installed to do the migration properly.

Prerequisites:

- You need to have .NET 6 SDK or higher installed.
- Install Visual Studio 2022 or Visual Studio Code with the necessary extensions for .NET MAUI.

Application Review:

- Review the architecture and dependencies of the Xamarin.Forms application you want to migrate.
- Verify what third party libraries and custom features you are using in your application.

Step 2: Creating the Project in .NET MAUI

In this step, we will explain how to create our new project in .NET MAUI, and also how to define the basic information of our project.

Create Project:

- In Visual Studio 2022, select "`Create a New Project`."
- Choose the appropriate .NET MAUI template (for example, .NET MAUI App, which is the most common).

Initial Settings:

- Define the elementary project settings (name, location, and so on).
- Select the target platforms (iOS, Android, and Windows).

Step 3: Code Migration

In this step, we will explain how to migrate our parts of code according to the component we are migrating, such as business logic, views, and dependencies.

Migrate Business Logic:

- Copy the code from your shared project (ViewModels, models, and services) from Xamarin.Forms to the new .NET MAUI project, we created in the previous step.
- Take advantage of the affinity with .NET 6 and C# 10 to improve the code if necessary and if you want to take advantage of the new features and improvements of this one.

Migrate the Views:

- Copy and adapt the XAML pages, and their corresponding code files for each of the views.
- Adjust the namespaces and references according to the structure of the new project, if you changed them.

Update Dependencies:

- Review and update third-party dependencies to versions that are fully compatible with .NET MAUI.
- Consider replacing deprecated libraries with more up-to-date options that are compatible with .NET MAUI.

Step 4: Testing and Debugging

In this step, we will explain the importance of debugging and testing our application to ensure that everything works properly.

Unit and integration testing:

- Use unit and integration testing to make sure that all major features of the application continue to function optimally.

Debugging and Tuning:

- Run comprehensive tests on all target platforms (iOS, Android, and Windows).
- Resolve any design or performance issues that may occur during the migration.

Step 5: Deployment and Distribution

In this step, we will explain the subsequent activities after we check that the migration has been done correctly. One of them is the compilation, another one is the distribution, and additional resources that are available for your use are mentioned.

Compilation and Packaging:

- Compiles the application for each of the target platforms.
- Creates package files (IPA, APK, and so on) for distribution in app stores or internal deployment.

Distribution and Ongoing Support:

- Ship the new version of the application already in .NET MAUI and make sure to provide ongoing support for users.

Additional Resources:

- Refer to the official .NET MAUI and Xamarin documentation to check specific details about the migration.
- You can collaborate with the .NET MAUI community to get help and share your experiences with other developers about the migration once it is done.
- Migrating an application from Xamarin.Forms to .NET MAUI may take some time, depending on the features and functions of your existing application. But the performance optimizations, new features, and development capabilities are well worth it.

Conclusion

To sum up, .NET has today emerged as a powerful and versatile platform, evolving to meet the dynamic needs of modern software development. Its journey, from the original .NET Framework to the robust .NET MAUI, illustrates a commitment to creating unified solutions for cross-platform application development. With its single codebase, modular architecture, and extensive tooling, .NET MAUI not only simplifies the process for developers but also enhances performance and user experience across diverse platforms such as iOS, Android, Windows, and macOS. As the landscape of software development continues to evolve, .NET stands out as a vital framework that empowers developers to build efficient, high-quality applications while reducing time and cost. Embracing .NET and its capabilities could be a game-changer for developers seeking to create innovative solutions in today's competitive market.

In the next chapter, we will show the main advantages and disadvantages of using .NET MAUI, explain some key libraries that we can incorporate into our projects using this technology, and will also see in detail the .NET MAUI architecture.

CHAPTER 2

Main Features of .NET MAUI

Introduction

In this chapter, you will learn the advantages and disadvantages of .NET MAUI to understand its strengths and weaknesses. We will go through the most common libraries that cannot be missed in any .NET MAUI project, since these libraries will help in the aspects of infrastructure, languages, common functionalities, and so on. Finally, it will explain what composes the architecture of .NET MAUI.

Structure

In this chapter, we will discuss the following topics:

- Advantages and Disadvantages of Using .NET MAUI
    - Advantages of .NET MAUI
    - Disadvantages of .NET MAUI
    - Other Important Considerations
- Libraries of .NET MAUI
    - Nuget Manager
    - `CommunityToolkit.Maui`
    - `CommunityToolkit.Mvvm`
    - `LocalizationResourceManager.Maui`
- Architecture of .NET MAUI
    - Structure of a Project

Advantages and Disadvantages of Using .NET MAUI

Like any technology, .NET MAUI has both advantages and disadvantages that are important to consider before adopting it for any software development project. Following is an analysis of the aspects to be considered:

Advantages of .NET MAUI

The following are the main advantages of using .NET MAUI:

- **Cross-Platform Development:** .NET MAUI allows developers to create applications that work optimally on multiple platforms, which are iOS, Android, Windows, and macOS, by developing a single set of code. This capability significantly decreases both the time and resources it takes to build native applications for each platform individually. Instead of occupying multiple teams working on individual versions of an application, one can only manage and maintain the entire project, simplifying the time of development, coordination, and project management.
- **Improved Productivity:** Working with .NET MAUI helps developers take advantage of the C# language and the Visual Studio IDE environment, tools that are used and known by many developers. This helps facilitate the integration of a team and improves productivity in development. In addition, integration with XAML greatly simplifies user interface design, as it is a highly practical tool. By using XAML, developers can design and develop interfaces in a more declarative and efficient way, streamlining the development process.
- **Optimal Performance:** .NET MAUI offers a performance quite close to the native one because it compiles the code directly on the target platforms that the developer indicates. This ensures that applications are faster and highly responsive, resulting in a smoother user experience. Performance optimization is important for applications that require high interactivity and faster response times, such as games or applications in the financial sector. By offering performance highly similar to native performance, .NET MAUI allows developers to create high-quality applications without slowing down or reducing efficiency.
- **Unified Ecosystem:** Because everything is integrated within the .NET ecosystem, .NET MAUI makes it easy to use existing libraries and tools in the .NET ecosystem. This makes it easy to reuse code and integrate with other .NET services and applications. Having this consistency in the ecosystem simplifies the management of dependencies and the implementation of additional functionalities. Developers will be able to take advantage of a large

set of tools and libraries already available in .NET, which reduces development time and helps make implementing complex features more convenient and easier.

- **Updates and Ongoing Support:** Microsoft is committed to the development and continuous improvement of .NET MAUI, providing regular updates and support. This commitment ensures that developers have access to the latest features, performance enhancements, and security solutions, keeping their applications up-to-date and secure. Frequent updates also ensure that .NET MAUI stays relevant and is able to compete with other emerging technologies in cross-platform application development.

Disadvantages of .NET MAUI

The following are the main disadvantages or difficulties that.NET MAUI provides:

- **Learning Curve:** Although .NET MAUI offers many advantages, it can present a somewhat steep learning curve, especially for those developers who do not have experience working or studying C# or the .NET ecosystem. The transition .NET MAUI may require a more extensive training time and good adaptation, which can delay the start of project development with this technology. Developers who are new to the platform should invest time in learning what encompasses the best practices and significant specificities of .NET MAUI, which can be a complex initial challenge.
- **Support and Community:** As a relatively new technology, as far as it goes, .NET MAUI does not yet have the same breadth of support and community resources as forums that other more established technologies may have due to the time they have already been in operation. The loss of more extensive documentation, examples that are 100% practical, and forums that are active can make it difficult to solve problems and implement advanced features, especially for new developers. The growing community may not be as large as that of older technologies, which can limit access to resources and solutions as specific problems arise.
- **Update Dependency:** The evolution of .NET MAUI will depend heavily on updates and ongoing support from Microsoft. Any delays you see in upgrades or major changes in technology can significantly affect backward compatibility and can lead to problems in projects that are currently being developed. This dependence can be a latent concern for some developers and companies that require greater stability in the long term. Long-term projects may be affected by unforeseen adjustments to the platform, which may require adjustments, migrations, and upgrades.
- **Platform Limitations:** Although .NET MAUI is potentially a cross-platform solution, there are some inherent differences between platforms that can lead

to limitations or inconsistent behavior. Developers may have some challenges when trying to implement certain features that are not fully supported uniformly across platforms, which may require additional tweaking and more extensive testing. Each platform handles its own features, quirks, and constraints, which can make it difficult to develop more specific functionalities and require slightly more customized solutions.

- **Customization and Access to Native Features:** In some cases, applications developed with .NET MAUI may need access to more platform-specific native features. Although MAUI provides an abstraction layer that helps simplify cross-platform development, the implementation of very specific features and functionality may require additional knowledge and the writing of native code, which can complicate the development and significantly increase the time needed to complete the project. The need to implement native code for each platform can contradict the main goal of having a single codebase, adding difficulty and extra effort to the development work.

Other Important Considerations

The following are some important extra considerations that we can consider when using .NET MAUI:

- **Maintenance and Scalability:** Maintaining cross-platform applications can become easier with .NET MAUI. This is due to the unification of the code into a single code and the coherence of the .NET ecosystem. However, as applications grow and evolve, code refactoring may become necessary to accommodate new needs and improve or optimize performance. Application scalability also relies heavily on the development team's ability to manage, refactor, and optimize code as new features and functionalities are added.
- **Integration with External Services:** Integration with external services and APIs is quite essential for most modern applications. .NET MAUI facilitates this integration by providing a relatively coherent interface for working with a wide variety of different services and technologies. However, integration can lead to several additional challenges when it comes to services that have restrictions that are particularly specific to certain platforms. Developers need to be informed to control these differences and adapt their code accordingly.
- **Testing and Debugging Strategies:** Testing and debugging strategies are important to the success of any modern software project. .NET MAUI offers built-in tools within the framework that can be used for testing and debugging that can facilitate these processes. However, due to the cross-platform nature of MAUI, developers must ensure that their tests support all target platforms to ensure the quality and consistency of the application. Automated testing and the use of CI/CD tools can significantly optimize the efficiency and reliability of the development process.

- **Adoption and Future of .NET MAUI:** The adoption of .NET MAUI will depend largely on its ability to create a competitive and efficient solution for cross-platform development. Market developments and the emergence of new, more modern technologies can influence the popularity and importance of MAUI. Microsoft should continue to invest in the development, optimization, and promotion of .NET MAUI to secure its position in the market for cross-platform development options. The developer community also plays a huge role in the adoption and success of the platform, providing feedback to Microsoft's support channels, creating new resources, and sharing experiences, they may have.

Libraries of .NET MAUI

Libraries in programming are a collection of codes that are packaged and that can be reused in different projects. Basically it is a set of functions that solve specific problems, helping programmers to develop software in a more agile way. For example, Json.NET is a library that we can incorporate into our project, allowing us to serialize and deserialize a JSON object in a more comfortable, organized, and faster way.

NuGet Manager

There is a huge number of compiled code packages, such as Dynamic Link Libraries (DLLs), so it is almost mandatory to use a package manager to facilitate the installation and implementation of these elements. This is where .NET provides NuGet, which is an open-source tool designed to create, consume, and share reusable and useful codes among developers.

It is easy to use the tool. Within Visual Studio, you must select the projects option and then manage NuGet packages; this should open a window, as shown in *Figure 2.1*.

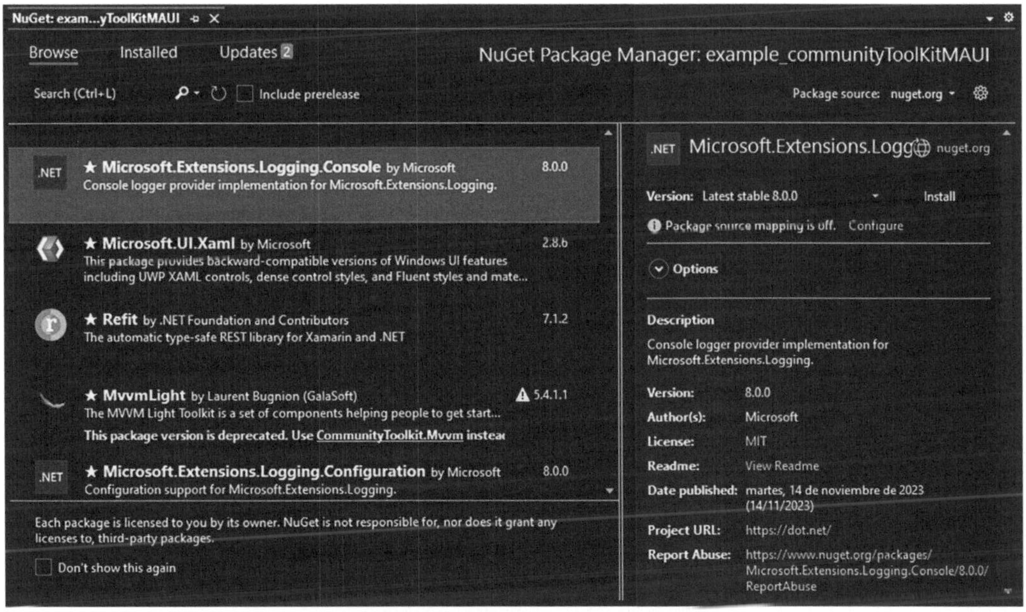

***Figure 2.1**: NuGet Package Manager*

The NuGet package manager shows the Browse section, where the list of all the packages that we can install in a project is shown. To carry out the installation, it is only necessary to search for the desired library, select it, and in the detail section, validate the version of the library as well as press install Another section is **`Installed`**, where you can see all the packages that are already installed, and finally **`Updates`**, which shows all the packages that need to be updated.

CommunityToolkit.MAUI

It is a toolkit that contains a collection of elements that are reusable for application development, providing animations, behaviors, effects, converters, and other features that allow agile development. The **`CommunityToolKit.MAUI`** kit is available within the .NET NuGet package manager.

To install the package from NuGet, it is necessary to search for it from the **`Browse`** with the name **`CommunityToolKit.MAUI`** developed by Microsoft; select it and install it.

After completing the installation of the kit, it must be initialized within **`MauiProgram.cs`**, where the library is declared with the following line of code:

```
using CommunityToolkit.Maui;
```

Within the **CreateMauiApp** method, **UseMauiCommunityToolkit** must be added below the **UseMauiApp<App>**, as shown in the following code example:

```
public static MauiApp CreateMauiApp()
{
var builder = MauiApp.CreateBuilder();
      builder
            .UseMauiApp<App>()
            .UseMauiCommunityToolkit()
            .ConfigureFonts(fonts =>
            {
                  fonts.AddFont("OpenSans-Regular.ttf",
"OpenSansRegular");
                  fonts.AddFont("OpenSans-Semibold.ttf",
"OpenSansSemibold");
            });
      }
}
```

Once the kit has been added, the only thing left to do is use it within the interface files, for example, the MainPage.xml within the file is the ContentPage tag; here the following attribute will be added:

```
xmlns:toolkit="http://schemas.microsoft.com/dotnet/2022/maui/
toolkit"
```

remaining the code in the following way:

```
<?xml version="1.0" encoding="utf-8" ?>
<ContentPage xmlns="http://schemas.microsoft.com/dotnet/2021/
maui"
            xmlns:x="http://schemas.microsoft.com/winfx/2009/
xaml"
            xmlns:toolkit="http://schemas.microsoft.com/dot-
net/2022/maui/toolkit"
            x:Class="example_communityToolKitMAUI.MainPage">
</ContentPage>
```

An example of using the Community would be to change the color of the status bar of a mobile device using the Behaviors within the **ContentPage**. The **ContentPage.Behaviors** tag would be added, **toolkit:StatusBehavior** would be added as content, and the attributes that we will use are **statusBarColor** to define the bar color and the **StatusBarStyle**, which is also used to modify the color of the icons. The styles offered by these attributes are **DarkContent**, **Default**, and **LightContent**, as presented in the following code:

```
<ContentPage xmlns="http://schemas.microsoft.com/dotnet/2021/maui"
             xmlns:x="http://schemas.microsoft.com/winfx/2009/xaml"
```

```
             xmlns:toolkit="http://schemas.microsoft.com/dotnet
/2022/maui/toolkit"
             x:Class="example_communityToolKitMAUI.MainPage">
    <ContentPage.Behaviors>
        <toolkit:StatusBarBehavior
             StatusBarColor="#ffff"
             StatusBarStyle="LightContent" />
    </ContentPage.Behaviors>
</ContentPage>
```

CommunityToolkit.Mvvm

The **CommunityToolkit.Mvvm** library is a tool that is currently widely used and very useful for developers who use MAUI and who want to implement the MVVM pattern in a simpler and more efficient way. Next, we will see the main features and how to use it in MAUI projects.

Main Features

These are the main functions that can be used in our projects provided by the **CommunityToolkit.Mvvm** library.

- **Automatic Change Notifications:** **CommunityToolkit.Mvvm** allows us to use attributes such as **[ObservableObject]** and **[ObservableProperty]**, which are automatically responsible for implementing **INotifyPropertyChanged**. This significantly reduces having to write repetitive code to notify changes to properties.
- **Asynchronous Commands:** The library allows the use of **[ICommand]** and **[AsyncRelayCommand]** for the handling of actions by the user asynchronously, and thus be able to prevent the user interface from becoming inoperative during operations that can take some time, such as calls to web services usually.
- **Messaging:** Includes a messaging system that facilitates communication between different parts of the application without the need to create direct dependencies. This is useful for sending notifications and commands between **ViewModels** efficiently.

Use in MAUI

Integrating **CommunityToolkit.Mvvm** into a project that uses MAUI technology is a straightforward and easy process to perform. Here are the steps on how to do it:

1. **Initial Configuration:** The first thing to do is to add the library to the MAUI project using the following command:

   ```
   dotnet add package CommunityToolkit.Mvvm
   ```

2. **Creating ViewModels:** To create a **ViewModel**, the ideal is to use the attributes provided by the library itself, making the process simpler:

```
using CommunityToolkit.Mvvm.ComponentModel;
using CommunityToolkit.Mvvm.Input;

public partial class MainViewModel : ObservableObject
{
      [ObservableProperty]
      private string _title;

      public MainViewModel()
      {
            Title = "Hello, MAUI with MVVM!";
      }

      [RelayCommand]
      private void UpdateTitle()
      {
            Title = "Title Updated!";
      }
}
```

3. **Data Binding in the View:** We can then bind the **ViewModel** to the view in XAML to ensure that changes to the **ViewModel** are displayed properly and automatically in the user interface:

```
<ContentPage xmlns="http://schemas.microsoft.com/dotnet/2021/
maui"
      xmlns:x="http://schemas.microsoft.com/winfx/2009/xaml"
      xmlns:local="clr-namespace:MyApp"
      x:Class="MyApp.MainPage">

      <ContentPage.BindingContext>
            <local:MainViewModel />
      </ContentPage.BindingContext>

      <StackLayout>
            <Label Text="{Binding Title}" />
            <Button Text="Update Title" Command="{Binding
            UpdateTitleCommand}" />
      </StackLayout>
</ContentPage>
```

4. **Messaging Implementation:** For the exchange of messages between the **ViewModels** of our application, the **CommunityToolkit.Mvvm** messaging system

can be used through **WeakReferenceMessenger**, which is more memory-safe than the default Messenger:

```
// In the ViewModel emitter
WeakReferenceMessenger.Default.Send(new UpdateMessage("New
Title"));

// On the Receiving ViewModel
public class AnotherViewModel : ObservableObject,
IRecipient<UpdateMessage>
{
    public AnotherViewModel()
    {
        WeakReferenceMessenger.Default.Register<Update
        Message>(this);
    }

    public void Receive(UpdateMessage message)
    {
        // Handling the message
        var newTitle = message.Value;
        // For example: Title = newTitle;
    }
}
```

Observed Benefits

These are the main benefits of using the **CommunityToolkit.Mvvm** library:

- **Less Repetitive Code**: Attributes and commands help greatly simplify the creation of observable properties and commands which significantly reduces repetitive code.
- **Easier to Maintain:** The clear separation between what would be the presentation logic and what is the user interface helps facilitate the maintenance and scalability of the application that is developed.
- **More Reactive User Interface:** Asynchronous commands make it easier to keep the user interface reactive, even if operations are quite long.

LocalizationResourceManager.Maui

LocalizationResourceManager.Maui is a very useful and necessary library for developers who are looking to implement multilingual support in their applications created with MAUI. Its main features and how to uses them in projects with MAUI will be shown.

Main Features

These are the main functions that can be used in our projects provided by the **LocalizationResourceManager.Maui** library:

- **Language Resource Management:** The library can make it easier to manage resource files (**.resx**) for multiple languages. This allows developers to host all text strings in one place and quickly adjust them according to the selected language.
- **Dynamic Language Update:** Allows you to adjust the language of the app in real-time, without any need to restart the app. This is quite good as it allows for a much smoother user experience.
- **Easy Integration: LocalizationResourceManager.Maui** has a very easy integration with MAUI and uses common practices such as data binding, which allows you to automatically translate text strings in the user interface.

Use in MAUI

Integrating **LocalizationResourceManager.Maui** into a project developed with MAUI is quite simple and fast. Here are the steps to do it:

1. **Initial Setup:** The first thing is to add the library to the MAUI project:

   ```
   dotnet add package LocalizationResourceManager.Maui
   ```
2. **Resource File Configuration:** Resource files (**.resx**) must be created for each of the languages that you want the application to be able to support. For example, you could have what is a **Resources.es.resx** file for Spanish and one called **Resources.en.resx** for the English language.
3. **Configuring LocalizationResourceManager:** Next, you must configure the **LocalizationResourceManager** in what is the **App.xaml.cs** file:

   ```
   using LocalizationResourceManager.Maui;

   public partial class App : Application
   {
         public App()
         {
               InitializeComponent();

               LocalizationResourceManager.SetDefaultCulture(new
               CultureInfo("en"));
               LocalizationResourceManager.Init(this, "MyApp.
               Resources");
   ```

```
            MainPage = new MainPage();
        }
    }
```

4. **Data Binding in the View:** Text strings in the XAML interface views could then be linked so that they are automatically translated into the selected language:

```
<ContentPage xmlns="http://schemas.microsoft.com/dotnet/2021/maui"
xmlns:x="http://schemas.microsoft.com/winfx/2009/xaml"
xmlns:local="clr-namespace:MyApp"
x:Class="MyApp.MainPage">

        <StackLayout>
            <Label Text="{Binding LocalizationResourceManager.
            Instance['Hello']}" />
            <Button Text="{Binding LocalizationResourceManager.
            Instance['ChangeLanguage']}"
            Command="{Binding ChangeLanguageCommand}" />
        </StackLayout>
</ContentPage>
```

5. **Real-Time Language Switching:** To adjust the language of the application in real-time, there is a command that can be used within the **`ViewModel`**:

```
using CommunityToolkit.Mvvm.ComponentModel;
using CommunityToolkit.Mvvm.Input;
using LocalizationResourceManager.Maui;
using System.Globalization;

public partial class MainViewModel : ObservableObject
{
        [ICommand]
        public void ChangeLanguage()
        {
            var newCulture = LocalizationResourceManager.
            Instance.CurrentCulture.Name == "en" ? "es" : "en";
            LocalizationResourceManager.Instance.SetCulture(new
            CultureInfo(newCulture));
        }
}
```

Observed Benefits

These are the main benefits of using the **`LocalizationResourceManager.Maui`** library:

- **Ease of Language Management:** Keeping all text strings in one place helps facilitate the management and subsequent updating of texts in multiple languages.

- **Dynamic Update:** It allows you to adjust the language of the application in real time in a simple and practical way, improving user experience.
- **Intuitive Integration:** It has a simple integration with MAUI, using practices that are commonly used in the development world, such as data linking.

Architecture of .NET MAUI

As previously mentioned, .NET MAUI is a framework for creating cross-platform applications that share the same code base for different platforms.

But what is the architecture of .NET MAUI? It basically separates the business logic (application code) from the user interface. This is because each of the APIs of the platforms interacts in a completely different way with the components and features of the device. It is for this reason that .NET MAUI unifies each platform-specific framework, which is .NET for Android, .NET for Mac, .NET for iOS, and WinUI 3 for Windows, where each framework is allowed to interact with the base case library (BCL) , allowing common business logic to be shared between platforms by providing execution environments for the code. Android, iOS, Mac depend on Mono Runtime, which is a runtime implementation of .NET and the CoreCLR runtime system.

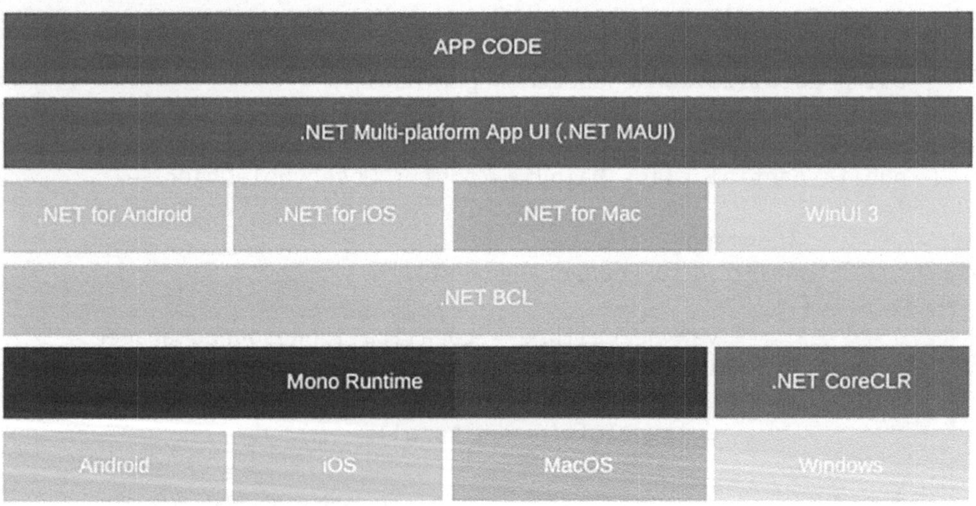

***Figure 2.2**: .NET technology stack*

Structure of a Project

Before creating a new project in .NET MAUI, it is necessary to understand how a newly created project is structured. This will provide us with the knowledge to configure the platforms, improve the organization, and create our resources such as styles, images, texts, and more.

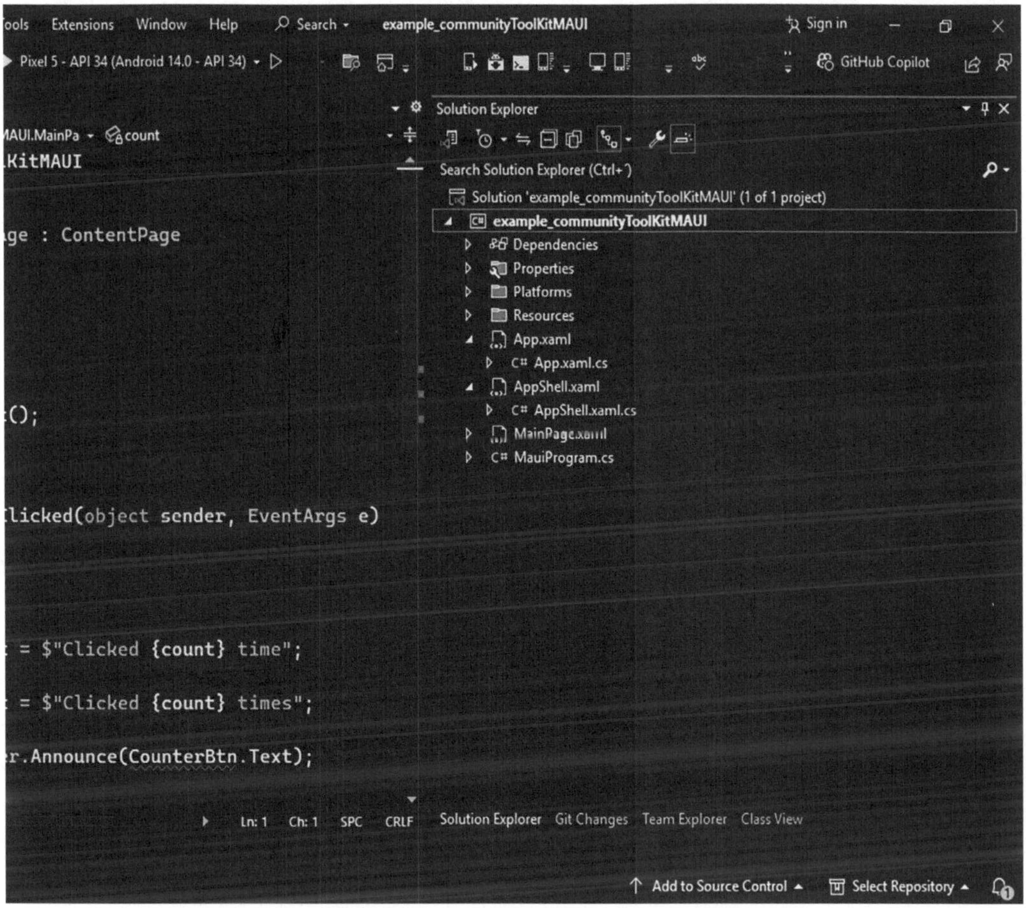

Figure 2.3: *Content of a newly created project*

As can be seen in *Figure* 2.3, within the project folder is the content of elements of our application; it is made up of the following:

Platforms: This directory contains files and resources necessary for initialization of supported platforms. Here you will find Android, iOS folders, MacCatalyst, Tizen, and Windows. Each folder contains resources necessary for the correct functioning of an application; for example, within the Android directory is the AndroidManifest.xml XML file where the metadata of an application is found, such as configurations, permissions to access some specific functionalities, compatibility of versions, hardware compatibility, packages, among other things.

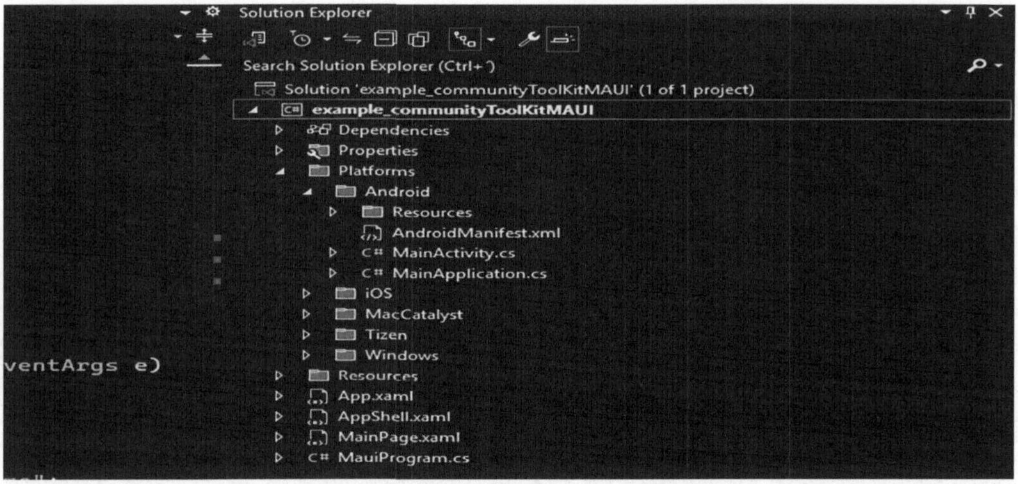

Figure 2.4: *Contents of Platforms folder*

Resources: This folder stores the resources of an application, for example, styles, images, and so on. It contains the following folders:

- **`AppIcon`**: Contains the icon of our application. It is recommended to use files with the **`svg`** extension in order to have the best quality resources and to avoid the problems that may arise with other extensions, for example, pixelation of images.
- **`Fonts`**: Saves the text fonts used for the project.
- **`Images`**: Contains the images that the application will use. The use of SVG is recommended, but you can use any other extension, such as PNG or JPG.
- **`Raw`**: Generic files, for example, JSON and TXT.
- **`Splash`**: It will contain the welcome screen of our application.
- **`Styles`**: .Net MAUI provides two files, one **`Colors.xaml`** that helps standardize the different types of colors that our project will use and **`Styles.xaml`** labels with component styles such as **`Button`**, **`BoxView`**, **`CheckBox`**, among others.

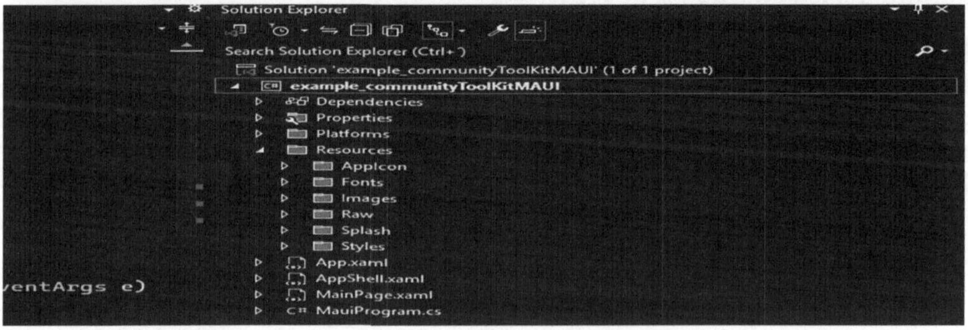

Figure 2.5: *Resources folder contents*

`.csproj`: This is the main file of the project, where the application configurations are made. Within the file is the **`PropertyGroup`** section. Here, the platforms that will be compatible with the app are specified. The way to do it is very simple: you only need to remove or comment on the unwanted platform **`TargetFrameworks`**. Within the **`ApplicationTitle`**, the name of our app is specified. **`SupportedOSPlatformVersion`** has the configuration of the operating system versions that the project will support. You can also modify the version from the **`ApplicationDisplayVersion`** and **`ApplicationVersion`**. Another section is the **`ItemGroup`**, which allows you to specify the icon, color screen, and loading image (splash). If we remember, within the Resources folder there is the **`AppIcon`** folder that contains SVG files that are the application icon. Taking this into account, within our **`ItemGroup`** there is the **`MauiIcon`** tag that contains the Include and **`ForegroundFile`** attributes, where you can change the icon that the application will have when it is deployed on the platform.

`App.xaml`: Defines the resources that the application will use. For example, within the **`ResourceDictionary`**, the color and style files that the project will use will be defined. The **`APP.xaml`** contains an underlying file **`APP.xaml.cs`**, which is a class that defines within the constructor which page will start first on the **`MainPage`**.

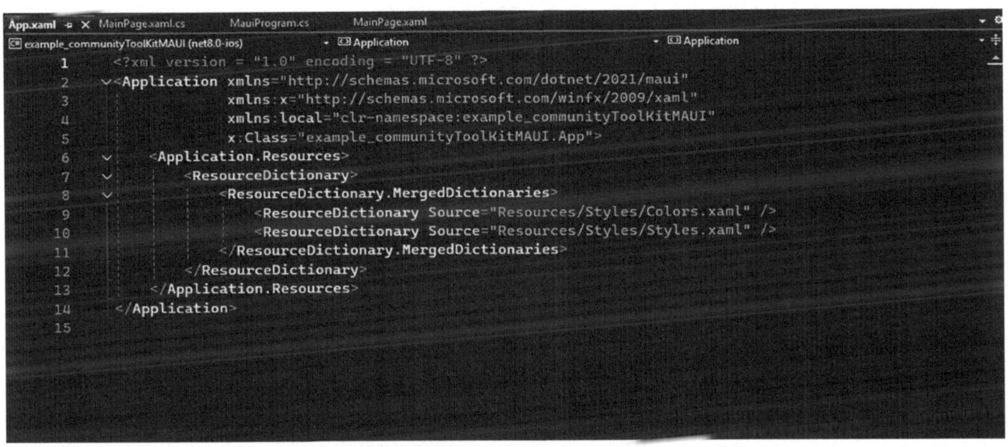

Figure 2.6: *Contents of the APP.xaml file*

`AppShell.xaml`: Defines the URL-based navigation structure of the application, where you can add which page will be the first from the **`ShellContent`**, add the items of a drop-down menu, among other things.

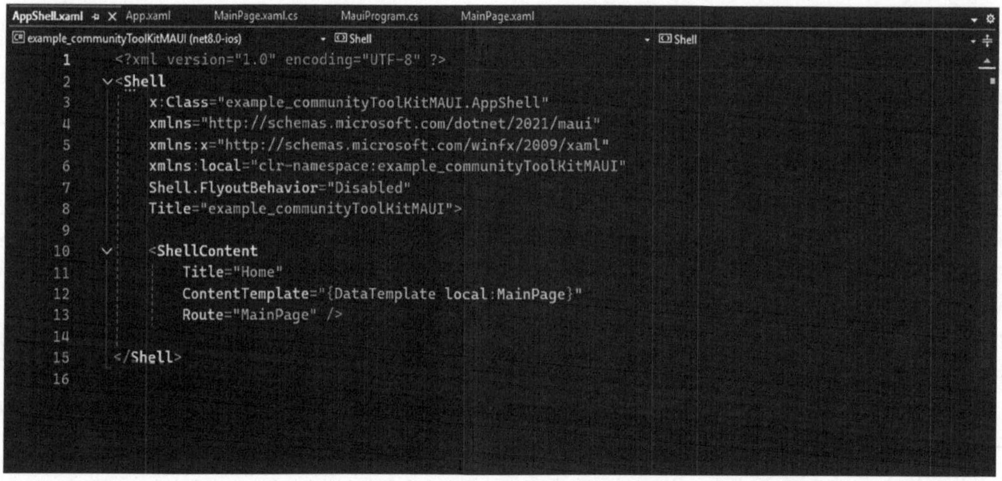

Figure 2.7: *App Shell file content*

`MauiProgram.cs`: This file is the starting point to initialize an application. Here you can define resources such as text sources, dependency injection, driver registration, service configuration, and more.

`MainPage.xml`: Basically, this file represents the user interface. It is an example generated when we created our project in .NET MAUI where some components are presented, such as **`ScrollView`**, **`VerticalStackLayout`**, and **`Button`**, **`Label`**. A design that helps understand how an interface is created and works. It contains an underlying file, **`MainPage.xaml.cs`**, that displays code for the **`OnCounterClicked`** event that is triggered when the button is clicked.

Conclusion

Thus, .NET MAUI presents a compelling solution for cross-platform application development, offering significant benefits such as reduced development time through a unified codebase, enhanced productivity with familiar tools, and optimal performance closely resembling native applications. The extensive support from Microsoft ensures that developers have access to regular updates and a robust ecosystem. However, the potential learning curve, limited community resources, and challenges with platform-specific features cannot be overlooked. As with any technology choice, organizations must weigh these advantages against the disadvantages to determine if .NET MAUI aligns with their project requirements and long-term goals. For developers considering .NET MAUI, investing time in learning and adapting to the framework will be crucial for unlocking its full potential and building high-quality, responsive applications that meet diverse user needs across platforms. Ultimately, the future of .NET MAUI hinges on its ability to evolve and address the challenges of cross-platform development, reaffirming its relevance in a rapidly changing technological landscape.

In the next chapter, we will show you how to create our first .NET MAUI project. We will learn about the components that can be used inside our tool, and also cover more about the **`LocalizationResourceManager.Maui`** library.

CHAPTER 3
Getting Started with .NET MAUI

Introduction

In this chapter, we will learn more about .NET MAUI. We will create our first project, understand XAML, and learn what they are and how to create the pages of an application. We will learn about the different design structures and the types of layouts. We will discover the different types of components and learn how to create our own custom components. We will understand how data binding works through commands and how to send parameters. Furthermore, we will explore the different ways of using styles, and how to translate our application into different languages.

Structure

In this chapter, we will discuss the following topics:

- Creating a .NET MAUI Application
- XAML
- C#
- Pages
- Layouts
- Components
- Styles
- Commands
- Localization

Creating a .NET MAUI Application

In the previous chapter, we talked about the structure of a project in .NET MAUI, analyzed some libraries, and also its NuGet package manager. Now knowing this part, it is time to create and run our first application in this framework.

To begin, we must have Visual Studio 2022 installed with version 17.8 or later, and the .NET MAUI framework should also be installed.

1. When starting Visual Studio in the start window, we will create a new project in the option **`Create a new project`**. Select the **`.NET MAUI App`** template in the project type list and then click the **`Next`** button.

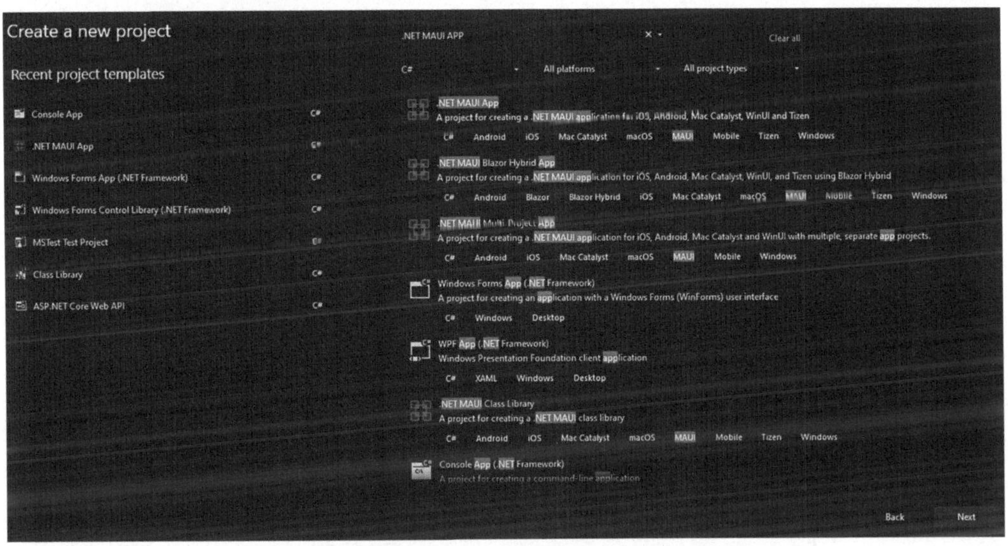

***Figure 3.1**: Selection of .NET MAUI app*

2. The next step is the configuration of the project. Here we configure the name of the project, the location, and the name of the solution. When the configuration is done, click on the **`Next`** button.

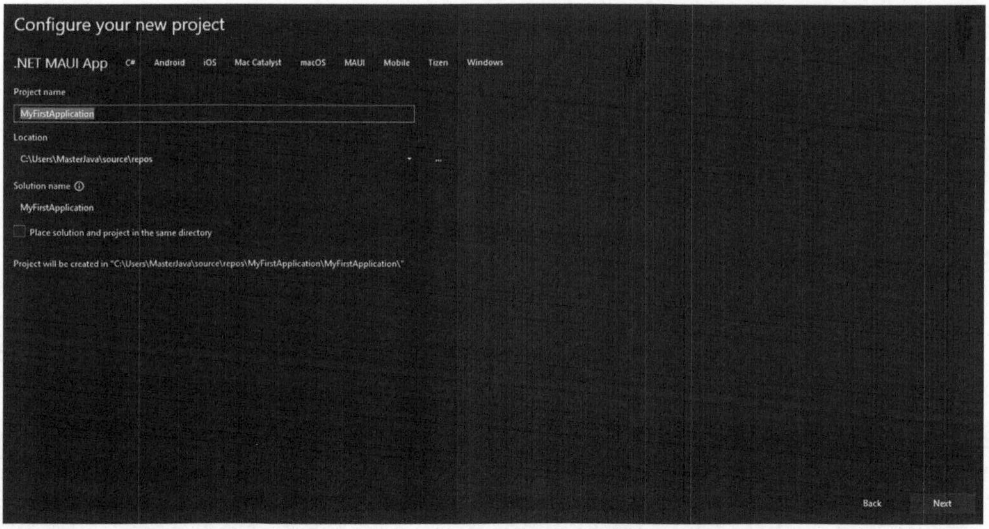

Figure 3.2: *Example of the project configuration*

3. In the additional information window, we will select the **`.NET 8.0`** framework, and click on the **`Create`** button. In this way, the application will be created and the project dependencies will be restored.

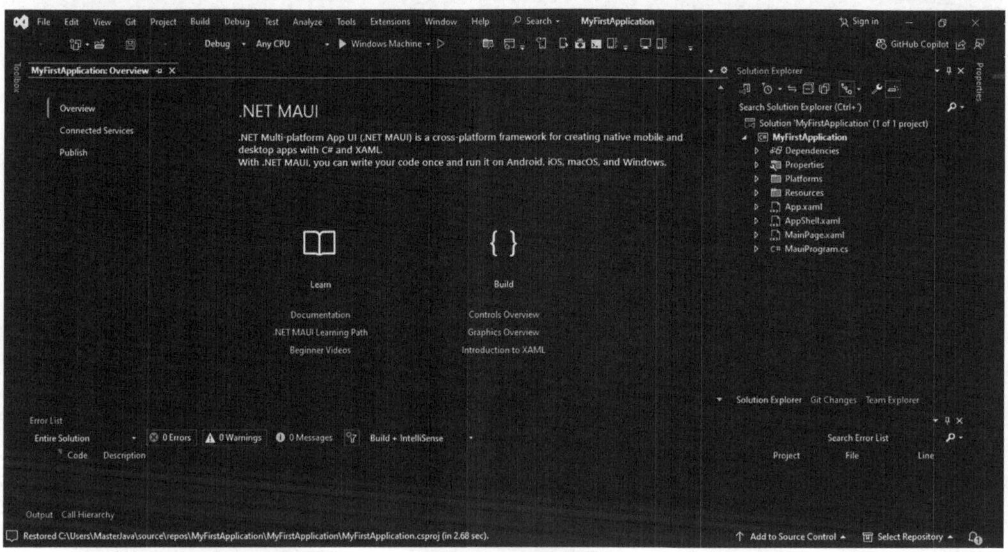

Figure 3.3: *The newly created project*

4. The next step would be to run the application. For this example, we will use an Android emulator, but you can also use a local device. If it is an Android device, the developer options and the USB debugging must be enabled. If it is an iPhone device, the iTunes application should be installed on the computer, and you must have your Issuer ID and Key ID in hand.

To run the project in the emulator, in the debug destination list, select the option **`Android Emulator`** and then the emulator input.

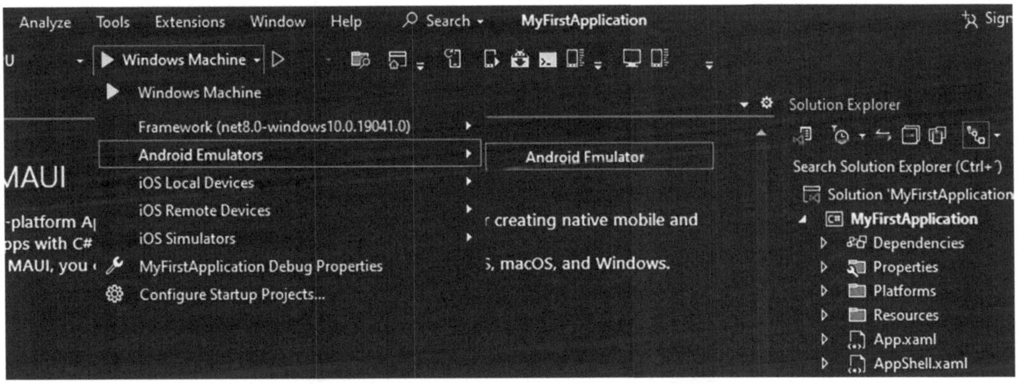

Figure 3.4: *Selecting Android Emulator*

5. Visual Studio will start the installation of the SDK and the emulator. You must accept the Android SDK license Then, in the user account dialog box, press the **`Yes`** button, and we will accept the license agreement The **`Android Emulator`** will be selected again, and a dialog box will open the **`Android Device Manager`**. Press **`Yes`**—this allows Visual Studio to download, unzip, and create the instance of the Android emulator. Sometimes, the emulator starts, but if not, we just press the **`Start`** button to start the emulator.

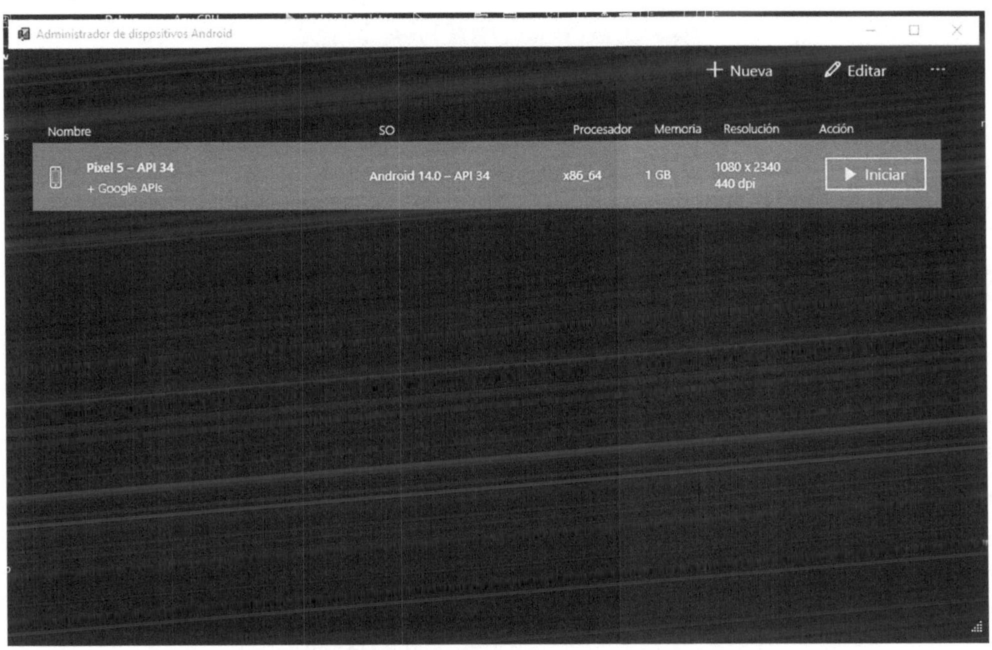

Figure 3.5: *Android Device Manager*

6. In Visual Studio, within the toolbar, press the **`Pixel 5`** button to start the emulator Compile the code and deploy the application.

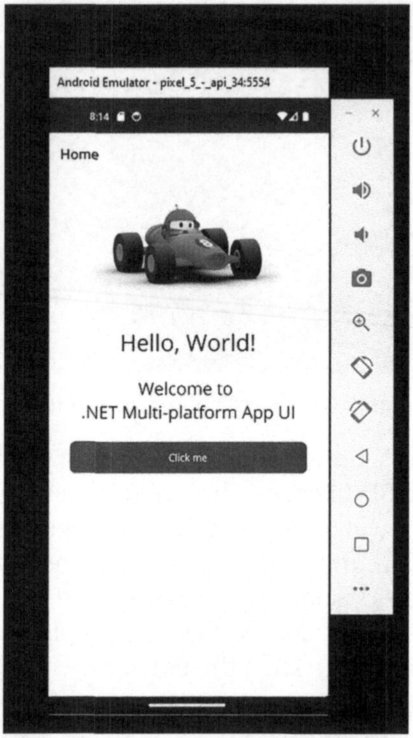

***Figure 3.6**: Application run on the Android Emulator*

As you can see in the previous figure, once the application has been compiled, it will run on our emulator or device. In the next section, we will explore XAML, the extensible markup language used for user interface development.

XAML

To define the user interface of an application developed in .NET MAUI that can run on multiple platforms, XAML is used, which is an Extensible Application Markup Language that allows developers to design and create user interfaces declaratively within the .NET ecosystem.

XAML, being declarative, allows you to focus on the desired result instead of how to get to that result, helping to simplify the creation and management of an interface, allowing the view to be separated from the logic that is usually written in C# from the application.

```
<Button Content="Click Me" Width="80" Height="50"
Clicked="OnButtonClick"/>
```

The previous example represents a button component that, when clicked, will launch the **OnButtonClick** event found in the C# code file.

```
private void OnButtonClick(object sender, EventArgs e)
{
    Console.WriteLine("Hello World");
}
```

To define a component in XAML, they are represented through tags. Within a tag, the control or interface element and the component's properties are specified. Interface elements communicate with the **ViewModel**; among other things, there are tags that allow nesting controls such as layouts that provide the structure of the application.

```
<VerticalStackLayout
    Padding="30,0"
    Spacing="15">
    <Label  Text="{Binding Title}"/>
    <Button
        Text="Click me"
        Clicked="OnCounterClicked"/>
</VerticalStackLayout>
```

XAML allows you to include and organize different library elements through the **xmlns** attribute, allowing the integration of external libraries, custom controls, or standards for the operation of an interface. An example of its use is when we include a class that inherits the **IDrawable** to be able to draw in a **GraphicsView** component.

```
<ContentPage xmlns="http://schemas.microsoft.com/dotnet/2021/
maui"
             xmlns:x="http://schemas.microsoft.com/winfx/2009/
xaml"
             xmlns:local="clr-namespace:YourAppNamespace"
             x:Class="YourAppNamespace.MainPage">

    <GraphicsView x:Name="canvas"
                  HeightRequest="200"
                  WidthRequest="200"
                  Drawable="{x:Static local:CircleDrawable.
Instance}" />
</ContentPage>
```

C#

It is a multi-paradigm programming language, which means that it works for different programming paradigms such as object-oriented, functional, generic, structured, event-driven, and reflective programming. It is a multifunctional technology for the development of various types of software and useful for web development, desktop, mobile, video games, API development, multiplatform application development, and other applications.

In this book, we will not talk about all the features of C#, such as the basic programming concepts; rather, we will focus on dealing with slightly more advanced concepts that are usually very useful when developing a cross-platform application in .NET MAUI, such as classes, objects, interfaces, dependency Injection, polymorphism, among other important features.

Classes and Objects

A class is the structure of an object; basically, it is a model or template that defines properties that are variables or methods that represent some behavior, while the object represents things in the real world, abstract concepts, and specific behaviors. An object must be related to an internal structure that is a class; for example, we have the Sale class, which has two properties: Price of type double and Total of type double.

```
public class Sale
{

    public double Price { get; set; }

    public double Total { get; set; }

}
```

To use this class, we will create two and then add them to obtain a result.

```
var Soda = new Sale();
var Potatoes = new Sale();

Soda.Price = 18.90;
Potatoes.Price = 12;

var NewSale = Soda.Price + Potatoes.Price;
Console.WriteLine(NewSale);
```

Constructor

A constructor is a function that is called the same as the class and is invoked when creating an object. It is very useful, when initiating values of the class or executing some specific behavior; for example, in a .NET MAUI **ContentPage** Object, the Page is always initialized in the class constructor. As such, the constructor does not have the ability to return values, but if it can receive parameters, an example of this would be when wanting to reuse an object that was created on a page and be able to send it to another page for the use of its values.

We have the **Sale** class that has its constructor defined, which is responsible for updating the sale price.

```
public class Sale
{
      public Sale (double newPrice = 0)
      {
        this.UpdatePrice(newPrice);
      }

      public void UpdatePrice(double newPrice = 0)
      {
          if (newPrice != 0)
               Price = newPrice;
      }

     public double Price { get; set; }
}
```

To test the constructor, an object of type **Sale** was created where a new value was sent as a parameter.

```
var Soda = new Sale(21.96);
Console.WriteLine(Soda.Price);
```

Inheritance

Inheritance is when we can inherit the characteristics of a class that is considered a parent class to other classes that will become children, which helps the code reuse and have more cleanliness in a project.

To create an inheritance, you must add a colon (:) after the name of the child class, and after the colon, you must add the parent class, as shown in the following example:

```
public class Product : Sale
{
    public double NewPrice
    {
        set
        {
            UpdatePrice(value);
        }
    }
}
```

Encapsulation

In summary, encapsulation is the quality of hiding to protect properties or behaviors of objects. As we already know, objects can communicate with each other which, although a very useful quality, can also bring some security problems. So it is necessary to protect the data. To do this, we must know how to use them. To hide a property or behavior, it will only be enough to add the private field. With this, the element will no longer be accessible outside the class. As a good practice, it is necessary to add an underscore and the first letter of the name of the class. The variable:

```
private double _sale;
```

Static

When we need to call a property or a specific method of some class but without the need to create a new object of the class because we do not need all the characteristics of that class, we can modify the call of that element to a Static, a very useful characteristic for creating global elements that can be used throughout the project.

```
public static double Price;
```

Overload

Overloading is the characteristic of having multiple methods called in the same way but having different parameters; it is useful for the development of API resources.

```
public class Sale
{
    public void UpdatePrice(double newPrice = 0)
    {
        if (newPrice != 0)
            Price = newPrice;
    }

    public void UpdatePrice(double newPrice, double tax)
    {
        Price = newPrice + tax;
    }

    public double Price { get; set; }
}
```

Polymorphism

In summary, polymorphism is the ability of an object to function depending on the context in which it is located. This brings benefits in the development of an application, such as code reuse, flexibility in being able to modify or extend a function, legibility, decoupling, and so on.

```
using System;
using System.Collections.Generic;

// Base class
public class Animal
{
    public virtual void Speak()
    {
        Console.WriteLine("The animal makes a sound.");
    }
}

// Derived class 1
public class Dog : Animal
{
    public override void Speak()
    {
        Console.WriteLine("The dog barks.");
    }
}

// Derived class 2
public class Cat : Animal
{
    public override void Speak()
    {
        Console.WriteLine("The cat meows.");
    }
}

// Main program
public class Program
{
    public static void Main()
    {
        // List of animals, but declared as the base class type
        List<Animal> animals = new List<Animal>
        {
            new Dog(),
            new Cat(),
            new Animal()
        };
```

```
            // Each object behaves differently based on its actual
    class
            foreach (var animal in animals)
            {
                animal.Speak();
            }
        }
    }
```

Interface

An interface can be described as an entity that provides a contract for the elements that must exist within a class, ensuring that the elements are present and promoting an appropriate abstraction.

```
interface IPerson
{
    public string Name { get; set; }
    public string FullName { get; set; }
}

class Person : IPerson
{
    public string Name { get; set; }
    public string FullName { get; set; }
}
```

Dependency Injection

Dependency injection is a design pattern that is based on the principle of dependency inversion, where it is suggested that a class should not depend on a concrete implementation. For example, an instance of a class, but rather that classes should depend on an abstraction, for instance, example one interface: injecting from the outside.

For example, first we define an interface:

```
interface IPerson
{
    public string Name { get; set; }
}
```

Then, an implementation of the interface will be created:

```
class Person : IPerson
{
    public void Name(string name)
    {
```

```
            Console.WriteLine($"What is your name? {name}");
        }
    }
```

Now, we directly inject the dependency without the need to create an instance.

```
    public class OrderName
    {
        private readonly IPerson _person;

        public OrderName(IPerson person)
        {
            _person = person;
        }

        public void ProcessOrder(string name)
        {
            _person.Name(name);
        }
    }
```

Finally, we construct the object by sending an instance of the Person object.

```
    IPerson person = new Person();
    OrderName orderProcessor = new OrderName(person);
    orderProcessor.ProcessOrder("My name is MAUI");
```

Pages

Normally, a user interface is built with one or more pages. Using a Hierarchy navigation system that allows the user to move between different Pages within an application.

A Page is built through objects to which a group of native controls is assigned so that the user can interact with the functions of the application; in short, a Page is a screen or window where our components will live.

To create an interface, main controls are used, starting from pages, layouts, and views as follows.

So, the Pages are our screen, which will have one or more layouts. The layout is the visual structure that will contain several views with logic to establish the positioning and size of elements; an example would be the grid. And finally, the views are objects of the user interface, such as **Buttons**, **Label**, **Frame**, **Map**, **DatePicker**, **CheckBox**, **BoxView**, **ContentView**, and others.

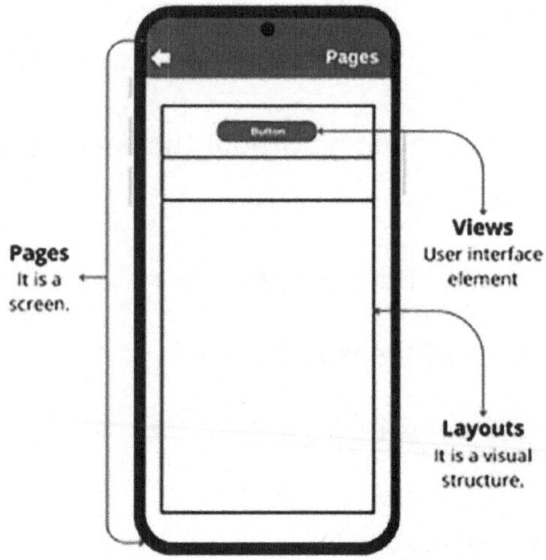

Figure 3.7: *Example of elements of a user interface*

.NET MAUI offers four types of pages: **`ContentPage`**, **`FlyoutPage`**, **`NavigationPage`**, and **`TabbedPage`**. Each Page is used according to the design of the application. If you need a hamburger-type menu, the appropriate page can be the **`FlyoutPage`**, or if a type menu is required, Tabbed will be used.

ContentPage

It is a screen that shows a single view that is usually the most used page when creating an application. It allows adding layouts such as Grid or StackLayout. This type of page only allows adding a single layout as a parent in the case that we add two layouts in the same hierarchy. This will be marked as an error that the content is set more than once.

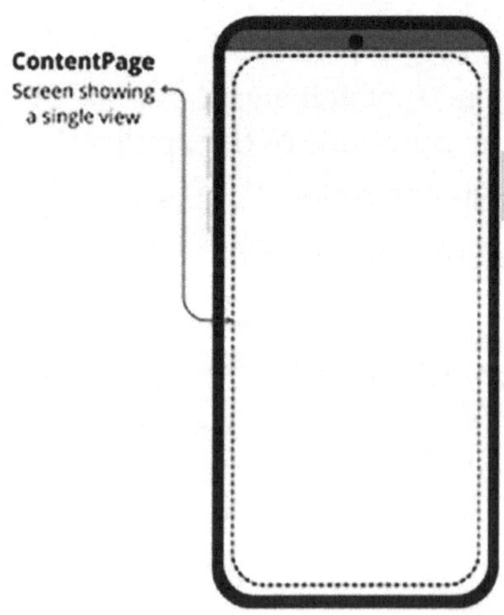

Figure 3.8: *Representation of a ContentPage page*

To create a **ContentPages** page, in Visual Studio, within the Solution Explorer, select the project or a folder where we will create our document; we will right-click and within the menu, select the option add and then new element. The dialog box **Add New Item** will open; within the C# items, we will look for the .NET MAUI option, and then you must select the element template **.NET MAUI ContentPage (XAML)**. In the name **TextBox**, we can modify the name of the file and finally click on the **Add** button to create the new document.

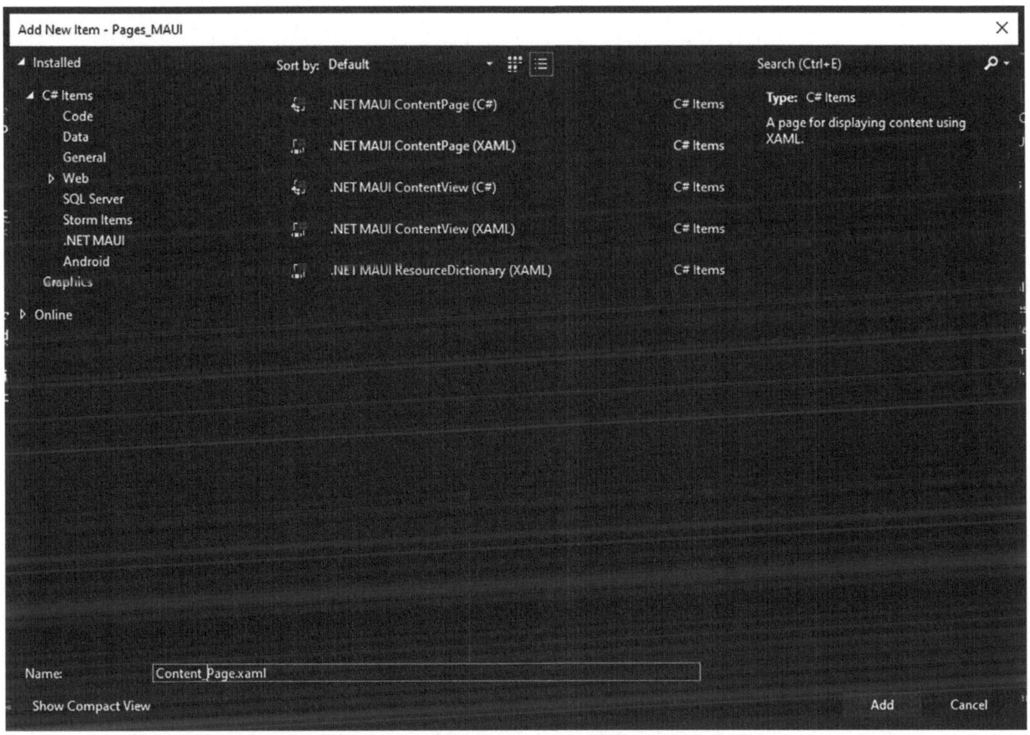

***Figure 3.9**: Representation of creating a new ContentPage in Visual Studio*

The file created is derived from the **ContentPage** with code similar to the following example:

```
<ContentPage xmlns="http://schemas.microsoft.com/dotnet/2021/maui"
             xmlns:x="http://schemas.microsoft.com/winfx/2009/xaml"
             x:Class="Pages_MAUI.Content_Page">
       <VerticalStackLayout>
             <Label Text="Welcome to .NET MAUI!"
                    VerticalOptions="Center"
                    HorizontalOptions="Center" />
       </VerticalStackLayout>
</ContentPage>
```

All that remains is to test this new page. To do so, you must modify the

App.xaml.cs file within the constructor and add the new instance of the page created in the **MainPage** variable.

```
namespace Pages_MAUI
{
    public partial class App : Application
    {
        public App()
        {
            InitializeComponent();
            //MainPage = new AppShell();
            MainPage = new Content_Page();
        }
    }
}
```

After this configuration, all that remains is to run it, remembering that you must have an emulator installed or a mobile device already configured.

***Figure 3.10**: ContentPage executed*

As you can see in the previous figure, once the application has been compiled, it will run on our emulator or device.

FlyoutPage

It is a drop-down screen in charge of managing two pages One of the pages is a drop-down and is displayed in a divided design, and on the left, it presents a menu of elements that can be related to other pages, and the second page represents the detail on the selected element of the drop-down page and has the layout of a pop-up window.

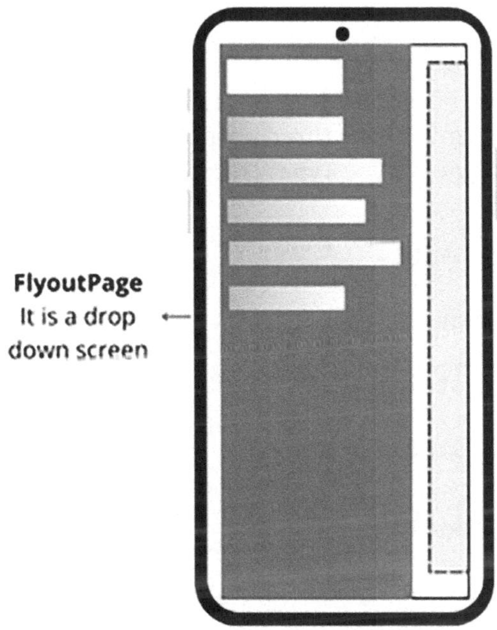

Figure 3.11: *Representation of a page FlyoutPage*

The Page **`FlyoutPage`** has the following properties described as follows:

Detail	Defines the detail page that will be displayed.
Flyout	It is the drop-down page.
`FlyoutLayoutBehavior`	Indicates the type of behavior that the drop-down page and the detail page will have.
`IsGestureEnabled`	Defines whether the swipe will be different between the drop-down page and the detail.
`IsPresented`	Indicates whether the drop-down page or the detail page is displayed.

Table 3.1: *Properties defined by FlyoutPage*

To create a window of type **FlyoutPage**: First, a new element will be added to our project. This element will be **.NET MAUI ContentPage (XAML)**. Within the newly created XAML file, the property is overridden for **ContentPage** for **FlyoutPage**. Likewise, in the file adjacent to the XAML, the .cs file in which the inheritance of the class will be modified.

The second step is to create a new **ContentPage**, also of type XAML, to be the definition of the **Flyout**, which will provide the elements of the dropdown page. In this case, name the file as **Items.xaml**, but it can be any name as long as it helps describe the uses of that file for future reference.

The third step would be to create a new **.cs** file; for this example, it was named **Object_Items**. This class must have three properties: Title of type string, **IconSource** type string, and **TargetType** of type **Type**. This class will help define the properties for the **ItemsSource**.

```
namespace Pages_MAUI
{
    internal class Object_Items
    {
        public string Title { get; set; }

        public string IconSource { get; set; }

        public Type TargetType { get; set; }
    }
}
```

In the second step, the **Item.xaml** file was created. Inside the **ContentPage**, the **CollectionView** inside this element has added the **CollectionView.ItemsSource** and the **CollectionView.ItemTemplate**. Within the **ItemsSource**, the elements that establish the items are defined, which are the pages to which the user will navigate when selecting the item, and the properties of the class **Object_Items**, which was created in step three, are used. The **ItemTemplate** is assigned a **DataTemplate** that has a grid containing an image (**IconSource**) and the label (**Title**). The following code shows an example of the definition of the **FlyoutMenuPage** of type **ContentPage**.

```
<?xml version="1.0" encoding="utf-8" ?>

<ContentPage xmlns="http://schemas.microsoft.com/dotnet/2021/maui"
             xmlns:x="http://schemas.microsoft.com/winfx/2009/xaml"
             xmlns:local="clr-namespace:Pages_MAUI"
             x:Class="Pages_MAUI.Items"
             Padding="0,40,0,0"
             IconImageSource="hamburger.png"
             Title="Items">
```

```
    <CollectionView x:Name="CollectionView"
                    x:FieldModifier="public"
                    SelectionMode="Single">

        <CollectionView.ItemsSource>
            <x:Array Type="{x:Type local:Object_Items}">

                <local:Object_Items Title="MainPage"
                                    IconSource="dotnet_bot.png"
                                    TargetType="{x:Type local:Main-
                                    Page}" />

                <local:Object_Items Title="NewPage1"
                                    IconSource="dotnet_bot.png"
                                    TargetType="{x:Type local:New-
                                    Page1}" />

            </x:Array>
        </CollectionView.ItemsSource>

        <CollectionView.ItemTemplate>
            <DataTemplate>

                <Grid Padding="5,10"
                      ColumnDefinitions="30,*">

                    <Image Source="{Binding IconSource}" />

                    <Label Grid.Column="1"
                           Margin="20,0"
                           Text="{Binding Title}"
                           FontSize="20"
                           FontAttributes="Bold"
                           VerticalOptions="Center" />
                </Grid>

            </DataTemplate>
        </CollectionView.ItemTemplate>
    </CollectionView>
</ContentPage>
```

In the file that was defined as **`FlyoutPage`** in step one, the property is established as **`FlyoutPage.Flyout`** where you set a ContentPage object that was named **`items.xaml`**. In step two, you also set the property as **`FlyoutPage.Detail`**, which will establish a **NavigationPage** that contains a **ContentPage** object; as an example, the default file that is created when creating the **MainPage.xaml** project will be used.

```
<FlyoutPage xmlns="http://schemas.microsoft.com/dotnet/2021/maui"
            xmlns:x="http://schemas.microsoft.com/winfx/2009/xaml"
            xmlns:local="clr-namespace:Pages_MAUI"
            x:Class="Pages_MAUI.Flyout_Page">

    <FlyoutPage.Flyout>
        <local:Items x:Name="flyoutPage" />
    </FlyoutPage.Flyout>

    <FlyoutPage.Detail>
        <NavigationPage>
            <x:Arguments>
                <local:MainPage />
            </x:Arguments>
        </NavigationPage>
    </FlyoutPage.Detail>

</FlyoutPage>
```

In the **code.cs** of the **FlyoutPage**, we will add navigation to the selected menu items. For this, the **OnSelectionChanged** event is added, and then in the constructor it is subscribed to the **SelectionChanged**, as shown in the following example:

```
namespace Pages_MAUI;

public partial class Flyout_Page : FlyoutPage
{
public Flyout_Page()
       {
              InitializeComponent();
              flyoutPage.CollectionView.SelectionChanged +=
              OnSelectionChanged;
       }

       void OnSelectionChanged(object sender, SelectionChanged
       EventArgs e)
       {
              //Object_Items class
              var item = e.CurrentSelection.FirstOrDefault() as
              Object_Items;

              if (item != null)
              {
                     // Detail is the property of the FlyoutPage
```

```
                        Detail = new
NavigationPage((Page)Activator.CreateInstance(item.TargetType));

                        if (!((IFlyoutPageController)this).Should-
                        ShowSplitMode)
                              IsPresented = false;
                  }
            }
      }
```

The last step is to create a new instance of the **FlyoutPage** for the **MainPage** inside the App class.

```
namespace Pages_MAUI
{
    public partial class App : Application
    {
        public App()
        {
            InitializeComponent();
            MainPage = new Flyout_Page();
        }
    }
}
```

All you need to do is run it, remembering that you must have an emulator installed or a mobile device already configured.

***Figure 3.12**: FlyoutPage executed*

As seen in the previous figure, once the application has been compiled, it will run on our emulator or device. In the next section, we explore the **NavigationPage**, a fundamental component of navigation in mobile applications.

NavigationPage

It is a screen that offers the experience of hierarchical navigation between the pages of an application, which allows the user to move back and forth using a navigation stack (LIFO).

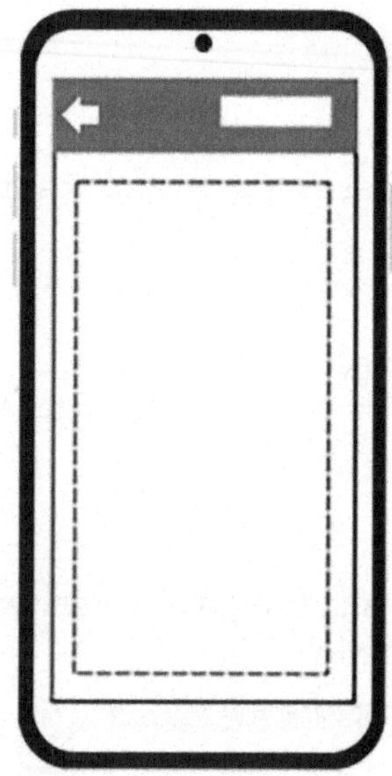

***Figure 3.13**: Representation of a page NavigationPage*

The **NavigationPage** has the following properties described in the following table:

BarBackground	Defines the background of the navigation bar.
BarBackgroundColor	Defines the background color of the navigation bar.
BackButtonTitle	Text that will be used by the back button.
BarTextColor	Navigation bar text color.
CurrentPage	Indicates the top page in the navigation stack.
HasNavigationBar	Defines whether there is a navigation bar.
HasBackButton	Defines whether the bar will have the back button.
IconColor	Defines the background color of the navigation bar icon.
RootPage	Represents the root page.

TitleIconImageSource	Defines the icon that represents the title of the navigation bar.
TitleView	Defines the view that will be displayed in the navigation bar.

Table 3.2: *Properties defined by NavigationPage*

The **NavigationPage** has three events defined: Pushed which inserts a page into the navigation stack; Popped which is responsible for extracting the page from the stack; and **PoppedToRoot** which is generated, when the last Page is extracted.

To create a **NavigationPage**, a .NET MAUI project will be created, and two ContentPages will be added. For this example, one **ContentPage** was named **Home.xaml**, and the second **ContentPage** was named **Page_1.xaml**.

In both the **Home.xaml** and the **Page_1.xaml**, the content will be replaced, and a **VerticalStackLayout** will be added with a button component that will have the properties Text that represents the button text, Clicked, which is the event when clicking, and Margin which represents the margin of the component.

In the **Home.xaml.cs**, a method will be created that provides navigation to Page **Page_1**. This event will be called **btnGoToPage_Clicked**, and within this method, we will assign a page to the navigation stack with the Pushed event using the **Navigation.PushAsync**. The following code shows the example of the created method:

```
namespace Navigation_Page;

public partial class Home : ContentPage
{
   public Home()
   {
        InitializeComponent();
   }

    private void btnGoToPage_Clicked(object sender, EventArgs e)
    {
        Navigation.PushAsync(new Page_1());
    }
}
```

In the **Home.xaml**, in the button properties, the Text is modified by adding the button text, and Clicked will be assigned the **btnGoToPage_Clicked** method, which was added in the **Home.xaml.cs**.

```
<ContentPage xmlns="http://schemas.microsoft.com/dotnet/2021/maui"
             xmlns:x="http://schemas.microsoft.com/winfx/2009/xaml"
             x:Class="Navigation_Page.Home"
             Title="Home">
    <VerticalStackLayout>
        <Button Text="Go to Page 1"
```

```
                Clicked="btnGoToPage_Clicked"
                Margin="10" />
    </VerticalStackLayout>
</ContentPage>
```

In **Page_1.xaml.cs**, a method will be created that will be responsible for extracting the page from the navigation stack. This event will be called **btnGoToHomePage_Clicked**, and within this method, the Popped event will be added using **Navigation.PopAsync**. The following code shows the example of the created method:

```
public partial class Page_1 : ContentPage
{
    public Page_1()
    {
        InitializeComponent();
    }

    private void btnGoToHomePage_Clicked(object sender, EventArgs e)
    {
        Navigation.PopAsync();
    }
}
```

In **Page_1.xaml**, in the button properties, the **Text** is modified by adding the button text, and **Clicked** will assign the **btnGoToHomePage_Clicked** method, which was added in **Home.xaml.cs**.

```
<ContentPage xmlns="http://schemas.microsoft.com/dotnet/2021/maui"
             xmlns:x="http://schemas.microsoft.com/winfx/2009/xaml"
             x:Class="Navigation_Page.Page_1"
             Title="Page_1">
    <VerticalStackLayout>
        <Button Text="Go to Home"
                Clicked="btnGoToHomePage_Clicked"
                Margin="10" />
    </VerticalStackLayout>
</ContentPage>
```

As a last step, you have to define the **Home.xaml** as the root of the navigation stack. Within the **App.xaml.cs** page constructor, the **NavigationPage** is installed in the **MainPage**, as shown in the following code example.

```
public partial class App : Application
{
        public App()
        {
            InitializeComponent();
            MainPage = new NavigationPage(new Home());
```

```
    }
}
```

All you need to do is run it, remembering that you must have an emulator installed or a mobile device already configured.

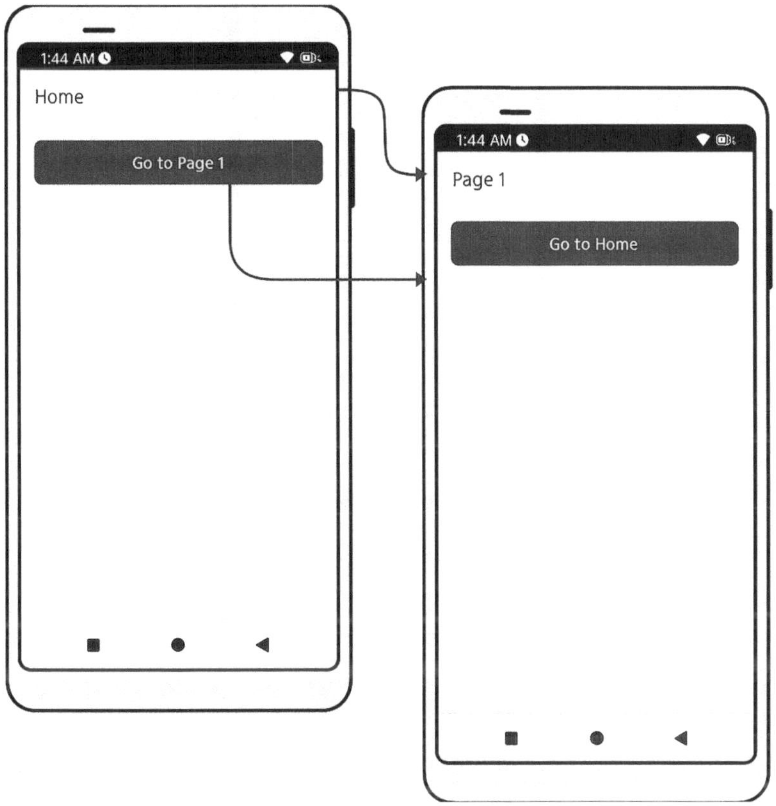

Figure 3.14: *Representation of how the NavigationPage works*

As seen in the previous figure, once the application has been compiled, it will run on our emulator or device. In the next section, we explore the **TabbedPage**, a fundamental component of mobile app navigation.

TabbedPage

It is a user interface that maintains a collection of Pages elements in a secondary way that are usually **ContentPage**, allowing only one to be completely visible but allowing navigation between tabs that are at the top or bottom of the window.

***Figure 3.15**: Representation of a TabbedPage page*

The **TabbedPage** has the following properties described as follows:

BarBackground	Defines the background of the tab bar.
BarBackgroundColor	Defines the background color of the tab bar.
BarTextColor	Defines the text color of the tab bar.
SelectedTabColor	Defines the color of the selected tab.
UnselectedTabColor	Indicates the color of the tab when it is not selected.

***Table 3.3**: Properties defined by TabbedPage*

To create a **TabbedPage**, a project will be created in .NET MAUI, and in the Solution Explorer, three new **ContentPages** were added. For this example, the files were named as follows: **Tabbed.xaml**, **Page_1.xaml**, and **Page_2.xaml**.

In the **Tabbed.xaml** file, the **ContentPage** object will have to be modified by the **TabbedPage**, and within the **.cs** code, the inheritance of the class will be modified.

The entire contents of the **Tabbed.xaml** will be replaced, and the collection of child Pages objects will be added, as shown in the following example:

```
<?xml version="1.0" encoding="utf-8" ?>
<TabbedPage xmlns="http://schemas.microsoft.com/dotnet/2021/maui"
            xmlns:x="http://schemas.microsoft.com/winfx/2009/xaml"
```

```
            xmlns:pages="clr-namespace:Tabbed_Page"
            x:Class="Tabbed_Page.Tabbed">

    <pages:MainPage />
    <pages:Page_1 />
    <pages:Page_2 />

</TabbedPage>
```

In the previous files, **Page_1.xaml**, **Page_2.xaml**, and **MainPage.xaml** (a file created by default when creating the project), the attributes **IconImageSource** and **Title** will be added, which will define both the icon and the title of the tab that will be created. will show in the tab bar.

```
<ContentPage xmlns="http://schemas.microsoft.com/dotnet/2021/maui"
             xmlns:x="http://schemas.microsoft.com/winfx/2009/xaml"
             x:Class="Tabbed_Page.Page_2"
             IconImageSource="dotnet_bot.png"
             Title="Page_2">
    <VerticalStackLayout>
        <Label
            Text="Welcome to .NET MAUI!"
            VerticalOptions="Center"
            HorizontalOptions="Center" />
    </VerticalStackLayout>
</ContentPage>
```

The last step is to create a new instance of the Tabbed object for the **MainPage** within the App class.

```
namespace Tabbed_Page
{
    public partial class App : Application
    {
        public App()
        {
            InitializeComponent();

            MainPage = new Tabbed();
        }
    }
}
```

All you need to do is run it, remembering that you must have an emulator installed or a mobile device already configured.

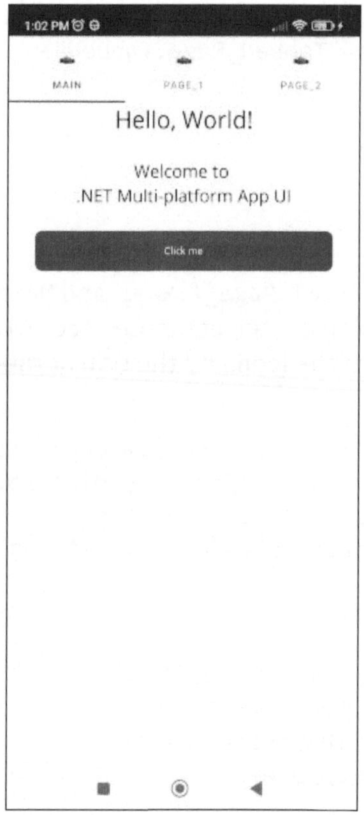

***Figure 3.16**: TabbedPage executed*

As seen in the previous figure, once the application has been compiled, it will run on our emulator or device. In the next section, we will explore Layouts which are essential for organizing and structuring visual elements in the user interface.

Layouts

Layouts are visual structures that allow you to organize and group visual elements; through logic, you can define the position and size of the components of an application.

.NET MAUI contains the following visual structures: **`AbsoluteLayout`**, **`BindableLayout`**, **`HorizontalStackLayout`**, **`StackLayout`**, **`VerticalStackLayout`**, **`FlexLayout`**, **`Grid`**.

StackLayout

The **`StackLayout`** is a one-dimensional stack element that allows components to be positioned horizontally or vertically.

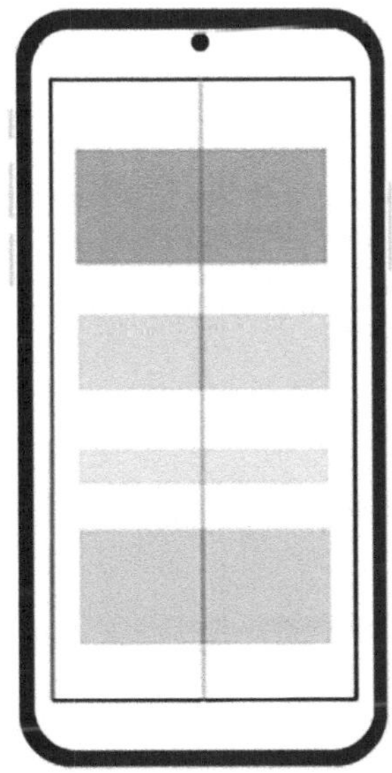

***Figure 3.17**: Representation of a visual StackLayout structure*

The **StackLayout** has the Orientation property, which represents the Horizontal or Vertical direction that the components will have. Spacing indicates the space between each component, and **BindableProperty** is the destination between data binding and styles.

```
<StackLayout Orientation="Horizontal" Spacing="10" Margin="15">
    <Label Text="Welcome to .NET MAUI!" />
    <Label Text="Hello word!"/>
</StackLayout>
```

HorizontalStackLayout

The **HorizontalStackLayout** is a one-dimensional horizontal stack element that allows components to be positioned horizontally, offering better performance than the **StackLayout**. The **HorizontalStackLayout** defines the Spacing property that specifies the space between the secondary visual components and the **BindableProperty** that can be the destination between links of data and styles.

```
<HorizontalStackLayout Spacing="10" Margin="15">
    <Label Text="HorizontalStackLayout" />
    <Label Text="Hello word!" />
</HorizontalStackLayout>
```

VerticalStackLayout

The **VerticalStackLayout** is a one-dimensional vertical stack element that allows components to be positioned vertically, offering better performance than the

StackLayout. The **VerticalStackLayout** defines the Spacing property that specifies the space between the secondary visual components and the **BindableProperty** that can be the destination between links of data and styles.

```
<VerticalStackLayout Spacing="10" Margin="15">
    <Label Text="VerticalStackLayout" />
    <Label Text="Hello word!" />
</VerticalStackLayout>
```

Grid

The **Grid** structure is a grid that displays view elements in rows and columns that can have proportional or absolute sizes.

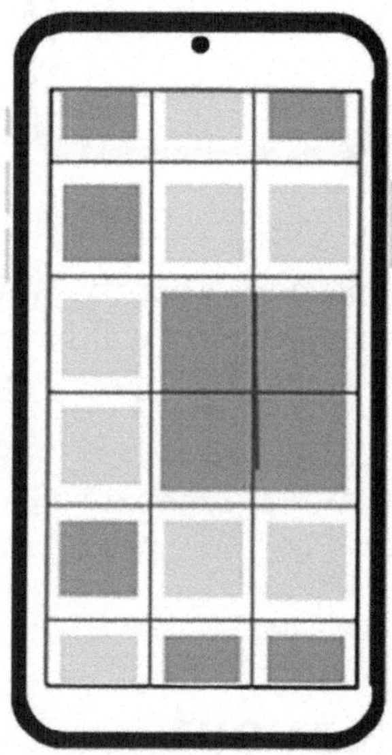

***Figure 3.18**: Representation of a visual Grid structure*

Grid has the following properties described as follows:

Column	Defines the alignment of the column within the Grid; it is of type int and its value must be greater than or equal to 0.
ColumnDefinitions	It is the collection of columns that will be defined in the Grid.
ColumnDefinition	Defines the width of the Grid columns.
ColumnSpacing	Defines the space between the columns of the Grid.
ColumnSpan	Indicates the number of columns that an element of the view will take; it is of type int and must be greater than or equal to 1.
Row	Defines the alignment of the rows within the Grid; it is of type int and its value must be greater than or equal to 0.

RowDefinitions	It is the collection of rows that will be defined in the Grid.
RowDefinition	Defines the height of the Grid rows.
RowSpacing	Defines the distance between the rows of the Grid.
RowSpan	Indicates the number of rows that an element of the view will take; it is of type int and must be greater than or equal to 1.

Table 3.4: *Properties defined by Grid*

These rows and columns are defined using the **RowDefinitions** and **ColumnDefinitions** properties, and for each child component, the cell where it will be located is specified with the **Grid.Column** for the column and the **Grid.Row** for the row. The following code example shows a 2-by-2 grid, and in each cell, a frame element with different colors is established.

```
<Grid ColumnDefinitions="20,auto"
      RowDefinitions="20,auto"
      Margin="15">

    <Frame Grid.Column="0"
           Grid.Row="0"
           WidthRequest="20"
           HeightRequest="20"
           BackgroundColor="Red">
    </Frame>
    <Frame Grid.Column="1"
           Grid.Row="0"
           WidthRequest="20"
           HeightRequest="20"
           BackgroundColor="Green">
    </Frame>
   <Frame Grid.Column="0"
          Grid.Row="1"
          WidthRequest="20"
          HeightRequest="20"
          BackgroundColor="Pink">
   </Frame>
   <Frame Grid.Column="1"
          Grid.Row="1"
          WidthRequest="20"
          HeightRequest="20"
          BackgroundColor="Blue">
   </Frame>

</Grid>
```

FlexLayout

The **FlexLayout** structure allows secondary elements to be positioned horizontally or vertically, very similar to the **StackLayout**, but at the same time it can encapsulate them in rows and columns depending on whether there are too many elements, allowing adaptation to different screen sizes. **FlexLayout** defines the following properties:

AlignContent	Defines how the layout engine distributes the spaces and surroundings of the elements, using the **FlexAlignContent** data type.
AlignItems	Defines how the layout engine distributes the spaces and surroundings of the elements on the transverse axis, using the **FlexAlignItems** data type.
Direction	Defines the direction and axis of the elements; uses the **FlexDirection** data type.
JustifyContent	Defines how the spaces and surroundings of the elements are distributed on the main axis, using the **FlexJustify** data type.
Position	Indicates the position of the children in a relative or fixed value manner; of type **FlexPosition**.
Wrap	Controls the elements that are arranged in one line in several; **FlexWrap** type.
AlignSelf	Defines how the layout engine distributes the spaces and surroundings of specific elements on the transverse axis; of type **FlexAlignSelf**.
Basis	Defines the initial size of the element before distributing spaces.
Grow	Specifies the available space that an element on the main axis should use.
Order	Determines which element should be placed before or after another element.
Shrink	Determines how an element should be reduced within the container.

Table 3.5: *Properties defined by FlexLayout*

The following code example shows three visual elements: A **Label**, **Image**, and a **Button** inside a **FlexLayout**.

```
<FlexLayout Direction="Column"
        AlignItems="Center"
        JustifyContent="SpaceEvenly">
    <Label Text="Hello"
           FontSize="18" />
    <Image Source="dotnet_bot.png"
```

```
            HeightRequest="300" />
        <Button Text="I am button" />
    </FlexLayout>
```

AbsoluteLayout

The **AbsoluteLayout** structure allows positioning child elements in an explicit way or with relative values. The position is specified from the top left of the component with the relationship of the top left corner of the structure; the **AbsoluteLayout** class only defines two properties: the **LayoutBounds** that represents the position and size of a visual component and the **LayoutFlags** property that attaches and represents the boundaries of the layout used for the child element's dimensions.

The following example represents four **BoxView** components of an explicit size of 100 x 100 and is displayed as centered and horizontal. Within each **BoxView**, the Rotation property is used to rotate each element by certain degrees and the color to represent each element in a different way. You can use the **AbsoluteLayout.LayoutFlags** property and set a proportion of the remaining space to the **PositionProportional**.

```
<AbsoluteLayout Margin="40">
        <BoxView Color="Pink"
                 AbsoluteLayout.LayoutFlags="PositionProportional"
                 AbsoluteLayout.LayoutBounds="0.5, 0, 100, 100"
                 Rotation="60" />
        <BoxView Color="Green"
                 AbsoluteLayout.LayoutFlags="PositionProportional"
                 AbsoluteLayout.LayoutBounds="0.5, 0, 100, 100"
                 Rotation="40" />
        <BoxView Color="Blue"
                 AbsoluteLayout.LayoutFlags="PositionProportional"
                 AbsoluteLayout.LayoutBounds="0.5, 0, 100, 100"
                 Rotation="20" />
        <BoxView Color="Red"
          AbsoluteLayout.LayoutFlags="PositionProportional"
          AbsoluteLayout.LayoutBounds="0.5, 0, 100, 100" />
 </AbsoluteLayout>
```

BindableLayout

The **BindableLayout** structure allows any Layout class to be bound to a collection of elements through the **ItemSource** and with the option to set the appearance of the component from the **DataTemplate**.

The following example links a **StackLayout** with a collection of elements. For this, we will use **MainPage.xaml.cs** where an **ObservableCollection<string>** object will be created that will contain a list of strings that will represent the image names.

```
public partial class MainPage : ContentPage
{
        public ObservableCollection<string> ImagesString { get; set; }
        public MainPage()
        {
              InitializeComponent();
              ImagesString = new ObservableCollection<string>
              {
                  "dotnet_bot.png",
                  "dotnet_bot.png",
                  "dotnet_bot.png"
              };
              BindingContext = this;
        }
}
```

In the **MainPage.xaml**, in the **BindableLayout.ItemsSource** property of the **StackLayout**, the Binding is established with the collection of **ImagesString** elements that was defined in the .cs, and within the **BindableLayout.ItemTemplate**, the style that the element will take will be established within the **DataTemplate**.

```
<StackLayout BindableLayout.ItemsSource="{Binding ImagesString}"
             Orientation="Horizontal">
    <BindableLayout.ItemTemplate>
        <DataTemplate>
            <Frame CornerRadius="50" Padding="5" Margin="5">
                <Image Source="{Binding}"
                       Aspect="AspectFill"
                       WidthRequest="44"
                       HeightRequest="44"/>
            </Frame>
        </DataTemplate>
    </BindableLayout.ItemTemplate>
</StackLayout>
```

Components

Views are objects of a user interface (UI); these controls are labels, buttons, and sliders that provide the point of contact with the user.

.NET MAUI contains a large number of views that are very useful and efficient in developing an application.

ActivityIndicator

It is a user interface that shows an indicator of prolonged activity without indicating progress. The appearance of this component will depend on the platform it is running on. On Android, it is displayed as a loading spinner.

The **ActivityIndicator** defines two properties: Color that defines the color of the indicator and the **IsRunning** of type bool indicates whether the component will be visible and animated or hidden.

```
<ActivityIndicator IsRunning="true"
                   Color="Blue" />
```

Border

It is a container whose property is to draw borders around a control. This container can only contain a single object, so it will be necessary to add a Layout object to add more than one secondary element. **Border** defines the following properties.

- **Content:** Represents the content that will be displayed in the component.
- **Padding:** Indicates the distance between the edges of the container and the children.
- **StrokeShape:** Describes the shape of the edge.
- **IShape:** Defines the default value of the Border, which is Rectangle.
- **Stroke:** Defines the border painting brush.
- **StrokeThickness:** Indicates the width of the Border, default is 1.0.
- **StrokeDashArray:** It is a collection of double elements that define patterns of spaces and dashes that form the border.
- **StrokeDashOffset:** Indicates the distance between the dash pattern.
- **StrokeLineCap:** Defines the shape of the lines.
- **StrikeLineJoin:** Defines the type of union of the vertices.
- **StrokeMiterLimit:** Defines the space limit of the stroke length and thickness.

The following example defines a Border container that contains a Label component:

```
<Border Stroke="Red"
        StrokeThickness="4"
        StrokeShape="RoundRectangle 60,60,60,0"
        Background="White"
        Padding="10,8"
        HorizontalOptions="Center">
```

```
        <Label Text="Hello"
               TextColor="Black"
               FontSize="18"/>
    </Border>
```

BoxView

It is a user interface that is represented as a square or rectangle, allowing you to create horizontal or vertical lines that are defined through the following properties: the **WidthRequest** and **HeightRequest**.

```
<BoxView Color="Red"
         Margin="10"
         WidthRequest="160"
         HeightRequest="5"
         VerticalOptions="Center"
         HorizontalOptions="Center" />
```

Button

It is a user interface that is represented as an object that displays a text or image and responds to a click or touch to fire an event. The **Button** defines the following events:

- **BorderColor**: Defines the border color.
- **BorderWidth**: Defines the width of the border.
- **CharacterSpacing**: Defines the space between characters in the text.
- **Command**: Defines a command that will be executed when the button is touched.
- **CommandParameter**: Parameters that are sent to the Command.
- **ContentLayout**: Controls the position of the image and button text.
- **CornerRadius**: Defines the corner radius of a button.
- **FontAttributes**: Defines the style of the button text.
- **FontAutoScalingEnabled**: Sets the operating system's scaling preferences for button text.
- **FontFamily**: Defines the font of the text.
- **FontSize**: Defines the font size.
- **ImageSource**: Defines the image that appears on the button.
- **LineBreakMode**: Defines the handling of text when it does not fit on the line.
- **Padding**: Determines the padding of the button.
- **Text**: Defines the text to be displayed on the button.

- **`TextColor`**: Defines the button text color.
- **`TextTransform`**: Defines whether the button text will be in upper or lower case.

The following example defines a button in XAML code:

```
<Button Text="I am Button"
        VerticalOptions="Center"
        HorizontalOptions="Center"/>
```

ContentView

It is a user interface that allows the creation of custom components or controls that can be reused. This object defines a content property that will represent the content of the **`ContentView`**. It also has the **`BindableProperty`** property to be able to bind data and have styles.

The process for creating a custom control with the **`ContentView`** is very simple. First, you must add a class of the type .NET MAUI **`ContentView`** (XAML); then you will have to define a control or event from the underlying **`.cs`** file. The interface of the custom control will be defined, and finally the instance of the custom control will be created.

First, the **`ContentView`** class will be added, which in this example will be called **`ProfileView`**, and then underneath, two properties will be defined: **`TitleView`**, which will be for a Label component, and **`IconView`**, which will be used for the Image component.

```
public partial class ProfileView : ContentView
{
    public static readonly BindableProperty TitleProperty =
        BindableProperty.Create(
            nameof(TitleView),
            typeof(string),
            typeof(ProfileView),
            string.Empty);

    public static readonly BindableProperty ImgProperty =
        BindableProperty.Create(
            nameof(IconView),
            typeof(string),
            typeof(ProfileView),
            string.Empty);

    public string TitleView
    {
        get => (string)GetValue(TitleProperty);
```

```
            set => SetValue(TitleProperty, value);
        }

        public string IconView
        {
            get => (string)GetValue(ImgProperty);
            set => SetValue(ImgProperty, value);
        }

        public ProfileView()
        {
            InitializeComponent();
        }
    }
```

The next step is to add the interface components of the custom component. In this case, a Frame was added that will be the parent container. Within the frame, the **BindingContext** property must be defined; otherwise, the custom component will not work. The content of the frame was added to an Image component where a Binding was performed with the IconView property defined in the **.cs**. A Binding was also performed within the Label component to the **TextView**.

```
<ContentView xmlns="http://schemas.microsoft.com/dotnet/2021/maui"
             xmlns:x="http://schemas.microsoft.com/winfx/2009/xaml"
             x:Class="Tabbed_Page.ProfileView"
             x:Name="this">

    <Frame BindingContext="{x:Reference this}"
           WidthRequest="150"
           Margin="10">

        <VerticalStackLayout>

            <Frame CornerRadius="50"
                   WidthRequest="50"
                   HeightRequest="50">

                <Image Source="{Binding IconView}"
                       Scale="5" />
            </Frame>

            <BoxView BackgroundColor="Red"
                     WidthRequest="150"
                     HeightRequest="2"
                     Margin="5" />
```

```
                <Label Text="{Binding TitleView, FallbackValue='Name'}"
                       HorizontalTextAlignment="Center" />

            </VerticalStackLayout>

        </Frame>
    </ContentView>
```

To finish, all that remains is to create the instance of the custom control within an Object, for example, a **ContentPage**. To create this instance, you must first reference or import the custom control with the **xmlns** and its prefix.

```
    <ContentPage xmlns="http://schemas.microsoft.com/dotnet/2021/maui"
                 xmlns:x="http://schemas.microsoft.com/winfx/2009/xaml"
                 xmlns:controls="clr-namespace:Tabbed_Page"
                 x:Class="Tabbed_Page.MainPage"
                 IconImageSource="dotnet_bot.png"
                 Title="Main">

        <ScrollView>

            <StackLayout>

                <controls:ProfileView
                    IconView="dotnet_bot.png"
                    TitleView="User name" />

            </StackLayout>

        </ScrollView>

    </ContentPage>
```

DatePicker

The **DatePicker** is a user interface control that allows you to display and select a date. The **DatePicker** defines the following properties:

- **MinimumDate:** It is the starting date of the calendar.
- **MaximumDate:** It is the final date on the calendar.
- **Date:** It is the selected date.
- **Format:** It is a standard or custom format string.
- **TextColor:** Defines the color of how the date will appear.
- **FontFamily:** Defines the source.

- **FontSize:** Defines the font size.
- **CharacterSpacing:** Defines the space between characters in the date text.

The following example represents the **DatePicker** handler in XAML code:

```
<DatePicker
   MinimumDate="01/01/2024"
   MaximumDate="12/31/2024"
   Date="07/21/2024" />
```

Editor

The **Editor** is a control that allows the entry and editing of several lines of text. The editor has properties for the **BindableProperty** to have a data link. In addition, the **Editor** class adds the properties of the **InputView**, providing more view options for the component. The defined properties of the Editor are as follows:

- **AutoSize:** Defines whether to change the size for text input.
- **HorizontalTextAlignment:** Defines the horizontal alignment of the text; alignment type **Start**, **Center**, and **End**.
- **VerticalTextAlignment:** Defines the vertical alignment of the text; alignment type **Start**, **Center**, and **End**.

The following example represents the Editor controller in XAML code:

```
<Editor Placeholder="Text"
        VerticalTextAlignment="Center"
        HeightRequest="250"/>
```

Entry

The **Entry** is a control that allows the entry and editing of a single line of text and has the following properties:

- **ClearButtonVisibility:** Allows the user to clear the content of the control.
- **HorizontalTextAlignment:** Defines the horizontal alignment of the text; alignment type **Start**, **Center**, and **End**.
- **VerticalTextAlignment:** Defines the vertical alignment of the text; alignment type **Start**, **Center**, and **End**.
- **IsPassword:** Hides the text.
- **ReturnCommand:** Command that is executed when pressing **Return**
- **ReturnCommandParameter:** Parameters for the **ReturnCommand** command.
- **ReturnType:** It is the style of the return button.

The following example represents the **Entry** controller in XAML code:

```
<Entry Placeholder="Enter password"
       IsPassword="True" />
```

Frame

The **Frame** is a control that works as a container, allowing you to configure colored borders, shadows, and rounded corners; which is useful when creating user interfaces. The following are its properties:

- **HasShadow:** Defines whether the control frame casts a shadow.
- **BorderColor:** Defines the border color.
- **CornerRadius:** Defines the rounding of the corners of the control.

The following example represents the **Frame** controller in XAML code:

```
<Frame CornerRadius="50" Padding="5" Margin="5">
    <Image Source="dotnet_bot.png"
           Aspect="AspectFill"
           WidthRequest="44"
           HeightRequest="44"/>
</Frame>
```

Frame is deprecated in .NET MAUI, starting with .NET 9. Use Border instead.

GraphicsView

The **GraphicsView** is a special control because it allows drawing 2D graphics within a space called a canvas. This control defines the "Drawable" that represents the content that will be drawn. The control defines the following properties:

- **EndHoverInteraction:** Event that fires when the pointer leaves the area.
- **StartHoverInteraction:** Event that fires when the pointer enters the area.
- **MoveHoverInteraction:** Event that is triggered when the pointer moves within the area.
- **StartInteraction:** Event that is triggered when pressing the **GraphicsView**.
- **DragInteraction:** Event that is fired when dragging the **GraphicsView** .
- **EndInteraction:** Event that is triggered when the **StartInteraction** is released.
- **CancelInteraction:** It is activated when contact with the **GraphicsView** is lost.

To start drawing within the **GraphicsView**, the Drawable is used. It implements the Draw method, which allows the use of the ICanva interface. It is the canvas for drawing, and ReactF is responsible for determining the size and location of the canvas through the **Bottom, Center, Height, IsEmpty, Left, Location, Right, Size, Top, Y, X**, and **Width** properties.

After this, you must first create a new class. In this example, it will have the name **GraphicsDrawable.cs** and it will inherit the ICanva interface. Within the class constructor, a color was defined for the drawing. With the **DrawArc** method, we will draw an arc on the canvas. The parameter that will be sent on the X axis, clockwise = false, represents whether the arc is drawn clockwise, and closed = true represents whether the starting point of the arc is connected to the end.

```
public class GraphicsDrawable : IDrawable
{
    public void Draw(ICanvas canvas, RectF dirtyRect)
    {
        canvas.StrokeColor = Colors.Red;
        canvas.DrawArc(150,150, 100,50, 0,360,false,true);
    }
}
```

After defining the class, it is time to instantiate it within a **ContentPage**. It will be imported from where the class is located using **xmlns**, and the drawable prefix was added. Within the Resource property of the **ContentPage**, the instance of the class was created, and the **GraphicsView** control was added inside the Layout.

```
<ContentPage xmlns="http://schemas.microsoft.com/dotnet/2021/maui"
             xmlns:x="http://schemas.microsoft.com/winfx/2009/xaml"
             xmlns:drawable="clr-namespace:Tabbed_Page"
             x:Class="Tabbed_Page.Canva_page"
             Title="Canva_page">

    <ContentPage.Resources>
        <drawable:GraphicsDrawable x:Key="drawable" />
    </ContentPage.Resources>

    <VerticalStackLayout BackgroundColor="Salmon">

        <GraphicsView Drawable="{StaticResource drawable}"
                      HeightRequest="300"
                      WidthRequest="400" />

    </VerticalStackLayout>

</ContentPage>
```

Image

The **Image** is a user interface that allows images to be displayed locally to a sequence or through a URL, supporting traditional image formats, GIF and SVG. This control defines the following properties:

- **Aspect:** Defines the scale of the image.
- **IsAnimationPlaying:** Determines whether the GIF plays or stops.
- **IsLoading:** Indicates the loading status of the image.
- **IsOpaque:** Determines whether the image can be rendered.
- **Source:** It is the source of the image.

The following example represents the Image controller in XAML code:

```
<Image Source="dotnet_bot.png" />
```

ImageButton

The **ImageButton** is a user interface that allows images to be displayed within a button component, allowing pressing the image to execute a function of the application. This control defines the following properties:

- **Aspect:** Defines the scale of the image.
- **IsLoading:** Indicates the loading status of the image.
- **IsOpaque:** Determines whether the image can be rendered.
- **Source:** It is the source of the image.
- **BorderColor:** Determines the border color.
- **BorderWidth:** Defines the width of the border.
- **Command:** Command that is executed when the button is pressed.
- **CommandParameter:** Parameters that will be sent to the command.
- **IsPressed:** Defines whether the button is being pressed.
- **Padding:** It is the button padding.

The following example represents the **ImageButton** handler in XAML code:

```
<ImageButton Source="dotnet_bot.png"
             Clicked="ButtonClicked"
             HorizontalOptions="Center"
             VerticalOptions="Center"
 />
```

Label

The **Label** is a user interface that allows displaying text, it defines the following properties

- **CharacterSpacing:** It is the space between the characters of the text.
- **FontAttributes:** Text style.
- **FontAutoScalingEnabled:** Determines whether to use the operating system's text scaling.
- **FontFamily:** Determines the source.
- **FontSize:** Determines the font size.
- **FormattedText:** Determines the format that the text will have.
- **HorizontalTextAlignment:** Defines the alignment of the text horizontally.
- **VerticalTextAlignment:** Defines the alignment of the text vertically.
- **LineBreakMode:** Determines how the text will wrap when it does not fit on the line.
- **LineHeight:** Determines the line height of the text.
- **MaxLines:** Defines the maximum number of lines allowed.
- **Padding:** It is the filler of the label.
- **Text:** Defines the content text.
- **TextColor:** Defines the color of the text.
- **TextDecorations:** Defines what decoration the text will have.
- **TextTransform:** Determines whether the text will be uppercase or lowercase.

The following example represents the **ImageButton** handler in XAML code:

```
<Label Text="Hello world" />
```

Picker

The **Picker** is a user interface element that displays a list of elements in order to select an element. The **Picker** defines the following properties:

- **FontFamily:** Determine the source.
- **FontSize:** Determines the font size.
- **FormattedText:** Determines the format that the text will have.
- **HorizontalTextAlignment:** Defines the alignment of the text horizontally.
- **VerticalTextAlignment:** Defines the alignment of the text vertically.
- **Text:** Defines the content text.

- **TextColor:** Defines the color of the text.
- **TextDecorations:** Defines what decoration the text will have.
- **TextTransform:** Determines whether the text will be in uppercase or lowercase.
- **CharacterSpacing:** Defines the space between characters.
- **ItemSource:** It is a data source of type IList.
- **SelectedItem:** It is the selected element.
- **ItemDisplayBinding:** Selects the property displayed on each element.
- **Title:** Represents the Picker's title.
- **TitleColor:** Defines the color of the title.

The following example represents the **Picker** handler in XAML code:

```
<Picker x:Name="picker"
        Title="Select a Color">
    <Picker.ItemsSource>
        <x:Array Type="{x:Type x:String}">
            <x:String>Red</x:String>
            <x:String>Pink</x:String>
            <x:String>Blue</x:String>
            <x:String>Green</x:String>
            <x:String>Black</x:String>
            <x:String>Silver</x:String>
        </x:Array>
    </Picker.ItemsSource>
</Picker>
```

ProgressBar

The **ProgressBar** is a user interface element that is a progress bar that fills according to a percentage. It defines two properties: Progress, which is the representation of the process through a value of type double, and **ProgressColor**, which represents the color of the progress bar.

```
<ProgressBar Progress="0.5"
             ProgressColor="Red"/>
```

RadioButton

The **RadioButton** is a button type control that allows you to select an element from a group.

- **FontFamily:** Determines the source.
- **FontSize:** Determines the font size.

- **TextColor**: Defines the color of the text.
- **TextTransform**: Determines whether the text will be in upper or lower case.
- **Content**: Defines the content to be displayed by the component.
- **IsChecked**: Defines whether the button is selected or not.
- **GroupName**: Determines which **RadioButton** are mutually exclusive.
- **Value**: Defines a single value associated with the **RadioButton**.
- **BorderColor**: Defines the border color.
- **BorderWidth**: Defines the width of the border.
- **CharacterSpacing**: Defines the space between characters in the text.
- **CornerRadius**: Defines the radius of the corner.

The following example represents the **RadioButton** controller in XAML code:

```
<StackLayout>
    <Label Text="Select a Color" />
    <RadioButton Content="Red" />
    <RadioButton Content="Blue" />
    <RadioButton Content="Pink" />
    <RadioButton Content="Silver"
                 IsChecked="true" />
</StackLayout>
```

RefreshView

The **RefreshView** is a container that allows updating its scrollable content, such as a **ScrollView**, **CollectionView**, or **ListView**. The **RefreshView** uses few properties, such as Command, to execute an update; **CommandParameter**, which are the parameters that will be sent when activating the **Command**; **IsRefreshing**, which indicates the current state of the component; and the **RefreshColor**, which defines the color of the update loading circle.

```
<RefreshView IsRefreshing="{Binding IsRefreshing}"
             Command="{Binding RefreshCommand}">
    <ScrollView>
        <FlexLayout Direction="Row"
                    BindableLayout.ItemsSource="{Binding Items}"
                    BindableLayout.ItemTemplate="{StaticResource
ColorItemTemplate}" />
    </ScrollView>
</RefreshView>
```

ScrollView

The **ScrollView** is a container that allows the movement of its content through a scroll; the scroll defines the following properties:

- **Content**: Defines the content of the **ScrollView**.
- **ContentSize**: Defines the size of the content.
- **HorizontalScrollBarVisibility**: Determines whether the horizontal bar is visible.
- **VerticalScrollBarVisibility**: Determines whether the vertical bar is visible.
- **Orientation**: Defines the direction of movement.
- **ScrollX**: Indicates the scroll on the current X axis.
- **ScrollY**: Indicates the current scroll on the Y axis.

The following example represents the **ScrollView** controller in XAML code:

```
<ScrollView HeightRequest="150">
    <StackLayout  Orientation="Vertical">
        <Label Text="Red" FontSize="40"/>
        <Label Text="Pink" FontSize="40"/>
        <Label Text="Blue"  FontSize="40"/>
        <Label Text="Silver" FontSize="40" />
        <Label Text="Black" FontSize="40"/>
        <Label Text="White" FontSize="40"/>
        <Label Text="Green" FontSize="40"/>
    </StackLayout>
</ScrollView>
```

SearchBar

The **SearchBar** is a control that allows entering a text entry for a search, allowing text entry, execution of a function, and cancellation of the search. It uses properties such as **CancelButtonColors**, which defines the color of the cancel button; **HorizontalTextAlignment**, which sets the horizontal alignment of the text; **VerticalTextAlignmentes**, which allows the text to be aligned vertically; and **SearchCommandes**, which allows linking an action to the moment of touch or click.

```
<SearchBar Placeholder="Search..." />
```

The **SearchBar** is a control that allows you to manipulate a bar horizontally in order to select a range on that bar.

The **SearchBar** defines the properties:

- **Minimum**: Defines the minimum of the bar range.

- **Maximum:** Defines the maximum range of the bar range.
- **Value:** It is the value of the selected range.
- **MinimumTrackColor:** It is the color of the bar on the left side of the thumb.
- **MaximumTrackColor:** It is the color of the bar on the right side of the thumb.
- **ThumbColor:** Defines the color of the thumb.
- **ThumbImageSource:** Defines the image that will be used in the thumbnail.
- **DragStartedCommand:** Command that is executed when starting the movement.
- **DragCompletedCommand:** Command that is executed when the movement is completed.

The following example represents the **SearchBar** controller in XAML code:

```
<StackLayout>
    <Label Text="Turn up the volume" HorizontalOptions="Center" />
    <Slider Maximum="100" />
</StackLayout>
```

Stepper

The **Stepper** is a control that allows you to select a value over a range of numerical values. It is shown as two buttons: one with the increase sign and the other with the subtract sign. The component defines the Increment properties, which are the values that change, increasing the value according to how they are selected. "**Minimum**" represents the minimum value, "**Maximum**" represents the maximum value that can be selected, and "**Value**" is the value of the **Stepper**. It also has the **ValueChange** property that allows data linking with a method.

```
<Stepper Maximum="360"
         Increment="30"
         HorizontalOptions="Center"/>
```

Switch

The **Switch** is a user interface control that allows you to display a horizontal toggle button to switch between two states, on and off. It only has three properties: **IsToggles**, which represents whether it is on or off; **OnColor**, which defines the color of the activated state of the switch; and the **ThumbColor**, which determines the color of the thumb.

```
<Switch IsToggled="true"
       OnColor="Pink"
       ThumbColor="Red"/>
```

TableView

The **TableView** is a user interface component for creating tables, allowing elements to be displayed through cells. The **TableView** has the Intent properties that the table provides only on iOS devices. **HasUnevenRows** defines the height of the rows according to the table element. Root is the child of the **TableView** and **RowHeight** that determines the height of the rows.

```
<TableView>
    <TableRoot>
        <TableSection Title="Examples">
            <TextCell Text="Example 1"
                      Detail="text row 1" />
            <TextCell Text="Example 2"
                      Detail="text row 2" />
        </TableSection>
    </TableRoot>
</TableView>
```

TimePicker

The **TimePicker** is a control to be able to select the time within a platform, it has the following properties.

- **Time:** Determines the selected time and returns a **TimeSpan** data type.
- **Format:** It is the time format whether standard or custom.
- **TextColor:** Defines the color of the selected time.
- **CharacterSpacing:** It is the space between the characters of the text.
- **FontAttributes:** Text style.
- **FontFamily:** Determine the source.
- **FontSize:** Determines the font size.

The following example shows the **TimePicker** label;

```
<TimePicker Time="3:51:18" />
```

CollectionView

The **CollectionView** is a view that allows displaying a list through a data link. The **DataTemplate** defines the design style that the element will have.

First, a collection is created within a class. In this case, the file underlying the **ContentPage** was used as an example:

```
public partial class Page_1 : ContentPage
{
    public ObservableCollection<string> ImagesString { get; set; }

    public Page_1()
    {
        InitializeComponent();

        ImagesString = new ObservableCollection<string>
        {
            "dotnet_bot.png",
            "dotnet_bot.png",
            "dotnet_bot.png"
        };

        BindingContext = this;
    }
}
```

Then, in the **ContentPage**, a **CollectionView** bound to the data collection was added, and finally the appearance of the elements was defined.

```
<CollectionView ItemsSource="{Binding ImagesString}">
    <CollectionView.ItemTemplate>
        <DataTemplate>
            <Frame CornerRadius="50"
                   Padding="5"
                   Margin="5">
                <Image Source="{Binding}"
                       Aspect="AspectFill"
                       WidthRequest="44"
                       HeightRequest="44" />
            </Frame>
        </DataTemplate>
    </CollectionView.ItemTemplate>
</CollectionView>
```

Styles

.NET MAUI allows the use of styles, whether they can be defined within the **Styles.xaml**, from the Style attribute, Globally or through Resource Variables. Styles allow UI components to have a coherent appearance, facilitating use of an application.

To define a style from the **Resources/Styles/Styles.xaml** file or any type of XAML file that works as a resource dictionary (**ResourceDictionary**), the style must be defined to do so by creating a **Style** tag where they will define the **x:key** properties that will help reference the style from the component where it will be applied. The **TargetType** that defines the type of component, we will add the **Setter** tag where the property and the value of the style will be defined.

```
<Style x:Key="ActivityIndicatorRed" TargetType="ActivityIndicator">
    <Setter Property="Color" Value="Red" />
    <Setter Property="IsRunning" Value="True" />
</Style>
```

Afterwards, we must apply the **ResourceDictionary** in the **App.xaml**. Usually, when we create a new project, a **Styles.xaml** file is already defined, but in the case of creating one, it would only be enough to define it.

```
<Application xmlns="http://schemas.microsoft.com/dotnet/2021/maui"
             xmlns:x="http://schemas.microsoft.com/winfx/2009/xaml"
             xmlns:local="clr-namespace:Tabbed_Page"
             x:Class="Tabbed_Page.App">
    <Application.Resources>
        <ResourceDictionary>
            <ResourceDictionary.MergedDictionaries>
                <ResourceDictionary Source="Resources/Styles/Colors.
                xaml" />
                <ResourceDictionary Source="Resources/Styles/Styles.
                xaml" />
            </ResourceDictionary.MergedDictionaries>
        </ResourceDictionary>
    </Application.Resources>
</Application>
```

Finally, all that remains is to use the style in the appropriate component from the style property. For example, if we create a new style for an **ActivityIndicator** tag in the **Style.xaml**, it would only be enough to define it in the **ActivityIndicator** component of our user interface.

```
<ActivityIndicator Style="{StaticResource ActivityIndicatorRED}" />
```

Commands

A command in Maui is known as an object that implements the **ICommand** interface. This interface has as its main feature. The definition of two key methods are as follows:

- **Execute:** This method defines what happens when the command is executed.
- **CanExecute:** This method gives you a Boolean value that tells us whether the command can be executed at any given time. This is useful for enabling or

disabling UI controls based on the state of the application at any given time. This is determined according to what we define.

Commands are mainly used to link some action to UI controls, such as buttons, menus, and other elements that are interactive to the user.

The most important advantages of using commands are as follows:

- **Decoupling:** Commands have a good feature, which allows us to separate the UI logic from the business logic. This greatly facilitates the maintenance and scalability of applications.
- **Reuse:** By encapsulating the logic in a command. It can be reused in what are the different parts of the application.
- **Control:** Commands have greater control over when and how actions are executed, thanks to the `Execute` method.

Implementing Commands

Next, we will explain how to implement the commands, as well as the different features that can be applied.

Definition in the `ViewModel`

The first step in being able to use commands in Maui is to define them in the `ViewModel`. That's where the logic of the application lies. Assuming we want to implement a command to save data:

```
public class MiViewModel : INotifyPropertyChanged
{
    public ICommand SaveCommand { get; }

    public MiViewModel()
    {
        SaveCommand = new Command(Save, CanSave);
    }

    private void Save()
    {
        // Logic for saving data
    }

    private bool CanSave()
    {
        // Conditions for enabling the Save button
        return true;
    }
}
```

In this example, **SaveCommand** is defined as a simple property in the **ViewModel** and initialized with a new Command, to which the following two methods are passed: Save and Save.

Command Binding in the View

Once the command is fully defined in the **ViewModel**, it can be linked to a control in the view. In XAML, it would look like the following example:

```
<Button Text="Save"
        Command="{Binding SaveCommand}" />
```

When a user clicks on what the button is, the command will be executed automatically, invoking the Save method that was defined within the **ViewModel**.

Using Parameters in Commands

Commands in **MAUI** can also accept various parameters, which is quite positive as it adds more flexibility. For example, if you are looking to pass a specific object or value when the command is executed in a specific context, you can do it as follows:

Defining the Command with Parameter

```
public ICommand DeleteCommand { get; }

public MiViewModel()
{
    DeleteCommand = new Command<int>(Delete);
}

private void Delete(int id)
{
    // Logic for deleting an item by its ID
}
```

Command Binding with Parameter in View

```
<Button Text="Delete"
        Command="{Binding EliminateCommand}"
        CommandParameter="{Binding Id}" />
```

In this case, the **DeleteCommand** command, as we can see, requires a parameter of a specific type which is int, which is passed from the view by **CommandParameter**.

Updating Commands

When the conditions that determine whether a command is allowed to execute change, it is important to notify the UI to modify it. This is done by invoking the **ChangeCanExecute** method of the command:

```
public void ChangeState()
{
    // Change a condition
    (SaveCommand as Command)?. ChangeCanExecute();
}
```

This method helps force the UI to reevaluate the conditions of the command and whether it can ever be executed, which in turn updates what is the enabled or disabled state of the controls that are linked.

Localization

Localization is defined as the process of adapting what an application is so that it works in a few different languages and regions that are defined. This includes not only what text translation is but also the adaptability of date, time, number, and other types of cultural convention formats. In MAUI, localization can be managed mainly through what are the resource files (**.resx**), which contain the translated text strings specified for each of the languages.

Localization Implementation

Next, we will explain how to implement localization.

Creating Resource Files

The first step in localizing your application on MAUI is to create some resource files (**.resx**). These can act as containers for text strings and can be organized by language. For example, you can have one **Resources.resx** file for your application's default language and multiple other files, such as **Resources.es.resx** for Spanish, **Resources.fr.resx** for French, and so on.

1. **Create the default resource file:**
   a. Add a new **.resx** file to your project and name it **Resources.resx**.
   b. Add some key-value text strings that you will use in your application. For example:
      `HelloWorld = Hello, World!`
2. **Create resource files for other languages:**
   a. Copy the **Resources.resx** file and rename it to reflect the specific language it will be, such as **Resources.es.resx** for Spanish.

b. Translate some text strings within this file:

```
HelloWorld = Hello, World!
```

Location Settings in MAUI

In order for .NET MAUI to use these resource files we've created, you need to configure them in your application:

1. **Update the `.csproj` file:** Make sure that these resource files are correctly referenced in what is the **`.csproj`** file:

```
<ItemGroup>
   <EmbeddedResource Include="Resources.resx" />
   <EmbeddedResource Include="Resources.es.resx" />
   <!-- Add more files as needed -->
</ItemGroup>
```

2. **Set the Default Language:** In the file **`App.xaml.cs`** or where your app is initialized, set the default culture. This is done to make sure that the app uses the language you define as correct:

```
using System.Globalization;
using System.Threading;

CultureInfo.DefaultThreadCurrentCulture = new CultureInfo("en");
CultureInfo.DefaultThreadCurrentUICulture = new Culture
Info("es");
```

Use of Localized Resources in the UI

Once all the resource files are set up correctly, you can use them in your UI. In XAML, this can be done by linking to resources:

```
<Label Text="{x:Static local:Resources.HelloWorld}" />
```

Here, **`local`** is the name segment where your resources get to be defined, and **`HelloWorld`** is the key to the string you want to show.

Dynamic Language Switching

In some applications, it may be necessary to be able to change the language at runtime. To do this, you must change the current culture and update what is shaken up as the user interface:

```
CultureInfo.DefaultThreadCurrentCulture = new CultureInfo("fr");
CultureInfo.DefaultThreadCurrentUICulture = new CultureInfo("fr");
```

Then, you have to reload or update what the views are to reflect a new language.

Date, Time, and Number Formats

In addition to text strings, it is very important to be able to consider the localization of date, time, and number formats. .NET MAUI has a feature that automatically handles these conversions when the right culture is established:

```
var date = DateTime.Now.ToString("D", CultureInfo.CurrentCulture);
var number = (123456.78). ToString("N", CultureInfo.CurrentCulture);
```

This makes it easier for us to display dates, times, and numbers appropriately for each of the cultures, for example, 12,345.67 are shown in English and 12.345,67 in Spanish.

Conclusion

In conclusion, creating an application with .NET MAUI not only gives developers the ability to efficiently build user interfaces using XAML and C#, but also optimizes the user experience through a variety of interactive controls and customizable components. From the use of resources such as images and buttons to the implementation of advanced features such as commands and internationalization, .NET MAUI stands as a powerful tool for cross-platform application development. As each element is integrated into the structure of the application, creativity is encouraged and the aesthetics of the final product are enhanced. With these fundamentals, developers are equipped to move forward in creating ingenious and effective applications, highlighting the importance of continuing to explore the capabilities that .NET MAUI offers to stay at the forefront of modern software development.

In the next chapter, we will explore design patterns, compare monolithic architecture with MVVM, learn about bindings and their types, and create our first application, using MVVM architecture.

Chapter 4
Design Patterns in .NET MAUI

Introduction

In this chapter, we will learn what a design pattern is, and what the existing types of design patterns are. We will see a comparison of the monolithic architecture and the MVVM, understand the bindings and their different types, and also create our first application using the MVVM architecture.

Structure

In this chapter, we will discuss the following topics:

- Knowing Design Patterns
- Types of Design Patterns
  - Creational Patterns
  - Structural Patterns
  - Patterns of Behavior
- Monolithic Architecture
  - Advantages of the Monolithic
  - Disadvantages of the Monolithic
- Model-View-ViewModel (MVVM)
  - MVVM Components
  - MVVM Advantages
  - Disadvantages of MVVM
- Introduction to Binding
  - `BindingContext`
  - `OneWay`

  - `TwoWay`
  - `OneWayToSource`
  - Command
  - Value Converters
- Types of Binding
  - MVVM
- First App with MVVM

Knowing Design Patterns

When we talk about design patterns in the realm of software engineering, we are referring to reusable and extensively tested solutions to common problems that arise during software development. Imagine that you face a problem in something that is specifically technical. Instead of reinventing the wheel, you can turn to what is known as a design pattern, a kind of template which outlines how to solve that problem effectively.

A design pattern is what is known as a general, repeatable solution to a problem that is common in a fairly particular design context. It is not off-the-shelf code but rather a kind of guide or model that tells you how to solve a recurring problem in software design.

Design patterns are critical because they allow developers to solve generally common problems with proven solutions, avoiding bugs and reducing development time. In addition, they encourage code reuse and standardization across development teams, as team members share a common language and set of best practices.

In addition, design patterns promote greater flexibility and scalability of the code. By following established patterns, code is easier to maintain, extend, and refactor, which is crucial in long-term software projects.

Types of Design Patterns

Design patterns are organized into three main different categories: Creational Patterns, Structural Patterns, and Behavioral Patterns. Each of these categories abounds in a different aspect of software design, from creating objects to organizing classes and interacting with them.

Creational Patterns

Creational patterns aim at how objects are created. Instead of instantiating objects directly, these patterns have mechanisms that improve the flexibility and reusability of the code.

- **Singleton:** Ensures that at least one class has more than one instance and provides a global access point to that instance. This pattern is quite useful when a single object must coordinate actions across the system, such as a configuration handler or logger.
- **Factory Method:** Defines an interface for creating an object but also makes it easier for subclasses to decide which class to instantiate. This pattern is of high value when classes don't know in advance what kind of objects they should create or when object creation logic needs to be centralized.
- **Abstract Factory:** Provides an interface for creating families of related or somewhat dependent objects without specifying their specific classes. This pattern is ideal for systems that need to be more independent of the particular implementation of their components.
- **Builder:** Separates the construction of a complex object from its representation so that the same construction process has a high facility to create different representations. This pattern is quite useful when building an object requires multiple steps or when there are multiple ways to construct the object.
- **Prototype:** Allows the creation of new objects by copying what is an existing instance, or "prototype." This pattern is useful when instances of a class only have a few possible combinations of states, and it's easier to clone an existing object than to create a new one from scratch.

Structural Patterns

Structural patterns deal with the composition of classes and objects to form much larger structures. These patterns facilitate the organization of systems and ensure that the relationships between the different components are clear and manageable.

- **Adapter:** Allows classes with completely incompatible interfaces to work together. It acts as a bridge between two different interfaces. This pattern is useful when you need to use an existing class that doesn't fit with the interface your code expects.
- **Bridge:** Separates an abstraction from its implementation, making it easier for both to evolve independently. It is ideal for situations where both abstractions and implementations can vary, providing flexibility in their combination.
- **Composite:** Allows you to treat individual and compound objects in a uniform manner. This pattern is useful in tree structures, such as menus or file systems, where items may contain other items of the same nature.
- **Decorator:** Allows you to add responsibilities to an object dynamically. It is

useful when you want to extend the functionality of classes flexibly without inheritance.

- **Facade:** Provides a simplified interface to a complex set of interfaces in a subsystem. This pattern is useful for reducing complexity when interacting with large systems, hiding internal details.
- **Flyweight:** Reduces memory usage by sharing as much information as possible between similar objects. It is useful when a large number of objects must be handled efficiently, such as in graphics systems where many similar elements are rendered.
- **Proxy:** Provides a surrogate or placeholder to control access to another object. This pattern is useful for controlling access to expensive or remote resources.

Patterns of Behavior

Patterns of behavior focus on how objects interact and how they distribute responsibility. These patterns define how objects communicate, and how they collaborate to accomplish complex tasks.

- **Chain of Responsibility:** Allows multiple objects to have the opportunity to handle a request, avoiding coupling between the sender and receiver. This pattern is useful when multiple entities can process a request, but you do not know which one will ultimately handle it.
- **Command:** Encapsulates a request as an object, allowing clients to be parameterized with different requests, queues or request logs, and supports operations that can be rolled back. It is useful, when you need to perform operations on objects in a flexible and extensible way.
- **Interpreter:** Defines a representation for the grammar of a language and an interpreter who uses the representation to interpret sentences in that language. This pattern is useful for constructing interpreters for simple languages, such as mathematical expressions or configuration scripts.
- **Iterator:** Provides a way to sequentially access items in a collection without exposing their underlying representation. This pattern is essential for going through collections in an even and abstract way.
- **Mediator:** Defines an object that encapsulates the way a set of objects interacts. The mediator promotes a weak coupling between objects, preventing them from directly referring to each other. It is useful in systems where it is necessary to centralize communication between multiple objects.
- **Memento:** Captures and externalizes the internal state of an object without violating its encapsulation, so that the object can be restored to this state later. This pattern is ideal for implementing undo or versioning capabilities in applications.

- **Observer:** Defines a one-to-many dependency between objects so that when an object changes state, all of its dependents are automatically notified and updated. This pattern is common in systems where changes in one object must be reflected in others, such as in graphical user interfaces.
- **State:** Allows an object to alter its behavior when its internal state changes. The object will appear to change its class. This pattern is useful for systems where objects can have multiple states, and the object's behavior should vary based on its current state.
- **Strategy:** Defines a family of algorithms, encapsulates each one, and makes them interchangeable. It allows the algorithm to vary regardless of the customers who use it. This pattern is useful, when you need to choose between multiple algorithms at runtime.
- **Template Method:** Defines the skeleton of an algorithm in an operation, letting subclasses redefine certain steps of the algorithm without changing their structure. It's ideal for when multiple methods in a class need to follow the same pattern but with differences in some steps.
- **Visitor:** Allows you to define new operations without changing the classes of the elements on which it operates. It is useful in systems that must process complex object structures and where it is desirable to maintain operations separate from the object structure.

Monolithic Architecture

Monolithic architecture is one of the most traditional approaches in software development. In a monolithic application, all of the code in the application is unified into a single project or set of files. This includes the user interface, business logic, and data access. Basically, everything is intertwined into a single piece.

Advantages of the Monolithic Architecture

Here are some of the most important advantages of monolithic architecture.

- **Initial Simplicity:** The monolithic architecture is simple to understand and easy to set up at the start of a project. All developers work on the same codebase, which makes it easy to collaborate and integrate.
- **Easy Deployment:** As a single unit, deploying a monolithic application is a relatively straightforward process. It packages everything into a single artifact (an executable file, a Docker container, and so on) and deploys it as a single piece.
- **Performance:** By not having to manage communication between different services or distributed components, monolithic applications can offer better

performance in certain situations, as all logic and data access are in the same memory space.

Disadvantages of the Monolithic

Here are some of the most significant disadvantages of monolithic architecture:

- **Long-Term Maintenance:** As the application grows, monolithic code tends to become difficult to maintain. Dependencies between different parts of the system can become complex and fragile, increasing the risk of introducing errors when making changes.
- **Limited Scalability:** Scaling a monolithic application can be tricky. Since everything is in a single block, it is difficult to scale only the parts that need the most resources. This can lead to wasted resources and performance issues.
- **Impediments to Innovation:** The fact that all developers are working on the same codebase means that any changes to one part of the system can affect other parts, slowing down the ability to innovate and experiment with new technologies or approaches.

Model-View-ViewModel (MVVM)

MVVM is an architectural pattern that originated in Windows application development (WPF and Silverlight) but has found its place in many modern platforms, including mobile and web development. MVVM is based on separation of concerns, organizing code into three main components: Model, View, and **`ViewModel`**.

MVVM Components

These are the components of the MVVM architecture:

- **Model:** Represents the data and business logic of the application. The Model is UI-agnostic and must have no knowledge of the View or the **`ViewModel`**. Their responsibility is to manage the application data, whether from a database, an API, or any other source.
- **View:** It is the visual representation of information. In MVVM, the View is responsible for defining the layout and appearance and is closely linked to the **`ViewModel`** through data binding mechanisms. The View should be as "silly" as possible, focused solely on the presentation.
- **`ViewModel`:** Acts as an intermediary between the View and the Model. It manages presentation logic, processes user input, and updates the View when the Model data changes. The **`ViewModel`** communicates with the Model and exposes the data to the View through properties and commands, making it easy to bind data.

MVVM Advantages

Here are some of the most important advantages of MVVM architecture:

- **Separation of Concerns:** MVVM encourages a clear separation between business logic, presentation logic, and user interface. This makes the code more modular, easy to test, and easy to maintain.
- **Scalability and Maintainability:** Since each component has a clear responsibility, MVVM-based applications are easier to scale and maintain. Changes to the business logic or user interface can be made independently without affecting other components.
- **Unit Tests:** MVVM makes it easy to write unit tests, especially for the `ViewModel`, which is in charge of the presentation logic. This improves code quality and reduces the chance of errors in production.

Disadvantages of MVVM

Here are some of the most significant disadvantages of MVVM architecture:

- **Initial Complexity:** Implementing MVVM can be more complex at first, especially for teams that are unfamiliar with the pattern. Creating `ViewModels` and configuring data bindings requires more upfront effort.
- **Data Link Overhead:** While data binding is a powerful tool, it can introduce performance overhead, especially in applications with highly dynamic user interfaces or on platforms with limited resources.
- **Learning Curve:** For developers new to the pattern, MVVM can have a steep learning curve. Understanding how to organize and communicate components can take time.

Introduction to Binding

Data Binding is a link between the user interface (UI) and a data model or `ViewModel`. In a more specific context, data binding allows updates to the UI when the data model presents a change or vice versa. For example, suppose that in our user interface we have a button component that has established a connection with a `ViewModel` that has an event that displays an alert. This indicates that every time the button is clicked, the alert will be displayed.

When developing an application in .NET MAUI, we can use this technique to facilitate the synchronization between the interface components and the application's data model. But you may be wondering how we can perform a binding. Before starting, there are some types of binding, such as the `OneWay`, which is used when the UI reflects changes to the model. `TwoWay` data flows both in the UI to the ViewModel and vice versa and are very useful for text inputs. **OneWayToSource** only reflects UI changes in the ViewModel, **BindingContext**, and setting the data source for the controls for an MVVM application. **Commands** are used for event handling (for example, buttons) and **Value Converters**, which allow converting data between the model and the UI.

BindingContext

The **BindingContext** is a property that allows you to bind specific data sources or models, defining a data context to a user interface element. It offers a lot of advantages, especially when working with the MVVM design pattern. **ViewModel** allows the decoupling of the business logic of the view, promotes a clean and modular design implementation, facilitates the maintenance of the same code, facilitates data link synchronization, allows the use of inheritance to a hierarchy of controls, and reduces redundancy .

Let's see an example in the code of how to use the **BindingContext**, the class created **AmountViewModel**, which handles the logic and data binding, to add two numbers each time a change is detected and return the result of that sum in a property.

```
using System.ComponentModel;
using System.Runtime.CompilerServices;

namespace ExampleBinding
{
    //AmountViewModel class inherits INotifyPropertyChanged
interface
    public class AmountViewModel : INotifyPropertyChanged
    {

        private double _numberOne;
        private double _numberTwo;
        private double _result;

        //This property manages and reports changes to the value.
        public double NumberOne
        {
            get => _numberOne;
            set
            {
                if (value != _numberOne)
                {
                    _numberOne = value;
                    OnPropertyChanged();
                    OnPropertyChanged(nameof(Result));
                }
            }
```

```
        }
        //This property manages and reports changes to the value.
        public double NumberTwo
        {
            get => _numberTwo;
            set
            {
                if (value != _numberTwo)
                {
                    _numberTwo = value;
                    OnPropertyChanged();
                    OnPropertyChanged(nameof(Result));
                }
            }
        }
        //This property is read-only and computed dynamically.
        public double Result => _numberOne + _numberTwo;


        private void AddNumbers()
        {
            Result =  _numberOne + _numberTwo;
        }

        //This function allows you to implement the INotify
PropertyChanged interface
        //allows the view to update automatically when the
ViewModel properties change
        public event PropertyChangedEventHandler PropertyChanged;
        protected virtual void OnPropertyChanged([CallerMember-
Name] string propertyName = null)
        {
            PropertyChanged?.Invoke(this, new PropertyChanged
EventArgs(propertyName));
        }

    }
}
```

For the view, a **ContentPage** was created with the name **BindingContextPage**. In the class constructor, the class is instantiated with the **AmountViewModel** in the **BindingContext** property. This way, the binding with the **ViewModel** was created.

```
namespace ExampleBinding;

public partial class BindingContextPage : ContentPage
{
```

```
        public BindingContextPage()
        {
                InitializeComponent();
                BindingContext = new AmountViewModel();
        }
    }
```

Continuing with the view within the **NumberTwo**, and finally, the Label component's Text property is established with the Result property and a **StringFormat** to specify how the property value should be displayed.

```
<?xml version="1.0" encoding="utf-8" ?>
<ContentPage xmlns="http://schemas.microsoft.com/dotnet/2021/maui"
             xmlns:x="http://schemas.microsoft.com/winfx/2009/xaml"
             x:Class="ExampleBinding.BindingContextPage"
             Title="BindingContextPage">
    <StackLayout Padding="20">
        <Entry Placeholder="Enter number 1"
               Keyboard="Numeric"
               Text="{Binding NumberOne}" />
        <Entry Placeholder="Enter number 2"
               Keyboard="Numeric"
               Text="{Binding NumberTwo}" />
        <Label Text="{Binding Result, StringFormat='Result: {0:N2}'}"
               FontSize="24"
               HorizontalOptions="Center" />
    </StackLayout>
</ContentPage>
```

In the previous example, you can see the MVVM where the view logic is decoupled, allowing the synchronization of UI properties with the **ViewModel**.

OneWay

The **OneWay** is a type of link between the UI and the **ViewModel** within the context of the binding. This link indicates that if changes are made to the UI, they do not affect the **ViewModel**, but the **ViewModel** does update the UI. For example, we have a **Label** component that will display a value of a property of the **ViewModel**. The value of the property may be changing, and this change will affect the value of the **Label**. But if the user could change the value of the **Label**, this will not affect the value of the property; let's see an example in XAML code and C#:

In a **ContentPage**, a **Label** is added inside a **StackLayout**. The **Label** is bound to a **ViewModel** property called **CurrentTime**.

```
<?xml version="1.0" encoding="utf-8" ?>
<ContentPage xmlns="http://schemas.microsoft.com/dotnet/2021/maui"
             xmlns:x="http://schemas.microsoft.com/winfx/2009/xaml"
```

```
            x:Class="ExampleBinding.MainPage">

    <StackLayout VerticalOptions="Center" HorizontalOptions="
Center">
        <Label Text="{Binding CurrentTime}"
               VerticalTextAlignment="Center"
               HorizontalTextAlignment="Center"
               FontSize="45" />
    </StackLayout>
</ContentPage>
```

In the associated code-behind file (**MainPage.xaml.cs**), the binding context (**BindingContext**) is assigned to an instance of the **ViewModel**.

```
namespace ExampleBinding;
public partial class MainPage : ContentPage
{
    public MainPage()
    {
        InitializeComponent();
        BindingContext = new TimeViewModel();
    }
}
```

The **ViewModel** contains a **CurrentTime** property that is automatically updated every second using **System.Timers.Timer**. Each time the value changes, the **PropertyChanged** event is triggered, allowing the UI to update the **Label**.

```
using System.ComponentModel;
using System.Timers;

namespace ExampleBinding;

public class TimeViewModel : INotifyPropertyChanged
{

    private readonly Timer _timer;

    private string _currentTime;
    public string CurrentTime
    {
        get => _currentTime;
        set
        {
            if (_currentTime != value)
            {
                _currentTime = value;
                OnPropertyChanged(nameof(CurrentTime));
```

```
                }
            }
        }

        public TimeViewModel()
        {
            _timer = new Timer(1000);
            _timer.Elapsed += (s, e) =>
            {
                MainThread.BeginInvokeOnMainThread(() =>
                {
                    CurrentTime = DateTime.Now.ToString("HH:mm:ss");
                });
            };
            _timer.Start();
        }

        public event PropertyChangedEventHandler PropertyChanged;

        protected void OnPropertyChanged(string propertyName) =>
            PropertyChanged?.Invoke(this, new PropertyChangedEven-
    tArgs(propertyName));
    }
```

The previous code will allow us to create a label that shows the time every second, allowing us to understand how the **Oneway** link works.

TwoWay

The **TwoWay** binding mode synchronizes the user interface (UI) with the **ViewModel**. This means the UI can update any property of the data model, and the model can also update properties in the UI.

For example, suppose we have an Entry component and a Label component. Whenever the text in the **Entry** is updated, the value in the Label should be updated as well. Let us look at an example using XAML and C# code.

In a **ContentPage**, an **Entry** and a **Label** are placed inside a **StackLayout**. The **Label** binds to the same property as the **Entry**:

```
<ContentPage xmlns="http://schemas.microsoft.com/dotnet/2021/maui"
             xmlns:x="http://schemas.microsoft.com/winfx/2009/xaml"
             x:Class="ExampleBinding.TwowayPage"
             Title="TwoWayPage">

    <StackLayout Padding="10">
        <Entry Text="{Binding Text, Mode=TwoWay}" />
        <Label Text="{Binding Text}" />
```

```
        </StackLayout>
    </ContentPage>
```

Next, we assign the **BindingContext** to an instance of the **ViewModel** in the code-behind file (**TwowayPage.xaml.cs**).

```
namespace ExampleBinding;

public partial class TwowayPage : ContentPage
{
    public TwowayPage()
    {
        InitializeComponent();
        BindingContext = new TwowayViewModel();
    }
}
```

We created a **ViewModel** that implements the **INotifyPropertyChanged** interface so that changes are automatically reflected in the UI.

```
using System.ComponentModel;
using System.Runtime.CompilerServices;

namespace ExampleBinding;

public class TwowayViewModel : INotifyPropertyChanged
{
    private string _text;

    public string Text
    {
        get => _text;
        set
        {
            if (_text != value)
            {
                _text = value;
                OnPropertyChanged();
            }
        }
    }

    public event PropertyChangedEventHandler PropertyChanged;
protected void OnPropertyChanged([CallerMemberName] string
propertyName = null) =>
        PropertyChanged?.Invoke(this, new PropertyChanged
EventArgs(propertyName));
}
```

The previous code allows the **Entry** component to be bound to a property of the **ViewModel**. Every time the **Entry**'s content is updated, the property in the **ViewModel** is automatically modified, and that change is also reflected in the UI, in this case in the Label. This is how two-way binding works.

OneWayToSource

The **OneWayToSource** binding mode is used to bind a **ViewModel** property to a UI component, but in only one direction: from the user interface to the **ViewModel**. It means that changes the user makes to the UI are reflected in the **ViewModel**, but changes to the **ViewModel** do not update the UI.

In a **ContentPage**, we define two controls: an **Entry** for the user to enter text and a **Label** that will display said text.

- The **Entry** is bound in **OneWayToSource** mode so that changes made by the user are updated in the **ViewModel**'s **EntryTextInput** property. But if the **ViewModel** changes that property, the text in the **Entry** will not change.
- The **Label** is bound to the **DisplayText** property which returns the value of **EntryTextInput**, and will be automatically updated when this property changes.

The following code shows the example in XAML:

```
<?xml version="1.0" encoding="utf-8" ?>
<ContentPage xmlns="http://schemas.microsoft.com/dotnet/2021/maui"
             xmlns:x="http://schemas.microsoft.com/winfx/2009/xaml"
             x:Class="ExampleBinding.OneWayToSourcePage"
             Title="OneWayToSourcePage">

    <StackLayout Padding="10">
<!-- Binding OneWayToSource: UI sends data to the ViewModel -->
        <Entry Text="{Binding EntryTextInput, Mode=OneWayToSource}"
/>

<!-- The Label is automatically updated from the ViewModel -->
        <Label Text="{Binding DisplayText}"
               VerticalOptions="CenterAndExpand"
               HorizontalOptions="CenterAndExpand" />
    </StackLayout>

</ContentPage>
```

Next, we assign the **BindingContext** to an instance of the **ViewModel** in the code-behind file (**OneWayToSourcePage.xaml.cs**).

```
namespace ExampleBinding;

public partial class OneWayToSourcePage : ContentPage
{
    public OneWayToSourcePage()
    {
        InitializeComponent();
        BindingContext = new OneWayToSourceViewModel();
    }
}
```

The **ViewModel** implements the **INotifyPropertyChanged** interface so that the UI can react when properties change (in this case, the **Label** is updated because it depends on **EntryTextInput**).

```
using System.ComponentModel;
using System.Runtime.CompilerServices;

public class OneWayToSourceViewModel : INotifyPropertyChanged
{
    private string entryTextInput;

    public string EntryTextInput
    {
        get => entryTextInput;
        set
        {
            if (entryTextInput != value)
            {
                entryTextInput = value;
                OnPropertyChanged();
                OnPropertyChanged(nameof(DisplayText));
     }
        }
    }

    public string DisplayText => EntryTextInput;

    public event PropertyChangedEventHandler PropertyChanged;

    protected void OnPropertyChanged([CallerMemberName] string
name = null) =>
        PropertyChanged?.Invoke(this, new PropertyChanged
EventArgs(name));
}
```

In the previous example, you can see how the **Entry** component that has the binding defined as **OneWayToSource** can modify the **Label** component, allowing a simple update of the property.

Command

The Command is an interface that allows you to define actions that will be executed in response to an event; for example, when selecting an element or clicking, there are several UI components that can have this property, such as **Button**, **MenuItem**, **ToolbarItem**, **CollectionView**, and **GestureRecognizers**, such as the **TapGestureRecognizer** that allows controls and views to respond to an event, such as Label, Frame, Image, and so on.

Let's see a code example of the Command using MVVM. In the class **AmountViewModel**, which was created previously to explain the **BindingContext**, the **MyCommand** property of type **ICommand** was defined, and within the constructor, a new instance of the Command class is assigned, passing the **AddNumbers** method as a parameter. In the **NumberOner** and **NumberTwo** properties, we comment on **this.AddNumbers ()** to let the command perform the addition.

```
public ICommand MyCommand { get; }

public AmountViewModel()
{
    MyCommand = new Command(AddNumbers);
}
```

The change that was made to the view was that a button element was added where the link with the **MyCommand** is established in the **Command** property.

```
<?xml version="1.0" encoding="utf-8" ?>
<ContentPage xmlns="http://schemas.microsoft.com/dotnet/2021/maui"
             xmlns:x="http://schemas.microsoft.com/winfx/2009/xaml"
             x:Class="ExampleBinding.BindingContextPage"
             Title="BindingContextPage">
    <StackLayout Padding="20">
        <Entry Placeholder="Enter number 1"
               Keyboard="Numeric"
               Text="{Binding NumberOne}" />
        <Entry Placeholder="Enter number 2"
               Keyboard="Numeric"
               Text="{Binding NumberTwo}" />
        <Button Text="add numbers"
                Command="{Binding MyCommand}"/>
        <Label Text="{Binding Result, StringFormat='Result:
{0:N2}'}"
               FontSize="24"
```

```
                HorizontalOptions="Center" />
        </StackLayout>
    </ContentPage>
```

In this way, the binding with the Command of the button element has been established, where every time the click action is performed, the **AddNumbers** function is executed, which will add the value of **NumberOne** and **NumberTwo**, and the Result will update the value of Result.

Value Converters

The Value Converters is a class to transform data between the Model and the UI, allowing you to change the format of the data so that the model can understand it better or convert the data before displaying it in the user interface.

This class implements the interface **IValueConverter**, which defines two main methods: the **Convert** to transform the data that goes from the Origin to the destination and the **ConvertBack** from destination to origin. Let's see an example in the code:

For this example, the **BoolToStringConverter** class was created that implements the **IValueConverter** interface. This class has two methods, **Convert** and **ConvertBack**.

```
using System.Globalization;

namespace ExampleBinding
{
    public class BoolToStringConverter : IValueConverter
    {
        public object? Convert(object? value, Type targetType, 
object? parameter, CultureInfo culture)
        {
            if (value is bool booleanValue)
            {
                return booleanValue ? "Yes" : "No";
            }
            return "No";
        }

        public object? ConvertBack(object? value, Type target-
Type, object? parameter, CultureInfo culture)
        {
            throw new NotImplementedException();
        }
    }
}
```

For the view, the class was defined in an instance within the resource dictionary of a XAML file, and the converter was defined within the binding of a Label:

```
<?xml version="1.0" encoding="utf-8" ?>
<ContentPage xmlns="http://schemas.microsoft.com/dotnet/2021/maui"
             xmlns:x="http://schemas.microsoft.com/winfx/2009/xaml"
             x:Class="ExampleBinding.BindingContextPage"
             xmlns:local="clr-namespace:ExampleBinding"
             Title="BindingContextPage">

    <ContentPage.Resources>
        <ResourceDictionary>
            <local:BoolToStringConverter x:Key="BoolToString" />
        </ResourceDictionary>
    </ContentPage.Resources>

    <StackLayout Padding="20">
      <Label Text="{Binding IsActive, Converter={StaticResource
BoolToString}}" />
    </StackLayout>

</ContentPage>
```

The label applied the converter to the **IsActive** property of type Boolean, converting the value to a string.

Types of Binding

Within MAUI, we can use different ways to create our data links. For example, we can use the **BindingContext**, which was explored in the previous section. We can also create a **direct link**, which refers to being able to bind data without the need to establish it from a **BindingContext** but rather define it directly from XAML or through the **C# code link**. Working with the **BindingContext** with a direct binding, we can follow the design pattern **MVVM**, which will provide us with ease when working and maintaining our code by separating the logic from the view, but we can use any type of binding; we just have to take into account the type of project that is going to be developed.

MVVM

Throughout the last chapters, we have been referring to Model-View-ViewModel (MVVM), but we have not explored what it is and why it is so important in the development of applications.

MVVM is an architectural design pattern. They are general and reusable solutions to solve common problems in software design, focused on establishing structure and organization in software.

MVVM allows you to separate the business logic from the user interface, providing great advantages when scaling, maintaining, testing, and developing our application, offering cleanliness and comfort when writing code. MVVM interrelates its components, functioning in the following way: **Model** is in charge of containing the business logic but does not know anything about the UI; the **View** displays and captures interface data and binds to the **`ViewModel`**. The one responsible for notifying data changes is basically the intermediary.

Working with MVVM in a .NET MAUI application can be done in several ways. One is to work directly with additional libraries such as **`CommunityToolkit.Mvvm`** or to work without the use of any library.

Using `CommunityToolkit.Mvvm`

`CommunityToolkit.Mvvm` is a library developed by Microsoft that provides an ease of using MVVM by simplifying and streamlining the process of developing an application. This library provides classes such as **`ObservableObject`**, which implements the **`INotifyPropertyChanged`** interface automatically, and **`RelayCommand`**, which simplifies the implementation of commands in the **`ViewModel`**, among other features. But it should be taken into account that when using a library, we lose a little control of implementations, installations of external dependencies, and compatibility problems.

To work with **`CommunityToolkit.Mvvm`**, we must first add the package to the project. We will do this from NuGet through the searched NuGet package manager **`CommunityToolkit.Mvvm`**, as shown in *Figure 4.1*.

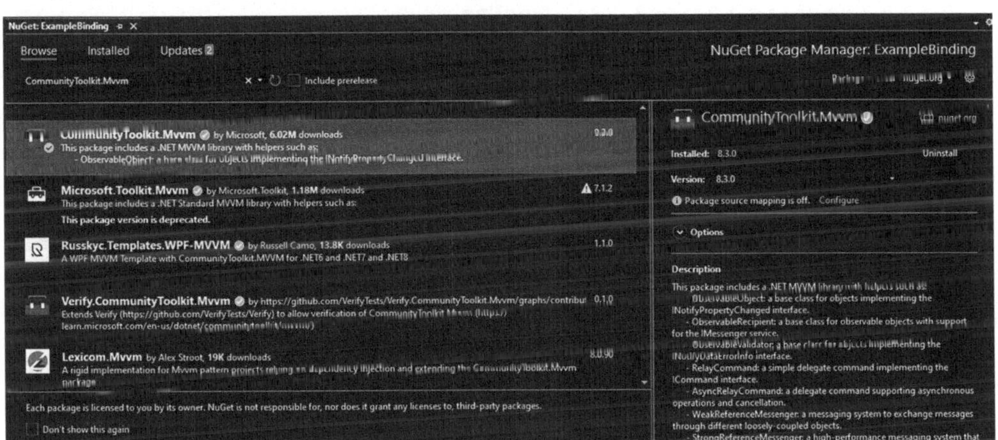

Figure 4.1: *Installing the CommunityToolkit.Mvvm package by administrator*

Another possibility is to do the installation through the package manager console with the command **`Install-Package CommunityToolkit.Mvvm`**, as shown in *Figure 4.2*.

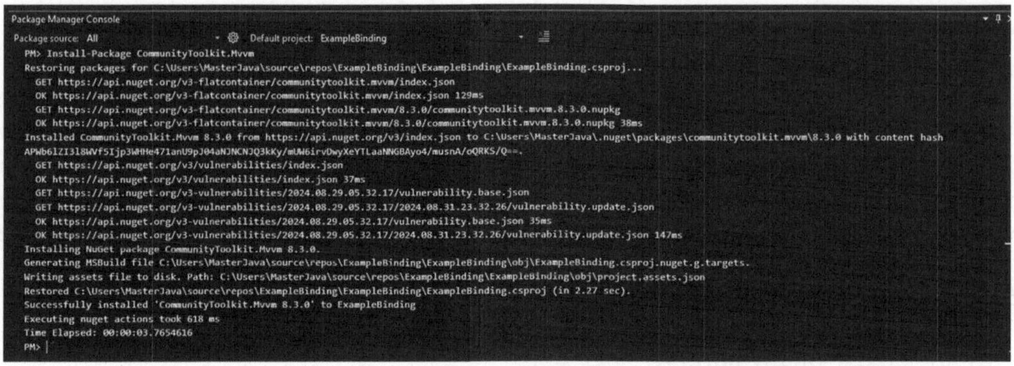

Figure 4.2: *Installing the CommunityToolkit.Mvvm package through the console*

Once the library is installed in the project, the way to use it is simple. The library has several classes; among them are **`ObservableObject`**, **`RelayCommand`**, and **`ICommand`**. To use the **`ObservableObject`**, you only have to implement it in our **`ViewModel`** class, which will allow us to update our properties automatically, for example:

```
using CommunityToolkit.Mvvm.ComponentModel;

namespace ExampleBinding
{
   internal class EmployeeViewModel : ObservableObject
   {
      private string? _employeeName;
      private double _employeeAge;

      public string? EmployeeName
      {
          get => _employeeName;
          set => SetProperty(ref _employeeName, value);
      }

      public double EmployeeAge
      {
          get => _employeeAge;
          set => SetProperty(ref _employeeAge, value);
      }

      public EmployeeViewModel()
      {
          this.EmployeeName = ".NET MAUI";
          this.EmployeeAge = 2.9;
```

```
            }
        }
    }
```

We can also use the **ObservableProperty**, which is a useful feature to simplify the implementation of properties. By defining the **ObservableProperty** attribute in the private properties, the public properties that will provide the change notification logic are automatically created. In addition, the class will be declared as partial to take advantage of the generation of code at compile time.

```
public partial class EmployeeViewModel : ObservableObject
{
    [ObservableProperty]
    public string? _employeeName;

    [ObservableProperty]
    public double _employeeAge;

    public EmployeeViewModel()
    {
        EmployeeName = ".NET MAUI";
        EmployeeAge = 2.9;
    }
}
```

To use the **RelayCommand**, we should only implement **IRelayCommand** to the command, and in the constructor, implement the **RelayCommand**, for example:

```
public class EmployeeViewModel : ObservableObject
{
        public IRelayCommand MyCommand { get; set; }

        public EmployeeViewModel()
        {
            MyCommand = new RelayCommand(TextValue);
        }

        private void TextValue()
        {
            // Implement TextValue logic here }
        }
}
```

As we can see, the implementation of the library is very simple, simplifying the link process, facilitating command management, and updating properties.

Without Using Any Toolkit Libraries

We can also work with MVVM without the need to incorporate additional libraries into our project. By working in this way, we will have full control over how the application design pattern will be implemented without the need to depend on third-party libraries, but it will require more effort to implement the **INotifyPropertyChanged** features. We will have less code cleanup, which can lead to repetitive code that can become more complex if the application grows, affecting the maintenance and scalability of the application.

In order to work with MVVM without libraries, our classes must have the following characteristics: the class that will be our **ViewModel** must implement the interface **INotifyPropertyChanged**. This interface declares the event **PropertyChanged**. The event must be invoked every time the object of a property changes. The event will be declared within the class using **PropertyChangedEventHandler**. This event will help the view receive notifications when the property changes, and the method **OnPropertyChanged** is added to invoke the **PropertyChanged** event to notify event subscribers that the property has changed by passing the name of the property that underwent the change:

```
public class ExampleViewModel : INotifyPropertyChanged
{
    private double _numberOne;
    //This property manages and reports changes to the value.
    public double NumberOne
    {
        get => _numberOne;
        set
        {
            if (value != _numberOne)
            {
                _numberOne = value;
                OnPropertyChanged();
            }
        }
    }

    //This function allows you to implement the INotifyProperty-
Changed interface
    //allows the view to update automatically when the ViewModel
properties change
    public event PropertyChangedEventHandler PropertyChanged;

protected virtual void OnPropertyChanged([CallerMemberName]
string propertyName = null)
    {
```

```
        PropertyChanged?.Invoke(this, new PropertyChangedEvent
Args(propertyName));
    }
}
```

The previous example shows how the **NumberOne** property calls the **OnPropertyChanged** method. Using this method to notify any subscriber that ownership has changed.

To use the **ICommand** without a library, we will first have to declare a type property **ICommand**, which is established in one **getter** representing that the property will be read-only and cannot be modified outside the class. In the class constructor, a new command is created by creating the instance with the keyword **new Command**, and as a parameter, the method that will be executed, when the command is executed or sent.

```
public class ExampleViewModel : INotifyPropertyChanged
{
      public ICommand MyCommand { get; }
      public ExampleViewModel ()
      {
           MyCommand = new Command(AddNumbers);
      }
      private void AddNumbers()
      {
           Result = _numberOne + _numberTwo;
      }
}
```

All that remains is to implement the **ViewModel**. To do this, it is necessary to create a new object of the class that will be our **ViewModel** and assign it to the **Bindingcontext** from our site.

Direct Link without Using MVVM

Also, we can create the application with direct links without the need to implement MVVM. This is done using the **code-behind** which is the C# code adjacent to our Page—a nice option for simple applications that do not require scalability. However, if the application grows in complexity, it will have several disadvantages that can affect the development and maintenance of the application. Therefore, it is something to take into account when deciding how to develop our applications.

```
<StackLayout>
      <Label x:Name="MyLabel" Text="Default Text" />
      <Entry x:Name="MyEntry" />
      <Button  Text ="Clicked" Clicked="OnChangeLabel" />
</StackLayout>
```

In the code-behind, the link is configured with the name of the controls, and through the control properties, it can be manipulated. The following example will be responsible for modifying the Label Text every time the Entry undergoes a change. The **OnChangeLabel** event was also added that will be executed when the button component is clicked and will be responsible for changing the Label text:

```
namespace ExampleBinding;

public partial class Example : ContentPage
{
   public Example()
   {
      InitializeComponent();

      MyLabel.Text = "Hello, World!";

       MyEntry.TextChanged += (s, e) =>
       {
           MyLabel.Text = e.NewTextValue;
       };
    }

    public void OnChangeLabel(object sender, EventArgs e)
    {
      MyLabel.Text = "Hello, World!";
    }
}
```

Working with direct linking may be suitable for small, simple applications or prototypes, but it is advisable to use the MVVM pattern, either using libraries or without using libraries, because we will have more benefits for the development and maintenance of our applications.

First App with MVVM

After reading the previous sections, we are ready to develop our first application using the MVVM design pattern and the **CommunityToolkit.Mvvm** library.

This application will have two text inputs, which will be numerical. A button that, when pressed, will execute a function that will calculate the sum of the input values, and the result will be reflected in the Label component.

Let's get started! First, we will create a new project. For this example, we will call it **MyFirstApplicationWithMVVM**, and we will use the Framework, **.NET 8.0**. Once our project is created, we will install the library **Community Toolkit.Mvvm** via package manager **NuGet**, once the library installation is complete. We are going to modify the folder and file structure of the project. We are going to create two folders: **ViewModels**, which stores the **ViewModel** classes that our application will use, and **Pages**, which will contain the views of the application. Inside the folder **ViewModels**, the class **SumOfQuantitiesViewModel.cs** will be created, and in the folder **Pages**, the **ContentPage SumOfQuantitiesPage.xaml** will be created, which will be the view of the application. Finally, for this example, we will delete the file **MainPage.xaml**. Remember, this XAML file was created automatically when we created our project.

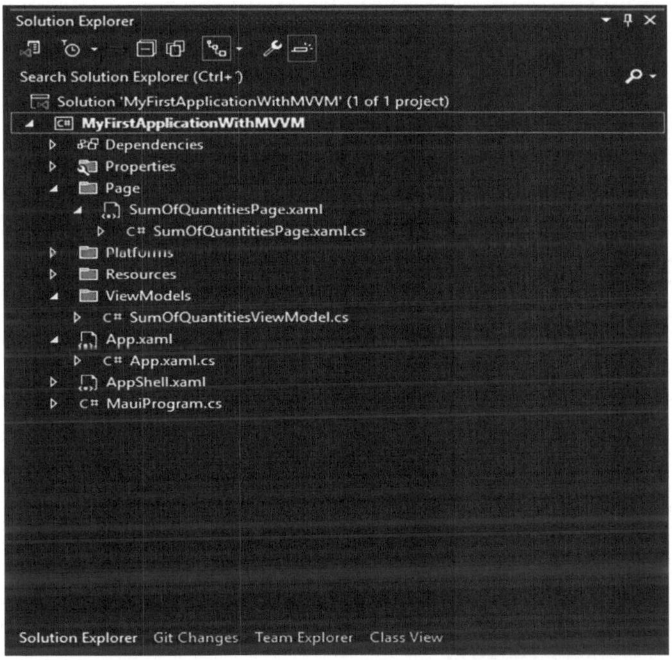

***Figure 4.3**: Project folder and file structure*

Now, let us configure **ShellContent** from **APPShell.xaml** to modify the attribute **ContentTemplate** to use a **DataTemplate** that references **SumOfQuantitiesPage**, and when loading the application, it can start with our page. Before testing, remember to create the reference of the **Pages** folder in the local prefix within the XML namespace (xmlns:local).

```
<?xml version="1.0" encoding="UTF-8" ?>

<Shell
    x:Class="MyFirstApplicationWithMVVM.AppShell"
    xmlns="http://schemas.microsoft.com/dotnet/2021/maui"
    xmlns:x="http://schemas.microsoft.com/winfx/2009/xaml"
    xmlns:local="clr-namespace:MyFirstApplicationWithMVVM.Page"
    Shell.FlyoutBehavior="Disabled"
    Title="MyFirstApplicationWithMVVM">
```

```
    <ShellContent Title="Sum Of Quantities"
        ContentTemplate="{DataTemplate local:SumOfQuantitiesPage}"
        Route="SumOfQuantitiesPage" />

</Shell>
```

Once our application has been tested, we will continue with the **ViewModel**. First, we will implement inheritance from **ObservableObject**, and let us define our type class **partial**. The following properties were created with the private property and by using the attribute **ObservableProperty**:

```
[ObservableProperty]
private double _numberOne;

[ObservableProperty]
private double _numberTwo;

[ObservableProperty]
private double _result;
```

Now, let us define a public property called **AddCommand** of type **IRelayCommand**. Within the **ViewModel** constructor, the **AddCommand** is initialized by creating a new instance of the **RelayCommand**, and the **CalculateSum** method is taken as a parameter. This method was created to add the **NumberOne** and **NumberTWo** properties, and the result of the calculation will be saved in the **Result** property.

```
public IRelayCommand AddCommand { get; set; }

public SumOfQuantitiesViewModel() => AddCommand = new Relay
Command(CalculateSum);

private void CalculateSum()
{
      Result = NumberOne + NumberTwo;
}
```

Once the previous step is done, our **ViewModel** is finished and should look like the following code example:

```
using CommunityToolkit.Mvvm.ComponentModel;
using CommunityToolkit.Mvvm.Input;

namespace MyFirstApplicationWithMVVM.ViewModels
{

    public partial class SumOfQuantitiesViewModel : Observable
    Object
    {
```

```
        [ObservableProperty]
        private double _numberOne;

        [ObservableProperty]
        private double _numberTwo;

        [ObservableProperty]
        private double _result;

        public IRelayCommand AddCommand { get; set; }

public SumOfQuantitiesViewModel() => AddCommand = new Relay
Command(CalculateSum);

        private void CalculateSum()
        {
            Result = NumberOne + NumberTwo;
        }

    }

}
```

Once our **ViewModel** is finished, it is time to design our User Interface. The view is made up of the following components:

- **ContentPage:** It will be the type of page that we will use in our application.
- **StackLayout:** It will be the main Layout of our components.
- **Frame:** It will serve as a container for some controls.
- **Label:** To show the result of the addition.
- **HorizontalStackLayout:** A container to accommodate our Entry and Button.
- **Entry:** Text input with the Keyboard property of type Numeric.
- **Button:** You will have a Command link to execute the Add action.

Next, we are going to define some styles within the **Styles.xaml** file, which is located within **Resources/Styles/Styles.xaml**. This file was generated automatically when creating the project. Defining our styles in this document will help us avoid writing boilerplate code within our view. The following styles were created within the **ResourceDictionary**:

```
<Style x:Key="StyledEntryKeyboard"
       TargetType="Entry">
    <Setter Property="BackgroundColor"
            Value="White" />
    <Sets Property="TextColor"
```

```
                Value="Black" />
        <Setter Property="FontSize"
                Value="16" />
        <Setter Property="Keyboard"
                Value="Numeric" />
</Style>

<Style x:Key="StyledButton"
       TargetType="Button">
        <Setter Property="FontSize"
                Value="16" />
        <Setter Property="Padding"
                Value="10,0" />
        <Setter Property="Margin"
                Value="0" />
        <Setter Property="HeightRequest"
                Value="55" />
        <Setter Property="WidthRequest"
                Value="100" />
</Style>

<Style x:Key="StyledFrame"
       TargetType="Frame">
        <Setter Property="BorderColor"
                Value="DarkSlateGray" />
        <Setter Property="CornerRadius"
                Value="10" />
        <Setter Property="HasShadow"
                Value="true" />
        <Setter Property="Padding"
                Value="5" />
        <Setter Property="Margin"
                Value="0,10" />
</Style>
```

After adding our styles, we are going to create the data binding with our **ViewModel** in the **code-behind** from the **SumOfQuantitiesPage** constructor. Inside it, we are going to instantiate our class in the **BindingContext** property, as shown in the following example.

```
using MyFirstApplicationWithMVVM.ViewModels;

namespace MyFirstApplicationWithMVVM.Page;
public partial class SumOfQuantitiesPage : ContentPage
{
    public SumOfQuantitiesPage()
    {
```

```
            InitializeComponent();
            BindingContext = new SumOfQuantitiesViewModel();
        }
    }
```

We already have our data binding defined. Now we are going to create our interface components. We are going to assign the corresponding style to the created components that we defined in the **Style.xaml** through the **Style** attribute of the component, and we are going to establish the Binding of the **Label** and **Entry** controls, and the **Command** of the **Button**. The design is as follows:

```
    <?xml version="1.0" encoding="utf-8" ?>

    <ContentPage xmlns="http://schemas.microsoft.com/dotnet/2021/maui"
                 xmlns:x="http://schemas.microsoft.com/winfx/2009/xaml"
                 x:Class="MyFirstApplicationWithMVVM.Page.SumOfQuan-
                 titiesPage"
                 Title="Sum Of Quantities">

        <StackLayout>

            <Frame Style="{StaticResource StyledFrame}" Margin="20">
                <Label Text="{Binding Result}" Margin="10" />
            </Frame>

           <HorizontalStackLayout HorizontalOptions="Center" Spacing=
    "10" Margin="20">

    <Frame Style="{StaticResource StyledFrame}">
                 <Entry Style="{StaticResource StyledEntryKeyboard}"
                        Placeholder="Number One"
                        Text="{Binding NumberOne}"/>
           </Frame>

           <Frame Style="{StaticResource StyledFrame}">
                 <Entry Style="{StaticResource StyledEntryKeyboard}"
                        Placeholder="Number Two"
                        Text="{Binding NumberTwo}"/>
           </Frame>

           <Button Style="{StaticResource StyledButton}"
                   Command="{Binding AddCommand}"
                   Text="Add" />

           </HorizontalStackLayout>
```

```
        </StackLayout>

    </ContentPage>
```

These are the final changes to be made to our project. If we debug our application, the result should be as shown in *Figure* 4.4 and working; we can now add two numbers.

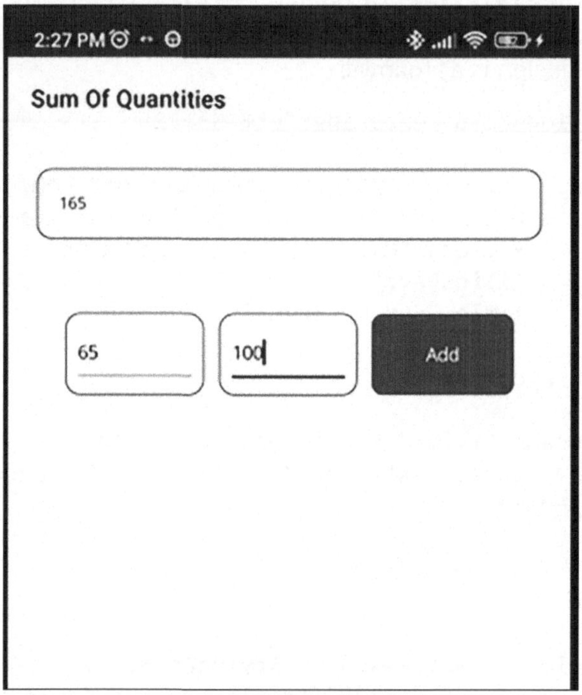

***Figure 4.4**: Final result, when debugging the project*

Congratulations, we have already finished our first application using MVVM, developing our application in an organized way, using quality practices, and in a fun way.

Conclusion

In conclusion, understanding and utilizing design patterns is paramount for any software engineer aiming to enhance their coding efficiency, maintainability, and collaboration within teams. By leveraging established solutions such as Creational, Structural, and Behavioral patterns, developers can tackle common challenges without reinventing the wheel. Furthermore, exploring architectural frameworks such as MVVM emphasizes the importance of separating business logic from user interfaces, ultimately resulting in cleaner, more scalable applications. As remote work becomes increasingly prevalent, adopting these patterns and practices allows developers to write robust, easily modifiable code, facilitating seamless collaboration across distributed teams. Embrace the power of design patterns and architectures in your projects, not only to streamline development but to foster innovation and adaptability in an ever-evolving tech landscape.

In the next chapter, we will explore how to use Blazor technology within our MAUI application, how it works, and show an example of its use.

Chapter 5
Using Blazor Components in .NET MAUI

Introduction

In this chapter, we will show what Blazor is and how it works. We will also understand how it can be used in conjunction with .NET MAUI. At the end of the chapter, we will develop an application, using .NET, MAUI to which we will integrate Blazor components to demonstrate their use by using them together.

Structure

In this chapter, we will discuss the following topics:

- Understanding Blazor
  - Types of Blazor
  - Integration with the .NET Ecosystem
  - Limitations of Blazor
- Functioning of Blazor
  - Blazor WebAssembly
  - Blazor Server
  - Component Life Cycle
- First App with Blazor

Understanding Blazor

Blazor is a technology used for web development, created by Microsoft that allows the creation of interactive client-side applications, using C# instead of JavaScript. That is, Blazor allows you to write web applications entirely with technologies that are more common, such as .NET and C#, eliminating the need to write a large part of the code using JavaScript. It is a huge advantage for developers who commonly work in the .NET ecosystem, as it allows them to leverage the same language and tools on the frontend and backend.

Commonly, web development has been mostly dominated by technologies such as HTML, CSS, and JavaScript. While JavaScript is powerful, most of the time it can be tedious for developers who are used to a more structured language such as C#. In addition, due to the increasing complexity of modern web applications, maintaining and structuring large and robust JavaScript codebases can be a major challenge.

Blazor changes everything completely by allowing web developers to write all client-side logic coding, using C#, with all the benefits that come with it: Static typing, highly advanced development tools in Visual Studio, and the reuse of all knowledge in .NET.

Types of Blazor

Blazor offers two main types of models for creating a web application:

- **Blazor WebAssembly (WASM):** In this model, the application runs entirely in the browser using WebAssembly. The C# application is compiled in WebAssembly, and the application is run in the browser as if it were native code, which is very useful. The advantage here is that all of the application logic, including UI rendering, runs on what is client-side, which goes a long way in reducing the load on the server.
- **Blazor Server:** In this approach, the application logic runs entirely on the server, but the UI is updated in real-time in the browser via what is known as a SignalR connection. This means you can take advantage of the power of C# and .NET on the server where your application is hosted while still delivering an interactive in-browser experience. The main advantage is that Blazor Server applications can be much lighter on the client, as resource-intensive work is done on the server.
- At its core, Blazor allows you to create reusable components that encapsulate both logic and user interface. These components are defined using .razor files, where you can mix HTML with C# code to give a definition to the structure and behavior of the UI.

Basic example of a component in Blazor:

```
<h3>Counter</h3>

<p>Current value: @contador</p>
```

```
<button @onclick="IncreaseCounter">Increase</button>

@code {
    private int counter = 0;

    private void IncrementCounter()
    {
        counter++;
    }
}
```

In this example, we define a component that has a button to increment a counter. We use **`@onclick`** to handle the button click event, and the logic to update the counter is written in C#. All this without any need to write a single line of JavaScript.

Integration with the .NET Ecosystem

One of Blazor's greatest strengths is its direct integration with everything that is the .NET ecosystem. This means you can use .NET libraries and tools, such as database access using the Entity Framework, shared logic between the backend and frontend, and access to the dependency injection infrastructure, which is very useful, making it easier to organize your code.

In addition, Blazor allows code sharing between the client application and the server. This is useful when working with validation logic, data access, or services, since you can reuse the same code at both ends, reducing duplications and keeping everything in a more coherent way.

Blazor is ideal for web applications that require an interactive and high-value user experience, such as dashboards, management applications, or any type of application where a reactive interface is of vital importance. Plus, it is a useful option if you already have experience working in the .NET ecosystem and are looking to reduce the need to handle multiple languages and technologies in your development stack.

Limitations of Blazor

Despite its advantages, Blazor has some limitations that should be considered:

- **Application Size:** In Blazor WebAssembly, the first time the application is loaded, the browser has the need to download the .NET runtime, which can greatly increase the initial load time, although this has improved over time.
- **Backward Browser Compatibility:** Since Blazor WebAssembly relies on newer technologies such as WebAssembly, older browsers may not be fully compatible or have performance issues.

Functioning of Blazor

Blazor's architecture is based on the creation of components. A component in Blazor is a reusable unit of UI that can encapsulate both logic and rendering. These components are defined in .razor files, and contain a combination of C# and HTML

Blazor WebAssembly

Blazor WebAssembly (WASM) is Blazor's model in which the entire application can be run directly in the browser, without the need for a server to process client-side logic. WebAssembly is a technology that allows the execution of compiled code within the browser at speeds close to native applications.

WebAssembly Execution Process

1. **Downloading the Application**: When a user loads a Blazor WebAssembly application, the browser downloads the (compiled) assembly of the .NET application, along with the WebAssembly runtime. Although the initial download may be heavier than in traditional applications, this is compensated for by the fact that most of the logic is executed on the client.
2. **Browser Execution**: Once the application is downloaded, all C# code is processed in the browser within the WebAssembly environment. The browser acts as a kind of "virtual machine" that executes .NET code, making it easy for developers to use the full power of C# and .NET without having to rely on JavaScript.
3. **Interaction with the DOM**: Although the application is written in C#, the browser still interacts with the Document Object Model (DOM), which is the internal structure of the web page. Blazor manages this interaction using its rendering engine, allowing the UI to update efficiently without the need to reload the page.
4. **PWA Capabilities**. Blazor WebAssembly also supports Progressive Web Apps (PWA), which means that apps can run smoothly offline, ship as installable web apps, and take advantage of all the browser's advanced features.

Advantages of Blazor WebAssembly

Here are some key benefits of Blazor WebAssembly:

- **Client Autonomy**: Everything that is logic is executed in the browser, which reduces dependence on the server.
- **Full Client Reactivity**: UI interactions do not require constant back-and-forth to the server.

- **Full Use of C#**: Allows you to use the full power of C# and .NET libraries directly in the browser.

Blazor Server

Blazor Server takes a different approach, where the application logic runs on the server, but UI updates are synchronized in real-time with the browser. This is done through **SignalR**, a library that helps maintain a real-time, two-way connection between the server and the client.

Execution Process on Blazor Server

1. **Running on the Server**: Instead of running the application on the client, Blazor Server runs all of the logic on the server. Each time the user interacts with the application (for example, clicks a button), the event is immediately sent to the server for processing.
2. **Real-Time Update with SignalR**: Blazor Server uses SignalR to maintain a much more constant connection between the server and the client. When the server needs to update the user interface, it sends the changes to the browser, which applies them without reloading the page.
3. **Interaction with the DOM**: Although the logic is solely on the server, Blazor Server interacts with the DOM more than efficiently. SignalR only sends the diffs between what is known as the current UI state and the new state, significantly minimizing what data traffic is.

Advantages of Blazor Server

Here are some key benefits of Blazor Server:

- **Fast Initial Loads**: Since there is no need to download the WebAssembly runtime or .NET assemblies, the application loads much faster than Blazor WebAssembly.
- **Complete Server Control**: All application updates are handled on the server, which can be more useful for applications that require full control over server resources.
- **Support for Legacy Devices**: Since the client only needs what it takes to render HTML and handle events, even older or more resource-constrained devices can easily run Blazor Server applications without any limitations.

Component Life Cycle

Blazor follows a component lifecycle that allows you the ability to control what happens in each phase of its execution. This includes methods such as:

- **`OnInitialized`**: Invoked only when the component has been initialized for the first time.
- **`OnParametersSet`**: Executed whenever the component's parameters are updated.
- **`OnAfterRender`**: Called after the component has been rendered in the DOM, ideal for performing actions after minimal UI updates.

These methods allow you to customize your application's behavior at each stage of a component's life, providing greater full control over how the interface is managed.

First App with Blazor

After reading the previous sections, we are now ready to develop our first application in Blazor MAUI using the MVVM design pattern with the library **`CommunityToolkit.Mvvm`**. It is worth mentioning that the use of the library is very similar to how it is done with XAML. The application that we are going to develop will be a calculator that will be responsible for performing simple mathematical operations such as addition, subtraction, multiplication, and division.

Let's get started! First, we will create a new project. For this project, we will use the template **MAUI Blazor**, as shown in *Figure* 5.1.

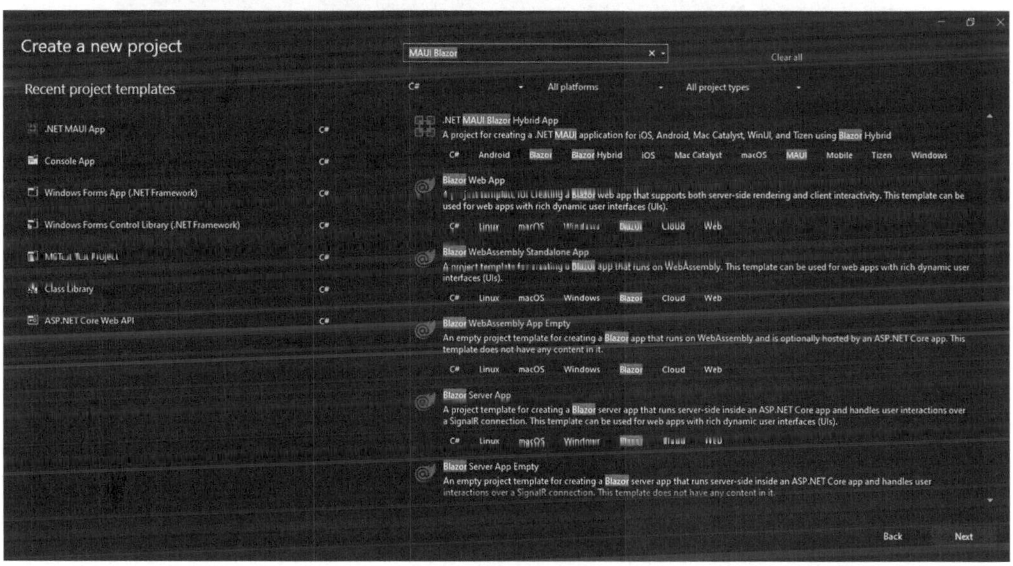

Figure 5.1: *Creating a MAUI Blazor project*

The project will be named **MyFirstAppMauiBlazor**, and we will use the.**NET 8.0** framework. Once our project is created, we will install the library **Community Toolkit.Mvvm** via the package manager **NuGet**. Once the library installation is complete, we are going to modify the folder and file structure of the project. We are going to create the folder **ViewModels.** This folder stores the **ViewModel** classes that our application will use. We will also create the folder **styles** within **wwwroot/css**. Within the **styles** folder, let us create the style sheet **Calculator.css** This file will define the style of our calculator. In the folder **ViewModels**, a class will be created named **CalculateViewModel.cs**; it will be the **ViewModel** of our application. Finally, we are going to delete the razor files that are located in **Components/Pages**, and we are going to create a new razor file with the name **CalculatePage.razor**. This file will be the main view.

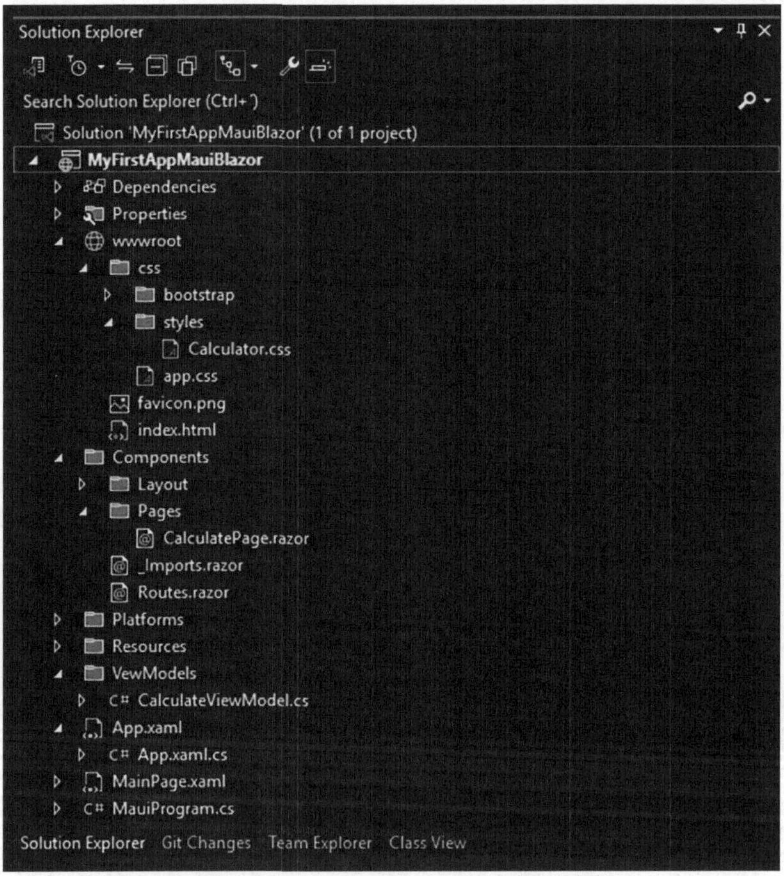

***Figure 5.2**: Representation of the project's folder and file structure*

Next, we are going to perform some configuration. We will search for the files **MainLayout.razor** and **NavMenu.razor**, which are found in **Components/Layout**. These files play important roles in organizing and navigating the user interface of our application. The file **MainLayout.razor** is the one in charge of defining the design of the application, providing a structure of headers, sidebars, and content pairs. For this example, we eliminate the header, leaving the code as follows:

```
@inherits LayoutComponentBase
<div class="page">
    <div class="sidebar">
        <NavMenu />
    </div>
    <main>
        <article class="content px-4">
            @Body
        </article>
    </main>
</div>
```

The file **NavMenu.razor** contains the navigation menu of an application. It is responsible for providing the varied links to select the different pages that our application will contain. This is where we are going to modify our menu. If you remember, we deleted three razor files; therefore, we have to delete the link of the files. For this, we will only delete the tag **NavLink** that linked any of these files, and we are going to create a new tag **NavLink** in the attribute **href**. The link to our Page is added. This time, we are going to leave it blank because our application will only have one page. After this configuration, we are going to run our application to see the result.

```
<div class="top-row ps-3 navbar navbar-dark">
    <div class="container-fluid">
        <a class="navbar-brand" href="">Calculator</a>
    </div>
</div>
<style>
    .nav-link {
        display: flex;
        align-items: center;
    }
</style>
<input type="checkbox" title="Navigation menu" class="navbar-toggler" />
<div class="nav-scrollable"
 onclick="document.querySelector('.navbar-toggler').click()">
    <nav class="flex-column">
        <div class="nav-item px-3">
            <NavLink class="nav-link d-flex align-items-center"
href="" Match="NavLinkMatch.All">
                <span>Calculator</span>
            </NavLink>
        </div>
```

```
    </none>
</div>
```

Once our application has been tested, we will continue with the **ViewModel**. In the class **CalculateViewModel.cs**, let's implement inheritance **ObservableObject** and define our type class **partial**. The following properties of type private were created, using the attribute **ObservableProperty** on two properties:

```
private string _pattern = "^[\\/*]+$";

private string _message = "Invalid expression";

[ObservableProperty]
private string displayValue;

[ObservableProperty]
private List<string> buttonValues;
```

Then, we are going to define a public property named **OperationsCommand**, of type **IRelayCommand**. Within the **ViewModel** constructor, the **OperationsCommand** is initialized by creating a new instance of the **RelayCommand**, and the **Operations** method is taken as a parameter, which receives a string value as a parameter. This method will be in charge of validating and carrying out the operations according to what is entered in the buttons. The property **ButtonValues** will also be initialized in the constructor. This will be a list of string characters and will represent the values of our calculator. The complete class should look like this:

```
using CommunityToolkit.Mvvm.ComponentModel;
using CommunityToolkit.Mvvm.Input;
using System.Text.RegularExpressions;
using System.Data;

namespace MyFirstAppMauiBlazor.VewModels
{
    public partial class CalculateViewModel : ObservableObject
    {
        private string _pattern = "^[\\/*]+$";

        private string _message = "Invalid expression";

        [ObservableProperty]
        private string displayValue;

        [ObservableProperty]
        private List<string> buttonValues;

        public IRelayCommand<string?> OperationsCommand { get;
set; }
```

```
        public CalculateViewModel()
        {
            DisplayValue = "";

            OperationsCommand = new RelayCommand<string?>
(Operations);

            ButtonValues = new List<string>
            {
                "7", "8", "9", "+",
                "4", "5", "6", "-",
                "1", "2", "3", "*",
                "0", "C", "=", "/"
             };
        }

        private void Operations(string? value)
        {
            DisplayValue = DisplayValue.Equals(_message) ?
string.Empty : DisplayValue ?? string.Empty;

            if (!string.IsNullOrWhiteSpace(value))
            {
                bool isValid = Regex.IsMatch(DisplayValue,
_pattern);
                if (!isValid && value != "C")
                {
                    if (value == "=")
                    {
                        var data = new DataTable();
                var result = data.Compute(DisplayValue, String.
Empty).ToString();
                        DisplayValue = result ?? "";
                    }
                    else
                        DisplayValue += value;
                    return;
                }
            }
            DisplayValue = value == "C" ? string.Empty :
_message;
        }

    }
}
```

Next, we are going to define some styles within the file **Calculator.css** that were created in the previous steps. This CSS style sheet will have the following styles:

```
.calculator {
    display: grid;
    grid-template-rows: auto 1fr;
    gap: 1rem;
}

.display {
    border: 1px solid #ccc;
    padding: 1rem;
    text-align: right;
    font-size: 2rem;
    background-color: #eee;
}

.buttons {
    display: grid;
    grid-template-columns: repeat(4, 1fr);
    gap: 0.5rem;
}

button {
    padding: 1rem;
    font-size: 1.5rem;
}
```

Once our styles have been added to our document **Calculator.css**, we are going to link this resource to the **index.html** found inside the **wwwroot**. To create the link, we are going to add the following line inside the head of the html:

```
<link rel="stylesheet" href="css/styles/Calculator.css"/>
```

After adding our styles, we are going to create our interface components. In the **CalculatePage.razor**, the attribute was defined as **@page** This attribute indicates that the file is an important page for URL navigation. When the attribute has the root path (/), it indicates that this file will be displayed first. The directives **@using** import the classes that the page code will use. The **@inject** directive will inject an instance of the **ViewModel** that is used to handle the calculator logic and provide data and commands to the user interface, and will be responsible for linking with our **ViewModel**.

```
@page "/"

@using System.Collections.Generic
@using System.ComponentModel
@using System.Windows.Input
```

```
@using MyFirstAppMauiBlazor.ViewModels

@inject CalculateViewModel ViewModel

<div class="calculator">

    <div class="display">
        <p>@ViewModel.DisplayValue</p>
    </div>

    <div class="buttons">

        @foreach (string? button in ViewModel.ButtonValues)
        {

<button @onclick="() => ViewModel.OperationsCommand.Execute(but-
ton)">
    @button
</button>

        }

    </div>

</div>
```

Now, all we have to do is debug our application. The result should be as shown in *Figure* 5.3; a simple and functional calculator should be displayed.

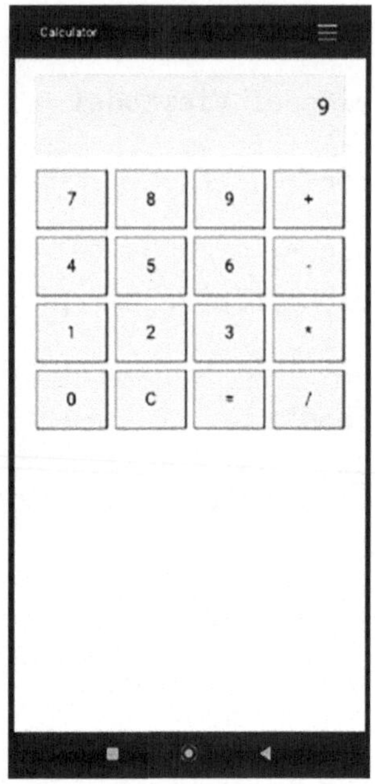

***Figure* 5.3**: *Representation of what the finished application should look like*

Congratulations, we have already finished our first application, using MVVM and MAUI Blazor, developing our application in an organized way, using quality practices, and in a fun way.

Conclusion

In conclusion, Blazor stands out as a transformative technology for web development, empowering developers within the .NET ecosystem to create interactive client-side applications, using familiar C# instead of JavaScript. By offering two distinct models—Blazor WebAssembly and Blazor Server—Blazor accommodates diverse project needs, whether prioritizing client autonomy or server control. Its seamless integration with the .NET framework enhances code reusability, and simplifies the development process, ensuring a coherent structure for the frontend and the backend. The journey of building our first application, a simple yet effective calculator, underscores Blazor's flexibility and the power of the MVVM architecture.

As we move forward in the evolving landscape of web technologies, embracing Blazor can streamline workflows, innovate user experiences, and ultimately redefine how we approach modern web application development. Therefore, now is the time to explore Blazor further, and harness its potential for your next project.

In the next chapter, we will talk about SQLite, and how it works. We will also talk about what APIs are, and how to connect them from .NET MAUI. Finally, we will elaborate on an application that uses both SQLite and an API connection.

CHAPTER 6
Internal DB and API Connection

Introduction

In this chapter, we will talk about SQLite, what it is, key features, and how it works. We will also cover the definition of API, and its main features. We will learn how to encode and decode JSON, which is very useful for sending and receiving information through an API. And finally, we will create an app that uses SQLite and an API.

Structure

In this chapter, we will discuss the following topics:

- Understanding SQLite
    - Key Features of SQLite
- Functioning of SQLite
- Understanding an API
    - Types of APIs
    - Benefits of Using APIs
- Ways to Connect to an API
    - Traditional Connection
    - Refit Library
- Encoding and Decoding a JSON
- First App with SQLite and Connection to API

Understanding SQLite

SQLite is known as a lightweight, quick, and fully contained relational database management system (RDBMS) in a single library. Unlike some other database systems such as MySQL or PostgreSQL, SQLite does not require a separate server configuration, nor does it require constant administration. For this reason, it is mostly used in mobile applications, desktop applications, and smaller or medium-sized projects where a lighter database is required and easier to implement.

SQLite has the main advantage of being self-contained, configuration-free, and transactional. This means that a complete database with all the ACID (Atomicity, Consistency, Isolation, and Durability) features can be used without having to install or configure a server system. Simply include the database file, along with your application, and it's ready to run. Because of these features, SQLite becomes an ideal choice for scenarios where an embedded database is required, such as in mobile apps (it's the default database system on Android and iOS) or small desktop apps.

SQLite uses a single database file that stores all the information you enter. When you work with an SQLite database, all operations are performed on this file, which is portable and can be easily copied or moved between multiple systems without losing integrity.

An SQLite database is basically a file with a .sqlite or .db extension, and all tables, indexes, triggers, and views are stored within it. The SQLite engine handles queries and transactions very efficiently, despite being a bit smaller and less complex than other well-known database systems. In fact, just because SQLite is stored in a single file does not mean it lacks robustness. In fact, SQLite supports complete transactions, which ensures that any operation on the data is atomic and maintains the integrity of the data.

Key Features of SQLite

The following are some of the most important features of SQLite:

- **Lightweight and Embedded:** SQLite is designed to be a lightweight database with almost no configuration required, which means it does not require a separate server. This makes it a pretty good choice for mobile apps, embedded devices, and resource-constrained solutions.
- **No External Dependencies:** SQLite is autonomous. Everything that is needed to interact with an SQLite database is within the same library, and does not depend on any server processes or external configurations.
- **ACID Transactions:** Despite being lightweight, SQLite complies with all ACID properties, ensuring that all operations on data are secure and consistent. Transactions are either fully completed or not executed at all, ensuring that the data is not left in an intermediate state.
- **Portability:** Since an SQLite database is simply a single file, you have the freedom to move that file between different platforms (Windows, Linux, and Mac) without concerns about compatibility.

- **Full SQL Support:** SQLite supports a full subset of SQL, including the main functions of creating, modifying, and manipulating data. It allows us to work with SQLite in the same way you would with any other RDBMS, using SQL commands such as **SELECT**, **INSERT**, **UPDATE**, and **DELETE**.
- **High Performance for Specific Scenarios:** Although SQLite is not well suited for large multi-user applications, its performance capability in read and write operations in single-user applications or mobile applications is quite excellent.

Functioning of SQLite

The steps for implementing SQLite within a system will be listed:

1. **Create a Database:** To start working with SQLite, the first thing you need is to create a database file. This can be done directly from the command line using the SQLite interface:

   ```
   sqlite3 miBaseDeDatos.db
   ```

   What this command does is create a database file called **miBaseDeDatos.db** and opens an interactive console where you can execute SQL commands directly.

2. **Create Tables and Basic Operations**: Once inside the database, you can start creating tables and manipulating data using standard SQL. For example, to create a table:

   ```
   CREATE TABLE Users (
   Id INTEGER PRIMARY KEY,
   Name TEXT,
   Email TEXT
   );

   And to insert data:

   INSERT INTO Users (Name, Email) VALUES ('Jorge Pérez', 'jorge.
   perez@email.com');
   ```

3. **Query Data:** You can run common SQL queries for database data retrieval:

   ```
   SELECT * FROM Users;
   SQLite will run the query and return the results directly.
   ```

4. **Integration with Programming Languages:** SQLite supports various programming languages, including C#, Python, Java, and many more. In C#, for example, you can use the **System.Data.SQLite** package to work with SQLite databases.

Basic example in C#:

```
using (var connection = new SQLiteConnection("Data Source=miBa-
seDeDatos.db"))
{
	connection. Open();

	var command = new SQLiteCommand("SELECT * FROM Users",
	connection);

	using (var reader = command. ExecuteReader())
	{

		while (reader. Read())
		{
			Console.WriteLine($"Name: {reader["Name"]},
			Email: {reader["Email"]}");
		}
	}
}
```

Understanding an API

Application Programming Interface (API) is a set of different rules and protocols that allow us to communicate with different applications. It is, in essence, an intermediate layer that defines how software components interact. APIs make it possible for programs to access multiple functionalities or data from other services without having to understand their internal code or how it works. They are critical to systems integration and greatly allow developers to take advantage of many services, platforms, or libraries without having to "reinvent the wheel." In simple terms, an API acts as an intermediary between two parties: a client application that requests or sends data or services and an application or system that provides it. When the client makes a request to the API, the API processes the request, translates it if necessary, and returns the information or result of the request to the client.

Types of APIs

There are several types of APIs, but the most common are the following:

- **Representational State Transfer (REST) APIs:** REST is a class of architectural style that is widely used in web development. A RESTful API is based on what standard HTTP methods are and follows some principles such as statelessness, that is, each API request is independent of all the others. REST APIs typically use formats that are lightweight, such as JSON, to send and receive data.

The most common actions in a RESTful API correspond to HTTP methods:

- **GET:** Get resources or data.
- **POST:** Create new resources.
- **PUT:** Update existing resources.
- **DELETE:** Delete resources.

Example: A RESTful API for managing users might have the following endpoints:

- **GET /users:** Returns a list of users.
- **POST /users:** Create a new user.
- **PUT /users/1:** Updates the user's data with ID 1.
- **DELETE /users/1:** Deletes the user with ID 1.

- **Simple Object Access Protocol (SOAP) APIs:** SOAP is a protocol with more formal principles than REST, with a specific message format (usually XML) and more complex and strict rules. It is known for its high robustness in enterprise applications, but it is also heavier compared to REST. SOAP is used in scenarios where more security is required, such as in banking transactions or where high security is needed.

  Example: A SOAP request to get a user to look something like this:

```
<soapenv:Envelope
xmlns:soapenv="http://schemas.xmlsoap.org/soap/envelope/"
xmlns:web="http://www.example.com/webservices">
      <soapenv:Header/>
      <soapenv:Body>
            <web:GetUser>
                  <web:UserId>1</web:UserId>
            </web:GetUser>
      </soapenv:Body>
</soapenv:Envelope>
```

- **Library APIs:** In addition to web-based APIs, there are APIs that are part of libraries or frameworks. These APIs are what allow developers to interact with the internal functionalities of a specific software or library. For example, an API in the .NET framework allows access to various functionalities such as file handling, mathematical operations, or manipulation of data strings.
- **System APIs:** APIs that are part of the operating system environment, such as the Windows API, allow developers to interact with hardware and other internal system services. Through these APIs, tasks such as opening files, managing different processes, or interacting with peripheral devices can be implemented.

Benefits of Using APIs

The use of APIs brings several important benefits:

- **Feature Reuse:** APIs allow different apps and services to reuse various features without having to duplicate the code. For example, a geolocation service can be integrated into several applications, using an API instead of having to develop that functionality from scratch in each one.
- **Abstraction and Simplicity:** APIs allow developers to interact with systems that are often much more complex in a simplified way. The API abstracts all the logic that is handled internally, exposing only the essential operations that the user may need.
- **Integration between Systems:** APIs allow applications from different environments or technologies to communicate internally with each other. For example, a mobile application may interact with a remote server to retrieve or send data through an API.
- **Scalability:** APIs make it easier to create systems that are mostly scalable. Developers can easily add functionality or connect to a myriad of new services without affecting the core of the application.

Ways to Connect to an API

Once we understand what an API is, it is time to connect to one. In .NET MAUI with C#, the process to connect to an API is very simple, and we will have different ways to make this connection, from a traditional way to the implementation of libraries that can bring multiple advantages when implementing it. For example, some libraries allow automatic serialization and deserialization of a JSON object, cleaner syntax, simplified error handling, among others.

When you want to connect to an API with C#, you must take the following points into account:

- **API Type:** Each type of API has different characteristics and connection methods, so it is important to know if it is a REST API, SOAP, GraphQL, and so on.
- **API Documentation:** It is important to understand the parameters, response formats, endpoints, data model, and authentication required for the API implementation.
- **HTTP Status Codes:** Proper implementation of response states for error handling and management of the status of correct responses, for example, codes 200, 201, and so on.

- **Authentication Handling:** Implement the appropriate authentication and credentials submission method.
- **Using Asynchrony:** Using async to make asynchronous calls and prevent the application from hanging.

On this occasion, we are going to explore two methods to connect to an API: the traditional approach and the use of the Refit library. In the following example, we used **jsonplaceholder.typicode.com**, which is an online service that provides a fake API that helps in testing and prototyping.

Traditional Connection

To make an HTTP request in a traditional way, the **HttpClient** class allows you to make requests and receive a response from an API by performing type operations **`GET`**, **`POST`**, **`PUT`** and **`DELETE`**.

Suppose we need to make a connection to the API **`JSONPlaceholder`**. The resource to use is https://jsonplaceholder.typicode.com/posts/ and the **`GET`** method.

First, the model that represents a publication will be defined:

```
namespace ApiConnection.Models;

public class Post
{
    public int Id { get; set; }
    public int UserId { get; set; }
    public string? Title { get; set; }
    public string? Body { get; set; }
}
```

Next, we are going to create our ApiServices service. This service will be responsible for generating the GET request to consult our API.

```
// Interface to abstract the service - this enables testing and
decoupling
namespace ApiConnection.Services;

using ApiConnection.Models;

public interface IApiService
{
    Task<List<Post>> GetUserListAsync();
}

// Concrete implementation of the API service
namespace ApiConnection.Services;
```

```
using ApiConnection.Models;
using System.Net.Http;
using System.Net.Http.Json;

public class ApiService : IApiService
{
    private readonly HttpClient _httpClient;

    // HttpClient is injected via dependency injection
    public ApiService(HttpClient httpClient)
    {
        _httpClient = httpClient;

        // Set base address only once. Optional if configured
elsewhere.
        _httpClient.BaseAddress = new Uri("https://jsonplace
holder.typicode.com/");
    }

    // Fetches a list of posts from the API
    public async Task<List<Post>> GetUserListAsync()
    {
        var response = await _httpClient.GetAsync("posts/");
        response.EnsureSuccessStatusCode();

        // Returns deserialized list or an empty one if null
        return await response.Content.ReadFromJsonAsyn-
c<List<Post>>() ?? new List<Post>();
    }
}


// Register the service and HttpClient in your MauiProgram.cs or
Startup.cs
builder.Services.AddHttpClient<IApiService, ApiService>();
```

As can be seen in the previous code, an instance of the class was created in the class constructor **HttpClient**, and the base address for the instance is set on the **BaseAddress** property. This means that all requests you make with **_client** will use this URL as a prefix. The function **GetUserListAsync** is an asynchronous method that makes a GET request to the API to get a list of posts. The request is sent to the route "**posts/**," and then it verifies that the response is successful. It is responsible for deserializing the JSON content into a list of Post objects.

To see an example of how to use the **ApiServices**, we can create an async method, where an instance of the **ApiServices** will be created. **ApiServices** is used to call

`GetUserListAsync` and obtain the data, where it is validated if the list is not null. If it is not null, each element is traversed and the ID, Title, and Body of each publication are printed in the console.

```
using ApiConnection.Services;
using CommunityToolkit.Mvvm.ComponentModel;
using CommunityToolkit.Mvvm.Input;

public partial class UsersViewModel : ObservableObject
{
    private readonly IApiService _apiService;

    public UsersViewModel(IApiService apiService)
    {
        _apiService = apiService;
    }

    // Command to fetch user list from API
    [RelayCommand]
    private async Task GetListUserAsync()
    {
        var list = await _apiService.GetUserListAsync();

        if (list != null)
        {
            foreach (var item in list)
            {
                Console.WriteLine($"id: {item.Id}, Title: {item.
Title}, Body: {item.Body}");
            }
        }
    }
}
```

The previous example allows us to see how a connection to the API is made in a simple and functional way.

Refit Library

Suppose we need to make a connection to the API **`JSONPlaceholder`**. The resource to use is https://jsonplaceholder.typicode.com/posts/ and the **`GET`** method.

To make an HTTP request with Refit, we must first have the Refit package installed in our project through NuGet.

```
dotnet add package Refit
```

Once the installation of our package is complete, the model that represents a publication will be defined:

```
namespace ApiConnection.Models
{
    public class Post
    {
        public int Id { get; set; }
        public int UserId { get; set; }
        public string? Title { set; get; }
        public string? Body { set; get; }
    }
}
```

Then, an interface is defined that represents the API calls and that Refit will be used.

```
using ApiConnection.Models;
using Refit;
namespace ApiConnection.Services
{
    public interface IApiServices
    {
         //method and resource where the request will be made
        [Get("/posts/")]
        Task<List<Post>> GetPostListAsync();
    }
}
```

Next, we are going to create our Refit client in the **ApiService** service that is responsible for interacting with the API.

```
// ===============================
// CLASS: ApiService
// Implements logic and delegates to the injected Refit client
// ===============================

using ApiConnection.Models;

namespace ApiConnection.Services;

public class ApiService
{
    private readonly IApiServices _apiService;

    // The Refit client (IApiServices) is injected via constructor
    public ApiService(IApiServices apiService)
    {
```

```
        _apiService = apiService;
    }

    // Fetches the list of posts via the Refit client
    public async Task<List<Post>> GetPostsAsync()
    {
        return await _apiService.GetPostListAsync();
    }
}

// ================================
// MAUIPROGRAM.CS
// Registers Refit, services, and ViewModel for DI
// ================================

using ApiConnection.Services;
using Refit;

public static class MauiProgram
{
    public static MauiApp CreateMauiApp()
    {
        var builder = MauiApp.CreateBuilder();

        builder
            .UseMauiApp<App>()
            .ConfigureFonts(fonts =>
            {
                fonts.AddFont("OpenSans-Regular.ttf",
"OpenSansRegular");
            });

        // Register the Refit interface with a base URI
        builder.Services.AddRefitClient<IApiServices>()
                        .ConfigureHttpClient(c =>
                        {
                            c.BaseAddress = new Uri("https://
jsonplaceholder.typicode.com");
                        });

        // Register the concrete service and ViewModel
        builder.Services.AddTransient<ApiService>();
        builder.Services.AddTransient<UsersViewModel>();

        return builder.Build();
    }
}
```

To see an example of how to use the **ApiService**, we can create an async method, where an instance of the **ApiService** will be created. **ApiServices** is used to call the **GetPostsAsync** and get the data.

```
// ViewModel or code-behind class
using ApiConnection.Services;

public class PostsViewModel
{
    private readonly ApiService _apiService;

    // ApiService is injected via constructor (DI)
    public PostsViewModel(ApiService apiService)
    {
        _apiService = apiService;
    }

    // Method to fetch posts and handle errors
    public async Task GetListUserAsync()
    {
        try
        {
            var posts = await _apiService.GetPostsAsync();

            foreach (var post in posts)
            {
                Console.WriteLine($"ID: {post.Id}, Title: {post.
Title}");
            }
        }
        catch (Exception ex)
        {
            Console.WriteLine($"Error: {ex.Message}");
        }
    }
}
```

The aforementioned example simplifies how to create a GET request to an API and get a list of posts. Refit simplifies call definition and handles deserialization automatically.

Encoding and Decoding a JSON

In the previous section, we established a connection to an API, and using a simple example, we decoded the content of the response. JSON encoding and decoding are essential when working with endpoints, as they allow us to extract and send data efficiently and easily. But what is a JSON? **JavaScript Object Notation** (JSON) is a lightweight text format for data exchange, which makes writing, reading, and processing easier. Commonly, a JSON is made up of two structures: the first is the object that is represented by curly braces "`{ }`", and contains key and value, as shown in the following example:

```
{ "key": "value" }
```

The second structure is the array and this is represented by brackets "`[ ]`" and they can have a list of values, for example:

```
[ "value_1", "value_2", "value_3" ]
```

A JSON can be made up of nested objects and arrays, allowing complex data to be represented where each key is a string between quotes. The data type of the values can be strings, numbers, booleans, objects, arrays, or null, as shown in the following example representing a collection of books along with their category:

```
{
        "book":
        [
                {
                        "id": 1,
                        "title": "Title1"
                },
                {
                        "id": 2,
                        "title": "Title2"
                }
        ],
        "Category" : "Science fiction"
}
```

Once we understand what a JSON is, it's time to explore how we can encode and decode this object format with C#.

In C#, we have several ways to work with JSON. Following are the most common methods to encode and decode this object format:

- **`System.Text.Json`:** It is a library integrated into .NET for efficiently serializing and deserializing JSON. To encode, the **`JsonSerializer.Serialize()`** method is used, and to decode, **`JsonSerializer.Deserialize<T>()`** is used.
- **`Newtonsoft.Json`:** It is the most popular library to work with JSON in .NET. To encode, the **`JsonConvert.SerializeObject()`** method is used, and to decode, the **`JsonConvert.DeserializeObject<T>()`** method is used.
- **`DataContractJsonSerializer`:** It is a class in the **`System.Runtime.Serialization.Json`** namespace of .NET. It is mainly used in WCF applications and web services to serialize and deserialize JSON objects. To encode, the

DataContractJsonSerializer.WriteObject() method is used, and to decode, **DataContractJsonSerializer.ReadObject()** is used.

- **JavaScriptSerializer**: It is a simple class to work with JSON in ASP.NET applications. To encode, the **JavaScriptSerializer.Serialize()** method is used, and to decode, **JavaScriptSerializer.Deserialize<T>()** is used.
- **Utf8Json**: It is a high performance library, mainly optimized for UTF-8 encoding. To encode, the **JsonSerializer.Serialize()** method is used, and to decode, the **JsonSerializer.Deserialize<T>()** method is used.

Remember that the choice to use a library will depend on the specific needs of the project such as performance, ease, compatibility, and so on.

Let's see a simple example of how to decode a JSON using the **System.Text.Json** library; the JSON to decode would be the following:

```
[
	{
		"id": 1,
		"title": "Title1"
	},
	{
		"id": 2,
		"title": "Title2"
	}
]
```

The first step would be to create our data model. Defining the model is important because it represents the structure of the JSON once it is decoded.

```
public class Book
{
    public int Id { get; set; }
    public string Title { set; get; }
}
```

Having our model, the next step would be to decode this JSON format using the **JsonSerializer.Deserialize<T>( )** method.

```
 string jsonString =
   "[{ \"id\": 1, \"Title\": \"Title1\" }, { \"id\": 2, \
"Title\": \"Title2\" }]";

 List<Book> books = JsonSerializer.Deserialize<List<Book>>(json-
String);

 foreach(var item in books)
 {
     Console.WriteLine($"Id: {item.Id}");
```

```
        Console.WriteLine($"Title: {item.Title}");
    }
```

In conclusion, C# offers a variety of methods that make working with JSON easier, allowing the encoding and decoding of data efficiently and easily.

First App with SQLite and Connection to API

After reading the previous sections, we are ready to develop our first application using SQLite with a connection to an API.

This application will try to display a list of publications within a `CollectionView`. The application works as follows:

1. When launching the post listing page, a request will be made to the API. **https://jsonplaceholder.typicode.com/posts/**.
2. The response of the requests is decoded and will be saved in the SQLite database.
3. Finally, a query is made to the table and the query data is saved in an `ObservableCollection` to be presented in the user interface.

Once we understand how our app works, we will start with the development. The first step will be to create our project. For this example, it was named `FirstAppWithSQLiteAndApi`, and we will use the Framework **.NET 8.0+**. Once the project is created, the NuGet packages `CommunityToolkit.Mvvm`, `Microsoft.Data.Sqlite`, and `Refit` will be installed. Then we are going to modify the folder and file structure of the project as follows:

- **Models**
  - `Post.cs`
- **Services**
  - `ApiConnection.cs`
  - `Database.cs`
  - `IApiConnection.cs`
- **ViewModels**
  - `FirstAppWithSQLiteAndApi`
- **Views**
  - `CommentsPage.xaml`
  - `CommentsPage.xaml.cs`

Once we have created our folders and files, we will proceed to modify the **AppShell**. In this step, we will update the **ContentTemplate** property of the **ShellContent** to point to **CommentsPage**. This setting will allow us to have our page load first, when the application starts.

```
<?xml version="1.0" encoding="UTF-8" ?>
<Shell
    x:Class="FirstAppWithSQLiteAndApi.AppShell"
    xmlns="http://schemas.microsoft.com/dotnet/2021/maui"
    xmlns:x="http://schemas.microsoft.com/winfx/2009/xaml"
    xmlns:local="clr-namespace:FirstAppWithSQLiteAndApi.Views"
    Shell.FlyoutBehavior="Disabled"
    Title="FirstAppWithSQLiteAndApi">

    <ShellContent
        ContentTemplate="{DataTemplate local:CommentsPage}"
        Route="MainPage" />
</Shell>
```

Later, we will create our data model in the class **Post**, which will represent the structure of the JSON object and the corresponding table in our database. This model will be essential for our app to manage and manipulate information efficiently, ensuring that all data is integrated coherently into the user interface.

```
namespace FirstAppWithSQLiteAndApi.Models
{
    public class Post
    {
        public int Id { get; set; }
        public int UserId { get; set; }
        public string? Title { get; set; }
        public string? Body { get; set; }
    }
}
```

Next, we will create the service responsible for establishing the connection and handling requests to the https://jsonplaceholder.typicode.com API. To start, we will define the interface in **IApiConnection**, as shown in the following example.

```
// Import the Post data model
using FirstAppWithSQLiteAndApi.Models;

// Import the Refit library for easier API calls
using Refit;

namespace FirstAppWithSQLiteAndApi.Services
{
```

```
    // Define the IApiConnection interface for connecting to the
API
    public interface IApiConnection
    {
        [Get("/posts/")]
 // Returns a task containing a list of Post objects
        Task<List<Post>> GetPostListAsync();
    }
}
```

In class **ApiConnection**, which implements the **IApiConnection** interface, a service will be developed in charge of making requests and obtaining data.

```
using FirstAppWithSQLiteAndApi.Models;
using Refit;

namespace FirstAppWithSQLiteAndApi.Services
{
    public class ApiConnection : IApiConnection
    {
        private readonly IApiConnection _apiService;

        public ApiConnection()
        {
            var url = "https://jsonplaceholder.typicode.com";
            _apiService = RestService.For<IApiConnection>(url);
        }

        public async Task<List<Post>> GetPostListAsync()
        {
            return await _apiService.GetPostListAsync();
        }
    }
}
```

Now, we will proceed to create the service to manage the SQLite database. In the file **Database.cs**, we have defined the interface **IDatabase**, which specifies the methods needed to query, save, and delete records. Additionally, in this same file, we have implemented the service **Database**, which will be in charge of interacting with the database. This service will allow you to initialize the table, query records, insert or update data, delete records using their ID, and, if necessary, delete the entire table.

```
using Microsoft.Data.Sqlite;
using FirstAppWithSQLiteAndApi.Models;

namespace FirstAppWithSQLiteAndApi.Services
{
    public interface IDatabase
```

```
    {
        Task<List<Post>> GetPostsAsync();
        Task<int> SavePostAsync(Post post);
        Task<int> DeletePostAsync(int id);
    }



    public class Database : IDatabase
    {
        private readonly string _dbPath;

        public Database(string dbPath)
        {
            _dbPath = dbPath;
            InitializeDatabase();
        }

        private void InitializeDatabase()
        {
            //DropPostTable();
            using var connection = new SqliteConnection($"Data
Source={_dbPath}");
            connection.Open();
            var command = connection.CreateCommand();
            command.CommandText = @"
                CREATE TABLE IF NOT EXISTS Post (
                    Id INTEGER PRIMARY KEY AUTOINCREMENT,
                    UserId INTEGER NOT NULL,
                    Title TEXT NOT NULL,
                    Body TEXT NOT NULL
                );";
                command.ExecuteNonQuery();
        }

        public async Task<List<Post>> GetPostsAsync()
        {
            var posts = new List<Post>();
            using var connection = new SqliteConnection($"Data
Source={_dbPath}");
            await connection.OpenAsync();
            var command = connection.CreateCommand();
            command.CommandText = "SELECT * FROM Post";

            using (var reader = command.ExecuteReader())
            {
```

```
                while (reader.Read())
                {
                    var note = new Post
                    {
                        Id = reader.GetInt32(0),
                        UserId = reader.GetInt32(1),
                        Title = reader.GetString(2),
                        Body = reader.GetString(3),
                    };
                    posts.Add(nota);
                }
            }
            return posts;
        }

        public async Task<int> SavePostAsync(Post post)
        {
            using var connection = new SqliteConnection($"Data
    Source={_dbPath}");
            await connection.OpenAsync();
            var command = connection.CreateCommand();
           if(post.Id == 0)
            {   // Insert
                command.CommandText = @"
      INSERT INTO Post (UserId, Title, Body)
      VALUES ($userId, $title, $body);";
                command.Parameters.AddWithValue("$userId", post.
                UserId);
                command.Parameters.AddWithValue("$title", post.
                Title);
                command.Parameters.AddWithValue("$body", post.
                Body);
                return await command.ExecuteNonQueryAsync();
            }
            else
            {   // Update
                command.CommandText = @"UPDATE Post SET
                          UserId = $userId, Title = $title,
    Body = $body WHERE Id = $id;";
                command.Parameters.AddWithValue("$userId", post.
                UserId);
                command.Parameters.AddWithValue("$title", post.
                Title);
                command.Parameters.AddWithValue("$body", post.
                Body);
                command.Parameters.AddWithValue("$id", post.Id);
                return await command.ExecuteNonQueryAsync();
```

```
                }
            }

            public async Task<int> DeletePostAsync(int id)
            {
                //Deleted
                using var connection = new SqliteConnection($"Data
                Source={_dbPath}");
                await connection.OpenAsync();
                var command = connection.CreateCommand();
                command.CommandText = "DELETE FROM Post WHERE Id =
                $id;";
                command.Parameters.AddWithValue("$id", id);
                return command.ExecuteNonQuery();
            }

            private void DropPostTable()
            {
                //Drop Table
                using var connection = new SqliteConnection($"Data
                Source={_dbPath}");
                connection.Open();
                var command = connection.CreateCommand();
                command.CommandText = "DROP TABLE IF EXISTS Post;";
                command.ExecuteNonQuery();
            }
        }
    }
```

Once the previous steps are completed, we will proceed to inject the dependencies of the classes that we have created in the file **MauiProgram.cs**.

```
using Microsoft.Extensions.Logging;
using FirstAppWithSQLiteAndApi.Services;
using FirstAppWithSQLiteAndApi.ViewModels;
using FirstAppWithSQLiteAndApi.Views;

namespace FirstAppWithSQLiteAndApi
{
    public static class MauiProgram
    {
        public static MauiApp CreateMauiApp()
        {
            var builder = MauiApp.CreateBuilder();

            builder
                .UseMauiApp<App>()
                .ConfigureFonts(fonts =>
```

```
                {
                    fonts.AddFont("OpenSans-Regular.ttf",
"OpenSansRegular");
                    fonts.AddFont("OpenSans-Semibold.ttf",
"OpenSansSemibold");
                });

            var dbPath = Path.Combine(
    Environment.GetFolderPath(
        Environment.SpecialFolder.LocalApplicationData),
        "posts.db3");
            builder.Services.AddSingleton<IDatabase>(new
Database(dbPath));
            builder.Services.AddSingleton<IApiConnection,
ApiConnection>();
            builder.Services.AddSingleton<CommentsViewModel>();
            builder.Services.AddTransient<CommentsPage>();

#if DEBUG
            builder.Logging.AddDebug();
#endif

            return builder.Build();
        }
    }
}
```

Once the previous step is completed, we will define the **ViewModel** of the page in the file **CommentsViewModel.cs**. Since we are working with dependency injection, in this case, the interfaces **IDatabase** and **IApiConnection** will be executed. In the class constructor, two methods were defined in the class:

- **LoadPost:** It is responsible for loading applications from an API and then saving them to the database; it also activates and deactivates a process indicator and handles possible errors.
- **OnSavePost:** It takes care of saving an individual post to the database and updates the post collection to reflect changes to the UI.

The **ViewModel** will look like this:

```
using System.Collections.ObjectModel;
using FirstAppWithSQLiteAndApi.Models;
using CommunityToolkit.Mvvm.ComponentModel;
using FirstAppWithSQLiteAndApi.Services;

namespace FirstAppWithSQLiteAndApi.ViewModels
{
```

```
    public partial  class CommentsViewModel : ObservableObject
    {
        private readonly IDatabase _database;

        private readonly IApiConnection _connection;

        [ObservableProperty]
        private ObservableCollection<Post>? _posts;

        [ObservableProperty]
        private bool _activate;

        public CommentsViewModel(IDatabase database, IApiConnec-
tion connection)
        {
            _database = database;
            _connection = connection;
            Task task = LoadPost();
        }

        private async Task LoadPost()
        {
            Activate = true;
            try
            {
                var posts = await _connection.GetPostListAsync();
                foreach (var post in posts)
                {
                   await OnSavePost(post);
                }
            }
            catch (Exception ex)
            {
                Console.WriteLine(ex.ToString());
            }
            Activate = false;
        }

        private async Task OnSavePost(Post post)
        {
            await _database.SavePostAsync(post);
            var list = await _database.GetPostsAsync();
            Posts = new ObservableCollection<Post>(list);
        }
    }
}
```

Now, we will proceed to create the **BindingContext** of our page inside the class constructor **CommentsPage.xaml.cs** to be able to use our **ViewModel**.

```
using FirstAppWithSQLiteAndApi.ViewModels;
namespace FirstAppWithSQLiteAndApi.Views;

public partial class CommentsPage : ContentPage
{
    public CommentsPage(CommentsViewModel commentsViewModel)
    {
        InitializeComponent();
        this.BindingContext = commentsViewModel;
    }
}
```

Now, let's create our interface components on **CommentsPage.xaml**. The user interface has the following component structure:

- <ContentPage>
    - <StackLayout>
        - <Label>
        - <ActivityIndicator>
        - <ScrollView>
            - <CollectionView>
                - <CollectionView.ItemTemplate>
                    - <DataTemplate>
                        - <Frame>
                            - <StackLayout>
                                - <Label>
                                - <Label>

By analyzing the preceding structure, we can understand a little more about the design of our user interface.

```
<?xml version="1.0" encoding="utf-8" ?>
<ContentPage xmlns="http://schemas.microsoft.com/dotnet/2021/maui"
             xmlns:x="http://schemas.microsoft.com/winfx/2009/xaml"
             x:Class="FirstAppWithSQLiteAndApi.Views.CommentsPage"
             BackgroundColor="#f7f7f7">

    <StackLayout Padding="10">
        <Label Text="User Comments"
               FontSize="24"
               FontAttributes="Bold"
```

```
                HorizontalOptions="Center"
                Margin="0,10,0,20" />

     <ActivityIndicator IsRunning="{Binding Activate}"
    IsVisible="{Binding Activate}"/>

            <ScrollView VerticalOptions="FillAndExpand">
                <CollectionView ItemsSource="{Binding Posts}">
                    <CollectionView.ItemTemplate>
                        <DataTemplate>
                            <Frame BorderColor="#d3d3d3"
                                   CornerRadius="8"
                                   Padding="10"
                                   Margin="5"
                                   BackgroundColor="White"
                                   HasShadow="True">

                                <StackLayout Orientation="Vertical"
                                             VerticalOptions="Center"
                                             Spacing="10">
                                    <Label Text="{Binding Title}"
                                           FontSize="18"
                                           FontAttributes="Bold"
                                           VerticalOptions="Center"
                                           HorizontalOptions="StartAnd
                                           Expand" />
                                    <Label Text="{Binding Body}"
                                           FontSize="16"
                                           VerticalOptions="Center"
                                           HorizontalOptions="StartAnd
                                           Expand" />
                                </StackLayout>

                            </Frame>
                        </DataTemplate>
                    </CollectionView.ItemTemplate>
                </CollectionView>
            </ScrollView>

        </StackLayout>
    </ContentPage>
```

Congratulations, you have already finished your first application, using MVVM, SQLite, and API! All that remains is to debug the application, and see the result.

Conclusion

In conclusion, understanding and working with APIs is essential for modern software development, especially in a world that increasingly relies on seamless integration of services and data. This guide has provided a comprehensive overview of APIs, highlighting their critical role as intermediaries that facilitate communication between diverse systems. From exploring various API types such as REST and SOAP to illustrating how to connect to APIs using C# and frameworks such as Refit, the journey into API integration is both enlightening and empowering. Moreover, incorporating databases such as SQLite into applications enhances data management, enabling effective storage and retrieval of information obtained through APIs. By developing a sample application that showcases how to connect to an API, retrieve data, and present it using the MVVM pattern, we have demonstrated a practical approach that developers can replicate in their projects. As we move forward in this ever-evolving technological landscape, embracing APIs will not only streamline the development process, but also foster innovation.

In the next chapter, we will cover the best practices to create an app in .NET MAUI. This will involve libraries you cannot afford to miss, performance improvement, the best practices using C#, and the best components that .NET MAUI provides.

CHAPTER 7
Best Practices in .NET MAUI

Introduction

Building high-quality applications with .NET MAUI goes far beyond just making things work—it is about making them efficient, scalable, and easy to maintain over time. Whether you are creating a small utility app or a full-fledged cross-platform solution, following best practices can dramatically improve performance, reduce bugs, and ensure a better experience for both developers and users.

In this chapter, we will explore the most effective strategies, tools, and patterns that will help you get the best out of your .NET MAUI projects. We will begin by reviewing some essential libraries that simplify development and add powerful capabilities to your applications. These libraries—from UI toolkits to HTTP clients and object mappers—will become part of your daily toolkit, and understanding their strengths will save you hours of work and countless bugs.

Structure

In this chapter, we will discuss the following topics:

- Libraries you Cannot Miss in Your App
  - `CommunityToolkit.Maui`
  - `SQLite-Net-PCL`
  - `Newtonsoft.Json`
  - `RestSharp`
  - `MediatR`
  - `Polly`
  - `FFImageLoading.Maui`
  - `AutoMapper`

- Improving Performance
  - User Interface (UI) Optimization
  - Efficient Resource Management
  - Business Logic Optimization
  - Performance Monitoring and Diagnostics
- Best Practices with C#
  - Nomenclature
  - Design Principles
  - Code Management
  - Efficiency and Performance
- Best Components of .NET MAUI

Libraries you Cannot Miss in Your App

We will show some essential libraries that cannot be missing in any .NET MAUI project, either for their usefulness, stability, or because they solve problems that you will inevitably encounter.

CommunityToolkit.Maui

The .NET MAUI Community Toolkit is one of those libraries that becomes almost essential in any project due to the functionalities it has. It is a set of utilities and controls that facilitate the development of user interfaces and also solve common needs without having to write code from scratch. It includes everything from converters and behaviors to animations and advanced controls.

Some of the most useful functionalities include:

- **`Snackbar and Toast`:** They make it easy to create non-invasive notifications for the user.
- **`StateContainer`:** Allows you to elegantly handle interface states (loading, error, and empty).
- **`MediaElement`:** A control that allows you to play audio and video easily.

```
dotnet add package CommunityToolkit.Maui
```

Also, the fact that it is developed and maintained by the community makes it a very reliable tool.

SQLite-Net-PCL

For any app that requires local storage, SQLite is an excellent choice, and **sqlite-net-pcl** is one of the most widely used libraries for integrating SQLite databases into .NET MAUI. It is very easy to use, lightweight, and works perfectly on iOS, Android, and Windows.

The good thing about this library is that it could abstract much of the complexity of working with SQLite databases. You just need to define the models that you will use, and from there, you can perform CRUD operations very simply.

Example of use:

```
using SQLite;

public class User
{
    [PrimaryKey, AutoIncrement]
    public int Id { get; set; }
    public string Name { get; set; }
}
dotnet add package sqlite-net-pcl
```

Newtonsoft.Json

Working with data in JSON format is practically inevitable, as it is quite common to do so in any modern application. If your app communicates with APIs or handles complex configurations, you will need to serialize and deserialize JSON almost mandatorily. **Newtonsoft.Json** is the de facto standard library for working with JSON in .NET. Although .NET has its own functionality for JSON (**System.Text.Json**), **Newtonsoft.Json** is still a favorite of many for its flexibility and ability to handle more advanced scenarios, and it is easy to use; hence, it does not require much configuration.

```
using Newtonsoft.Json;

var json = JsonConvert.SerializeObject(myObject);
var object = JsonConvert.DeserializeObject<MyClass>(json);
dotnet add package Newtonsoft.Json
```

RestSharp

If your app connects to web services, you need a good library for handling HTTP requests, and **RestSharp** is a great choice for interacting with REST APIs. It simplifies the creation of **GET**, **POST**, **PUT**, and **DELETE** requests, and makes it much easier to handle authentication, headers, and response content.

For example, to make a GET request:

```
var client = new RestClient("https://api.example.com");
var request = new RestRequest("users", Method.Get);
var response = await client. ExecuteAsync(request);
```

RestSharp makes working with APIs much cleaner and more readable.

```
dotnet add package RestSharp
```

MediatR

MediatR is a library that is quite useful for implementing design patterns such as the Mediator pattern or Command Query Responsibility Segregation (CQRS). If your application grows in complexity, it will allow you to decouple the components you use in your app, making it easier to maintain and test business logic. Instead of your views or controllers communicating directly with services or databases, you can use commands, events, and queries, delegating all of these responsibilities through **MediatR**.

A basic example of how a command is defined and handled in **MediatR** would be:

```
public class CreateUserCommand : IRequest<int>
{
    public string Name { get; set; }
}

public class CreateUserHandler : IRequestHandler<CreateUserCom-
mand, int>
{
    public Task<int> Handle(CreateUserCommand request,
CancellationToken cancellationToken)
    {
        Logic for creating a user
        return Task.FromResult(1); Returns the Id of the created
user
    }
}
dotnet add package MediatR.Extensions.Microsoft.Dependency
Injection
```

Polly

Network failures are inevitable and quite common in applications that constantly attempt to send or obtain information, especially when your app consumes APIs or makes HTTP requests. **Polly** is a library that helps you implement resilience patterns, such as automatic retries, circuit breakers, and timeouts. This is key to improving the robustness of your application and offering a better user experience in situations of unstable connectivity.

For example, to retry an operation up to 3 times:

```
var policy = Policy
    . Handle<HttpRequestException>()
    . WaitAndRetryAsync(3, retryAttempt => TimeSpan.From
Seconds(retryAttempt));

await policy. ExecuteAsync(() => client. GetAsync("https://api.
example.com"));
dotnet add package Polly
```

FFImageLoading.Maui

Images are a key component in many apps, and **FFImageLoading.Maui** is a library that optimizes image loading and manipulation. It allows you to cache images, supports animations, and offers a lot of transformations, such as rounding edges or making fades very efficiently. If your app has dynamic images or downloads images from an API, this library is your best bet for significantly improving performance.

```
dotnet add package FFImageLoading.Maui
```

AutoMapper

In applications with complex business logic, quite often you have to map objects from one type to another (for example, it is common for it to be from entities to DTOs). Doing this manually can become tedious and error-prone. **AutoMapper** automates this process, mapping properties from one class to another in an automatic, user-friendly, and efficient way.

```
var config = new MapperConfiguration(cfg = > {
    cfg. CreateMap<Source, Destination>();
});
IMapper mapper = config. CreateMapper();
Destination dest = mapper. Map<Source, Destination>(sourceObj);
dotnet add package AutoMapper.Extensions.Microsoft.Dependency
Injection
```

Improving Performance

When you are developing an application in .NET MAUI, performance is a pretty key element. An app that responds quickly and smoothly not only offers a better user experience, but at the same time also consumes fewer system resources, which translates into less battery consumption and better memory usage, which is critical on mobile devices that lack some resources.

User Interface (UI) Optimization

The first impression of performance the user has is through the user interface. If your UI is not agile, the user will perceive the entire app to be slow, even if your backend is fast. Here are some tips for keeping the UI smooth.

Avoid Heavy Operations on the Main Thread

.NET MAUI, like many graphics' platforms, uses a single main thread (or UI thread) to handle interface updates and user interactions. If you make calculations or network calls in this thread, the UI will freeze until the operation is finished, resulting in a poor user experience.

To avoid this, use async/await and run heavy tasks in the background. An example:

```
Heavy Operation
await Task.Run(() => LoadData());
```

This ensures that the operation does not crash the UI while it is still working in the background.

Use Compiled Bindings Instead of Conventional Bindings

Compiled bindings are much faster than conventional bindings because they eliminate the need for reflection. Not only does this improve speed, but it also helps catch compile-time errors.

```
<Label Text="{Binding Name, Mode=OneWay}" />
<!-- Improved to: -->
<Label Text="{Binding Name, Mode=OneWay}" x:DataType="models:
User" />
```

This ensures that bindings are faster and safer.

Reduce the Use of Nested Layouts

Overuse of nested layouts (such as **StackLayout** within another **StackLayout**) increases the complexity of interface metering and layout, which affects performance. Use more efficient layouts such as **Grid** or **FlexLayout**, which allow you to arrange components more optimally.

Instead of doing something like this:

```
<StackLayout>
    <StackLayout Orientation="Horizontal">
        <Label Text="Name:" />
        <Label Text="{Binding Name}" />
    </StackLayout>
</StackLayout>
```

You could use a Grid:

```
<Grid>
    <Grid.ColumnDefinitions>
        <ColumnDefinition Width="Auto" />
        <ColumnDefinition Width="*" />
    </Grid.ColumnDefinitions>
    <label text="name:" grid.column="0" />
    <label text="{binding name}" grid.column="1" />
</Grid>
```

This optimizes the use of layouts and improves performance.

List Virtualization

When using long lists, such as **CollectionView** or **ListView**, make sure to turn on virtualization. This means that only visible elements are rendered in the UI, and not the entire list. This minimizes memory usage and improves speed.

```
<CollectionView ItemsSource="{Binding Users}" />
```

The **CollectionView** in .NET MAUI, unlike the older **ListView**, already has virtualization enabled by default, making it a better choice for large lists.

Efficient Resource Management

Resources, such as images or fonts, can be one of the biggest causes of poor performance in an application, especially on mobile devices with limited memory.

Using Images in the Right Format

Use images in suitable formats such as WebP or SVG whenever possible. WebP offers excellent compression without noticeable loss of visual quality, helping to reduce app size and memory consumption.

.NET MAUI supports vector images (**.svg**), which are much lighter compared to images in **.png** or **.jpg** format when we talk about graphics that do not need complex details.

Asynchronous Image Loading and Lazy Loading

If your app has a lot of images, do not load them all at once. Use lazy loading to load images only when needed or when they come on screen. Also, make sure that the images are uploaded asynchronously.

```
<ffimageloading:CachedImage Source="{Binding ImageUrl}" />
```

Use a library such as **FFImageLoading.Maui** for efficient image caching and loading.

Data Caching

When your app works with external data (such as web services), it is essential to implement a caching system. This way, you do not have to make repetitive requests to the network if you already have the data available locally.

You can use libraries like **MonkeyCache** to handle caching in .NET MAUI applications easily.

```
dotnet add package MonkeyCache
```

Business Logic Optimization

Performance depends not only on the UI, but also on how you manage business logic.

Minimizes the use of LINQ

LINQ is very convenient, but in scenarios with many queries or intensive data processing, it can negatively impact performance. Consider replacing it with traditional loops when working with large volumes of data or when performance is critical.

Instead of:

```
var result - UserList.Where(u => u.Active). ToList();
```

You could use a more efficient loop:

```
var result = new List<User>();
foreach (var user in Userslist)
{
    if (user. Active)
        result. Add;
}
```

Avoid Unnecessary Use of Reflection

While reflection is powerful in .NET, it is costly in terms of performance. If you can avoid it, do so. Whenever possible, use alternative approaches such as Compiled Bindings or Expression Trees to avoid overheating reflection.

Performance Monitoring and Diagnostics

You cannot improve what you do not measure. Use the right tools to monitor and diagnose performance issues.

Profiling Tools

.NET MAUI benefits from the same profiling tools as other .NET applications. Use Visual Studio Profiler or Xamarin Profiler to identify bottlenecks in your application. These tools show you which methods are consuming the most CPU or memory and allow you to make informed decisions.

Performance Tracing

You can use performance tracking to analyze execution times and optimize the performance of your applications. On Android, you can use **`Android.OS.Trace`** to track execution and find potential optimizations.

```
Android.OS.Trace.BeginSection("Data Load");
Load logic
Android.OS.Trace.EndSection();
```

Using Ahead-of-Time (AOT) Compilation

AOT compilation converts your .NET code into native code before the application is run. This improves your app's launch times and overall execution on mobile platforms by eliminating the need for Just-In-Time (JIT) to compile code at runtime.

To enable AOT on Android:

```
<PropertyGroup>
  <RunAOTCompilation>true</RunAOTCompilation>
</PropertyGroup>
```

Best Practices with C#

When we write code, it is important to follow good practices in any programming language, as this significantly improves the quality of the software. These practices are essential, allowing the maintenance, readability, and reuse of our code. It also helps us reduce errors and have better scalability, facilitating testing and being able to meet the desired standards. In this subtopic, we will address some of the best practices that we can carry out in C# and that will help to have clean, maintainable, and efficient code.

Nomenclature

When we talk about nomenclature in C#, we are referring to writing clean and understandable code. It is recommended to use **`PascalCase`**, which consists of compound words without spaces, with the first letter of each word capitalized. **`PascalCase`** is usually used when naming classes, types, methods, properties, namespaces that are structured hierarchically, interfaces that generally begin with "I", and enumerations, for example:

- **Class and types:** `Employee`, `EmployeeData`.
- **Methods:** `GetEmployee`.
- **Properties:** `FirstName`.
- **Interfaces:** `IEmployee`.
- **Enumerations:** `OrderStatus`.
- **Namespaces:** `MyProject.Utilities`.

Other recommendations are the use of **camelCase,** which is a writing style where words are combined without spaces and except for the first word, each word begins with an uppercase letter. This style is used in **Private fields**, which usually begin with an underscore (_), followed by **camelCase**. For example, **`_totalAmount`**. **Local variables and parameters** also use **camelCase**. For example, **`totalAmount`**. When we work with constants, they must be written in capital letters with underscores separating the words, for example, **`MAX_LENGTH`**.

It is preferable to use complete names that clearly describe the purpose of the class, variable, and so on, always avoiding abbreviations. The use of good nomenclature will improve the readability of the code and facilitate collaboration with other developers.

Design Principles

Design principles are guidelines that help create robust, maintainable, and easy-to-understand software, seeking to improve code quality.

Among the design principles is the **separation of concerns**, indicating the use of design patterns, for example, **MVC**, **MVVM**, and so on. It is also recommended to use the model **SOLID,** which is a set of five fundamental principles for object-oriented programming, where each letter of **SOLID** is represented by the following principles:

- **S (SRP):** The Single Responsibility Principle indicates that a class should only have one responsibility or reason for changing.

- **O (OCP):** Open/closed principle indicates that classes must be open for extension, but must be closed for modification.
- **L (LSP):** Liskov Substitution Principle indicates that the subclasses must be able to replace the base class without altering the behavior of the program.
- **I (ISP):** The Principle of Interface Segregation indicates that it is much better to have several interfaces in one place than one general interface.
- **D (DIP):** The Dependency Inversion Principle indicates that dependencies should be in abstractions and not in concrete classes.

The use of the principle **SOLID** will help develop robust and scalable projects, improving software quality.

Code Management

Code management refers to the way of structuring, organizing, and managing our code, which aims to improve the quality, readability, and maintainability of the software. Some of the key aspects are the following:

- **Folder structure:** Organize your code in logical folders where the functionality of that code is described, for example, Models, Controllers, Services, Pages, ViewModels, Repositories, and so on.
- **Use of Descriptive Names:** For the naming of classes, folders, files, and methods, it is advisable to use clear and meaningful names, which help better understanding for other developers.
- **Code format:** The use of automatic formatting tools is recommended to ensure that the code is correctly indented and structured.
- **Comments:** Include comments to explain the logic of a code fragment, which may be complex to understand, avoiding obvious comments, and always focusing on the why.
- **Unit Tests:** Write unit tests to validate methods and classes.
- **THERE:** Continuous integration; the use of this system will help automate test execution and ensure that code updates do not affect existing functionality.
- **Continuous refactoring:** It is basically spending time improving the structure and readability of the code without affecting its functionality.

Code management is a good practice because it helps us improve the development environment, providing better quality, team collaboration, and long-term maintainability of the software.

Efficiency and Performance

Efficiency and performance are class concepts that refer to how resources are used to run an application efficiently. Optimization in C# is implemented through strategies that improve the performance of the code, from the use of appropriate algorithms, programming asynchronously, proper use of Language Integrated Query (LINQ), and minimization of unnecessary objects, among other practices.

- **Choosing efficient algorithms**: Algorithms with lower temporal and spatial complexity should be selected, such as O(n log n) type algorithms instead of $O(n^2)$, because the execution time is increased in a more controlled manner than $O(n^2)$. For example, if we need to sort a large list, it is more efficient to use the Merge Sort (0(n log n)) algorithm than the Bubble Sort ($O(n^2)$).
- **Asynchronous:** The use of async and await allows the main thread not to block during the processing of a function, for example, when an API call is made, we access a database or read files.
- **Proper use of LINQ:** It is important to evaluate the situation and use it in a balanced way. Use LINQ to filter and select data in a clear way, avoid having very complex queries, use **`ToList()`** or **`ToArray()`** only when it is necessary to execute the query and obtain results, use LINQ for data in memory, and for database, use data that uses an ORM, for example, Entity Framework.
- **Unnecessary objects**: Having objects in an unnecessary way can lead to high resource consumption. To avoid this situation, you can reuse objects or create temporary objects (**`ArrayPool<T>`**).

There are more ways to improve the efficiency of our programs, such as understanding garbage collection, use of concurrent data structures, such as the use of **`ConcurrentDictionary`**, use of ORM, among other strategies that can help your application.

Best Components of .NET MAUI

When working with .NET MAUI, we have a wide range of user interface components that give us a powerful and flexible option for developing cross-platform applications. This allows us to create rich and attractive interfaces that adapt to various platforms, offering a consistent and immersive user experience. The following list represents some of the best components that can be used in .NET MAUI:

- **UI controls**: These interface components are essential for iteration with the user, displaying information, text input, handling data, and executing functions efficiently.
  - **`Button`**: Executes actions when pressed, allowing simple interactivity.

  - **`Label`**: Allows text to be displayed in the user interface, allowing customization of styles and behaviors.
  - **`Entry`**: Allows text entry, style customization, and user interaction.
  - **`ListView`**: For the management of simple lists, allowing the handling of selection events.
  - **`CollectionView`**: For list management, but has better optimization for performance, supports layouts, element customization, and data management.
  - **`Shell`**: Improves application navigation organization into an effective hierarchical structure for building complex applications.
  - **`Image`**: Allows you to display images, supporting different formats and visual configurations.
- **Layouts:** The choice of layout should be based on the specific needs of the project, where different layouts should be managed in a strategic way, allowing the development of attractive and functional interfaces. Some recommendations will be presented below:
  - **`Grid`**: Allows the creation of complex layouts using rows and columns, useful for structured layouts.
  - **`FlexLayout`**: Essential for responsive designs that automatically adjust to the screen size.
  - **`AbsoluteLayout`**: Essential when you need full control over the positioning of elements.
- **Data Binding**: This feature is essential for modern application development, as it improves code organization, optimizes user experience, and facilitates maintenance. The use of **`BindingContext`** enables data binding between the user interface and the **`ViewModel`**, which encourages the separation of presentation logic. Furthermore, by implementing **`INotifyPropertyChanged`**, notification of changes to model properties is ensured, allowing the interface to update automatically.
- **Styles**: To manage styles, it is recommended to use **`ResourceDictionary`** to facilitate resource management and reuse, with storage of styles, colors, and other resources to improve design consistency.

These components offer the possibility of design and functionality, which improve the overall developer experience in user interfaces. With a wide range of tools and controls for creating cross-platform applications.

Conclusion

In conclusion, the integration of essential libraries and best practices in your .NET MAUI projects can significantly enhance both performance and user experience. By leveraging powerful tools such as **`CommunityToolkit.Maui`**, **`SQLite-Net-PCL`**, and **`RestSharp`**, developers can streamline functionality while ensuring robust application performance. Additionally, embracing design principles such as SOLID and efficient resource management strategies can lead to clean, maintainable code, essential for long-term success. As you embark on your .NET MAUI journey, remember that the key to building outstanding applications lies not only in the tools you choose but also in your commitment to efficient coding practices and thoughtful design. Empower your projects today with these indispensable libraries and strategies, and elevate the quality and responsiveness of your applications to new heights. In the following chapter, we will create an application that exemplifies what e-commerce is; we will see the different parts that compose it at a general level and the most common functionalities that it can have.

CHAPTER 8
Building an E-Commerce App

Introduction

In this chapter, we focus on developing an e-commerce application, one of the most widely used models today. During the process, we explore key aspects of software development, such as file organization and structure, essential elements for the maintenance and scalability of any project. We also implemented dependency injection and set up a path-logging system to facilitate navigation between screens.

Structure

In this chapter, we will discuss the following topics:

- App Description
- Definition of APIs
- Creating Applications
- SQLite Data Access Class
- Product Service
- `HomeView`
- `ProductDescriptionView`
- `AccountView`
- `ShoppingCartView`
- `UserView`
- `PurchaseViewModel`
- `MenuView`
- Practice Exercise, Order History Page

App Description

In the previous chapters, we delved into cross-platform application development with .NET MAUI. We studied its main components, explored best development practices, and completed practical exercises in database connections, API consumption, and user interface design.

The time has come to develop a more complex application than the previous exercises: an e-commerce application. Basically, e-commerce is a business model that allows people to buy and sell products or services over the internet. With this concept in mind, we will develop a mobile application that will allow users to browse a product catalog, add products to favorites, create orders, and make payments.

The application will have a design based on a `TabBar`, where the following sections will be displayed:

- `Home`: This page will include a product search engine, a horizontal menu to filter by category, and a list of available products.
- `Account`: Here, users will be able to see their username and the products they have marked as favorites.
- `Shop Cart`: This section will display the list of products added to the cart, with the option to make the purchase.
- `Menu`: This page will include several options, such as purchase history, user account view, and the option to log out.

With the above out of the way, without further ado, let us get started developing our e-commerce app!

Definition of APIs

In this project, we will not be using a real API to retrieve data. Instead, we will simulate an API response using a JSON file. This JSON file will contain the data we need, such as products, images, prices, and descriptions, and we will use it to represent the API response locally.

The JSON we are going to use is a JSON of a list of **objects**. Where each object in the list represents a product with various properties associated with it. In this case, the JSON has a product structure that includes:

- `Id`: A unique identifier for each product (in GUID format).
- `Image`: The name of the image associated with the product (assuming the images are in the project).
- `Name`: The name of the product.

- **Category**: The category to which the product belongs (for example, "**Home**", "**Electronics**").
- **Description**: A brief description of the product.
- **Price**: The price of the product.
- **Stock**: The available quantity of the product.

The following example shows the JSON representation that we will use in this project to simulate an API response.

```
[
    {
        "Id": "00000000-0000-0000-0000-000000000001",
        "Image": "house.png",
        "Name": "House",
        "Category": "Home",
        "Description": "Enjoy high-quality furniture and accessories
        for your
        home.  Find the perfect coffee table for your living room.",
        "Price": 250,
        "Stock": 3
    },
    {
        "Id": "00000000-0000-0000-0000-000000000002",
        "Image": "tecno.png",
        "Name": "Technology",
        "Category": "Electronics",
        "Description": "Latest gadgets and tech devices. Discover
the newest
  smartphones, computers, and accessories.",
        "Price": 100,
        "Stock": 2
    }
]
```

This JSON must be saved in the project within the directory **Raw**, usually located in the folder **resources**. This will be done after creating the project, so the file can be accessed from the code. Later, to simulate an API, we will create a service dedicated to reading this JSON file and deserializing it. This will allow the application to dynamically interact with the data, similar to how it would with a real API.

Creating Applications

We will create a new project using the template **.NET MAUI App** and the framework **.NET 8** or higher. In this case, we will call the project **EcommerceApp**, but remember that you can name it whatever you prefer. Just be sure to maintain consistency with the name throughout the development process to avoid confusion.

Once our project is created, we will proceed to install the necessary packages for its development using NuGet. These packages are essential for implementing various functionalities in our application. The packages we will use are listed below:

- **`CommunityToolkit.MAUI`:** Provides a set of additional tools that extend the capabilities of MAUI, such as controls, extensions, and common functionality.
- **`CommunityToolkit.Mvvm`:** It facilitates the implementation of the Model-View-ViewModel (MVVM) pattern, providing a more efficient and clean way to handle business logic and the user interface.
- **`Refit`:** A library to facilitate the use of REST APIs in our applications. It allows us to automatically generate HTTP clients from interfaces.
- **`Microsoft.Data.Sqlite`:** Official Microsoft library for working with SQLite databases. It offers robust tools for managing and manipulating local data.
- **`Sqlite-net-pcl`:** A lightweight library for working with SQLite in .NET applications, specifically designed for cross-platform use. Although not detailed in depth in this book, it is worth mentioning that this library is useful for simpler interaction with SQLite databases, providing a basic Object-Relational Mapping (ORM).

With these packages, we will have a solid foundation for developing our application, integrating advanced user interface features, REST API consumption, and local database management.

If you have questions about any of these packages, you can refer to previous chapters where we explored these libraries. For example:

- In *Chapter 6, Internal DB and API Connection*, we review SQLite, API consumption, and Refit.
- In *Chapter 4, Design Patterns in .NET MAUI*, we delve deeper into the MVVM model.

It is essential to ensure that you install the most recent and compatible versions of the selected framework when creating your project and also select those developed by **Microsoft** except for **`Refit`**, whose author is **.NET Foundation and Contributors**, and **`sqlite-net-pcl`** developed by **SQLite-net**.

Once the installation is complete, your package list should look like the one shown in *Figure 8.1*.

***Figure 8.1**: Representation of the packages installed in the project*

Once the installation is complete, we will proceed to register the Community Toolkit for .NET MAUI in the application. This is done in the file **`MauiProgram.cs`**, where we must add the line **`UseMauiCommunityToolkit`** within the **`builder`** to enable the functionalities of the **toolkit**. This configuration ensures that the Community Toolkit tools and components are available.

```
namespace EcommerceApp
{
    public static class MauiProgram
    {
        public static MauiApp CreateMauiApp()
        {
            var builder = MauiApp.CreateBuilder();
            builder
                .UseMauiApp<App>()
                .UseMauiCommunityToolkit()
                .ConfigureFonts(fonts =>
                {
                    fonts.AddFont("OpenSans-Regular.ttf",
"OpenSansRegular");
                    fonts.AddFont("OpenSans-Semibold.ttf",
"OpenSansSemibold");
                });
#if DEBUG
```

```
                builder.Logging.AddDebug();
#endif
                return builder.Build();
            }
        }
    }
```

Next, we will set up the file structure needed for our project. We will start by creating the directories or subdirectories in the project root. The structure will be as follows:

- **Models:** It will contain the models that our application will use, representing the key entities and data.
- **Helpers:** It will store helper classes, methods, and functions that provide reusable functionality across multiple parts of the project.
- **Services:** It will include functionalities that interact with external resources, such as databases, APIs, or other services.
- **`ViewModels`:** The classes responsible for handling presentation logic and interaction with the UI will be stored here.
- **Views:** It will contain the views or user interfaces (UI) of the application, where the data managed by the **`ViewModels`** will be presented.
- **Data**: This folder contains classes related to the application's data management. It includes the implementation of the database context (**`DatabaseContext`**), which facilitates asynchronous access and manipulation of data in SQLite.

After creating our directories, we will create the project's main Views along with their respective **`ViewModels`**. Within the **`Views`** directory, the following pages of type will be created: **`ContentPage`.** If you have any questions about this type of pages, you can consult *Chapter 3, Getting Started With* .NET MAUI, where we explore the different types of Pages, Layouts, Components, and so on. The pages we are going to create are the following:

- **`HomeView.xaml`**: This page will include a product search engine, a horizontal menu to filter by category, and a list of available products.
- **`AccountView.xaml`**: Here, users can see their order history and the products they have marked as favorites.
- **`ShoppingCartView.xaml`:** This section will display a list of products added to your cart, with the option to make a purchase.
- **`MenuView.xaml`**: This page will include several options, such as purchase history, a view of the user's account, information about the app, and the option to log out.

Once the pages are finished, we will proceed to create their respective classes. **`ViewModel`** within the directory **`ViewModels`**, being organized as follows:

HomeViewModel, **AccountViewModel**, **MenuViewModel**, **ShoppingViewModel**, and finally the class **BaseViewModel**.

The class **BaseViewModel** will be used to provide common functionality to all other **ViewModels**. This class inherits from **ObservableObject**, which allows the user interface to be automatically notified of property changes, facilitating data binding and improving synchronization between logic and the UI. The **BaseViewModel** class should look like this:

```
using CommunityToolkit.Mvvm.ComponentModel;
namespace EcommerceApp.ViewModels;
public partial class BaseViewModel : ObservableObject { }
```

With our Views and **ViewModels** already created, the next step will be to delete the page generated by default when creating the project, called **MainPage.xaml**. This page serves as the initial view in new projects, but since we are defining our own structure and design, it is no longer necessary.

The structure of our project would be organized as follows, as shown in *Figure 8.2*:

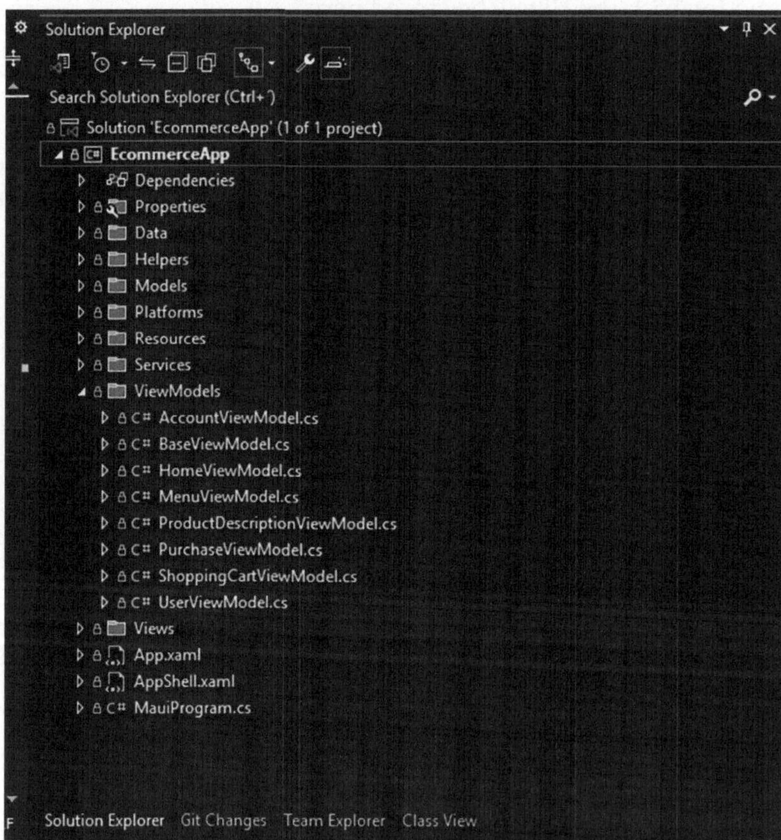

***Figure 8.2**: File structure required for the project*

If you try to run the application at this point, it will most likely fail to compile. This happens because we deleted the file **MainPage.xaml**, which was set as the home page by a **ShellContent** and **AppShell.xaml** as a result, the application cannot find a valid page to launch, generating an error.

To solve this problem, we are going to modify the file **AppShell.xaml** to use a design based on **TabBar** rather than **ShellContent.** The **TabBar** will allow us to implement a tab-type navigation menu, offering a more structured experience adapted to the needs of our application.

The file **AppShell.xaml** would be configured as follows:

```
<?xml version="1.0" encoding="UTF-8" ?>
<Shell
    x:Class="EcommerceApp.AppShell"
    ...
    xmlns:views="clr-namespace:EcommerceApp.Views"
    xmlns:toolkit="http://schemas.microsoft.com/dotnet/2022/maui/
toolkit"
    xmlns:local="clr-namespace:EcommerceApp"
    Shell.FlyoutBehavior="Disabled"
    Title="EcommerceApp">
<!-- Status bar behavior, changes color->
    <Shell.Behaviors>
        <toolkit:StatusBarBehavior StatusBarColor="#ffffff"
                                   StatusBarStyle="DarkContent" />
    </Shell.Behaviors>
<!-- TabBar based menu -->
    <TabBar>
        <Tab Title="Home"
             Icon="home.png">
            <ShellContent ContentTemplate="{DataTemplate views:
HomeView}" />
        </Tab>
        <Tab Title="Account"
             Icon="account.png">
            <ShellContent ContentTemplate="{DataTemplate views:
AccountView}" />
        </Tab>
        <Tab Title="Shop Cart"
             Icon="shopcart.png">
           <ShellContent ContentTemplate="{DataTemplate views:
ShoppingCartView}"/>
        </Tab>
        <Tab Title="Menu"
             Icon="menu.png">
```

```
                <ShellContent ContentTemplate="{DataTemplate views:
MenuView}" />
            </Tab>
    </TabBar>
</Shell>
```

The previous code defines the application navigation using a **TabBar**, which is a tabbed navigation bar. Each tab represents a different section of the application and allows the user to navigate between them quickly and easily.

Within the **TabBar**, four main tabs are defined:

- **Home**: Displays the home view, where you can browse products.
- **Account**: Displays the account view and favorite products.
- **Shop Cart:** Displays the shopping cart with the selected products.
- **Menu**: Displays the menu with additional options, such as purchase history and settings.

Each tab has a title (for example, "**Home**") and an icon (for example, "**home.png**"). Each is also linked to a specific view of the app by using **ShellContent**, which defines the content to be displayed when the tab is selected.

In the code shown above, each tab is assigned an icon. To add new icons, simply include them in the folder **Resources/Images** of your project. In this case, we used free icons obtained from the website **Iconfinder.com** in PNG format. In *Figure* 8.3, an example of the icons that have been added is shown, but remember that you can use any icon you prefer, as long as it is in the correct format and is located in the correct folder to be correctly referenced in your project.

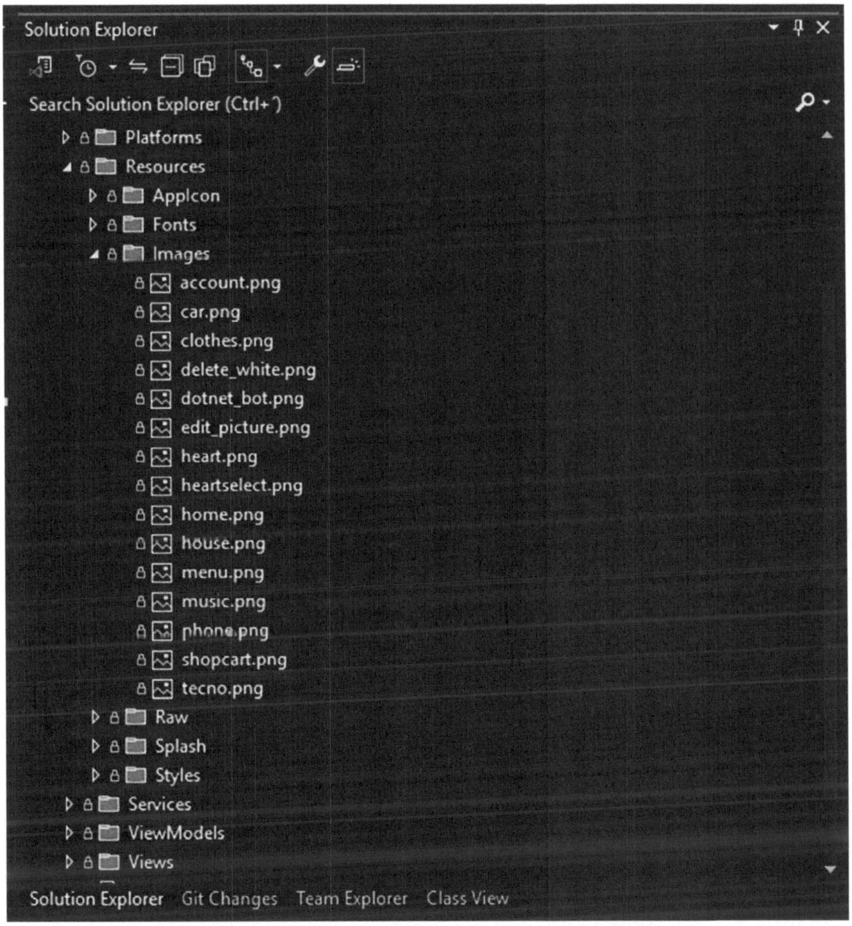

Figure 8.3*: Example of icons added to the project*

Once we have successfully added and defined the icons and completed the previous steps, we can run our application. Upon compilation, everything should work smoothly, and we will be able to see the tab menu in action, allowing us to navigate between different sections of the application without any issues. Remember to add the following line to the **AppShell.xaml** file so that the views bind correctly to the **DataTemplate**:

```
xmlns:views="clr-namespace:<EcommerceApp.Views>"
```

This namespace declaration is important because it allows the application to recognize the views defined in the project, such as **HomeView**, **AccountView**, **ShoppingCartView**, **MenuView**, and so on. Without this reference, the **ContentTemplate** will not be able to correctly point to views, and you may get errors when trying to run the application.

Next, we will implement dependency injection for our pages and their respective

ViewModels. The primary goal of this approach is to prevent the **ViewModel** from directly depending on the View, which improves the separation of responsibilities and makes unit testing easier. This way, the **ViewModel** can handle business logic and data interaction without needing to know specific details about the user interface.

To carry out the injection of the **ContentPages** and their **ViewModels**, we will configure the dependency container in the file **MauiProgram.cs** of the project. We will use the method **builder.Services.AddTransient**, which registers classes or services in the container with a transient lifecycle. This means that a new instance of the **ViewModel** will be created each time the corresponding page is accessed, ensuring that each page has a clean, fresh instance of its **ViewModel**.

This type of dependency injection not only makes code organization easier but also contributes to a cleaner and more maintainable design by reducing coupling between application layers.

Our archive **MauiProgram.cs** will be configured as follows:

```
namespace EcommerceApp
{
    public static class MauiProgram
    {
        public static MauiApp CreateMauiApp()
        {
            var builder = MauiApp.CreateBuilder();
            builder
                .UseMauiApp<App>()
                .UseMauiCommunityToolkit()
                .ConfigureFonts(fonts =>
                {
                    fonts.AddFont("OpenSans-Regular.ttf",
"OpenSansRegular");
                    fonts.AddFont("OpenSans-Semibold.ttf",
"OpenSansSemibold");
                });

#if DEBUG
               builder.Logging.AddDebug();
#endif          //Pages and ViewModels
            builder.Services.AddTransient<HomeView>();
            builder.Services.AddTransient<HomeViewModel>();
            builder.Services.AddTransient<AccountView>();
            builder.Services.AddTransient<AccountViewModel>();
            builder.Services.AddTransient<ShoppingCartView>();
            builder.Services.AddTransient<ShoppingCartViewModel>();
            builder.Services.AddTransient<MenuView>();
            builder.Services.AddTransient<MenuViewModel>();
```

```
            builder.Services.AddTransient<ProductDescriptionView>();
            builder.Services.AddTransient<ProductDescriptionView
Model>();
            return builder.Build();
        }
    }
}
```

When using dependency injection with **AddTransient** for both views and **ViewModels**, it allows you to decouple views from the presentation logic, which facilitates code reuse and improves application maintainability.

SQLite Data Access Class

Once the previous steps are complete, we will create a data access class, which will function as a service layer responsible for managing all interactions with the SQLite database, such as queries, modifications, deletions, table creation, among other operations. To do this, you must have the NuGet package installed, **sqlite-net-pcl**, which will help us efficiently manage the database, simplifying operations and providing us with a more accessible and robust interface.

Within the directory **Data**, the class **DatabaseContext** will be created, which will be responsible for managing all operations related to the SQLite database. This class will implement the interface **IAsyncDisposable**, which will allow us to efficiently manage the asynchronous release of resources upon completion of database operations. Next, let us look at the main parts of how our class will look.

First, we will define the database. We define the name and location of the database using a constant **DbName** and a property **DbPath**. We use **Path.Combine** to get the full path to the database in the application directory.

```
private const string DbName = "ecommercedb.db3";
private static string DbPath => Path.Combine(FileSystem.AppData
Directory, DbName);
```

Let us create a connection to the database using **SQLiteAsyncConnection**. Allowing us to perform asynchronous operations such as reading and writing to the database without blocking the user interface.

```
private SQLiteAsyncConnection _connection;
private SQLiteAsyncConnection Database =>
    (_connection ??= new SQLiteAsyncConnection(DbPath, SQLiteOpen-
Flags.Create | SQLiteOpenFlags.ReadWrite | SQLiteOpenFlags.Shared-
Cache));
```

Let us create the method **CreateTableIfNotExists**, which will be responsible for creating the table if it does not exist.

```
private async Task CreateTableIfNotExists<TTable>() where TTable :
class, new()
{
    await Database.CreateTableAsync<TTable>();
}
```

After creating the previous method, now we are going to create the **GetTableAsync**, which is used to obtain a table from the database, and if it is not found, create it using **CreateTableIfNotExists**

```
private async Task<AsyncTableQuery<TTable>> GetTableAsync<TTable>()
where TTable : class, new()
{
    await CreateTableIfNotExists<TTable>();
    return Database.Table<TTable>();
}
```

Once the previous steps are completed, we will create the methods for obtaining data:

- **GetAllAsync**: Retrieves all records from a table.
- **GetFileteredAsync**: Retrieves records that match a specific filter.

Both methods use **GetTableAsync**, to create the tables if they do not exist.

```
public async Task<IEnumerable<TTable>>
GetAllAsync<TTable>() where TTable : class, new()
{
    var table = await GetTableAsync<TTable>();
    return await table.ToListAsync();
}

public async Task<IEnumerable<TTable>>
GetFileteredAsync<TTable>(Expression<Func<TTable, bool>> predicate)
where TTable : class, new()
{
    var table = await GetTableAsync<TTable>();
    return await table.Where(predicate).ToListAsync();
}
```

Next, we will create the method **Execute**, which is a generic helper method used to perform actions on the database, such as inserting, updating, or retrieving records, asynchronously:

```
private async Task<TResult> Execute<TTable, TResult>(Func
<Task<TResult>> action) where TTable : class, new()
 {
```

```
        await CreateTableIfNotExists<TTable>();
        return await action();
    }
```

Next, we will create the methods responsible for performing the CRUD operations:

- **GetItemByKeyAsync**: Query a record using the primary key.
- **AddItemAsync**: Inserts a new record into the database.
- **UpdateItemAsync**: Updates an existing record.
- **DeleteItemAsync**: Deletes a specific record.
- **DeleteAllAsync**: Deletes all records from a table.
- **DeleteItemByKeyAsync**: Deletes a record using the primary key.

These operations will facilitate efficient and flexible manipulation and management of data in the database. You can find these methods within the application repository.

To finish, we will use the method **DisposeAsync**, which will be responsible for closing the connection to the database when it is no longer needed.

```
public async ValueTask DisposeAsync() => await _connection?.
CloseAsync();
```

In short, the class we created earlier acts as a "bridge" between the database and the application. It allows you to perform all basic (CRUD) operations on data stored in SQLite centrally.

Once completed, we must inject it into **MauiProgram.cs** to be able to use it in any part of the project. For this, we use **AddSingleton**, since we want that **DatabaseContext** to be a single instance throughout the application's lifecycle. This prevents the creation of multiple unnecessary instances.

```
//DataBase
builder.Services.AddSingleton<DatabaseContext>();
```

Also, remember to import the corresponding namespace:

```
using EcommerceApp.Data.
```

At this point, you might be wondering: what about the tables? To create them, we will use the concept of models. This means we will define some classes that will serve as representations of the data in our tables. It is important to note that we will not be creating the tables directly; they will be generated automatically when needed using the **DatabaseContext**.

Within the directory **Models**, the following classes will be created: **Users.cs**, **Favorites.cs**, and **ShopCart.cs**. The class **Users.cs** will be the data model to manage user information.

```
using SQLite;
namespace EcommerceApp.Models
{
    public class Users
    {
        [PrimaryKey]
        public Guid Id { get; set; }

        public string? Name { get; set; }

        public string? Email { get; set; }

        public string? Password { get; set; }

        public bool ActiveSession { get; set; }
    }
}
```

The class **Favorites.cs**: This object is responsible for storing the products that the user has marked as favorites.

```
using SQLite;
namespace EcommerceApp.Models
{
    public class Favorites
    {
        [PrimaryKey]
        public Guid Id { get; set; }
        public string? Product_Id { get; set; }
    }
}
```

The class **ShopCart.cs**: This file will contain two classes: **Item**, which will represent the products you want to buy, and **ShopCart**, which will store information related to the shopping cart.

```
using SQLite;
namespace EcommerceApp.Models
{
    public class ShopCart
    {
        [PrimaryKey]
        public Guid Id {  get; set; }
        public string? User_Id { get; set; }
        public string? Items { get; set; }
        public decimal SubTotal { get; set; }
        public decimal Tax { get; set; }
        public decimal Total { get; set; }
```

```
            public DateTime Created_at {  get; set; }
        }

        public class Item
        {
            [PrimaryKey]
            public Guid Id { get; set; }
            public string? Product_Id { get; set; }
            public string? Name { get; set; }
            public double Price { get; set; }
            public int? Quantity { get; set; }
            public string? Image { get; set; }
            public bool IsBuy { get; set; }
        }
    }
```

Remember that when implementing our classes for SQLite, we must include **`using SQLite`** at the beginning of each file. Also, as an important note, if you want to use a primary key, it is essential to name the variable with the attribute **`[PrimaryKey]`**.

As you can see, it is a simple database, but it will allow us to locally store the users who can access the app, manage their favorites list, create their shopping cart, and finally, save their purchases.

Product Service

At the beginning of this chapter, specifically in the subtitle "**API Definition**," we mentioned that we will not be implementing a real API in this project. But do not worry, we will simulate the process! We will create a service that will emulate API queries, so we can work with data as if it were being obtained from an external source.

To do this, we are going to create a JSON file called **`Products.json`**. Remember that in the "**API Definition**" subheading, we showed you how this file will be structured. The JSON file will be saved in the Raw directory, located within the project's Resources directory.

Once the JSON file is created and saved in the Raw directory, we will proceed to create the class **`Product.cs`**, which will serve as a data model. Remember that, as a model, this class must be saved in the directory **`Models`**. We will show you how this model will look:

```
namespace EcommerceApp.Models
{
    public class Product
    {
        public Guid Id { get; set; }
```

```
            public string? Name { get; set; }
            public string? Description { get; set; }
            public string? Image { get; set; }
            public string? Category { get; set; }
            public double Price { get; set; }
            public int Stock{ get; set; }
        }
    }
```

Then, we will create the class **ProductsService.cs**, which will act as a service in charge of reading the JSON file, deserializing it, and returning its contents in a list of Product objects. This class will be saved in the directory **Services.** Below, we show you how the service will look after the explanation of the code.

```
using EcommerceApp.Models;
using System.Text.Json;

namespace EcommerceApp.Services {
    public class ProductsService : IProductsServices {
        private List<Product>  products = new List<Product>();
        public async Task<List<Product>?> List()
        {
            await this.GetData();
            return products;
        }
        private async Task GetData()
        {
            products = new List<Product>();
            try
            {
                string fileName = "Products.json";
// Open the JSON file
              using var stream = await FileSystem.OpenAppPackage-
FileAsync(fileName);
                using var reader = new StreamReader(stream);
                var json = await reader.ReadToEndAsync();
// Configure options for the deserializer
                var options = new JsonSerializerOptions
                {
// Ignore case in properties
                 PropertyNameCaseInsensitive = true
               };
products = JsonSerializer.Deserialize<List<Product>>(json,
options) ?? new List<Product>();
            }
            catch (Exception ex) {  Console.WriteLine(ex.
ToString()); }
```

```
            }
        }

        public interface IProductsServices
        {
            Task<List<Product>?> List();
        }
    }
```

In this code snippet, we have the class **ProductsService**, which is responsible for reading a JSON file located in **Raw**, which is called **Products.json**, and returns a list of products (**List<Product>**). This class implements the interface **IProductsServices**, which defines the method **List()** to obtain the products, working as follows:

- **List() method**: This asynchronous method calls the private **GetData()** method to load the products from the JSON file and then returns the list of products.
- **GetData() method**: This method reads the JSON file, deserializes it to a list of Product objects, and handles possible read errors.

This service simulates retrieving products from a JSON file, allowing you to manage data locally without having to connect to an API or database. It is an efficient solution for small or developing projects where a real API is not yet available.

Once the service is finished, we record it in the file **MauiProgram.cs.** This will allow it to be used centrally throughout the application and its features to be accessed from anywhere in the project.

To achieve this, we use the method **AddSingleton**, which records **ProductsService** as the implementation of the interface **IProductsServices** within the application's dependency container. This ensures that the service remains a singleton instance throughout the application's lifetime, avoiding the creation of multiple unnecessary instances and optimizing resource usage.

```
//Services
builder.Services.AddSingleton<IProductsServices, Products
Service>();
```

With this, we will be ready to use our service efficiently and professionally anywhere in the application.

Once the previous steps have been completed, a class called **ItemHelper.cs**, which should be saved in the directory **Helpers** of the project, is designed to convert objects of type **Product** to objects of type **Item** in a simple and reusable way. This class is of type **static**, which means it does not require dependency injection or instantiation for use. Its purpose is to centralize and simplify conversion logic, improving code organization and maintenance. The class code is as follows:

```
using EcommerceApp.Models;
namespace EcommerceApp.Helpers
{
    public static class ItemHelper
    {
        public static Item CreateItemFromProduct(Product product)
        {
            return new Item
            {
Id = Guid.NewGuid(), // Generates a unique identifier for the Item
                Product_Id = product.Id.ToString(), // ID del
Product al Item
Name = product.Name, // Assigns the name of the product
Price = product.Price, // Copy the product price
Quantity = product.Stock, // Assign the stock as the initial
quantity
Image = product.Image // Copy the product image
            };
        }
    }
}
```

They are key development tools, as they encapsulate reusable functionality in static methods, facilitating the use of common tasks such as conversions, validations, or calculations.

The class **`ItemHelper.cs`** must be saved in the directory **`Helpers`** of your project, following an organized structure that allows you to quickly identify its purpose.

HomeView

Now we will move on to the page responsible for displaying the products. This page will present the available catalog to the user, using the data managed by the product service we created previously. Here, we will implement the user interface along with the logic necessary to dynamically load, display, and, if necessary, interact with the products.

The page **`HomeView`** will be designed to offer an intuitive and functional user experience. It will feature a **search engine** at the top, allowing the user to filter products quickly and easily, thus improving navigation.

It will also include a **category menu** located below the search engine, which will facilitate the exploration of products according to the user's preferences.

The central part of the page will be dedicated to a **`CollectionView`**, designed to display products in a visually appealing and well-organized manner. Each product will be contained within a frame, which will highlight it for easy viewing. The elements will include essential details such as name, price, image, and description, offering a clear and complete presentation of each item. In addition, each product will have a command that allows you to interact with it. Tapping on a product will activate navigation using a **NavigationPage**, which will display the complete product information where it can be added to favorites and to the cart. *Figure* 8.4 illustrates an example of the proposed design for this page.

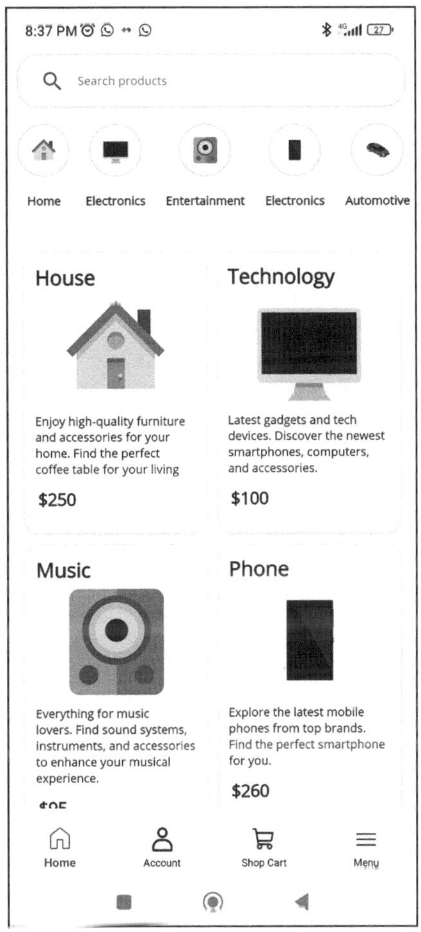

***Figure 8.4**: Example HomeView page layout*

Without further ado, let's get started developing our page.

ViewModel

At this point, we should have the following files: **HomeView.xaml** and its corresponding code-behind, **HomeView.xaml.cs**, located in the directory **Views**, and its viewmodel **HomeViewModel.cs**, which is located in the directory **ViewModels**.

Let us make sure all of these items are configured correctly before continuing.

First, we will start with the **ViewModel**. The class **HomeViewModel** must inherit from the class **BaseViewModel**, which, in turn, inherits from **ObservableObject**. The latter includes the implementation of **INotifyPropertyChanged**, which allows changes to the **ViewModel** properties to be automatically reflected in the user interface using the **ViewModel** mechanism **data binding**.

Remember that the class **BaseViewModel** we created previously in the '**Creating Applications**' section of this chapter serves as the basis for the **ViewModels** of our application.

```
public partial class HomeViewModel : BaseViewModel
```

First, we are going to import the libraries responsible for the functioning of our class.

```
using CommunityToolkit.Mvvm.ComponentModel;
using EcommerceApp.Models;
using System.Collections.ObjectModel;
using CommunityToolkit.Mvvm.Input;
using EcommerceApp.Views;
using System.Text.Json;
using EcommerceApp.Services;
```

After we declare the properties, we will use them within our **ViewModel**. These properties are linked to the user interface using the binding mechanism:

```
[ObservableProperty]
public List<Product> productsList;
[ObservableProperty]
public ObservableCollection<Product> filteredProductsList;
[ObservableProperty]
public ObservableCollection<Category> categories;
[ObservableProperty]
public bool isLoading = true;
[ObservableProperty]
public string? searchText;
```

Within the class constructor, we initialize the necessary properties and define the categories that will be available in the application. The property **ObservableCollection<Category>** will be responsible for storing the list of categories, and thanks to its dynamic nature, any changes to this collection are automatically reflected in the user interface.

```
public HomeViewModel(IProductsServices productsServices)
{
    ProductsList = new List<Product>();
    FilteredProductsList = new ObservableCollection<Product>();
```

```
    Categories = new ObservableCollection<Category>()
    {
new Category {Id=Guid.NewGuid(), Image ="house.png", Title =
"Home" },
new Category {Id=Guid.NewGuid(), Image ="tecno.png", Title =
"Electronics" },
new Category {Id=Guid.NewGuid(), Image ="music.png", Title =
"Entertainment" },
new Category {Id=Guid.NewGuid(), Image ="phone.png", Title =
"Electronics" },
new Category {Id=Guid.NewGuid(), Image ="car.png", Title =
"Automotive" },
new Category {Id=Guid.NewGuid(), Image ="clothes.png", Title =
"Apparel" }
    };
            _productsServices = productsServices;
}
```

You may be wondering about the object **Category**. This will be a class that will be responsible for being the data model for our categories. Remember that, as a model, you must save it in the directory **Models** of the project. The class should look like this:

```
public class Category
{
    public Guid Id { get; set; }
    public string? Image { get; set; }
    public string? Title { get; set; }
}
```

Then we will define the method **GetData**, which is responsible for obtaining the data from the service and filling in the product list:

```
public async void GetData()
{
    IsLoading = true;
    try{
      FilteredProductsList.Clear();
      ProductsList = await _productsServices.List() ?? new
List<Product>();
      if (ProductsList != null)
          foreach (var item in ProductsList)
             FilteredProductsList.Add(item);
    }
    catch (JsonException jsonEx){
       Console.WriteLine($"JSON Error: {jsonEx.Message}");
    }
    catch (Exception ex) {
```

```
            Console.WriteLine($"General Error: {ex.Message}");
        }
        finally {  IsLoading = false; }
    }
```

Once done, we will create a method command that allows us to navigate to the details page of a specific product. Remember to use **`[RelayCommand]`** for methods that will work as commands:

```
[RelayCommand]
public async Task Description(Guid Id){
    await Shell.Current.GoToAsync($"ProductPage?productId={Id}");
}
```

You may be wondering why we use the parameter **`ProductPage?productId={Id}`** in the method **`GoToAsync`**. The reason is that, for now, we still need to create the content pages that will serve as navigation pages to display the full product. Later, we will create and register them with the application router so the navigation works properly.

Now, let us create the **`OnSearchTextChanged`**. This method is automatically executed when the search text changes. Its purpose is to filter products based on the entered text:

```
partial void OnSearchTextChanged(string? value)
{
    if (string.IsNullOrWhiteSpace(value))
    {
        FilteredProductsList.Clear();
        foreach (var product in ProductsList)
       FilteredProductsList.Add(product);
    }
    else
    {
       var filtered =  ProductsList.Where(p =>
       (p.Name?.Contains(value,StringComparison.OrdinalIgnore-
Case) ?? false) || (p.Description?.Contains(value, String
Comparison.OrdinalIgnoreCase) ?? false)).ToList();
        FilteredProductsList.Clear();
        foreach (var product in filtered)
             FilteredProductsList.Add(product);
    }
}
```

Finally, we are going to create the command that will help us filter products according to the selected category:

```
[RelayCommand]
public void SearchByCategory(string value)
```

```
{
    if (!string.IsNullOrWhiteSpace(value)){
       var filtered = ProductsList.Where
(p => p.Category == value)
.ToList() ?? new List<Product>();
         FilteredProductsList.Clear();
         foreach (var product in filtered){
             FilteredProductsList.Add(product);
         }
    }
}
```

As you can see, the class **HomeViewModel** is responsible for managing the logic of the application's main view, handling the loading and filtering of products and categories. This pretty much covers everything related to the behavior and logic of our **ViewModel**.

View and code-behind

Within the code-behind of our **ContentPage**, we are going to set up the binding with our **ViewModel**. If you remember, we previously injected the view along with its **ViewModel** into the **MauiProgram** of the project. So now we just need to assign the **ViewModel** to the page's binding context. The code will look like this:

```
public partial class HomeView : ContentPage
{
        public HomeView(HomeViewModel viewModel)
        {
                InitializeComponent();
                this.BindingContext = viewModel;
        }
 }
```

Once we have established the **data binding**, we are going to implement the method **OnAppearing**. This method will be executed every time the page appears in the interface, and its purpose will be to call the method **GetData** of our **ViewModel** to ensure that the product listing is always up to date when the page loads.

```
protected override void OnAppearing()
{
    base.OnAppearing();

    if (this.BindingContext is HomeViewModel viewModel)
    {
        viewModel.GetData();
    }
}
```

This would be all we need to do in the **code-behind**. Now, let us move on to creating the view in the file **XAML**. Let us create the page according to *Figure* 8.4. First, we will import the necessary libraries for our XAML file to work correctly. In this case, this includes the **ViewModels**, Models, and other useful resource namespaces.

```
<?xml version="1.0" encoding="utf-8" ?>
<ContentPage xmlns="http://schemas.microsoft.com/dotnet/2021/maui"
             xmlns:x="http://schemas.microsoft.com/winfx/2009/xaml"
             xmlns:viewmodels="clr-namespace:EcommerceApp.ViewModels"
xmlns:toolkit="http://schemas.microsoft.com/dotnet/2022/maui/toolkit"
             xmlns:models="clr-namespace:EcommerceApp.Models"
             x:Class="EcommerceApp.Views.HomeView"
             x:DataType="viewmodels:HomeViewModel"
             Title="">
```

In this snippet, we have configured the page to use the **ViewModel HomeViewModel**, and we link the **DataType** with it, which allows for easier data linking.

Next, we have a **SearchBar** that allows the user to search for products. The entered text is linked to the property **SearchText** of the **ViewModel**:

```
<Frame CornerRadius="20"
       Padding="1,1,1,0"
       Margin="10">
    <SearchBar Placeholder="Search products"
               Text="{Binding SearchText}"/>
</Frame>
```

The following block is a **CollectionView**, which displays the available categories. Each category is presented with its image and title, and each item can be clicked to filter products by the selected category:

```
<CollectionView ItemsSource="{Binding Categories}"
                Margin="5,0,5,15"
                x:Name="CollectionCategories">
    <CollectionView.ItemsLayout>
        <LinearItemsLayout Orientation="Horizontal"/>
    </CollectionView.ItemsLayout>
    <CollectionView.ItemTemplate>
        <DataTemplate x:DataType="models:Category">
            <VerticalStackLayout>
                <Frame Style="{StaticResource AvatarFrameStyle}"
                       Padding="2">
                    <Image Source="{Binding Image}"
                           WidthRequest="25"
                           VerticalOptions="Center"
                           HorizontalOptions="Center"/>
                    <Frame.GestureRecognizers>
```

```
<TapGestureRecognizer Command="{Binding Path = BindingContext.
SearchByCategoryCommand, Source={Reference CollectionCategories}}"
CommandParameter="{Binding Title}" />
                    </Frame.GestureRecognizers>
                </Frame>
                <Label Text="{Binding Title}"
                       HorizontalTextAlignment="Center"
                       VerticalTextAlignment="Center"
                       FontAttributes="Bold"
                       Margin="10"/>
            </VerticalStackLayout>
        </DataTemplate>
    </CollectionView.ItemTemplate>
</CollectionView>
```

Then, we will define an **ActivityIndicator** that displays a spinner while data is loading, and its visibility and running state are bound to the **IsLoading** property of the **ViewModel**:

```
<ActivityIndicator IsVisible="{Binding IsLoading}"
                   IsRunning="{Binding IsLoading}"
                   VerticalOptions="Center"
                   HorizontalOptions="Center" />
```

Finally, we are going to create another **CollectionView** that shows the filtered products. Each product is presented with its name, image, description, and price. In addition, it is linked to a command **DescriptionCommand** to navigate to the product details page:

```
<CollectionView ItemsSource="{Binding FilteredProductsList}"
                VerticalOptions="FillAndExpand"
                x:Name="CollectionProduct" Margin="10">
    <CollectionView.ItemsLayout>
        <GridItemsLayout Orientation="Vertical" Span="2"/>
    </CollectionView.ItemsLayout>
    <CollectionView.ItemTemplate>
        <DataTemplate x:DataType="models:Product">
            <Frame CornerRadius="15" BackgroundColor="White"
                   BorderColor="#E0E0E0"  Padding="10"
                   Margin="5"  HasShadow="True">
                <VerticalStackLayout>
                    <Label Text="{Binding Name}"
                           FontAttributes="Bold"
                           FontSize="Title"
                           InputTransparent="True" />
                    <Image Source="{Binding Image}"
                           WidthRequest="100"
                           Margin="5,5,5,10"/>
                    <Label Text="{Binding Description}"
```

```
                                 HorizontalTextAlignment="Start"
FontSize="14"
                                 InputTransparent="True" />
                        <Label Text="{Binding Price, StringFor-
mat='${0:0}'}"
FontSize="20"
                                 FontAttributes="Bold"
                                 Margin="2,10"
                                 InputTransparent="True" />
                    </VerticalStackLayout>
                    <Frame.GestureRecognizers>
                        <TapGestureRecognizer Command="{Binding Path =
BindingContext.DescriptionCommand, Source={Reference Collection
Product}}"
                                              CommandParameter="{Binding
Id}"/>
                    </Frame.GestureRecognizers>
                </Frame>
            </DataTemplate>
        </CollectionView.ItemTemplate>
    </CollectionView>
```

If you have made it this far, congratulations! We have completed creating our **HomeView** page. Now, you have a functional interface that efficiently connects to the **ViewModel**, loading and displaying products and categories.

ProductDescriptionView

Now we will move on to creating the page responsible for displaying the information for the selected product. If you recall, in **HomeViewModel**, we have a command called **Description**. This command, when activated, is responsible for navigating to a new content page (**ContentPage**) using **Shell.Current.GeTAsync** to manage navigation within the app. We will proceed to create the new content page. This page will be injected and registered in our application router to ensure its integration with the navigation flow.

Without further ado, let us begin. *Figure* 8.5 shows the layout of this content page.

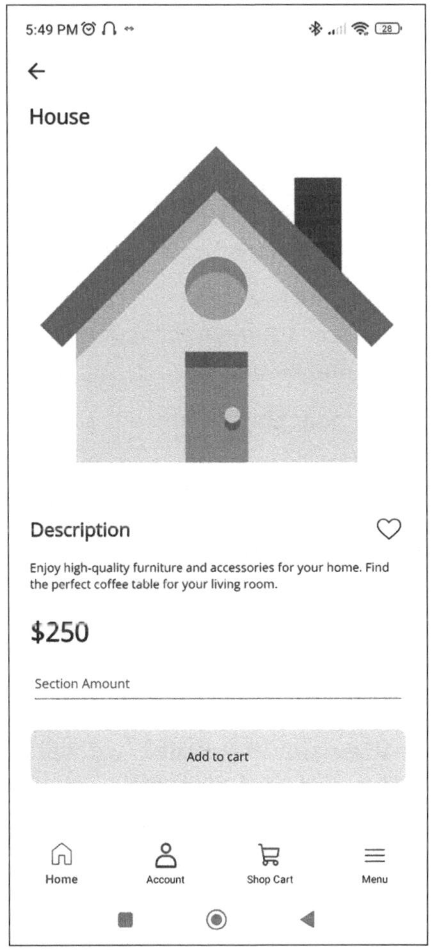

***Figure 8.5**: Design the content page to display product information*

Our product page will be clearly organized to provide a smooth and engaging user experience. Initially, a **Label** is highlighted with the **product name**, followed by the **corresponding photograph or image** that will allow the user to view the article in detail. After the image, a **detailed description** of the product, so that the user can know all its features and specifications.

Just below the description, you will find a **heart-shaped icon** that will allow the user to mark **the product as a favorite**. This icon will have two versions: one blank as the initial state and another colored one, to indicate that the product has been added to the favorites list. When making a **tap** in the heart, the icon will change, providing visual feedback that the product has been added to favorites.

The **price** of the product will be clearly shown below, and then a presentation will be made using **Picker** so that the user can select the desired **quantity of** the product. Finally, a button is prominent for adding **the product to the shopping cart**, facilitating the purchasing action and ensuring that the process is as simple as possible for the user.

First, we will create our **ContentPage** and its **ViewModel**. The **ContentPage** will bear the name of **ProductDescriptionView.xaml**, and it must be saved inside the directory **Views**. Once the page is ready, we will proceed to create its **ViewModel** with the name of **ProductDescriptionViewModel.cs**. This file must be created in the directory **ViewModels** of the project.

The class **ProductDescriptionViewModel** must inherit from the class **BaseViewModel** and the interface **IQueryAttributable** to implement the method **ApplyQueryAttributes**, remaining as follows:

```
public partial class ProductDescriptionViewModel:BaseViewModel,
IQueryAttributable {
    public void ApplyQueryAttributes(IDictionary<string, object>
    query){}
    public ProductDescriptionViewModel() {}
}
```

The method ApplyQueryAttributes: Its implementation will be necessary so that the **ViewModel** can receive parameters from the **View** through his **grandson ViewModel.**

After finishing creating our **View** and **ViewModel**, we will inject and register it in the router of our application within our **MauiProgram**.

To register it in the router of our application, we will use the **Routing** remaining as follows:

```
 Routing.RegisterRoute("ProductPage", typeof(ProductDes
criptionView));
```

The first parameter of **RegisterRoute**, in this case "**ProductPage**", represents the name of the route that we will use to navigate. The second parameter is the type of **View** that we want to associate with that route, in this case **typeof (ProductDescriptionView)**, which is the view that will be displayed when navigating to the route "**ProductPage**".

Then, we inject the **View** and the **Viewmodel** using **AddTransient**, shown as follows

```
builder.Services.AddTransient<ProductDescriptionView>(); builder.
Services.AddTransient<ProductDescriptionViewModel>();
```

With this finished, we can continue with the development of our Page **ProductDescriptionView**.

ViewModel

Let us declare the private properties and variables we will use within our **ViewModel**. The properties will be public and linked to the user interface using the binding mechanism:

```
private string? _productId { get; set; }
[ObservableProperty] public ObservableCollection<QuantityItem>
quantityItem;
[ObservableProperty] public List<Product> products;
[ObservableProperty] public QuantityItem selectedQuantity;
[ObservableProperty] public string buttonText;
[ObservableProperty] public Product product;
[ObservableProperty] public string heartIcon;
[ObservableProperty] public string productName;
[ObservableProperty] public string productDescription;
[ObservableProperty] public string productImage;
[ObservableProperty] public double productPrice;
[ObservableProperty] public bool isEnabledButton = false;
private readonly DatabaseContext _dateBaseContext;
private readonly IProductsServices _productsServices;
```

Then, within the method **ApplyQueryAttributes**, we are going to capture a query parameter called **productId** and store it in a class variable **_productId**, as follows:

```
public void ApplyQueryAttributes(IDictionary<string, object>
query {         _productId = query["productId"] as string; }
```

Inside the class constructor, we initialize the necessary properties and some important variables for the correct functioning of the class.

```
public ProductDescriptionViewModel(DatabaseContext dateBase
Context, IProductsServices productsServices){
    HeartIcon = "heart.png";
    ButtonText = "Add to cart";
    _dateBaseContext = dateBaseContext;
    _productsServices = productsServices;  }
```

Creation of the method ConsultProduct: This method will be responsible for querying a product's details, assigning the corresponding information to the class properties, and preparing the interface elements based on the product data. First, the button is disabled while the query is performed. Then, a list of products is obtained from the service **._productsServices** that we created earlier. If you have a **productId**, the corresponding product is filtered from the list, and its values are assigned to the class properties. In addition, if the product has **stock**, available quantity items are created (such as purchase quantity options). If the product is out of stock, only an option indicating that it is out of stock is added. Finally, **IsFavorite()** to check if the product is marked as a favorite.

You may be wondering about the object **QuantityItem**. This will be a class that will be in charge of being the data model for our quantities for the component **Picker**. Remember that, as a model, you must save it in the directory **Models** of the project. The class should look like this:

```
public class QuantityItem
{
    public string? Name { get; set; } // The name of the product
    or item
    public int Amount { get; set; } // The quantity available
}
```

Creation of the method IsFavorite: This method checks if the current product is in the favorites list. The product ID is obtained, and if valid, the database is queried to see if the product is in the favorites list. If the product is found in the list, the heart icon is changed to a selected one **("heartselect.png")**.

```
public async void IsFavorite()
{
    try
    {
        var idProd = Product.Id.ToString() ?? string.Empty;
        if(!string.IsNullOrWhiteSpace(idProd)) {
       var favorite = (await _dateBaseContext.GetFileteredAsync<-
Favorites>(
                x => x.Product_Id == idProd))
                .Select(x => (Guid?)x.Id) // Convertir a Nul-
lable<Guid>
                .FirstOrDefault()?.ToString();
            if (!string.IsNullOrWhiteSpace(favorite))
                HeartIcon = "heartselect.png";
        }
    }
    catch(Exception ex) { Console.WriteLine(ex.Message); }
}
```

Now, we are going to create the method **Select Quantity Changed**, which is an event handler that is triggered when a quantity is selected in the UI; in this case, the property will be **SelectedQuantity**. If the selected quantity is non-zero, the button is enabled.

```
partial void OnSelectedQuantityChanged(QuantityItem value){

    if (value != null ) {

        if(SelectedQuantity.Amount != 0)
```

```
                IsEnabledButton = true;
            }
        }
```

Next, we will create the method **HeartIconTap** that binds to a UI command, which is executed when the user taps the heart icon. Call the method **AddOrRemoveToFavorites** to add or remove the product from your favorites list.

```
[RelayCommand]
public async Task HeartIconTap() { await this.AddOrRemoveTo
Favorites(); }
```

Method AddOrRemoveToFavorites: This method handles the logic for adding or removing a product from the favorites list. If the product is not marked as a favorite (the heart icon is not selected), a new record is created in the database to add the product to the favorites. If it is already marked as a favorite, the corresponding records are deleted from the database, and the heart icon returns to its original state.

```
private async Task AddOrRemoveToFavorites() {
    try {
        if(HeartIcon.Equals("heart.png"))  {
            var favorite = new Favorites() {
                Id = Guid.NewGuid(),
                Product_Id = Product.Id.ToString()
            };
            if (await _dateBaseContext.AddItemAsync(favorite)) {
                HeartIcon = "heartselect.png";
            }
        } else  {
            var idProd = Product.Id.ToString();
var favorites = (await _dateBaseContext.GetFileteredAsync<Favor-
ites>(x => x.Product_Id == idProd)).Select(x => x.Id).ToList();
            if (favorites is null) return;
            foreach (var item in favorites){
   if (await _dateBaseContext.DeleteItemByKeyAsync<Favorites>(item))
{
                    HeartIcon = "heart.png";
                }
            }
        }
    }
    catch (Exception ex){  Console.WriteLine(ex.Message); }
}
```

Command TapButton: This is a command that adds or removes a product from the shopping cart. When you tap the button, the **ButtonText** property is checked. If the text is anything other than "**`remove from cart`**," it means the product is not in the cart and is therefore added. If the text is "**`remove from cart`**," it means the product is already in the cart and is therefore removed.

```
[RelayCommand]
public async void TapButton(){
    if (!ButtonText.Equals("remove from cart"))   await this.AddTo-
Cart();
    else await this.RemoveFromCart();  }
```

Method `AddToCart`: This method handles the logic for adding a product to the cart. It creates an item from the product and sets the selected quantity. Then, it saves it to the database, and changes the button text to "**`remove from cart`**" to indicate that the product is in the cart.

```
private async Task AddToCart() {
    try     {
        var item = ItemHelper.CreateItemFromProduct(Product);
        item.Quantity = SelectedQuantity.Amount;
        item.IsBuy = false;
        if (await _dateBaseContext.AddItemAsync(item)) {
            ButtonText = "remove from cart";
        }
    } catch(Exception ex) { Console.WriteLine(ex.Message);  }
}
```

Method `RemoveFromCart`: This method removes the product from the cart. The database is queried to obtain the **`items`** corresponding to the product, and they are removed one by one. If the product is successfully removed from the cart, the button text changes to "**`Add to cart`**".

```
private async Task RemoveFromCart() {
    try     {
        var iSRemove = false;
        var idProd = Product.Id.ToString();
        var items = (await _dateBaseContext.GetFileteredAsync<Item>
                    (x => x.Product_Id == idProd)
                 ).Select(x => x.Id).ToList();
        if (items is null) return;
        foreach ( var item in items)         {
          if(await _dateBaseContext.DeleteItemByKeyAsync<Item>
(item)) {
                iSRemove = true;
            }
        }
        if(iSRemove)
            ButtonText = "Add to cart";
    } catch(Exception ex){ Console.WriteLine(ex.Message); } }
```

With this, we finish our **viewModel**. Now we can continue with the development of our Page **ProductDescriptionView**.

View and Code-Behind

Within the code-behind of our **ContentPage**, we are going to set up the binding with our **ViewModel**. If you remember, we previously injected the view along with its **ViewModel** into the **MauiProgram** of the project. So now we just need to assign the **ViewModel** to the page's binding context. The code will look like this:

```
public ProductDescriptionView(ProductDescriptionViewModel viewModel)
{
  InitializeComponent();
  this.BindingContext = viewModel;
}
```

Once we have established the **data binding**, we are going to implement the method **OnAppearing**. This method will be executed every time the page appears in the interface, and its purpose will be to call the method **ConsultProduct** of our **ViewModel**.

```
 protected override void OnAppearing() {
     base.OnAppearing();
     if (this.BindingContext is ProductDescriptionViewModel viewModel)
         viewModel.ConsultProduct();
}
```

This would be all that we need to do in the **code-behind**. Now, let us move on to creating the view in the **XAML** file. Let us create the page according to *Figure* 8.5. First, we will import the necessary libraries for our XAML file to work correctly, and we will add the layouts that our page will use, a **ScrollViewy VerticalStackLayout**, shown as follows:

```
 <?xml version="1.0" encoding="utf-8" ?>
<ContentPage xmlns="http://schemas.microsoft.com/dotnet/2021/maui"
             xmlns:x="http://schemas.microsoft.com/winfx/2009/xaml"
             x:Class="EcommerceApp.Views.ProductDescriptionView"
             Title="">
    <ScrollView>
        <VerticalStackLayout Padding="20, 0">
        </VerticalStackLayout>
    </ScrollView>
</ContentPage>
```

Within the **VerticalStackLayout**, we will add a **Label** to display the product title, linked to the property **ProductName**, with a style that highlights the text using a large font size and bold. Then we will add an **Image** to display the product image, linked to the property **ProductImage**

```
<Label Text="{Binding ProductName}" FontSize="Title" FontAttri-
butes="Bold"/>
<Image Source="{Binding ProductImage}"/>
```

Then we will add a component **Grid**, within which we will define two elements. The first will be a **Label** that will display the product description text. The second will be an **Image** that will use the property **HeartIcon** to display the heart icon. This image will include a **GestureRecognizer** of the type **TapGestureRecognizer**, which will be linked to the command **HeartIconTapCommand**, allowing you to handle touch events to add or remove the product from your favorites.

```
<Grid HeightRequest="35"  Padding="0,5">
    <Label Text="Description"
FontSize="22"
           FontAttributes="Bold"
           VerticalOptions="Center"
           HorizontalOptions="StartAndExpand" />
    <Image Source="{Binding HeartIcon}"
           WidthRequest="30"
           HeightRequest="30"
           VerticalOptions="Center"
           HorizontalOptions="End" >
        <Image.GestureRecognizers>
            <TapGestureRecognizer Command="{Binding HeartIconTap
Command}"/>
        </Image.GestureRecognizers>
    </Image>
</Grid>
```

We will add the following components to display and manage product information:

First, a **Label** that will display the product description using the property **ProductDescription**. Then we will add another Label which will display the price of the product. This will be linked to the property **Product.Price** with a custom format to display the currency value. This text will be styled with a large font size and bold to highlight the price. Next, we will include a **Picker** which will allow you to select the quantity of the product. This will be linked to the property **QuantityItem** to fill your options and **SelectedQuantity** to reflect the current selection. Additionally, it will use the property **Name** as the text that will be displayed on each element and will have a descriptive title along with styles like a medium font size and bold. Finally, we will add a **Button** to perform actions related to the product. Your text will be linked to the property **ButtonText** to indicate the action (such as adding or removing from the cart). The button will be enabled or disabled depending on the property

IsEnabledButton and will execute the command **TapButtonCommand** when pressed. It looks like this:

```
<Label Text="{Binding ProductDescription}" Margin="0,10" />

<Label Text="{Binding Product.Price, StringFormat='${0:0}'}"
      FontSize="30"  FontAttributes="Bold"  Margin="0,10"/>
<Picker ItemsSource="{Binding QuantityItem}"
        SelectedItem="{Binding SelectedQuantity}"
        ItemDisplayBinding="{Binding Name}"  Title="Section Amount"
        FontSize="15" FontAttributes="Bold"/>
<Button Text="{Binding ButtonText}"  Margin="0,20"
        IsEnabled="{Binding IsEnabledButton}"
        Command="{Binding TapButtonCommand}" />
```

If you have made it this far, congratulations! We have completed creating our page.

AccountView

The content page **AccountView** will display relevant user information such as their name and email address. It will also offer a list of the user's favorite items. This window has a simple yet functional design, allowing the user to view products that interest them and that they may purchase in the future. Its main purpose is to provide a practical and personalized experience, making it easier to organize the user's interests within the platform.

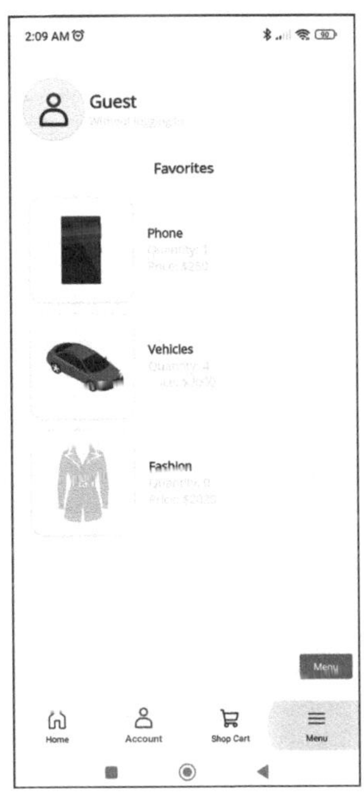

Figure 8.6: *AccountView content page design*

The page **AccountView** will have a simple design. It will have an element **Frame** which will serve as a container for an image representative of the user, a **Label** to display the title with the user's name, and another **Label** for the subtitle with additional information, such as email.

At the bottom, a will be included in **CollectionView** to display the list of favorite articles selected by the user. At this point, you should have created the view named **AccountView.xaml** along with its corresponding **ViewModel**, called **AccountViewModel.cs**.

ViewModel

The class **AccountViewModel** inherits from the class **BaseViewModel** and will be the bridge between the logic and the graphical interface of the view **AccountView.xaml**.

We declare the private properties and variables that we will use within our **ViewModel**.

```
private readonly DatabaseContext _dateBaseContext;
private readonly IProductsServices _productsService;
[ObservableProperty] public ObservableCollection<Item> items;
[ObservableProperty] public string? title;
[ObservableProperty] public string? subTitle;
```

Inside the class constructor, we initialize the necessary properties and some important variables for the correct functioning of the class.

```
public AccountViewModel(DatabaseContext dateBaseContext, IProducts-
Services productsService) {
    _dateBaseContext = dateBaseContext;
    _productsService = productsService;
    Items = new ObservableCollection<Item>();
}
```

Next, we will create the method **OnAppearingAsync**, which is responsible for initializing data and preparing the interface when the view appears. First, the method clears the Items collection and sets the initial title to "**Guest**" and a subtitle to "**Without logging in**," indicating that no one is logged in. Then, it queries the favorites stored in the database via**_dateBaseContext.GetAllAsync<Favorites>()**. If there are no favorites, the method ends. Then, you get the full list of products using **_productsService.List()**, if there are no products available, it also ends.

Next, iterate through each favorite. For each one, validate whether the property **Product_Id** is not empty, and convert this **ID** into a **GUID**. Find the corresponding product in the product list and, if found, create a new item using **ItemHelper.CreateItemFromProduct(product)** and adds it to the collection **Items**. Finally, it checks to see if there is a logged-in user by querying the database. If it finds one, it updates the title with the user's name and the subtitle with their email address. If an error occurs, it is captured and logged in the console, indicating the method name and error details.

```
public async void OnAppearingAsync(){
    try {
        Items.Clear();
        Title = "Guest";
        SubTitle = "Without logging in";
        var favorities = await _dateBaseContext.GetAllAsync
<Favorites>();
        if (favorities == null || !favorities.Any()) return;
        var products = await _productsService.List();
        if (products == null) return;
        foreach (var favorite in favorities) {
            if(!string.IsNullOrWhiteSpace(favorite.Product_Id)) {
                var id = new Guid(favorite.Product_Id);
                var product = products.FirstOrDefault(x => x.Id ==
id);
                if (product != null) {
                    var item = ItemHelper.CreateItemFromProduct
(product);
                    Items.Add(item);
                }
            }
        }
        //data user
        var result = (await _dateBaseContext.GetAllAsync<Users>())
            .Where(x => x.ActiveSession == true).FirstOrDefault();
        if(result != null) {
            Title = result.Name ?? Title;
            SubTitle = result.Email ?? SubTitle;
        }
    } catch (Exception ex){
        Console.WriteLine($"Error in {nameof(OnAppearingAsync)}:
{ex}");
    }
}
```

With this, we finish our **viewModel**; now we can continue with the development of our Page **AccountView**..

View and Code-Behind

Within the **code-behind** of our **ContentPage**, we are going to set up the binding with our **ViewModel**. If you remember, we previously injected the view along with its

`ViewModel` into the **`MauiProgram`** of the project. So now we just need to assign the **`ViewModel`** to the page's binding context. The code will look like this:

```
public AccountView(AccountViewModel viewModel) {
    InitializeComponent();
    BindingContext = viewModel;
}
```

Once we have established the **data binding**, we are going to implement the method **`OnAppearing`**.

```
protected override void OnAppearing()
{
    base.OnAppearing();
    if (this.BindingContext is AccountViewModel viewModel) {
        viewModel.OnAppearingAsync();
    }
}
```

This would be all we need to do in the **code-behind**. Now, let us move on to creating the view in the **XAML** file.

For the page first, we are going to import the necessary libraries for our XAML file to work correctly, and we are going to add the layouts that our page will use; as the main container, we will use **`VerticalStackLayout`**, remaining as follows:

```
<ContentPage xmlns="http://schemas.microsoft.com/dotnet/2021/maui"
             xmlns:x="http://schemas.microsoft.com/winfx/2009/xaml"
             xmlns:viewmodels="clr-namespace:EcommerceApp.ViewModels"
xmlns:toolkit="http://schemas.microsoft.com/dotnet/2022/maui/toolkit"
             xmlns:models="clr-namespace:EcommerceApp.Models"
             x:Class="EcommerceApp.Views.AccountView"
             Title="">
    <VerticalStackLayout Margin="10" Spacing="10">
    </VerticalStackLayout>
</ContentPage>
```

Within the **`VerticalStackLayout`**, the following components will be organized. First, a **`HorizontalStackLayout`**, which will contain a **`Frame`**. The **`Frame`** will host an Image, which will be displayed centered both horizontally and vertically. Next, a **`VerticalStackLayout`** will be added, which will have two Labels: the first will display the content title, linked to the **`Title`** property, and the second will display a subtitle, linked to the **`SubTitle`** property.

```
<HorizontalStackLayout Margin="0,20,0,0">
    <Frame Style="{StaticResource AvatarFrameStyle}"
           Padding="15" WidthRequest="70" HeightRequest="70"
           BackgroundColor="#E0E0E0">
        <Image Source="account.png"
```

```
                    VerticalOptions="CenterAndExpand"
                    HorizontalOptions="CenterAndExpand"/>
        </Frame>
        <VerticalStackLayout VerticalOptions="CenterAndExpand">
            <Label Text="{Binding Title}" FontSize="Title"
                    FontAttributes="Bold" />
    <Label Text="{Binding SubTitle}" FontSize="Subtitle"
   TextColor="Silver" />
        </VerticalStackLayout>
    </HorizontalStackLayout>
```

Another component in our main layout will be a **VerticalStackLayout**, which will house a Label. This Label will not be linked to any properties, and its sole purpose will be to display the "**Favorites**" title, serving as a header for the favorite products section.

```
        <VerticalStackLayout  Padding="10,5,10,0">
            <Label Text="Favorites" FontSize="20"
                   FontAttributes="Bold"  HorizontalOptions="Center"
                   VerticalOptions="Center" />
        </VerticalStackLayout>
```

Another component in our main layout will be a **CollectionView**, which will be linked to the Items property of our **ViewModel**. This component will be used to display a list of products. Within the **CollectionView**, each item will be defined using a **DataTemplate**.

Each item's template consists of a Frame surrounding a **HorizontalStackLayout**. This horizontal container will contain two elements:

- And **Frame** with rounded edges and a white background, which will contain an image of the product. The image will be bound to the Image property of the data model.
- And **VerticalStackLayout**, which will be vertically aligned to the center and will have three labels (Label):
  - The first label will display the name of the product, bound to the **Name** property.
  - The second label will display the available quantity, in the format "**Quantity: {0}**", linked to Quantity.
  - The third tag will display the price of the product, in the format "**Price: ${0}**", linked to Price.

This design allows each product to be presented clearly and orderly within the favorites list, with the code as follows:

```
    <CollectionView ItemsSource="{Binding Items}"
                    VerticalOptions="FillAndExpand"
```

```
                 Margin="5"
                 HeightRequest="550">
    <CollectionView.ItemTemplate>
        <DataTemplate x:DataType="models:Item">
            <Frame BorderColor="Transparent"
                   Padding="0">
                <HorizontalStackLayout>
                    <Frame CornerRadius="15"
                           BackgroundColor="White"
                           BorderColor="#E0E0E0"
                           Padding="8"
                           Margin="5"
                           HasShadow="True">
             <Image Source="{Binding Image}" WidthRequest="100" />
                    </Frame>
<VerticalStackLayout VerticalOptions="Center" Padding="10,0,0,0">
                        <Label Text="{Binding Name}"
FontSize="17"
                               FontAttributes="Bold" />
             <Label Text="{Binding Quantity, StringFormat='Quantity:
{0}'}"
FontSize="17"
                               TextColor="Silver" />
                 <Label Text="{Binding Price, StringFormat='Price:
${0}'}"
FontSize="17"
                               TextColor="Silver" />
                    </VerticalStackLayout>
                </HorizontalStackLayout>
            </Frame>
        </DataTemplate>
    </CollectionView.ItemTemplate>
</CollectionView>
```

If you have made it this far, congratulations! We have completed creating our page.

ShoppingCartView

The **ShoppingCartView** content page will be responsible for displaying the list of products added to the shopping cart. Each item will have a **SwipeView.LeftItems**, which will allow the user to swipe the product to reveal a button that will remove it from the cart. A prominent checkout button will also be included.

When the user taps the purchase button, the app will check if they are logged in. If the user is not authenticated, a window will open to log in or create an account. If the user is already logged in, the app will redirect to the purchase page, where they can enter their delivery location information and proceed with payment. This flow ensures a smooth and appropriate purchase process based on the user's session status.

***Figure 8.7**: Designing the ShoppingCartView content page*

The page **`ShoppingCartView`** will have a simple and organized design using a **`Grid.`** As the main container, the Grid will have two rows. In **row 0, `CollectionView`** will be displayed, with the product items added to the cart. In **row 1, the button** will be displayed. Buy to proceed with the purchase; the design ensures that the cart information is clear and accessible with a simple flow to the purchase action.

ViewModel

The class **`ShoppingCartViewModel`** inherits from the class **`BaseViewModel`**, and it will be a simple **`ViewModel`**. It will have three methods:

- **`BuyProccess`**: This method will trigger the event when the Buy button is tapped. First, it will validate whether the user is logged in. If so, it will navigate to the page. **`PurchasePage`** (which we have not created yet). If the user is not logged in, they will be redirected to the page **`UserPage`** (which we will create later).

- **DeletedItem**: This method will remove an item from the shopping cart list.
- **OnAppearing**: This method will be activated when the page loads and will be responsible for consulting the items that represent the shopping cart to show them to the user.

Additionally, this **ViewModel** uses the MVVM pattern with observable properties to reactively update the interface and **RelayCommand** commands to handle events. You can see the full implementation of this class in the project repository.

With this, we conclude the logic of the **ViewModel** and can continue with the development of the cart page interface.

View and Code-Behind

As in the previous code-behind, we are going to establish the binding with our **ViewModel** and implement the **OnAppearing** method.

```
public partial class ShoppingCartView : ContentPage {
    public ShoppingCartView()      {
    InitializeComponent();
    var _dataBaseContext = new DatabaseContext();
    this.BindingContext = new ShoppingCartViewModel(_dataBase
Context);
    }
    protected override void OnAppearing() {
       base.OnAppearing();
          if (this.BindingContext is ShoppingCartViewModel view
          Model){
             viewModel.OnAppearing();
          }
    }
}
```

That is all we need to do in the code behind. Now, let us move on to creating the view in the XAML file. First, we define the libraries our **ContentPage** will use and add the Grid as its main container. This Grid will have two rows. The first row will display the **CollectionView** containing the shopping cart items, and the second row will house the checkout button.

In the first row (row 0), we define a **CollectionView**, which is used to display the list of products in the shopping cart. Binds the **ItemsSource** property to the **Items** of the **ViewModel**. This means that the items displayed in the **CollectionView** are the products in the cart. Within each item in the cart, a **DataTemplate** is used to define how the product should be displayed. This **DataTemplate** contains a **SwipeView**, which allows the action of swiping the product to display additional options, such as removing the product from the cart. Within this **SwipeView**, there will be **SwipeView.LeftItems** that contains a **SwipeItem** that is displayed when the user swipes the product to the left. The **SwipeItem** has a delete icon (an image called "**delete_white.png**") with a red background. Clicking this icon executes the command **DeletedItemCommand**, which is in the **ViewModel**. This command will remove the product from the cart. The parameter to the command is the product itself, which allows you to delete that specific product. In the main part of the product, a **Frame** to style it and add margins, which contains a **HorizontalStackLayout**, which organizes the product image and additional information. Within the **HorizontalStackLayout**, the product has its image represented by an **Image**, which is linked to the product's Image property. A **VerticalStackLayout** is then included to display the product information in three labels. A **Label** that displays the product name (**Name**), another **Label** that shows the quantity of the product (**Quantity**), with a format that adds the text "**Quantity**" and finally a **Label** that shows the price of the product (**Price**), with the format "**Price: $**", in silver color.

You can check the complete code in the file **ShoppingCartPage.xaml** available in the repository.

In the second row (row 1) of our layout, we defined a button with the text "**Buy**." This button is bound to the property **BuyProccessCommand** in the **ViewModel**.

```
<Button Text="Buy" Grid.Row="1" Command="{Binding BuyProccess
Command}"/>
```

If you've made it this far, congratulations! We've completed creating our page.

UserView

The content page **UserView** will manage navigation to a new content page (**ContentPage**) using **Shell.Current.GoToAsync**. This page will include the following features: a login form, the option to register a new user, the ability to view authenticated user information, and the ability to edit user data.

First, the files necessary for the development of this page will be created. A new file will be created **UserView.xml**, which should be saved in the directory of **Views**, and then we will create its **viewModel** inside the directory **ViewModels** and will bear the name **UserViewModel.cs**. This page will be injected and registered in our application router to ensure its integration with the navigation flow within the file **MauiProgram.cs** of the project. To register the router, we will use the identifier '**UserPage**' associated with the page. **UserView** registration will be done as follows:

```
Routing.RegisterRoute("UserPage", typeof(UserView));
```

To inject the **View** and **ViewModel** dependencies, we will use the method **AddTransient**, leaving the configuration as follows:

```
builder.Services.AddTransient<UserView>();
builder.Services.AddTransient<UserViewModel>();
```

This ensures that **UserView** and **UserViewModel** instances are created transiently on each request.

Finishing the above, we will continue with the development. *Figure* 8.8 will represent the design that the page will have:

***Figure 8.8**: Designing the UserView content page*

This page features a simple design but key functionality. Its behavior will vary depending on how you use it:

- **User creation mode:** Entry fields for username, email, and password will be displayed, along with a button labeled **'Create Session'**.
- **User display and editing mode:** The same input fields will be visible, but the button text will change to **'Edit'** to reflect the functionality.

- **Login Mode:** Only the username and password input fields will be displayed, along with a button labeled '**Login**'.

This design ensures an intuitive experience for each available function.

ViewModel

As in the previous viewmodels, the class **UserViewModel** inherits from the class **BaseViewModel**.

Next, we declare the public properties and private variables that we will use within our **ViewModel**.

```
private DatabaseContext _databaseContext;
private string _idUser;
[ObservableProperty] public string userName;
[ObservableProperty] public string email;
[ObservableProperty] public string pass;
[ObservableProperty] public bool createSession;
[ObservableProperty] public bool isVisibleButtonLogin;
[ObservableProperty] public string message;
[ObservableProperty] public Color messageTextColor;
[ObservableProperty] public string? textButtonSaved;
```

Inside the class constructor, we initialize the necessary properties and some important variables for the correct functioning of the class.

```
public UserViewModel(DatabaseContext databaseContext){
     _databaseContext = databaseContext;
     UserName = string.Empty;
     Email = string.Empty;
     Pass = string.Empty;
     CreateSession = false;
     IsVisibleButtonLogin = true;
     Message = string.Empty;
     _idUser = string.Empty;
     MessageTextColor = new ColorMaui.Color(1, 0, 0); // RED
     TextButtonSaved = "Create Session";
 }
```

Next, we will create the method **OnAppearingAsync**, which is responsible for checking if there is a user logged in; if found, it fills out the form with their data and changes the form to edit mode.

```
public async Task OnAppearing(){
     try  {
         var result = (await _databaseContext.GetAllAsync<Users>())
             .Where(x => x.ActiveSession == true).FirstOrDefault();
         if (result != null)  {
```

```
                UserName = result.Name ?? string.Empty;
                Email = result.Email ?? string.Empty;
                Pass = result.Password ?? string.Empty;
                CreateSession = true;
                IsVisibleButtonLogin = false;
                _idUser = result.Id.ToString() ?? string.Empty;
                TextButtonSaved = "Edit";
            }
        } catch(Exception ex) { Console.WriteLine(ex.ToString()); }
    }
```

Next, we create the method **`TapSaved`**, decorated with the attribute **`[RelayCommand]`**, allowing it to be used directly as a command in the MVVM pattern.

This method has two main responsibilities:

- **Create a new user:** It validates that all fields are complete and that the user does not already exist (via email address). If everything is correct, it saves the user to the database.
- **Update an existing user:** If the field **`_idUser`** contains a value, it means we are editing a user. In this case, the method updates the user's information with the new data.

In both cases, visual feedback is provided to the user, displaying a message with a green color if the operation was successful or red if there was a problem (such as the email being already registered).

If you want to review the complete implementation of the method **`TapSaved`**, you can consult it directly in the repository.

Finally, we define the method **`TapLogin`**, also decorated with **`[RelayCommand]`**. This method validates the user's credentials to allow login. The main logic is:

- Verify that the user has entered a name and password.
- Query the database to see if a user with that information exists.
- If the user is found, the session is activated, and the user is redirected to the home page.
- Otherwise, it displays an error message indicating that the username or password is incorrect.
- If the user has not yet created a session, reset the variables to display the login form.

To see the detailed implementation of the method **`TapLogin`**, you can check the repository.

With this, we have finished our **`viewModel`**; now we can continue with the development of our Page.

View and Code-Behind

Within the **code-behind** of our **ContentPage**, we are going to set up the binding with our **ViewModel**. If you remember, we previously injected the view along with its **ViewModel** into the **MauiProgram** of the project. So now we just need to assign the **ViewModel** to the page's binding context. The code will look like this:

```
public UserView(UserViewModel viewModel) {
  InitializeComponent();
  this.BindingContext = viewModel; }
```

Once we have established the **data binding**, we are going to implement the method **OnAppearing**. This method will be executed every time the page appears in the interface, and its purpose will be to call the method **viewModel.OnAppearing** of our **ViewModel**.

```
protected override void OnAppearing() {
    base.OnAppearing();
    if (this.BindingContext is UserViewModel viewModel)
        viewModel.OnAppearing();
}
```

With this configuration completed, we continue with the design of the XAML file. First, the header is declared to establish the required namespaces, define the associated class, and assign a title to the page

```
<?xml version="1.0" encoding="utf-8" ?>
<ContentPage xmlns="http://schemas.microsoft.com/dotnet/2021/maui"
             xmlns:x="http://schemas.microsoft.com/winfx/2009/xaml"
             x:Class="EcommerceApp.Views.UserView"
             Title="Account">
```

Within the page, **ScrollView** is used to handle vertical scrolling of content. This contains a **VerticalStackLayout** that organizes the elements vertically, with a defined space between them and a general padding

```
<ScrollView>
    <VerticalStackLayout Spacing="20" Padding="20">
    </VerticalStackLayout>
</ScrollView>
```

In its **VerticalStackLayout**, at the top, the profile image is placed within a **Grid**. This allows you to center a decorative circle (**Ellipse**) and, above, an image that represents the user.

```
<Grid HorizontalOptions="Center" VerticalOptions="Start">
    <Ellipse WidthRequest="150" HeightRequest="150" Fill="LightGray"
/>
```

```
<Image Source="account" WidthRequest="100" HeightRequest="100"
VerticalOptions="Center" HorizontalOptions="Center" />
</Grid>
```

Input fields are added (**Entry**) bound to **ViewModel** properties. The username field is always visible. The email field only appears in user creation mode, controlled by the **CreateSession** property. The password field is set to protected.

```
    <Entry Placeholder="User Name" Text="{Binding UserName}" />
            <Entry Placeholder="Email Address" Keyboard="Email"
Text="{Binding Email}" IsVisible="{Binding CreateSession}" />
<Entry Placeholder="Password" IsPassword="True" Text="{Binding Pass}" />
```

Then, buttons are defined that perform the main actions. The login button is visible only when the property **IsVisibleButtonLogin** is active and executes the command **TapLoginCommand**. The other button dynamically changes its text with the property **TextButtonSaved** and executes the command **TapSavedCommand**.

```
<Button Text="Login" BackgroundColor="#3b5998" TextColor="White"
        CornerRadius="5" HorizontalOptions="Fill"
IsVisible="{Binding IsVisibleButtonLogin}"
Command="{Binding TapLoginCommand}" />

<Button Text="{Binding TextButtonSaved}" BackgroundColor="#3b5998"
TextColor="White" CornerRadius="5" HorizontalOptions="Fill"
Command="{Binding TapSavedCommand}" />
```

Finally, a tag is added (**Label**) to display messages to the user, whose content and color are controlled by the **ViewModel**

```
<Label Text="{Binding Message}" TextColor="{Binding MessageText
Color}" />
```

This design adapts to different states based on the properties bound to the **ViewModel**, allowing the interface to be reused for multiple functionalities.

If you have made it this far, congratulations! We have completed creating our login and user creation page.

PurchaseViewModel

The content page **PurchaseViewModel** will manage navigation to a new content page (**ContentPage**) using **Shell.Current.GoToAsync**. Basically, this page will handle payment for the products and adding the products to the cart in purchase status. The page design is shown in *Figure* 8.9:

***Figure 8.9**: Designing the PurchaseViewModel content page*

The design of the page **`PurchaseView`** will be composed as follows:

- A text showing the **total** of the purchase that will be the result of the sum of the prices of the total of the products.
- Several fields to capture user information, such as address, city, state, phone number, among other additional data.
- A section to select the payment method with a radio button for "**`Cash Payment`**"
- A big button at the bottom that says "**`Pay`**"

Everything is organized vertically with a clean design focused on functionality.

To create the pages, we must first create the file **`PurchaseView.xaml`** within the directory **`Views`** and the file **`PurchaseViewModel.cs`** in the directory **`ViewModels`**. Additionally, you need to inject the **`View`** and **`ViewModel`** as dependencies and proceed with registering them in the router within the **`MauiProgram.cs`** file.

```
Routing.RegisterRoute("PurchasePage", typeof(PurchaseView));
builder.Services.AddTransient<PurchaseView>();
builder.Services.AddTransient<PurchaseViewModel>();
```

This will ensure that they are properly configured for navigation and operation in the application.

ViewModel

As in the previous **viewmodels**, the class **PurchaseViewModel** inherits from the class **BaseViewModel.** This class implements the following libraries:

```
using CommunityToolkit.Mvvm.ComponentModel;
using CommunityToolkit.Mvvm.Input;
using EcommerceApp.Data;
using EcommerceApp.Models;
using System.Text.Json;
```

Next, we declare the public properties and private variables that we will use within our **ViewModel**.

```
private DatabaseContext _databaseContext;
[ObservableProperty] public string total;
[ObservableProperty] private string recipientName;
[ObservableProperty] private string street;
[ObservableProperty] private string exteriorNumber;
[ObservableProperty] private string interiorNumber;
[ObservableProperty] private string neighborhood;
[ObservableProperty] private string city;
[ObservableProperty] private string state;
[ObservableProperty] private string postalCode;
[ObservableProperty] private string phone;
private List<Item> _items;
public bool createSession;
[ObservableProperty] public bool isVisibleButtonLogin;
[ObservableProperty] public string message;
[ObservableProperty] public Color messageTextColor;
[ObservableProperty] public string? textButtonSaved;
```

Inside the class constructor, we initialize the necessary properties and some important variables for the correct functioning of the class.

```
public PurchaseViewModel (DatabaseContext databaseContext) {
_databaseContext = databaseContext; }
```

Next, we will create the method **OnAppearingAsync**, responsible for consulting the products that have been added to the shopping cart with the status **'pending purchase'** and calculating the total price of said products.

```
public async Task OnAppearing() {
     try {
         decimal count = 0;
_items = (await _databaseContext.GetAllAsync<Item>())
.Where(x => x.IsBuy == false).ToList();
         if (_items != null) {
             foreach (var item in _items) {
                 if (item.Quantity.HasValue) {
```

```
                    count += (decimal)item.Price * (decimal)item.
Quantity;
                    item.IsBuy = true;
                }
            }
            Total = count.ToString();
        }
    } catch (Exception ex){Console.WriteLine(ex.ToString());}
}
```

Next, we will create the method **TapBuy**, which will be decorated with the attribute **[RelayCommand]**. To enable its use as a command in the MVVM pattern, this method is basically responsible for validating the product delivery information form, validating the price, making the purchase, and displaying an alert with a message about the purchase status.

```
[RelayCommand]
public async Task TapBuy() {
    var message = string.Empty;
// Validate if all fields are filled in
if (string.IsNullOrWhiteSpace(RecipientName) ||
string.IsNullOrWhiteSpace(Street) ||
string.IsNullOrWhiteSpace(ExteriorNumber) ||
string.IsNullOrWhiteSpace(Neighborhood) ||
string.IsNullOrWhiteSpace(City) ||
string.IsNullOrWhiteSpace(State) ||
string.IsNullOrWhiteSpace(PostalCode) ||
string.IsNullOrWhiteSpace(Phone))
    { message = "incomplete form"; } else{
var result = (await _databaseContext.GetAllAsync<Users>())
.Where(x => x.ActiveSession == true).FirstOrDefault();
        if (result != null){
            decimal parsedTotal;
            if (!decimal.TryParse(Total, out parsedTotal)){
                message = "Invalid total value";
      Application.Current.MainPage.DisplayAlert("Success", message,
"OK");
                return;
            }
            var newBought = new ShopCart(){
                Id = Guid.NewGuid(),
                User_Id = result.Id.ToString(),
                Items = JsonSerializer.Serialize(_items),
                SubTotal = parsedTotal,
                Tax = 0.16m,
                Total = 0.16m * parsedTotal,
                Created_at = DateTime.UtcNow
```

```
            };
            if (await _databaseContext.AddItemAsync<ShopCart>
(newBought))
            {
                foreach (var item in _items)   {
                    await _databaseContext.UpdateItemAsync(item);
                }
                message = "purchase made successfully";
                await Shell.Current.GoToAsync("../");
            } else {
                message = "The purchase could not be completed
correctly";
            }
        } else{
            message = "The purchase could not be completed correctly";
        }
    }
    Application.Current.MainPage.DisplayAlert("Success", message,
"OK");
}
```

With this, we finish our **viewModel**; now we can continue with the development of our Page.

View and Code-Behind

Within the **code-behind** of our **ContentPage**, we are going to set up the binding with our **ViewModel**. If you remember, we previously injected the view along with its **ViewModel** into the **MauiProgram** of the project. So now we just need to assign the **ViewModel** to the page's binding context. The code will look like this:

```
public PurchaseView(PurchaseViewModel viewModel)
{
   InitializeComponent();
   this.BindingContext = viewModel;
}
```

Once we have established the **data binding**, we are going to implement the method **OnAppearing**. This method will be executed every time the page appears in the interface, and its purpose will be to call the method **viewModel.OnAppearing** of our **ViewModel**.

```
protected override void OnAppearing()
{
    base.OnAppearing();
    if (this.BindingContext is PurchaseViewModel viewModel)
```

```
        {
            viewModel.OnAppearing();
        }
    }
```

With this configuration completed we continue with the design of the XAML file. First, the XAML file is defined with the **namespaces** required, the class associated with the page, and the title of the view.

Within the page, a **ScrollView** is used to allow vertical scrolling of content. It contains a **VerticalStackLayout** that arranges elements vertically, with a spacing of 10 and a padding of 20.

```
<ScrollView>
    <VerticalStackLayout Padding="20" Spacing="10">
    </VerticalStackLayout>
</ScrollView>
```

At the top, the purchase total is displayed with a Label, which is linked to the **ViewModel**'s total property and displayed in currency format. The text is set to be centered and bold with font size of 20.

```
<Label Text="{Binding Total, StringFormat='$Total: {0:0}'}"
FontSize="20"
        FontAttributes="Bold"
        HorizontalOptions="Center" />
```

A dividing line is added with a **BoxView**, whose height is 1 and color is red. This is placed between the total and address sections.

```
<BoxView HeightRequest="1" Color="Red" Margin="0,10" />
```

Next, input fields are added for the shipping address. Each field is bound to **ViewModel** properties, such as **RecipientName**, **Street**, **ExteriorNumber**, and so on. These fields allow the user to enter their name, address, exterior and interior numbers, among other things.

```
<Label Text="Address"
FontSize="18"
        FontAttributes="Bold" />
<Entry Placeholder="Recipient's Name"
        Text="{Binding RecipientName}" />
<Entry Placeholder="Street"
        Text="{Binding Street}" />
<Entry Placeholder="Exterior Number"
        Text="{Binding ExteriorNumber}" />
<Entry Placeholder="Interior Number"
        Text="{Binding InteriorNumber}" />
<Entry Placeholder="Neighborhood"
        Text="{Binding Neighborhood}" />
```

```
<Entry Placeholder="City"
       Text="{Binding City}" />
<Entry Placeholder="State"
       Text="{Binding State}" />
<Entry Placeholder="Postal Code"
       Text="{Binding PostalCode}" />
<Entry Placeholder="Phone"
       Text="{Binding Phone}"
       Keyboard="Telephone" />
```

Another **BoxView** is then placed as a separator between the address section and the payment method section.

Below is a Label with the text "**Payment Method**" to indicate the payment method section. Below is a **RadioButton** that is selected by default, representing the cash payment option.

```
<Label Text="Payment Method"
FontSize="18"
       FontAttributes="Bold" />
<RadioButton Content="Cash Payment"
             Value="Cash Payment"
             IsChecked="True" />
```

A new **BoxView** is added to separate the payment section from the payment button.

Finally, a button to make the payment is included, which is linked to the command **TapBuyCommand**. The button has a blue background, white text, and takes up the full width of the page.

```
<Button Text="Pay" BackgroundColor="#3B5998" TextColor="White"
        FontAttributes="Bold" HorizontalOptions="Fill"
        Command="{Binding TapBuyCommand}" />
```

Congratulations on making it this far!

We have completed creating our payment page. We are almost ready to finish.

MenuView

The page **MenuView** is responsible for displaying the following options:

- **Purchase history:** This section will be a surprise in this chapter. It is an optional exercise that will allow you to put into practice everything you have learned so far. We will explain it in detail later.
- **View account:** This option will redirect the user to the page "**UserPage**", where you can manage your account and review your data.

- **Button to log in or out:** The user will be able to log in or out as needed, ensuring a personalized experience.

With this in mind, *Figure* 8.10 shows the design that this page will have.

Figure 8.10: *Designing the MenuView content page*

Our design is simple yet effective, designed to offer the user a clear and accessible experience. Intuitively, you can check your account, review your orders, and log out with ease. Everything is organized to ensure a convenient, quick, and hassle-free process.

`ViewModel`

As in the previous viewmodels, the class **`MenuViewModel`** inherits from the class **`BaseViewModel`**.

Next, we declare the public properties and private variables that we will use within our **ViewModel**.

```
private DatabaseContext _databaseContext;
private Users? _userLogin;
[ObservableProperty] public string? textLogin;
```

Inside the class constructor, we initialize the necessary properties and some important variables for the correct functioning of the class.

```
public MenuViewModel(DatabaseContext databaseContext) {
_databaseContext = databaseContext;
  TextLogin = string.Empty;
}
```

Next, we will create the method **OnAppearingAsync**, which is responsible for querying the logged-in user and detecting whether there is a logged-in user, and modify **TextLogin**.

```
public async void OnAppearing() {
   try {
         _userLogin = (await _databaseContext.GetAllAsync<Users>())
         .Where(x => x.ActiveSession == true).FirstOrDefault();
         TextLogin = _userLogin != null ? "Log out" : "Login";
   }catch (Exception ex){ Console.WriteLine(ex.ToString());}
}
```

We will create the method **TapButtonLogin**, which will be decorated with the attribute **[RelayCommand]**. This method will validate whether a user is logged in. If the user is logged in, it will close the user session and modify the text of the login button. Otherwise, it will navigate to the "**UserPage**".

```
[RelayCommand]
public async Task TapButtonLogin()
{  try {
         if (string.IsNullOrWhiteSpace(TextLogin)) return;
         if(TextLogin.Equals("Login")){
                     await Shell.Current.GoToAsync("UserPage");
         } else if(_userLogin != null) {
            _userLogin.ActiveSession = false;
            if (await _databaseContext.UpdateItemAsync(_userLogin)) {
  TextLogin = TextLogin.Equals("Log out") ? "Login" : "Log out";
            }
        }
   } catch(Exception ex){   Console.WriteLine(ex.ToString());}
}
```

We will create the method **TapButtonAccount**, which will be decorated with the **[RelayCommand]** attribute. This method will be responsible for sending the user to the **UserPage**.

```
[RelayCommand]
public async Task TapButtonAccount(){
 await Shell.Current.GoToAsync("UserPage");
}
```

View and Code-behind

Within the **code-behind** of our **ContentPage**, we are going to set up the binding with our **ViewModel**. If you remember, we previously injected the view along with its **ViewModel** into the **MauiProgram** of the project. So now we just need to assign the **ViewModel** to the page's binding context. The code will look like this:

```
public MenuView(MenuViewModel viewModel) {
    InitializeComponent();
    this.BindingContext = viewModel;
}
```

Once we have established the **data binding**, we are going to implement the method **OnAppearing**.

```
 protected override void OnAppearing(){
    base.OnAppearing();
    if (this.BindingContext is MenuViewModel viewModel)
viewModel.OnAppearing();
}
```

With this configuration completed the **code-behind**, we continue with the design of the XAML file. As shown in *Figure* 8.10, it is a very simple design consisting of only three buttons, with the code as follows:

```
<?xml version="1.0" encoding="utf-8" ?>
<ContentPage xmlns="http://schemas.microsoft.com/dotnet/2021/maui"
             xmlns:x="http://schemas.microsoft.com/winfx/2009/xaml"
             x:Class="EcommerceApp.Views.MenuView"
             Title="">
    <Grid RowDefinitions="*,auto"
          Padding="10">
        <StackLayout Spacing="10"
                     Margin="0,10">
            <Button Text="Order history" />

            <Button Text="View account"
                    Command="{Binding TapButtonAccountCommand}"/>
        </StackLayout>
```

```
            <Button Text="{Binding TextLogin}"
                    Grid.Row="1"
                    BackgroundColor="{StaticResource LogOut}"
                    Command="{Binding TapButtonLoginCommand}"/>
        </Grid>
    </ContentPage>
```

Practice Exercise, Order History Page

The exercise will consist of creating the page **`Order History`**. You will need to create your **`View`** and **`ViewModel`**, following the same approach as the previous pages. Remember that you will need to inject and register this page in the project routes within **`MauiProgram`**. As in this project, we keep the purchase records in the table **`ShopCart`**, the page must meet the following requirements:

- Display the name and email address of the logged-in user. If the user is not found, the text "**`Sign in`**" should be displayed.
- **`CollectionView`**: You will need to display a list of purchases, for example, in a Frame with the following data: Subtotal, Total, Tax, and Purchase Date. This data must be contained within a Label for each product.
- **`TapOrderHistory` Method**: Create this method inside **`MenuViewModel`** and make sure to add the **`OrderHistory`** property to the button.

This exercise aims to put into practice everything you have learned so far. It is very similar to what we have been working on throughout this chapter, so you now have the foundation to tackle it. We wish you good luck and success in this part of the process!

Conclusion

In this chapter, we developed an e-commerce application, one of the most widely used. Throughout the chapter, we analyzed and addressed key aspects of software development, such as file organization and structure, which are essential for project maintenance and scalability. We implemented dependency injection and a route logging system to optimize navigation. We worked with the MVVM design pattern, managed events such as **`OnAppearing`**, and performed CRUD operations on our database. We also delved into object management and, most importantly, enjoyed the creation process. In the next chapter, we will see how to create an ERP application and its main components that are usually found in this type of application.

Chapter 9
Building an ERP App

Introduction

In this chapter, we will develop an ERP-style application, a very common type of application in the business sector. Throughout the chapter, we will analyze and address key aspects of software development, such as organization, file structure, scalability, dependency injection, and a route logging system. We will work with the MVVM design pattern and perform CRUD operations on our SQLite database. By the end of the chapter, you will know how to create an ERP application and the most common parts that make up these applications.

Structure

In this chapter, we will discuss the following topics:

- App Description
- Creating the Application
- Project Structure
- Configuring `SQLite-net-PCL`
- Data Modeling
- Menu Flyout
- `LoginView`
- `UserView`
- `DashBoard`
- `CustomSearchControl`
- `ProductPopup`
- `FormViewModel`
- `SuppliersView`
- `CustomerView`
- `PurchaseView`

- `WarehouseView`
- `SaleView`

App Description

In the previous chapter, we developed an e-commerce application with a TabPages-style menu. Now it is time to create a common but essential application for business resource management. We will develop a simple but functional Enterprise Resource Planning (ERP).

ERP applications are systems designed for planning and managing a company's resources. Their main function is to integrate different processes into a centralized system, optimizing management and information flow. This offers multiple advantages, such as process automation, operational efficiency, error reduction, real-time access to data, and improved decision-making through reporting.

Most ERPs include a set of key features, such as:

- Purchasing for supplier and order control.
- Sales for customer management and billing.
- Warehouses for inventory management.
- Finance to improve account management and budgeting.
- Human Resources for employee and payroll control.

Based on the previous analysis, we will develop such an application. We will implement a Flyout-style menu through **`AppShell`**, and the project will include the following features:

Flyout/Menu:

- **`FlyoutHeader`**: Will display the authenticated user information.
- **`DashBoard`**: Main module that will bring together all the key functions of the ERP.
- **`Account`**: User account administrator.
- **`About`**: Information about the application.
- **`FlyoutFooter`**: Option to log out the user.

Dashboard/Modules:

- **`Suppliers`**: Supplier management (list, add, and delete records).
- **`Sales`**: Customer sales management, with impact on inventory.
- **`Purchase`**: Purchase record, with options to add or remove products from inventory.

- **`Customers`**: Customer management (list, add, and delete records).
- **`Warehouse`**: Inventory management.

As in previous chapters, we will continue using MVVM to develop our application. We will also implement SQLite to efficiently manage data. Without further ado, let us get started!

Creating the Application

We will create a new project using the template **.NET MAUI App** and the framework **.NET 8** or higher. In this case, we will call the project **`ERP_APP`**, but remember that you can name it whatever you prefer. Just be sure to maintain consistency with the name throughout the development process to avoid confusion.

Once our project is created, we will proceed to install the necessary packages for its development. The packages to be installed would be the following:

- **`CommunityToolkit.MAUI` by Microsoft:** Provides a set of additional tools that extend the capabilities of MAUI, such as controls, extensions, and common functionality.
- **`CommunityToolkit.Mvvm` by Microsoft:** It facilitates the implementation of the Model-View-ViewModel (MVVM) pattern, providing a more efficient and clean way to handle business logic and the user interface.
- **`Microsoft.Data.Sqlite` by Microsoft:** Official Microsoft library for working with SQLite databases. It offers robust tools for managing and manipulating local data.
- **`sqlite-net-pcl` by SQLite-net:** A lightweight library for working with SQLite in .NET applications, providing a basic Object-Relational Mapping (ORM).

With these packages, we will have a solid foundation for developing our application. It is essential to make sure we install the latest and most compatible versions of the selected framework when creating our project.

Once the installation is complete, we will proceed to register the **Community Toolkit** for .NET MAUI in the application. This is done in the file **`MauiProgram.cs`**, where we must add the line **`UseMauiCommunityToolkit`** within the **builder** to enable the functionalities of the **toolkit**.

```
var builder = MauiApp.CreateBuilder();
builder
    .UseMauiApp<App>()
    .UseMauiCommunityToolkit()
    .ConfigureFonts(fonts =>
    {
```

```
            fonts.AddFont("OpenSans-Regular.ttf", "OpenSansRegular");

            fonts.AddFont("OpenSans-Semibold.ttf", "OpenSansSemibold");
        });
```

In the next section, we will configure the file structure necessary for our project. We will begin by creating directories or subdirectories in the project root and files such as classes, models, views, and viewmodels.

Project Structure

We will start by creating subdirectories in the project root along with the files we will use and configure throughout development. The structure will be as follows:

- **Controls:** This directory will contain reusable components that are used on most pages.
    - `CustomSearchControl.xaml`
    - `CustomSearchControl.xaml.cs`
    - `ProductoPopup.xaml`
    - `ProductoPopup.xaml.cs`
- **Data**: The directory will contain the class that acts as an ORM to interact more comfortably with SQLite.
    - `DatabaseContext.cs`
- **Models:** It will contain the data models that will facilitate interaction with SQLite and will be used in the application logic.
    - `Customers.cs`
    - `DashBoard.cs`
    - `Item.cs`
    - `ProductsSold.cs`
    - `Sales.cs`
    - `Shopping.cs`
    - `Suppliers.cs`
    - `Users.cs`
    - `WareHouse.cs`
- **ViewModels:** This directory will contain the **`ViewModels`**, which will be responsible for managing the presentation logic and the interaction between the views and the data models.
    - `BaseViewModel.cs(adjust to singular)`

- `CustomerViewModel.cs`
- `DashBoardViewModel.cs`
- `FormViewModel.cs`
- `LoginViewModel.cs`
- `MainViewModel.cs`
- `PurchaseViewModel.cs`
- `SaleViewModel.cs`
- `SuppliersViewModels.cs`
- `UserViewModels.cs`
- `WarehouseViewModel.cs`

- **Views:** This directory will store the views and their code-behind of our application, which will be responsible for displaying the user interface and interacting with the **`ViewModels`**.
  - `AboutView.xaml`
  - `CustomerView.xaml`
  - `DashBoardView.xaml`
  - `FormView.xaml`
  - `LoginView.xaml`
  - `PurchaseView.xaml`
  - `SaleView.xaml`
  - `SuppliersView.xaml`
  - `UserView.xaml`
  - `WarehouseView.xaml`

Having finished creating our directories and files, the next step will be to delete the page generated by default when creating the project, called **`MainPage.xaml`**. This page serves as the initial view in new projects, but since we are defining our own structure and design, it is no longer necessary.

The next step will be to add icons inside the folder **`Resources/Images`** from our project. Below is a list of examples of icon names used in this implementation.

- **`about.png`**
- **`account.png`**
- **`add.png`**
- **`cancel.png`**
- **`customers.png`**

- **`dash.png`**
- **`delete.png`**
- **`sales.png`**
- **`search.png`**
- **`shop.png`**
- **`store.png`**
- **`supplier.png`**
- **`user.png`**
- **`avatar.png`**

Remember that you can customize the icons to your liking, as long as they are in the correct format and in the correct folder to be referenced correctly in your project.

In the next topic, we will configure SQLite-net-PCL as the ORM for our application, enabling efficient database management through an abstraction layer. We will implement a core class to handle CRUD operations and configure its integration into the project.

Configuring `SQLite-net-PCL`

We are going to create the data access class, which will function as a service layer in charge of managing all interactions with the SQLite database, such as queries, modifications, deletions, and table creation, among other operations. To do this, you need to have the NuGet package installed that we reviewed in the previous sections, such as **`Microsoft.Data.Sqlite`** and **`sqlite-net-pcl`**, which will help us efficiently manage the database, simplifying operations and providing us with a more accessible and robust interface.

Within the directory **`Data`**, we had created the class **`DatabaseContext`**, which will be responsible for managing all operations related to the SQLite database. This class will implement the interface **`IAsyncDisposable`**, which will allow efficient management of asynchronous resource release upon completion of database operations.

```
using SQLite;
using System.Linq.Expressions;
namespace ERP_APP.Data {
    public class DatabaseContext : IAsyncDisposable { }
}
```

First, we will define the database. We define the name and location of the database using a constant **`DbName`** and a property **`DbPath`**. We use **`Path.Combine`** to get the full path to the database in the application directory.

```
private const string DbName = "erp.db3";
private static string DbPath => Path.Combine(FileSystem.AppData
Directory, DbName);
```

Then we create a connection to the database using **SQLiteAsyncConnection**. Allowing us to perform asynchronous operations such as reading and writing to the database without blocking the user interface.

```
private SQLiteAsyncConnection _connection;
private SQLiteAsyncConnection Database =>
  (_connection ??= new SQLiteAsyncConnection
  (DbPath, SQLiteOpenFlags.Create | SQLiteOpenFlags.ReadWrite |
SQLiteOpenFlags.SharedCache));
```

Let us create the method **CreateTableIfNotExists**, which will be responsible for creating the table if it does not exist.

```
private async Task CreateTableIfNotExists<TTable>() where TTable :
class, new() {
    await Database.CreateTableAsync<TTable>();
}
```

After creating the previous method, now we are going to create the **GetTableAsync**, which is used to obtain a table from the database, and if it is not found, create it using **CreateTableIfNotExists**

```
private async Task<AsyncTableQuery<TTable>> GetTableAsync<TTable>()
where TTable : class, new() {
    await CreateTableIfNotExists<TTable>();
    return Database.Table<TTable>();
}
```

Once the previous steps are completed, we will create the methods to obtain data:

- **GetAllAsync**: Retrieves all records from a table.
- **GetFileteredAsync**: Retrieves records that match a specific filter.

Both methods use **GetTableAsync** to create the tables if they do not exist.

```
public async Task<IEnumerable<TTable>>
GetAllAsync<TTable>() where TTable : class, new() {
    var table = await GetTableAsync<TTable>();
    return await table.ToListAsync();
}

public async Task<IEnumerable<TTable>>
GetFileteredAsync<TTable>(Expression<Func<TTable, bool>> predicate)
where TTable : class, new() {
    var table = await GetTableAsync<TTable>();
    return await table.Where(predicate).ToListAsync();
}
```

Next, we will create the method **Execute,** which is a generic helper method used to perform actions on the database, such as inserting, updating, or retrieving records, asynchronously:

```
private async Task<TResult> Execute<TTable, TResult>(Func
<Task<TResult>> action) where TTable : class, new() {
     await CreateTableIfNotExists<TTable>();
     return await action();
 }
```

Next, we will create the methods in charge of performing the CRUD operations. The first method is the **GetItemByKeyAsync**, which will be responsible for querying records through the primary key.

```
public async Task<TTable> GetItemByKeyAsync<TTable>(object
primaryKey) where TTable : class, new() {
    try  {
        await CreateTableIfNotExists<TTable>();
        return await Execute<TTable, TTable>(async () => await
Database.GetAsync<TTable>(primaryKey));
    } catch (Exception ex) { Console.WriteLine(ex.ToString()); }
    return null;
}
```

Next, we will add the method **AddItemAsync**, which will be responsible for inserting a new record into the database.

```
public async Task<bool> AddItemAsync<TTable>(TTable item) where
TTable : class, new() {
      await CreateTableIfNotExists<TTable>();
             return await Execute<TTable, bool>(async () =>
               await   Database.InsertAsync(item) > 0);
  }
```

Method **UpdateItemAsync** is responsible for updating an existing record in the database.

```
public async Task<bool> UpdateItemAsync<TTable>(TTable item) where
TTable : class, new() {
     await CreateTableIfNotExists<TTable>();
     return await Database.UpdateAsync(item) > 0;
 }
```

Next, we will create the methods responsible for deleting records, either individually, as a whole, or using their primary key.

```
public async Task<bool> DeleteItemAsync<TTable>(TTable item) where
TTable : class, new() {
    await CreateTableIfNotExists<TTable>();
```

```
        return await Database.DeleteAsync(item) > 0;
    }

    public async Task<bool> DeleteItemByKeyAsync<TTable>(object
    primaryKey) where TTable : class, new() {
        await CreateTableIfNotExists<TTable>();
        return await Database.DeleteAsync<TTable>(primaryKey) > 0;
    }

    public async Task<bool> DeleteAllAsync<TTable>() where TTable :
    class, new() {
        await CreateTableIfNotExists<TTable>();
        return await Database.DeleteAllAsync<TTable>() > 0;
    }
```

Finally, we are going to create the method **DisposeAsync**, which will be responsible for closing the connection to the database when it is no longer needed.

```
public async ValueTask DisposeAsync() => await _connection?.
CloseAsync();
```

The above operations will facilitate the manipulation and management of data in the database in an efficient and flexible manner.

Finally, we inject our class into the file **MauiProgram.cs**, allowing its centralized use throughout the application and facilitating access from any part of the project. To do this, we will use **AddSingleton**, ensuring that **DatabaseContext** has a single instance throughout the life of the application. Injection is performed as follows:

```
builder.Services.AddSingleton<DatabaseContext>();
```

This avoids the unnecessary creation of multiple instances and optimizes the performance of our application.

In the next topic, we will focus on creating the classes that will represent the tables in our database.

Data Modeling

In this section, we will define the classes that will represent the data in our tables. It is important to note that we will not create the tables explicitly, but rather they will be generated automatically when necessary, thanks to the use of **DatabaseContext**.

Before diving into the implementation of the data model, it is important to explore our database's entity-relationship (ER) diagram. Although the model will be simple, we will focus on representing a structure that simulates a realistic situation, as would be used in an ERP system, to ensure that the data and its relationships are consistent and effective.

Our database will be structured with a total of seven tables, covering the main functionalities of the ERP system. The tables that will manage the different areas of the application are described below:

- **Users:** Stores records of system users, allowing authentication.
- **Suppliers:** It stores information related to our suppliers, facilitating purchasing management.
- **Shopping:** Records purchases made from suppliers, allowing inventory and payment control.
- **Warehouses:** It represents the inventory of our warehouses, related to the purchases and sales of products.
- **Customers:** Contains our customers' data, in order to manage sales and customer service.
- **Sales:** Records sales transactions, including details about products sold, prices, and customers.
- **Products_Sold:** It stores the products sold in each transaction, functioning as a sales detail, and is linked to the sales table.

This database schema is designed to simulate the management of the purchasing, sales, and warehouse administration processes of an ERP; the entity-relationship model of the tables is represented in *Figure* 9.1.

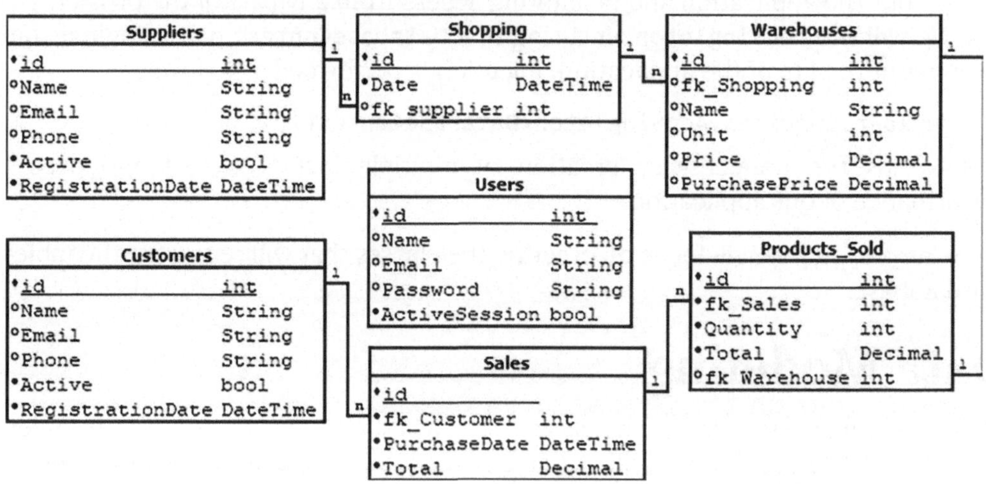

***Figure* 9.1**: *Entity Relationship Model of the ERP_APP database*

Based on the previous analysis, let us begin defining the classes that will represent the data in our tables. As mentioned before, we created the Models directory, which will house the classes that will model our data. In this case, we will start by defining the class **Customers.cs**, which will be used to represent our clients in the database. This class will have the following structure:

```
using SQLite;
namespace ERP_APP.Models
{
    public class Customers
    {
        [PrimaryKey, AutoIncrement]
        public int Id { get; set; }
        public string? Name { get; set; }
        public string? Email { get; set; }
        public string? Phone { get; set; }
        public bool Active { get; set; }
        public DateTime RegistrationDate { get; set; }
    }
}
```

Next, we will define the classes **Users.cs**, which will help us manage the users who can log in to our app. The class will be structured as follows:

```
public class Users
{
    [PrimaryKey, AutoIncrement]
    public int Id { get; set; }
    public string? Name { get; set; }
    public string? Email { get; set; }
    public string? Password { get; set; }
    public bool ActiveSession { get; set; }
}
```

We will define the class **WareHouses.cs**, which will allow us to manage our warehouse inventory. The class structure will be as follows:

```
public class WareHouses{
    [PrimaryKey, AutoIncrement]
    public int Id { get; set; }
    public int fk_Shopping { get; set; }
    public string? Name { get; set; }
    public int Unit { get; set; }
    public Decimal PurchasePrice { get; set; }
    public Decimal Price { get; set; }
    public DateTime RegistrationDate { get; set; }
}
```

We will continue defining the class **Suppliers.cs**. This class will allow us to manage our suppliers' information. This class will have the following structure:

```
public class Suppliers
{
    [PrimaryKey, AutoIncrement]
    public int Id { get; set; }
```

```
        public string? Name { get; set; }
        public string? Email { get; set; }
        public string? Phone { get; set; }
        public bool Active { get; set; }
        public DateTime RegistrationDate { get; set; }
    }
```

Next, we will create the class structure **Sales.cs**, which will be responsible for managing the registration of sales made.

```
public class Sales
{
    [PrimaryKey, AutoIncrement]
    public int Id { get; set; }
    public int fk_Customer { get; set; }
    public DateTime PurchaseDate { get; set; }
    public Decimal Total { get; set; }
}
```

Later, we will define the class **Shopping.cs**, which will allow us to manage purchases made from our suppliers.

```
public class Shopping
{

    [PrimaryKey, AutoIncrement]
    public int Id { get; set; }
    public string guid { get; set; }
    public int fk_supplier { get; set; }
    public string? Total { get; set; }
    public DateTime Date { get; set; }
}
```

Finally, we will define the class **ProductsSold.cs**, which will be responsible for recording the history of products sold, being directly related to the sales made.

```
public class ProductsSold {
    [PrimaryKey, AutoIncrement]
    public int Id { get; set; }
    public int fk_Sales { get; set; }
    public int fk_warehouses { get; set; }
    public int Quantity { get; set; }
    public Decimal Total { get; set; }
}
```

By defining the classes that represent our database tables, we have established the necessary structure for managing our ERP data. Each class is designed to facilitate the efficient management of user, supplier, purchasing, sales, product, and inventory information, meeting our system's requirements.

In the next topic, we will continue with the creation of our Flyout menu, inject the views and **`ViewModels`**, and register the routes of the pages we will navigate to.

Menu Flyout

As mentioned at the beginning of this chapter, we will now configure our menu type, **`Flyout`**, in the application. To do this, we will work directly in the file **`AppShell.xaml`**, where we will define the structure and behavior of the menu.

This menu will include key options such as **`Dashboard`**, **`Account`**, **`About`**, and an option for **`log out`** of the authenticated user. In addition, relevant information about the logged-in user will be displayed, thus improving the browsing experience within the application.

In *Figure* 9.2, the final design of our **`Flyout`** menu is as follows:

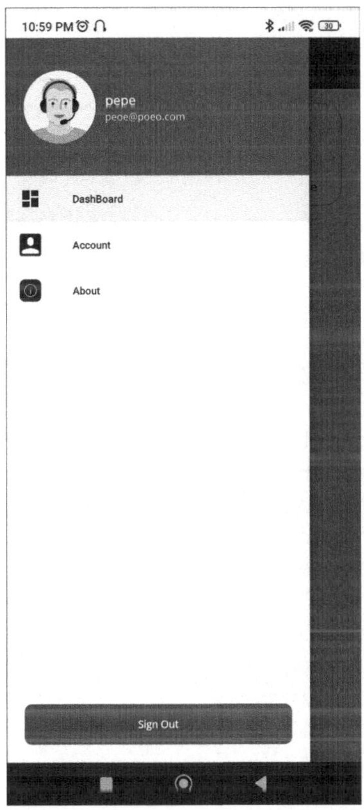

***Figure 9.2**: Flyout Menu Design*

The first thing we will configure in the **`Shell`** will be the appearance of the application. We will define the background color, the text color, and hide the tab bar using the property. **`Shell.TabBarIsVisible="False"`**.

In addition, we will apply styles to the **Status Bar** using the element "**Shell.Behaviors**", where we will set its color and style to maintain a uniform appearance in the user interface.

```
<Shell
    x:Class="ERP_APP.AppShell"
    xmlns="http://schemas.microsoft.com/dotnet/2021/maui"
    xmlns:x="http://schemas.microsoft.com/winfx/2009/xaml"
    xmlns:toolkit="http://schemas.microsoft.com/dotnet/2022/maui/
toolkit"
    xmlns:local="clr-namespace:ERP_APP"
    xmlns:view="clr-namespace:ERP_APP.Views"
    Shell.TabBarIsVisible="False"
    Shell.BackgroundColor="#6200EE"
    Shell.ForegroundColor="White"
    Shell.TitleColor="White"
    Shell.NavBarHasShadow="False">
    <Shell.Behaviors>
        <toolkit:StatusBarBehavior StatusBarColor="#ffffff"
                                   StatusBarStyle="DarkContent" />
    </Shell.Behaviors>
</Shell>
```

Next, we will create the menu header using **Shell.FlyoutHeader**. In this section, we will display the authenticated user's information, including their name (**UserName**) and email (**UserEmail**).

```
<Shell.FlyoutHeader>
    <Grid BackgroundColor="#6200EE"
          Padding="20"
          HeightRequest="150">
        <Grid.ColumnDefinitions>
            <ColumnDefinition Width="80" />
            <ColumnDefinition Width="*" />
        </Grid.ColumnDefinitions>
        <Image Source="avatar.png"
               WidthRequest="100"
               HeightRequest="100"
               Grid.Column="0"
               VerticalOptions="Center"
               HorizontalOptions="Center" />
        <StackLayout Grid.Column="1"
                     VerticalOptions="Center"
                     Padding="10">
            <Label Text="{Binding UserName}"
FontSize="18"
                   TextColor="White"
```

```
                    FontAttributes="Bold" />
                <Label Text="{Binding UserEmail}"
FontSize="14"
                    TextColor="White" />
            </StackLayout>
        </Grid>
    </Shell.FlyoutHeader>
```

Let us define the elements **ShellContent**, which will be responsible for managing the login and user creation screens. These elements are configured with **FlyoutItemIsVisible="False"** and **Shell.FlyoutBehavior="Disabled"**, which means that they will not appear in the side menu and that navigation within the **Flyout** will be disabled for these pages.

With this setting, before loading the main content of the application, the login screen will be displayed first (**LoginView**) or, if necessary, the user registration screen (**UserView**).

```
    <ShellContent Title="Login"
                  ContentTemplate="{DataTemplate view:LoginView}"
                  FlyoutItemIsVisible="False"
                  Shell.FlyoutBehavior="Disabled"
                  Route="LoginPage" />
     <ShellContent Title="CreateUserPage"
                  ContentTemplate="{DataTemplate view:UserView}"
                  FlyoutItemIsVisible="False"
                  Shell.FlyoutBehavior="Disabled"
                  Route="CreateUserPage" />
```

Next, we are going to add the element **FlyoutItem**, using the property **FlyoutDisplayOptions="AsMultipleItems"**, allowing pages defined within the element to appear independently in the menu.

```
<FlyoutItem Route="AccountsPageView"
            FlyoutDisplayOptions="AsMultipleItems">
    <ShellContent Title="DashBoard"
                  Icon="dash.png"
                  ContentTemplate="{DataTemplate view:DashBoardView}" />
    <ShellContent Title="Account"
                  Icon="account.png"
                  ContentTemplate="{DataTemplate view:UserView}" />
    <ShellContent Title="About"
                  Icon="about.png"
                  ContentTemplate="{DataTemplate view:AboutView}" />
</FlyoutItem>
```

Once the previous step is completed, we will add a **FlyoutFooter** to our menu. This item will include a button for logging out. This button will be linked to the command

TapButtonSingOutCommand, which will be responsible for executing the logic necessary to close the user's session when pressed.

```
<Shell.FlyoutFooter>
    <StackLayout Padding="20">
        <Button Text="Sign Out"
                TextColor="White"
                FontAttributes="Bold"
                BackgroundColor="{StaticResource Primary}"
                Command="{Binding TapButtonSingOutCommand}"/>
    </StackLayout>
</Shell.FlyoutFooter>
```

Once the previous steps are complete, the next step is to work on the Shell **ViewModel**. To do this, we will use the files **MainViewModel.cs**, **App.xaml.cs**, and **BaseViewModel.cs**, which we previously added to the project structure.

As a first step, we will modify the class **BaseViewModel** so that it may inherit from **ObservableObject**, a functionality provided by **CommunityToolkit.Mvvm**.

This implementation will allow us to use **INotifyPropertyChanged** without having to implement it manually in each **ViewModel**, optimizing the handling of the user interface state. It will also allow us to take advantage of attributes such as **[ObservableProperty]** and methods such as **SetProperty()**, avoiding unnecessary code repetition and following the principle **DRY (Don't Repeat Yourself).** The class would look like this:

```
using CommunityToolkit.Mvvm.ComponentModel;
namespace ERP_APP.ViewModels;
public partial class BaseViewModel : ObservableObject{ }
```

Now we are going to go to the **MainViewModel**. This class must implement the class **BaseViewModel**, and we will define the variables that we will use for the shell logic. We will also create a property called **_databaseContext**. Inside our constructor, we are going to inject the **DatabaseContext**, leaving the code as follows:

```
using ERP_APP.Models;
namespace ERP_APP.ViewModels;
public partial class MainViewModel : BaseViewModel {
    private DatabaseContext _databaseContext;
    [ObservableProperty] private string? userName;
    [ObservableProperty] private string? userEmail;
    public MainViewModel(DatabaseContext databaseContext) {
        _databaseContext = databaseContext;
    }
}
```

Next, we will add the method **TapButtonSingOut**, which will work as a **Command** using **RelayCommand** for our logout button in the **View** menu.

This method will be responsible for checking whether the user is currently authenticated. If so, it will update their status to log out and redirect the user to the login screen.

```
[RelayCommand]
public async Task TapButtonSingOut() {
    try {
        var result = (await _databaseContext.GetAllAsync<Users>())
              .Where(x => x.ActiveSession == true).FirstOrDefault();
        if (result != null) {
            result.ActiveSession = false;
            var update = (await _databaseContext.UpdateItemAsync
(result));
            if (update)
            {
                await Shell.Current.GoToAsync("//LoginPage");
            }
        }
    }
    catch(Exception ex) {
        Application.Current.MainPage.DisplayAlert("Error",
ex.Message, "OK");
    }
}
```

With the previous step, we finalize the **viewModel** that we will use in the Shell, inside the class **APP.xaml.cs**. We are going to instantiate the **MainViewModel** within the constructor to subsequently create the **bindingContext** in the code-behind of the **APPShell**

```
public partial class App : Application {
        public static MainViewModel ViewModel { get; private set; }
        public App() {
            InitializeComponent();
     //You can add this line, it will help us with dark mode.
            Application.Current.UserAppTheme = AppTheme.Light;
            ViewModel = new MainViewModel(new DatabaseContext());
            MainPage = new AppShell();
        }
    }
```

To finish in the Shell code-behind, we will create the **ViewModel**'s **BindingContext** as follows:

```
namespace ERP_APP {
    public partial class AppShell : Shell {
        public AppShell() {
            InitializeComponent();
```

```
                BindingContext = App.ViewModel;
            }
        }
    }
```

At this point, if you try to run the application, you may encounter compilation errors. This is because we still need some configuration and settings before we can properly test it. In the next topic, we will focus on creating the login and new user registration screens, ensuring the application has a complete and functional authentication flow.

LoginView

We are going to create the page so that the user can log in; this page will be composed of a simple form where it will only ask to add a username and password in addition to two buttons, one to log in and another to redirect the user to the create user page. *Figure* 9.3 shows the design that our page should have.

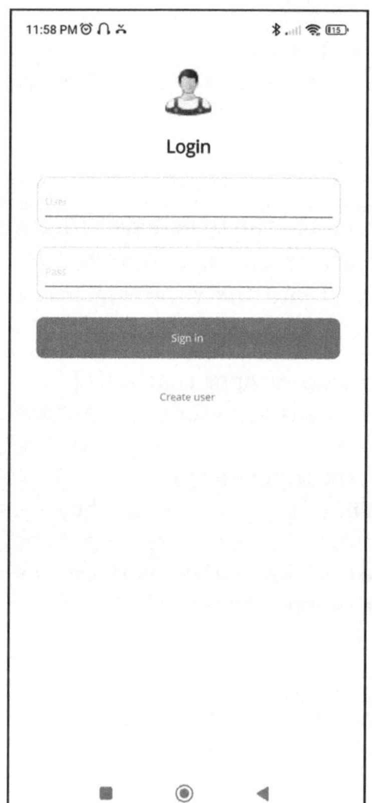

Figure 9.3: *Login page design*

Previously, in the Shell, we configured the **`ContentTemplate`** within the **`ShellContent`**, defining it as a **DataTemplate**. This allows us to ensure that the login page is automatically displayed when the application initializes.

View

Based on *Figure* 9.3, we will start with the design of our page, within the directory **Views** in the file **LoginView.xaml**. Let us configure the login screen layout. On this page, we disable the navigation bar using **Shell.NavBarIsVisible="False"**, which will allow us to have a cleaner and more personalized design for user authentication.

Let us create a login screen using a **VerticalStackLayout**, where we will arrange the elements vertically with spacing between them.

```
<VerticalStackLayout Padding="30" Spacing="20"> </VerticalStack
Layout>
```

Within the **VerticalStackLayout**, let us add an Image component, place a representative image (in this case, supplier.png) at the top, with a size of 50×50 pixels, centered horizontally, and then add the title "**Login**" in a large, bold font size, also centered horizontally.

```
<Image Source="supplier.png"
       HeightRequest="50"
       WidthRequest="50"
       HorizontalOptions="Center" />
<Label Text="Login"
FontSize="24"
       FontAttributes="Bold"
       HorizontalOptions="Center" />
```

Next, we will create the input fields. The first field is an **Entry** where the user can enter their username, and the second field is another **Entry** to enter the password; the latter will have the property **IsPassword="True"**, also wrapped in a **Frame**.

```
<Frame CornerRadius="10" Padding="5" BorderColor="#ccc">
    <Entry  Placeholder="User" TextColor="Black" Text="{Binding
UserName}"/>
</Frame>

<Frame CornerRadius="10" Padding="5" BorderColor="#ccc">
    <Entry Placeholder="Pass" IsPassword="True" TextColor="Black"
        Text="{Binding PassUser}"/>
</Frame>
```

Next, we will add two buttons: the first is "**Sign in**", which will execute the **TapButtonSignInCommand** command when the user clicks it, and the second button is “Create user”, which will execute the command **TapButtonCreateUserCommand**, allowing users to create an account if they do not already have one.

```
<Button Text="Sign in" BackgroundColor="#007AFF" TextColor="White"
       Command="{Binding TapButtonSignInCommand}"/>
<Button Text="Create user" BackgroundColor="#ffffff" TextColor="#007AFF"
       Command="{Binding TapButtonCreateUserCommand}" />
```

In this way, we finish the page of **login**, and we will continue with the creation of the **ViewModel**.

ViewModel

In the **LoginViewModel.cs** class located in the **ViewModels** directory, we are going to implement the class **BaseViewModel**, and we will define the variables that we will use for the logic of our login page. We will also create a property called **_databaseContext**, to inject the **DatabaseContext** inside the constructor, leaving the class as follows:

```
public partial class LoginViewModel : BaseViewModel
{
    private DatabaseContext _databaseContext;
    [ObservableProperty] private string? userName;
    [ObservableProperty] private string? passUser;
    public LoginViewModel(DatabaseContext databaseContext) {
        _databaseContext = databaseContext;
    }
}
```

Then we will create the **OnAppearing** method that will be in charge of executing when the page starts. This method is in charge of validating if a session is already started; if it is true, it will send the user to the **AccountsPageView** (it is the Route defined in the **FlyoutItem**). The following is how the code should look:

```
public async Task OnAppearing() {
    try {
        var result = (await _databaseContext.GetAllAsync<Users>())
            .Where(x => x.ActiveSession == true).FirstOrDefault();
        if (result != null) {
            App.ViewModel.UserName = result.Name;
App.ViewModel.UserEmail = result.Email;
            await Shell.Current.GoToAsync("//AccountsPageView");
        }
    }
    catch (Exception ex){Console.WriteLine(ex.ToString());}
}
```

Next, we will add the methods that will be responsible for serving as **`Command`**. The first is the **`TapButtonSignIn`**, which will be responsible for validating the data added in the form and logging in, and the second method, the **`TapButtonCreateUser`**, will be responsible for showing the create user page.

```
[RelayCommand]
public async Task TapButtonSignIn(){
    try{
 if (!string.IsNullOrWhiteSpace(UserName) && !string.IsNullOr-
WhiteSpace(PassUser))
    {
      var result = (await _databaseContext.GetAllAsync<Users>())
      .Where(x => x.Name == UserName && x.Password == PassUser).
FirstOrDefault();
            if(result != null){
                result.ActiveSession = true;
                var update = (await _databaseContext.UpdateItem
Async(result));
                if(update){
                    App.ViewModel.UserName = result.Name;
App.ViewModel.UserEmail = result.Email;
                    await Shell.Current.GoToAsync("//Accounts
PageView");
                    return;
                }
            }
        }
    }catch (Exception ex){
        Application.Current.MainPage.DisplayAlert("Error",
ex.Message, "OK");
    }
Application.Current.MainPage.DisplayAlert("Invalid user", "Incorrect
username or password", "OK");
}
[RelayCommand]
public async Task TapButtonCreateUser(){
    await Shell.Current.GoToAsync("//CreateUserPage");
}
```

The last steps are to inject our **`ViewModel`** and create the **`BindingContext`** in the View, in the **`MauiProgram`**. The View must be injected as the **`ViewModel`** as follows:

```
builder.Services.AddSingleton<LoginView, LoginViewModel>();
```

Finally, in the **code-behind** of the **`LoginView`** we are going to create the **`BindingContext`** and we will add the method **`OnAppearing`**.

```
public partial class LoginView : ContentPage {
   public LoginView(LoginViewModel viewmodel)    {
```

```
            InitializeComponent();
            this.BindingContext = viewmodel;
        }
         protected override void OnAppearing() {
             base.OnAppearing();
             if (this.BindingContext is LoginViewModel viewModel){
                 viewModel.OnAppearing();
             }
         }
    }
```

If you have made it this far, congratulations! We have completed creating our page. In the next topic, we will focus on creating the screens for registering new users, ensuring the application has a complete and functional authentication flow.

UserView

The **UserView** page will have two functionalities: updating and creating the user account. *Figure* 9.4 shows the design that our View will have.

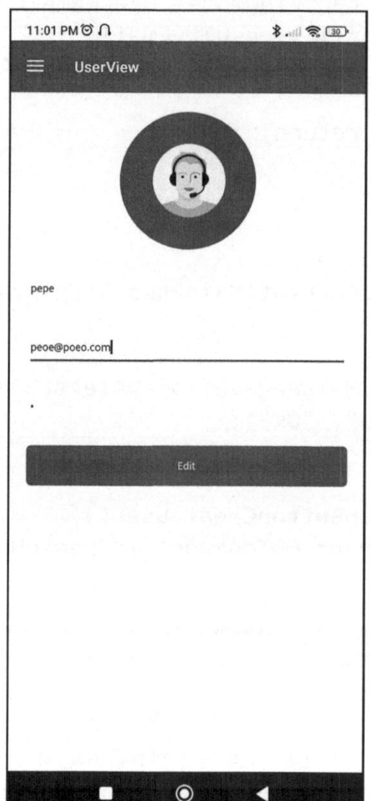

***Figure 9.4**: UserView page layout*

The **View** will only have a simple form composed of three entry elements to add and display user data and a button to save the form data.

View

Inside the **Views** directory, in the file **UserView.xaml**, we configure the structure of the user screen. On this page, we set a **Title** to define the name of the view.

```
<ContentPage xmlns="http://schemas.microsoft.com/dotnet/2021/maui"
             xmlns:x="http://schemas.microsoft.com/winfx/2009/xaml"
             x:Class="ERP_APP.Views.UserView"
             Title="UserView">
</ContentPage>
```

Next, we wrap all the content in a **ScrollView** to allow for vertical scrolling in case the elements do not fit on the screen. Within this, we use a **VerticalStackLayout** with a spacing of 20 and a padding of 20 to arrange the elements vertically and with separation between them.

```
<ScrollView>
    <VerticalStackLayout Spacing="20"
                         Padding="20">
    </VerticalStackLayout>
</ScrollView>
```

In the **VerticalStackLayout**, we will add a centered profile image, contained within a Grid. First, we add a 150×150 pixel ellipse as the background. On top of this, we place a 100×100 pixel image, aligned to the center.

```
<Grid HorizontalOptions="Center"
      VerticalOptions="Start">
    <Ellipse WidthRequest="150"
             HeightRequest="150"
             Fill="{StaticResource Primary}" />
    <Image Source="avatar.png"
           WidthRequest="100"
           HeightRequest="100"
           VerticalOptions="Center"
           HorizontalOptions="Center" />
</Grid>
```

After the profile picture, we added three input fields (**Entry**). The first allows you to enter the username (**UserName**), the second the email address (**Email**) with a keyboard specialized for email addresses (**Keyboard="Email"**), and the third is a password field (**Pass**) with the **IsPassword="True"** property to hide the entered text.

```
<Entry Placeholder="User Name" Text="{Binding UserName}" />
<Entry Placeholder="Email Address" Keyboard="Email" Text="{Binding
Email}"/>
<Entry Placeholder="Password" IsPassword="True" Text="{Binding Pass}"
/>
```

Finally, we add a button with dynamic text Binding **TextButtonSaved**. This button will execute the command **TapSavedCommand** when pressed.

```
<Button Text="{Binding TextButtonSaved}"
        BackgroundColor="#3b5998"
        TextColor="White"
        CornerRadius="5"
        HorizontalOptions="Fill"
        Command="{Binding TapSavedCommand}" />
```

With this, we finish building the user page, and in the next step, we will proceed to implement its **ViewModel**.

ViewModel

In class **UserViewModel**, as in the previous **viewModels**, this class must be **BaseViewModel**. We will create the properties and inject the **DatabaseContext** as shown in the following code:

```
public partial class UserViewModel : BaseViewModel
{
    private DatabaseContext _databaseContext;
    private int _idUser;
    [ObservableProperty] public string userName;
    [ObservableProperty] public string email;
    [ObservableProperty] public string pass;
    [ObservableProperty] public bool createSession;
    [ObservableProperty] public bool isVisibleButtonLogin;
    [ObservableProperty] public string? textButtonSaved;
    public UserViewModel(DatabaseContext databaseContext) {
        _databaseContext = databaseContext;
        UserName = string.Empty;
        Email = string.Empty;
        Pass = string.Empty;
        CreateSession = false;
        IsVisibleButtonLogin = true;
        TextButtonSaved = "Create Session";
    }
}
```

Then we will add the method **OnAppearing**, which runs when the view is displayed on the screen. Its purpose is to clear the input fields and check if there is an active user session. If a logged-in user is found, the data is populated in the interface, and the button text is changed to "**Edit**"; this will allow the form to act for editing the user's account. Otherwise, the button text will remain as "**Create Session**" and will be used to create users.

```
public async Task OnAppearing() {
    try {
        UserName = string.Empty;
        Email = string.Empty;
        Pass =string.Empty;
        _idUser = 0;
        var result = (await _databaseContext.GetAllAsync<Users>())
            .Where(x => x.ActiveSession == true).FirstOrDefault();
        if (result != null) {
            TextButtonSaved = "Edit";
            UserName = result.Name ?? string.Empty;
            Email = result.Email ?? string.Empty;
            Pass = result.Password ?? string.Empty;
            _idUser = result.Id;
        }

    } catch (Exception ex){Console.WriteLine(ex.ToString()); }
}
```

The command is added to **TapSaved**. It runs when the user presses the save button. First, it validates that the fields are not empty. Then, if the user does not exist in the database, a new record is created and the user is redirected to the login page. If the user already exists (in edit mode), their information is updated.

```
[RelayCommand]
public async Task TapSaved(){ try{
        var user = string.IsNullOrWhiteSpace(UserName);
        var email = string.IsNullOrWhiteSpace(Email);
        var pass = string.IsNullOrWhiteSpace(Pass);
        if (!user && !email && !pass){
            var newUser = new Users() {
                Name = UserName,
                Email = Email,
                Password = Pass,
                ActiveSession = TextButtonSaved == "Edit" ? true :
false
            };
            if (TextButtonSaved != "Edit"){
                var insert = (await _databaseContext.AddItem
Async(newUser));
                if(insert){
```

```
                    await Shell.Current.GoToAsync("//LoginPage");
                }else{
Application.Current.MainPage.DisplayAlert
("Create User", "Faild create user", "OK");
                }
            }else{
                newUser.Id = _idUser;
                var update = (await _databaseContext.UpdateItem
Async(newUser));
                if (update){
Application.Current.MainPage.DisplayAlert
("Update", "Update succefull", "OK");
                    App.ViewModel.UserName = newUser.Name;
App.ViewModel.UserEmail = newUser.Email;
                }else{
                    Application.Current.MainPage.DisplayAlert
("Update", "Error Update", "OK");
                }
            }
        }
    }catch (Exception ex){
        Application.Current.MainPage.DisplayAlert("Error",
ex.Message, "OK");
    }
}
```

As the last step is to inject the **View** and the **ViewModel** and create the **BindingContext** in the View, in the **MauiProgram**, the **View** and **ViewModel** must be injected as follows:

```
builder.Services.AddSingleton<UserView, UserViewModel>();
```

Finally, in the **code-behind** of the **UserView** we are going to create the **BindingContext** and we will add the method **OnAppearing**.

```
public partial class UserView : ContentPage {
    public UserView(UserViewModel viewModel){
     InitializeComponent();
     this.BindingContext = viewModel;
    }
    protected override void OnAppearing(){
        base.OnAppearing();
        if (this.BindingContext is UserViewModel viewModel){
            viewModel.OnAppearing();
        }
    }
}
```

If you have made it this far, congratulations! We have completed creating our page. In the next topic, we will focus on creating the **`Dashboard`** screen that will display the app's feature options.

DashBoard

The **`Dashboard`** page will be responsible for displaying the options for the different functionalities that the ERP will have. *Figure* 9.5 shows the design that our View will have.

***Figure* 9.5**: *UserView page layout*

The view uses a **`CollectionView`** to organize and display a grid of options, each represented by an image and a title.

Inside the file **DashBoardView.xaml**, we configure the interface using a **VerticalStackLayout** containing a **CollectionView**. This component allows you to display dashboard options in an organized manner in a three-column grid layout.

```
<ContentPage xmlns="http://schemas.microsoft.com/dotnet/2021/maui"
             xmlns:x="http://schemas.microsoft.com/winfx/2009/xaml"
             x:Class="ERP_APP.Views.DashBoardView"
             xmlns:models="clr-namespace:ERP_APP.Models"
             Title="DashBoard">
    <VerticalStackLayout>
        <CollectionView ItemsSource="{Binding OptionDashBoard}"
                        VerticalOptions="FillAndExpand"
                        x:Name="CollectionItems"
                        Margin="15">
            <CollectionView.ItemsLayout>
                <GridItemsLayout Orientation="Vertical"
                                 Span="3"
                                 VerticalItemSpacing="15"/>
            </CollectionView.ItemsLayout>
            <CollectionView.ItemTemplate>
                <DataTemplate x:DataType="models:DashBoard">
                </DataTemplate>
            </CollectionView.ItemTemplate>
        </CollectionView>
    </VerticalStackLayout>
</ContentPage>
```

In **DataTemplate**, we will add a structure with the component **frame** and a **VerticalStackLayout**, which will act as a container for the card.

```
<Frame Grid.Row="0" CornerRadius="20" BackgroundColor="White"Border-
Color="#E0E0E0"
       WidthRequest="110"  Padding="10" HasShadow="False">
    <VerticalStackLayout Spacing="2" HorizontalOptions="Center">
    </VerticalStackLayout>
</Frame>
```

Within the **VerticalStackLayout**, we will add an avatar that will display the representative image of the module's functionality. This avatar will be contained within a **Frame** circular to improve its presentation and also implements a **TapGestureRecognizer**, which will allow you to interact with the selected option.

```
<Frame Padding="15,5" WidthRequest="70" HeightRequest="70"
CornerRadius="40"
  BorderColor="Transparent" HorizontalOptions="Center" Vertical
Options="Center">
    <Image Source="{Binding Image}" Aspect="AspectFit"
           VerticalOptions="Center" HorizontalOptions="Center">
```

```
            <Image.GestureRecognizers>
                <TapGestureRecognizer Command="{Binding Path = Binding-
Context.TapButtonOptionCommand, Source={Reference CollectionItems}}"
                                      CommandParameter="{Binding Page}"
/>
            </Image.GestureRecognizers>
        </Image>
        <Frame.GestureRecognizers>
            <TapGestureRecognizer Command="{Binding Path = BindingCon-
text.TapButtonOptionCommand, Source={Reference CollectionItems}}"
                                  CommandParameter="{Binding Page}" />
        </Frame.GestureRecognizers>
</Frame>
```

Finally, we add a **Label** with the Binding Text to display the option titles.

```
 <Label Text="{Binding Title}" HorizontalTextAlignment="Center"
   FontSize="16" FontAttributes="Bold" TextColor="Black"Input
Transparent="True" />
```

With this, we finish building the page, and we will continue with the **ViewModel**.

ViewModel

In class **DashBoardViewModel**, just like in the previous **ViewModels**, this class must have a **BaseViewModel**, as shown in the following code:

```
public partial class DashBoardViewModel : BaseViewModel
{
   [ObservableProperty] ObservableCollection<DashBoard> optionDash-
Board;
}
```

The command is added **TapButtonOption**, which will allow asynchronous navigation to a page according to the received parameter.

```
 [RelayCommand]
        public async Task TapButtonOption(string page) =>
                await Shell.Current.GoToAsync($"{page}");
```

Then we will add the method **OnAppearing**. It runs when the view is displayed on screen and will be responsible for adding the elements to the **ObservableCollection**.

```
public void OnAppearing(){
     OptionDashBoard = new ObservableCollection<DashBoard>(){
          new DashBoard { Title = "Supplers", Image = "supplier.png",
                          Page = "SupplersPage"},
          new DashBoard { Title = "Sale", Image = "sales.png",
                          Page = "SalePage"},
```

```
            new DashBoard { Title = "Purchase", Image = "shop.png",
                            Page = "PurchasePage"},
            new DashBoard { Title = "Customer", Image = "customers.png",
                            Page = "CustomerPage"},
            new DashBoard { Title = "Warehouse", Image = "store.png",
                            Page = "WarehousePage"},
        };
    }
```

It is very problematic if you get an error in the last step; this is because we need to add the **DashBoard** model. Within the **Models** directory, we will create the **DashBoard** class with the following properties:

```
namespace ERP_APP.Models{
    public class DashBoard {
        public string? Title { get; set; }
        public string? Image { get; set; }
        public string? Page {  get; set; }
    }
}
```

The last steps are to inject the **View** and the **ViewModel**, create the page route record, and create the **BindingContext** in the View.

In the archive **MauiProgram.cs**, we record the navigation route for **DashBoardView**, and we will configure dependency injection for both the view and its ViewModel.

```
Routing.RegisterRoute(nameof(DashBoardView), typeof(DashBoardView));
builder.Services.AddSingleton<DashBoardView, DashBoardViewModel>();
```

Finally, in the **code-behind** of the **UserView**, we are going to create the **BindingContext** and we will add the method **OnAppearing**.

```
public partial class DashBoardView : ContentPage{
   public DashBoardView(DashBoardViewModel bindigViewModel){
         InitializeComponent();
         this.BindingContext = bindigViewModel;
   }
     protected override void OnAppearing(){
         base.OnAppearing();
         if (this.BindingContext is DashBoardViewModel viewModel){
             viewModel.OnAppearing();
         }
     }
}
```

If you have made it this far, congratulations! We have completed creating our dashboard page. In the next topic, we will focus on creating a **ContentView** Control that we can reuse on different ERP pages. Let us keep moving forward!

CustomSearchControl

We are going to build a reusable component similar to a **SearchBar**, which we can integrate into various pages of our application. An example of our control is shown in *Figure 9.6*.

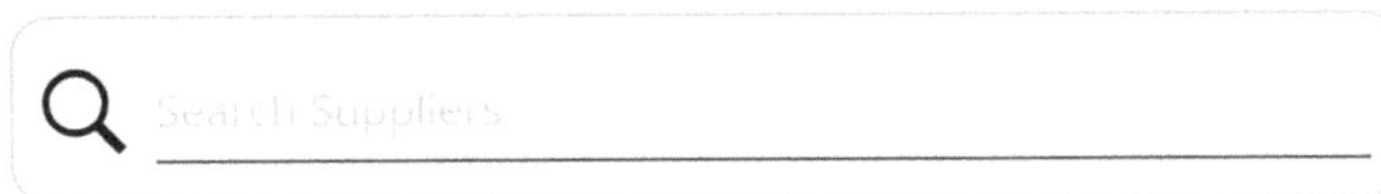

***Figure 9.6**: Design of the CustomSearchControl*

Inside the **CustomSearchControl.xaml** file, located in the Controls directory, we will add a **ContentView** that will contain the following layout:

A Frame, which will provide a container with rounded edges and visual separation.

A Grid with three columns, where:

- **Column 0**: Will contain an image (**search.png**) as a search icon.
- **Column 1**: Will include an Entry where the user can write their search.
- **Column 2**: Will display an image (**cancel.png**) with a **GestureRecognizer** that will allow you to cancel the search.

Next, we will show the implementation of the component:

```
<ContentView xmlns="http://schemas.microsoft.com/dotnet/2021/maui"
             xmlns:x="http://schemas.microsoft.com/winfx/2009/xaml"
             x:Class="ERP_APP.Controls.CustomSearchControl">
    <Frame Padding="5,2"
           Margin="10,10,10,0"
           CornerRadius="10">
        <Grid ColumnDefinitions="20, *,auto">
            <Image Source="search.png"
                   WidthRequest="30"
                   HeightRequest="30"
                   Margin="10,0,0,0"
                   VerticalOptions="Center" />
            <Entry Placeholder="Search Suppliers"
                   Grid.Column="1"
                   Text="{Binding SearchText}"
                   Margin="10,0,0,0"
FontSize="15"
                   VerticalOptions="Center"
                   HorizontalOptions="FillAndExpand"
                   BackgroundColor="Transparent" />
            <Image Source="cancel.png"  Grid.Column="2"
                   WidthRequest="25"
```

```
                    IsVisible="{Binding CancelIsVisible}"
                    HeightRequest="25"
                    Margin="5,0,5,0"
                    VerticalOptions="Center">
                 <Image.GestureRecognizers>
              <TapGestureRecognizer Command="{Binding TapButton
CancelCommand}" />
                 </Image.GestureRecognizers>
            </Image>
        </Grid>
    </Frame>
</ContentView>
```

So that the **CustomSearchControl** works correctly, we must add the logic in a **ViewModel**, where we will handle the state of the search text and the visibility of the cancel button. This indicates that in each **ContentPage** that we use the component, we must add the following elements to its **ViewModel**:

```
// Search text
    [ObservableProperty]private string? searchText = string.Empty;
// Controls the visibility of the cancel button
    [ObservableProperty] private bool cancelIsVisible = false;
//It will detect changes in the search text and execute an action
    partial void OnSearchTextChanged(string? value){}
//Command to clear the search text
    [RelayCommand]
    public void TapButtonCancel() {
      SearchText = string.Empty;
    }
```

Besides, so that the **ContentView** can use **ViewModel**, we must make sure to link it on the page where we use it. In the file **XAML** where we want to use the component **CustomSearchControl**, we need to add a namespace declaration (**xmlns**). For example:

```
xmlns:controls="clr-namespace:ERP_APP.Controls"
```

Once this line is added, we can use our **CustomSearchControl** inside the view as follows:

```
<controls:CustomSearchControl />
```

If you have made it this far, congratulations! We have completed creating the component.

ProductPopup

Within the directory **Control** in the file **ProductoPopup.xaml**. Let us create a popup window designed to efficiently capture new product data and be easy to use for entering the necessary information. This window includes the following fields:

- **`Product name`**
- **`Purchase price`**
- **`Sale price`**
- **`Units`**

And a button to save the entered data.

When the "**`Save`**" button is pressed, the form is validated, and if the data is correct, a custom event is fired that sends the data to the component that opened the window.

This allows the popup to be flexibly integrated into any view that needs to dynamically add products.

You can see the complete code for the popup, both in XAML and C#, in the project repository at **`Controls/ProductoPopup.xaml`**.

FormViewModel

This page will display a form based on the parameters received. Instead of creating separate pages for each form, we will create a dynamic view that displays the corresponding form based on the provided parameters, thus optimizing development time.

The page **`FormView`** will be responsible for displaying the forms corresponding to the different functionalities that the ERP will have, as shown in *Figure* 9.7.

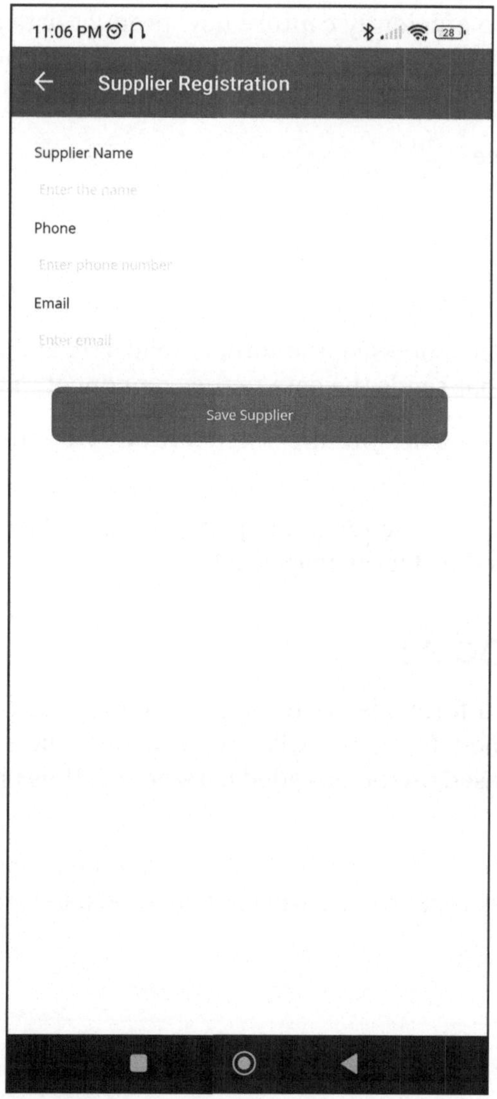

Figure 9.7: *FormView page design*

The design is organized in a **ScrollView** with a **StackLayout**, which contains several forms for the specific functionalities of the system (Supplier, Customer, Purchase, and Sale).

```
<ContentPage xmlns="http://schemas.microsoft.com/dotnet/2021/maui"
             xmlns:x="http://schemas.microsoft.com/winfx/2009/xaml"
             x:Class="ERP_APP.Views.FormView"
             Title="{Binding TitleView}">
    <ScrollView> <StackLayout></StackLayout> </ScrollView>
</ContentPage>
```

The view will use a **ScrollView** to allow the content to be scrollable, adapting to the screen size. Within this **ScrollView**, a **StackLayout** will be added that organizes the forms vertically.

The **StackLayout** will contain the different forms for **Supplier**, **Customer**, **Purchase**, and **Sales**. Each one is organized within a **VerticalStackLayout** and is dynamically displayed or hidden based on the value of the bindings (**IsSupplier**, **IsCustomer**, **IsPurchase**, **IsSale**). Each form will have input fields such as **Entry**, **Picker**, and **DatePicker**, as well as buttons that execute commands, such as **SaveDataCommand**, to save the form data.

The Supplier form contains fields for the supplier's name, phone number, and email address.

```
<!—Supplier Form →
<VerticalStackLayout Padding="20"
                     IsVisible="{Binding IsSupplier}">
    <Label Text="Supplier Name"
           FontSize="Medium" />
    <Entry Text="{Binding SupplierName}"
           Placeholder="Enter the name" />
    <Label Text="Phone"
           FontSize="Medium" />
    <Entry Text="{Binding SupplierPhone}"
           Placeholder="Enter phone number"
           Keyboard="Telephone" />
    <Label Text="Email"
           FontSize="Medium" />
    <Entry Text="{Binding SupplierEmail}"
           Placeholder="Enter email"
           Keyboard="Email" />
    <Button Text="Save Supplier"
            BackgroundColor="Green"
            TextColor="White"
            Margin="15"
            Command="{Binding SaveDataCommand}"
            CommandParameter="Supplier"/>
</VerticalStackLayout>
```

The Supplier Customer form will have fields for the customer's name, phone number, and email.

```
<!—Customer Form →
<VerticalStackLayout Padding="20"
                     IsVisible="{Binding IsCustomer}">
    <Label Text="Name"
           FontSize="Medium" />
    <Entry Text="{Binding CustomerName}"
```

```
                Placeholder="Enter name" />
        <Label Text="Email"
                FontSize="Medium" />
        <Entry Text="{Binding CustomerEmail}"
                Placeholder="Enter email"
                Keyboard="Email" />
        <Label Text="Phone"
                FontSize="Medium" />
        <Entry Text="{Binding CustomerPhone}"
                Placeholder="Enter phone number"
                Keyboard="Telephone" />
        <Button Text="Save Customer"
                 BackgroundColor="Blue"
                 TextColor="White"
                 Command="{Binding SaveDataCommand}"
                 CommandParameter="Customer" />
    </VerticalStackLayout>
```

Within the form of **Purchase**, the fields are used to select the supplier, date, and products purchased.

```
   <!—Purchase Form →
   <VerticalStackLayout Padding="20"
                        IsVisible="{Binding IsPurchase}">
       <Label Text="Supplier"
               FontSize="Medium" />

       <Frame Padding="10,1"
               Margin="0,10,0,10"
               CornerRadius="10">
           <VerticalStackLayout>
               <Picker Title="Select an Options"
                        ItemsSource="{Binding Options}"
                        ItemDisplayBinding="{Binding Name}"
                        SelectedItem="{Binding SelectedSupplier,
  Mode=TwoWay}" />
           </VerticalStackLayout>
       </Frame>

       <Label Text="Date"
               FontSize="Medium" />
       <DatePicker Date="{Binding PurchaseDate}" />

       <Button Text="Add product"
                Margin="0,10"
                BackgroundColor="Green"
                TextColor="White"
                Command="{Binding NewProductCommand}"
```

```
            CommandParameter="Purchase" />

    <Label Text="{Binding Produts}"
           LineBreakMode="WordWrap"
           Padding="10"
           Margin="0,10"/>

    <Label Text="Total"
           FontSize="Medium" />

    <Entry Text="{Binding PurchaseTotal}"
           Placeholder="$0.00"
           Keyboard="Numeric"
           IsEnabled="False"
           Margin="0,10" />

    <Button Text="Save Purchase"
            BackgroundColor="Purple"
            TextColor="White"
            Command="{Binding SaveDataCommand}"
            CommandParameter="Purchase" />
</VerticalStackLayout>
```

Finally, we will add the sales form with fields for selecting the product, unit, and warehouse-related data.

```
    <!—Sale Form →
     <VerticalStackLayout Padding="20"
                          IsVisible="{Binding IsSale}">
         <Label Text="Product"
                FontSize="Medium" />
         <Frame Padding="10,1"
                Margin="0,10,0,10"
                CornerRadius="10">
             <VerticalStackLayout>
                 <Picker Title="Select an Options"
                         ItemsSource="{Binding OptionsWareHouses}"
                         ItemDisplayBinding="{Binding Name}"
                         SelectedItem="{Binding SelectedWareHouses,
Mode=TwoWay}" />
             </VerticalStackLayout>
         </Frame>
         <Label Text="Unit"
                FontSize="Medium" />
         <Entry Text="{Binding UnitSales}"
                Placeholder="Enter location"
                Keyboard="Numeric" />
         <Button Text="Save Warehouse"
```

```
                  BackgroundColor="Teal"
                  TextColor="White"
                  Command="{Binding SaveDataCommand}"
                  CommandParameter="Warehouse" />
      </VerticalStackLayout>
```

With this, we finish building the page, and we will continue with the **ViewModel**.

ViewModel

The class **FormViewModel** inherits from **BaseViewModel** and implements the interface **IqueryAttributable**, which allows for the reception of navigation parameters. The implementation is shown below:

```
public partial class FormViewModel : BaseViewModel, IqueryAttribut-
able
{
    public void ApplyQueryAttributes(Idictionary<string, object>
query){}
    private DatabaseContext _databaseContext;
    public FormViewModel(DatabaseContext databaseContext) {
         _databaseContext = databaseContext;
    }
}
```

Next, we will define the variables and properties required for each of the forms. Since there are so many, we recommend checking the application repository for a detailed review.

Once the properties have been added, we will configure **ApplyQueryAttributes** to receive the navigation parameters, which will enable the corresponding form and execute the necessary functions. To do this, we will use a structure **switch**, ensuring that each type of form (**Supplier**, **Purchase**, **Sale**, and **Customer**) is handled correctly and the corresponding actions are executed in an organized and efficient manner.

```
Public void ApplyQueryAttributes(Idictionary<string, object> query){
IsPurchase = false;
    IsSale = false;
    IsCustomer = false;
    IsSupplier = false;
    _parameter = string.Empty;
    _formType = query["typeForm"] as string;
    TitleView = $"{_formType} Registration";
    if(!string.IsNullOrEmpty(_formType)) {
        switch (_formType)  {
            case "Supplier":
                IsSupplier = true;
                break;
```

```
            case "Purchase":
                IsPurchase = true;
                PurchaseDate = DateTime.Now;
                PurchaseTotal = string.Empty;
                Produts = string.Empty;
                _wareHouses = new List<WareHouses>();
                _ = GetSupplier();
                break;
            case "Sale":
                IsSale = true;
                UnitSales = string.Empty;
                SelectedWareHouses = new WareHouses();
                OptionsWareHouses = new ObservableCollection
<WareHouses>();
                _ = GetProducts();
                break;
            case "Customer":
                IsCustomer = true;
                break;
        }
    }
}
```

For now, you may see some errors, as we still need to add some functionality. Next, we will create a private **async** method called **GetSupplier**, which will be responsible for consulting the active providers in the table **Suppliers**.

```
Private async Task GetSupplier(){
    string message = string.Empty;
    try{
        Options = new ObservableCollection<Suppliers>();
       var result = (await _databaseContext.GetAllAsync<Suppliers>()).
Where(x =>
                x.Active == true).Select(x => new { x.Id, x.Name });
        if (result.Any()){
            foreach(var item in result){
                Options.Add(new Suppliers { Id = item.Id, Name =
item.Name });
            }
            return;
        }
message = "Suppliers could not be consulted. Please check if there are
            records created.";
    }catch (Exception ex){message = ex.Message;}
    Application.Current.MainPage.DisplayAlert("Forms", message,
"OK");
}
```

Afterwards, we will implement the method **GetProducts**, which will be responsible for querying the products stored in the table **WareHouses**, and save them in an **ObservableCollection**. This collection will be used later in the component **Picker** of sight.

```
 Private async Task GetProducts() {
      string message = string.Empty;
      try{
           OptionsWareHouses = new ObservableCollection<WareHouses>();
           var result = (await _databaseContext.GetAllAsync<Ware
Houses>());
           if (result.Any()){
                foreach (var item in result){
                  OptionsWareHouses.Add(new WareHouses { Id = item.Id,
Name =
                  item.Name, Unit = item.Unit, PurchasePrice = item.
PurchasePrice });
                }
                return;
           }
           message = "WareHouses could not be consulted. Please check
if there are
records created.";
      }catch (Exception ex){message = ex.Message;}
      Application.Current.MainPage.DisplayAlert("Forms", message,
"OK");
 }
```

IsValid: Is responsible for validating whether the provided fields are empty or null, returning false if all values are valid.

```
Private bool IsValid(params string[] fields) => fields.All(val =>
!string.IsNullOrEmpty(val));
```

SaveData: This method handles the save logic for different forms (**Supplier**, **Purchase**, **Sale**, **Customer**). Depending on the type of form, it validates the fields and executes the corresponding function.

```
[RelayCommand]
public async Task SaveData(string form)
{
    var message = "There are empty elements in the form";
    var status = "Success";
    switch (_formType){
        case "Supplier":
            if (IsValid(SupplierName, SupplierPhone, SupplierEmail))
                message = await SupplierFunction();           break;
        case "Purchase":
```

```
            if (IsValid(SelectedSupplier.Name ?? string.Empty,
PurchaseTotal,
                Produts))
                message = await PurchaseFunction();
            break;
        case "Sale":
            if (IsValid(SelectedWareHouses.Name ?? string.Empty,
UnitSales))
            {
                message = await this.SalesFunction();
                if (message == "product successfully added")
                    return;
            }
            break;
        case "Customer":
            if (IsValid(CustomerName, CustomerEmail, CustomerPhone))
{
                message = await CustomerFunction();
            }
            break;
        default:
            status = "Error";
            message = "invalid page";
            break;
    }
    Application.Current.MainPage.DisplayAlert("status", message,
"OK");
}
```

Afterwards, we will define the method **SupplierFunction**, which is responsible for registering a new supplier in the database if one does not already exist.

```
Private async Task<string> SupplierFunction()
{
    string message = string.Empty;
    try{
        var newSupplier = new Suppliers(){
            Name = SupplierName,
            Email = SupplierEmail,
            Phone = SupplierPhone,
            Active = true,
            RegistrationDate = DateTime.Now
        };
        var result = (await _databaseContext.GetAllAsync<Suppliers>())
            .Where(x => x.Name == newSupplier.Name &&
       x.Active == true).FirstOrDefault();
        if (result == null){
```

```
            if (await _databaseContext.AddItemAsync(newSupplier)){
                SupplierName = string.Empty;
                SupplierEmail = string.Empty;
                SupplierPhone = string.Empty;
                return "Supplier saved successfully";
            }
        }
        message = "This supplier is already registered";
    }catch (Exception ex){message = ex.Message;}
    return message;
}
```

PurchaseFunction: This function records a new purchase in the database, ensuring that the products are correctly associated.

```
Private async Task<string> PurchaseFunction(){
    string message = string.Empty;
    try{
        var shopping = new Shopping(){
            fk_supplier = SelectedSupplier.Id,
            guid = Guid.NewGuid().ToString(),
            Date = DateTime.Now,
            Total = PurchaseTotal
        };
        if (await _databaseContext.AddItemAsync(shopping)) {
var idNewShopping = (await _databaseContext.GetAllAsync<Shopping>())
                .Where(x => x.guid == shopping.guid)
                .Select(x => x.Id)
                .FirstOrDefault();
            foreach (var item in _wareHouses){
                item.fk_Shopping = idNewShopping;
                await _databaseContext.AddItemAsync(item);
            }
            PurchaseTotal = string.Empty;
            Produts = string.Empty;
            _wareHouses = new List<WareHouses>();
            return "Shopping saved successfully";
        }
        message = "This shopping is already registered";
    } catch (Exception ex) { message = ex.Message; }
    return message;
}
```

NewProduct: This method handles adding new products to a shopping list via a popup.

```
Public async Task NewProduct(){
    decimal total = 0;
    var popup = new ProductoPopup();
```

```
        popup.ProdutsSaved += (name, price, purchasePrice, unit) =>  {
            _wareHouses.Add(new WareHouses { Name = name, Unit = unit,
    Price = price,
                         PurchasePrice = purchasePrice });
            Produts += $"New product added: {name}.\n"; };
        await App.Current.MainPage.ShowPopupAsync(popup);
        foreach (var item in _wareHouses)    {
            total += (item.PurchasePrice * item.Unit);
        }
        PurchaseTotal = $"${total}";
    }
```

Let us create the method: **CustomerFunction**, which will be responsible for registering a new client in the database if one does not already exist.

```
    Private async Task<string> CustomerFunction(){
        string message = string.Empty;
        try{
            var newCustomer = new Customers()
            {
                Name = CustomerName,
                Email = CustomerEmail,
                Phone = CustomerPhone,
                Active = true,
                RegistrationDate = DateTime.Now
            };
            var result = (await _databaseContext.GetAllAsync<Customers>())
                .Where(x => x.Name == newCustomer.Name && x.Active ==
    true)
                .FirstOrDefault();
            if (result == null){
                if (await _databaseContext.AddItemAsync(newCustomer)) {
                    CustomerName = string.Empty;
                    CustomerEmail = string.Empty;
                    CustomerPhone = string.Empty;
                    return "Customer saved successfully";
                }
            }
            message = "This customer is already registered";
        }catch (Exception ex){message = ex.Message;}
        return message;
    }
```

Now we will create the method **SalesFunction**, which will manage the sales logic. It will validate that the number of units sold does not exceed available inventory and will prevent invalid values. If the sale is valid, it will send the corresponding product parameters to the previous page for processing.

```
Private async Task<string> SalesFunction(){
    string message = "Product successfully added";
    try {
        if (int.Parse(UnitSales) <= SelectedWareHouses.Unit){
            _parameter = $"..?" +
                $"id={SelectedWareHouses.Id}" +
                $"&Prod={SelectedWareHouses.Name}" +
                $"&Unit={UnitSales}" +
                $"&PurchasePrice={SelectedWareHouses.PurchasePrice}";
            await Shell.Current.GoToAsync(_parameter, true);
        } else {
            message = $"The added units exceed the available stock.
Only
    {SelectedWareHouses.Unit} in stock.";
        }
    } catch (Exception ex) { message = ex.Message; }
    return message;
}
```

The final steps are to create the route record and inject the **View** and **ViewModel** in **MauiProgram.cs** as follows:

```
Routing.RegisterRoute("FormPage", typeof(FormView));
builder.Services.AddSingleton<FormView, FormViewModel>();
```

After finishing the above, all that remains is to create the **BindingContext** in code-behind of the **Formview**.

```
Public partial class FormView : ContentPage}{
   public FormView(FormViewModel viewModel){
         InitializeComponent();
         this.BindingContext = viewModel;
   }
}
```

If you have made it this far, congratulations! We have completed the forms page. In the next topic, we will focus on creating the **SuppliersView** page. Let us keep going!

SuppliersView

This page will have the function of showing the registered suppliers, deleting and creating them. In *Figure* 9.8, you can see the design that the View will have.

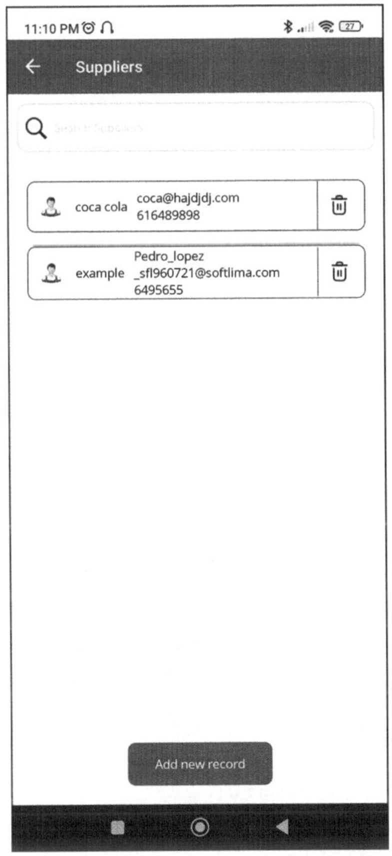

***Figure 9.8**: Suppliers page design*

The supplier screen interface has a simple and structured design. In the **SuppliersView.xaml** file, we created a **ContentPage** containing a **StackLayout**, within which a Grid with multiple rows is organized to distribute the visual elements.

- In row 0, the **CustomSearchControl** control, developed in previous topics, is placed.
- Row 1 includes an **ActivityIndicator** to indicate loading states.
- In row 2, inside a **VerticalStackLayout**, a **CollectionView** is added that will display the registered providers using an **ObservableCollection**.

Each supplier is represented by a card (Frame) displaying their name, email address, phone number, and a touch-enabled delete button. These cards are defined within the **CollectionView**'s **DataTemplate**, which uses the Suppliers model to bind data from the Items collection.

Finally, in row 3, a button is added that allows you to add new suppliers.

With this, we conclude the construction of the view. Next, we move on to the implementation of the **ViewModel**. The class **SuppliersViewModel** will inherit from **BaseViewModel** and use **DatabaseContext** to access the data. The properties needed to properly interact with the user interface will also be defined.

```
public partial class SuppliersViewModel : BaseViewModel
{
    private DatabaseContext _databaseContext;
    [ObservableProperty] private bool isVisible = false;
    [ObservableProperty] public string? searchText = string.Empty;
    [ObservableProperty] public bool cancelIsVisible = false;
    [ObservableProperty] public ObservableCollection<Suppliers> items;
    private List<Suppliers> _items;
    public SuppliersViewModel(DatabaseContext databaseContext) {
        _items = new List<Suppliers>();
        _databaseContext = databaseContext;
    }
}
```

The following 3 methods will be defined: First, an **OnAppearing** method that will be executed when the page starts; this method will be responsible for calling **GetData** so that the information is consulted in the database, and the method **FillItems**, which would fill in the data from the **ObservableCollection**.

```
public async Task OnAppearing() {
    IsVisible = true;
    SearchText = string.Empty;
    Items = new ObservableCollection<Suppliers>();
    await this.GetData();
    this.FillItems(_items);
    IsVisible = false;
}
private  async Task GetData() {
      var messge = string.Empty;
      try  {
          var result = (await _databaseContext.GetAllAsync
<Suppliers>())
                 .Where(x => x.Active == true);
          if (result.Any()) {
              _items.Clear();
              _items = result.ToList();
              return;
          }
          messge = "I couldn't see the information, have you
already tried to
                 create a new record?";
      } catch (Exception ex) { messge = ex.Message;}
      Application.Current.MainPage.DisplayAlert("Supplers Page",
```

```
messge, "OK");
   }
 private void FillItems(List<Suppliers> items){
     Items.Clear();
     foreach (var item in items) {
         Items.Add(new Suppliers { Email = item.Email, Phone = item.
Phone,
                                   Name = item.Name, Id = item.Id
});

}}
```

For the correct functioning of the component **CustomSearchControl**, the **OnSearchTextChanged** method will be created, which will be executed every time the property changes **SearchText**, executing the method **SearchAsync** and the **FillItems**. The **TapButtonCancel** command will also be implemented to clean the search engine.

```
partial void OnSearchTextChanged(string? value){
     CancelIsVisible = string.IsNullOrWhiteSpace(value) ? false :
true;
     if (!string.IsNullOrWhiteSpace(value))
         this.SearchAsync(value);
     else
         this.FillItems(_items)
}
private void SearchAsync(string query){
    var items = _items.Where(item =>
             (!string.IsNullOrEmpty(item.Name) && item.Name.
Contains(query,       StringComparison.OrdinalIgnoreCase)) ||
            (!string.IsNullOrEmpty(item.Email) && item.Email.
Contains(query, StringComparison.OrdinalIgnoreCase)) ||
            (!string.IsNullOrEmpty(item.Phone) && item.Phone.
Contains(query, StringComparison.OrdinalIgnoreCase))
        ).ToList();
    this.FillItems(items);
}
[RelayCommand]
public void TapButtonCancel(){SearchText = string.Empty;}
```

To complete the **ViewModel**, two command methods were added. **TapButtonAddNewRecords**, which will redirect the user to the supplier form, and **TapButtonItem**, which will be responsible for removing and disabling the selected provider

```
[RelayCommand]
public async Task TapButtonAddNewRecords() =>
await Shell.Current.GoToAsync($"FormPage?typeForm=Supplier");
[RelayCommand]
```

```
public async Task TapButtonItem(int id){
    IsVisible = true;
    _items.RemoveAll(i => i.Id == id);
    var rm = Items.FirstOrDefault(i => i.Id == id);
    if (rm != null) {
        var result = (await _databaseContext.GetAllAsync<Suppliers>())
                     .Where(x => x.Id == id && x.Active == true).
FirstOrDefault();
        if (result != null){
            result.Active = false;
            if (await _databaseContext.UpdateItemAsync(result)){
                Items.Remove(rm);
            }
        }
    }
    IsVisible = false;
}
```

The final steps are to create the route record and inject the **View** and **ViewModel** into **MauiProgram.cs** as follows:

```
Routing.RegisterRoute("SupplersPage", typeof(SuppliersView));
Routing.RegisterRoute("SupplersPage", typeof(SuppliersView));
```

After finishing the preceding code, all that remains is to create the **BindingContext** and add the method **OnAppearing** in the code-behind of the **SuppliersView**.

```
public partial class SuppliersView : ContentPage{
   public SuppliersView(SuppliersViewModel viewModel){
 InitializeComponent();
    this.BindingContext = viewModel;
    }
    protected override void OnAppearing(){
        base.OnAppearing();
        if (this.BindingContext is SuppliersViewModel viewModel){
            _ = viewModel.OnAppearing();
        }
    }
}
```

If you have made it this far, congratulations! We have completed the supplier management page.

CustomerView

This page will have the function of showing registered clients, deleting and creating them. In *Figure* 9.9, you can see the design that the View will have.

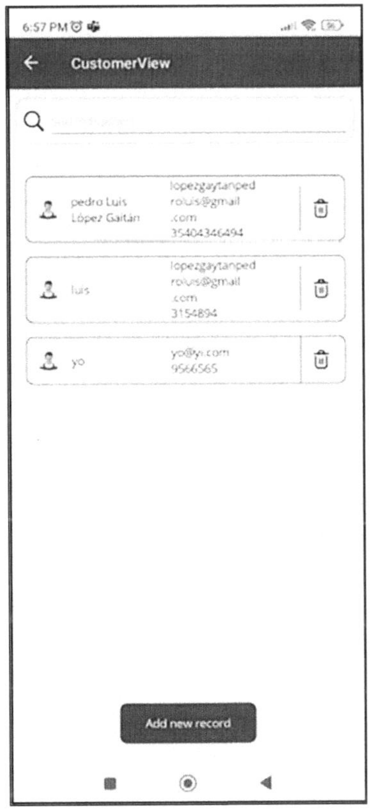

***Figure 9.9**: Designing the CustomerView page*

The page has a simple design. In the file **`CustomerView.xaml`**, we will create a **`ContentPage`** and within this, a **`StackLayout`** and a **`Grid`** to organize interface elements.

```
<Grid RowDefinitions="auto,30, *, auto" VerticalOptions="FillAnd
Expand"></Grid>
```

The Grid will have the following dContent distribution:

- **Row 0:** Control is added to CustomSearchControl, reused from previous topics. This allows you to search among registered customers.
- **Row 1:** An **`ActivityIndicator`** is included, linked to the property **`IsVisible`** of the **`ViewModel`**. This flag is set while data is being loaded.
- **Row 2:** Contains a **`VerticalStackLayout`** with a **`CollectionView`** that displays the list of customers. Each item comes from an **`ObservableCollection`** called Items, and uses the Customers model.
- **Row 3:** A button with the text "**`Add new record`**" is added, which allows you to add new records by pressing.

With this, we have completed the page build. To review the complete code and better understand the implementation details, checking out the project repository is recommended. We will continue with the implementation of the **ViewModel**. The class **CustomerViewModel** inherits the **BaseViewModel** and will use **DatabaseContext** to access the data. Additionally, the necessary properties for interacting with the view were added.

```
public partial class CustomerViewModel : BaseViewModel {
    [ObservableProperty] public string? searchText = string.Empty;
    [ObservableProperty] public bool cancelIsVisible = false;
    [ObservableProperty] public ObservableCollection<Customers> items;
    [ObservableProperty] public bool isVisible = false;
    private List<Customers> _items;
    private DatabaseContext _databaseContext;
    public CustomerViewModel(DatabaseContext databaseContext){
        _items = new List<Customers>();
        _databaseContext = databaseContext;
    }
}
```

The following 3 methods will be defined: First, an **OnAppearing** method that will be executed when the page starts; this method will be responsible for calling **GetData** so that the information is consulted in the database, and the method **FillItems**, which would fill in the data from the **ObservableCollection**.

```
public async void OnAppearing() {
    IsVisible = true;
    Items = new ObservableCollection<Customers>();
    await this.GetData();
    this.FillItems(_items);
    IsVisible = false;
}
private async Task GetData() {
    var messge = string.Empty;
    try{
        var result = (await _databaseContext.GetAllAsync
<Customers>())
                .Where(x => x.Active == true);
        if (result.Any()){
            _items.Clear();
            _items = result.ToList();
            return;
        }
        messge = "I couldn't see the information, have you already
tried to
                create a new record?";
    }catch (Exception ex){messge = ex.Message;}
```

```
     Application.Current.MainPage.DisplayAlert("Supplers Page",
messge, "OK");
 }
private void FillItems(List<Customers> items){
    Items.Clear();
    foreach (var item in items){
        Items.Add(new Customers { Email = item.Email, Phone = item.
Phone, Name = item.Name, Id = item.Id });
    }
}
```

For the correct functioning of the component **CustomSearchControl**, the method **OnSearchTextChanged** will be created, which will be executed every time the property changes **SearchText**, executing the method **SearchAsync** and the **FillItems**. The **TapButtonCancel** command will also be implemented to clean the search engine.

```
partial void OnSearchTextChanged(string? value){
    CancelIsVisible = string.IsNullOrWhiteSpace(value) ? false :
true;
    if (!string.IsNullOrWhiteSpace(value)){
        this.SearchAsync(value);
    }else{
        this.FillItems(_items);
    }
}

private void SearchAsync(string query){
     var items = _items.Where(item =>
             (!string.IsNullOrEmpty(item.Name) && item.Name.
Contains(query, StringComparison.OrdinalIgnoreCase)) ||
             (!string.IsNullOrEmpty(item.Email) && item.Email.
Contains(query, StringComparison.OrdinalIgnoreCase)) ||
             (!string.IsNullOrEmpty(item.Phone) && item.Phone.
Contains(query, StringComparison.OrdinalIgnoreCase))
         ).ToList();
     this.FillItems(items);
 }

[RelayCommand]
 public void TapButtonCancel(){
     SearchText = string.Empty;
 }
```

To complete the **ViewModel**, two command methods were added. **TapButtonAddNewRecords**, which will redirect the user to the customer form, and **TapButtonItem**, which will be responsible for removing and disabling the selected client.

```
[RelayCommand]
      public async Task TapButtonAddNewRecords() =>
      await Shell.Current.GoToAsync($"FormPage?typeForm=Customer");


[RelayCommand]
 public async Task TapButtonItem(you id){
     IsVisible = true;
     _items.RemoveAll(i => i.Id == id);
     var rm = Items.FirstOrDefault(i => i.Id == id);
     if (rm != null) {
         var result = (await _databaseContext.GetAllAsync
<Customers>())
                      .Where(x => x.Id == id && x.Active == true).
FirstOrDefault();
         if (result != null){
             result.Active = false;
             if (await _databaseContext.UpdateItemAsync(result)) {
                 Items.Remove(rm);
             }
         }
     }
     IsVisible = false;
 }
```

The final steps are to create the route record and inject the **View** and **ViewModel** into **MauiProgram.cs** as follows:

```
Routing.RegisterRoute("CustomerPage", typeof(CustomerView));
builder.Services.AddSingleton<CustomerView, CustomerViewModel>();
```

After finishing the preceding code, all that remains is to create the **BindingContext** and add the method **OnAppearing** in the code-behind of the **CustomerView**.

```
public partial class CustomerView : ContentPage{
       public CustomerView(CustomerViewModel viewmodel){
         InitializeComponent();
        this.BindingContext = viewmodel;
    }
    protected override void OnAppearing(){
        base.OnAppearing();
        if (this.BindingContext is CustomerViewModel viewModel){
            viewModel.OnAppearing();
        }
    }
}
```

If you have made it this far, congratulations! We have completed the customer management page.

PurchaseView

This page will have the function of showing the registered purchases and saving the products purchased through the form, deleting the purchases, and creating. In *Figure 9.10*, you can see the design that the View will have.

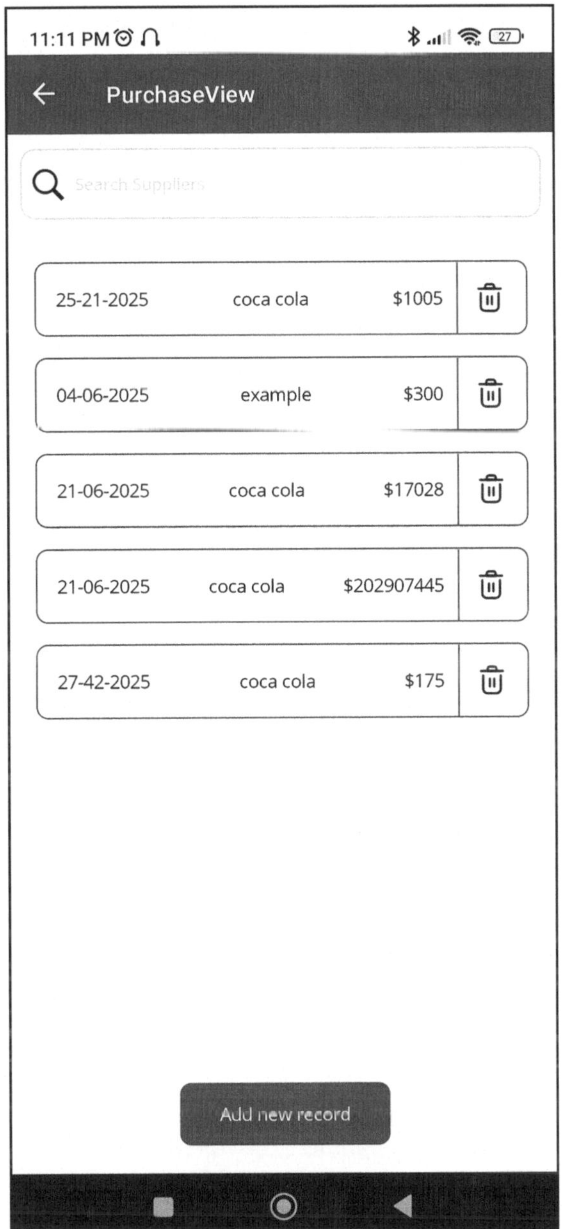

Figure 9.10: *PurchaseView page layout*

The page has a simple design. In the file **PurchaseView.xaml**, we will create a **ContentPage** and within this, a **StackLayout** and a **Grid** to organize interface elements.

```
<Grid RowDefinitions="auto,30,*,auto" VerticalOptions="Fill
AndExpand"></Grid>
```

In row 0 of the Grid, **CustomSearchControl** control will be added, created in previous sections, and within row 1, it will be defined **ActivityIndicator**

```
<controls:CustomSearchControl Grid.Row="0" />
<ActivityIndicator Grid.Row="1" IsVisible="{Binding  IsVisible}"
                   IsRunning="{Binding  IsVisible}" />
```

In row 2 inside a **VerticalStackLayout**, **CollectionView** will be added, which will be responsible for showing the elements of an **ObservableCollection**, which will have the data of the registered purchases.

```
<VerticalStackLayout Grid.Row="2" Margin="0,0,0,0"
Padding="20,0,20,20">
    <CollectionView ItemsSource="{Binding Items}"
                    HorizontalOptions="FillAndExpand"
                    x:Name="CollectionItems"
                    HeightRequest="500">
        <CollectionView.ItemTemplate>
            <DataTemplate x:DataType="models:ItemSupplier">
             </DataTemplate>
         </CollectionView.ItemTemplate>
     </CollectionView>
 </VerticalStackLayout>
```

Let us create the card represented by the **Frame,** designed so that each purchase displays the registration date, product name, purchase price, and a delete button with touch interaction. Each card will be presented within the **DataTemplate**, which will take the data from each record from an **ObservableCollection** named **Items** and using the model **ItemSupplier.**

```
<Frame Padding="15,0,15,0" Margin="0,0,0,15"BorderColor="{StaticRe-
source Primary}">
     <Grid ColumnDefinitions="auto,*,auto,1,auto"
           Padding="0">
         <Label Text="{Binding Date}"  Grid.Column="0"
                VerticalTextAlignment="Center" FontSize="Subtitle" />
         <Label Text="{Binding Name}" VerticalTextAlignment="Center"
                HorizontalTextAlignment="Center"
                FontSize="Subtitle" Grid.Column="1" />
         <Label Text="{Binding Total}" Margin="0,0,10,0"
                VerticalTextAlignment="Center"
                HorizontalTextAlignment="Center"
                FontSize="Subtitle"
```

```
                Grid.Column="2" />
         <BoxView WidthRequest="1" HeightRequest="50"
                  BackgroundColor="{StaticResource Primary}"
                  HorizontalOptions="Center" VerticalOptions="Center"
                  Grid.Column="3" />
         <Image Source="delete.png" Grid.Column="4" WidthRequest="25"
                Margin="10,0,0,0">
             <Image.GestureRecognizers>
                 <TapGestureRecognizer Command="{Binding Path =
BindingContext.TapButtonItemCommand, Source={Reference Collection-
Items}}"
                                       CommandParameter="{Binding Id}"
/>
             </Image.GestureRecognizers>
         </Image>
     </Grid>
 </Frame>
```

Finally, in row 3, a button is added to add new clients.

```
 <Button Grid.Row="3" WidthRequest="150" Text="Add new record"
         FontSize="16" Padding="5" Margin="0,0,0,20"
         Command="{Binding TapButtonAddNewRecordsCommand}"></Button>
```

With this, we have finished building the page. We will continue with the implementation of the **ViewModel**. The class **PurchaseViewModel** inherits the **BaseViewModel** and will use **DatabaseContext** to access the data. Additionally, the necessary properties for interacting with the view were added.

```
public partial class PurchaseViewModel : BaseViewModel
{
    private DatabaseContext _databaseContext;
    private List<ItemSupplier> _items;
    [ObservableProperty] public string? searchText = string.Empty;
    [ObservableProperty] public bool cancelIsVisible = false;
    [ObservableProperty] public ObservableCollection<ItemSupplier>
items;
    [ObservableProperty] public bool isVisible = false;
    public PurchaseViewModel(DatabaseContext databaseContext) {
        _databaseContext = databaseContext;
        _items = new List<ItemSupplier>();
        IsVisible = false;
    }
 }
```

The following 3 methods will be defined: First, an **OnAppearing** method that will be executed when the page starts; this method will be responsible for calling **GetData** so that the information is consulted in the database, and the method **FillItems**, which would fill in the data from the **ObservableCollection**.

```
public async Task OnAppearing() {
    IsVisible = true;
    Items = new ObservableCollection<ItemSupplier>();
    await this.GetData();
    this.FillItems(_items);
    IsVisible = false;
}
private async Task GetData() {
    try{
        _items.Clear();
        var shoppings = (await _databaseContext.GetAllAsync<Shop-
ping>());
        if (shoppings.Any()) {
            foreach (var item in shoppings) {
                var supplier = (await _databaseContext.GetAllAsync
<Suppliers>())
                    .Where(x => x.Id == item.fk_supplier).FirstOr
Default();
                if(supplier != null){
                    _items.Add(new ItemSupplier  {
                        Name = supplier.Name,
                        Total = item.Total ?? "$0.00",
                        Date = item.Date.ToString("dd-mm-yyyy"),
                        Id = supplier.Id
                    });
                }
            }
            return;
        }
    }catch(Exception ex){
        Application.Current.MainPage.DisplayAlert("Forms",
ex.Message, "OK");
    }
}
private void FillItems(List<ItemSupplier> items){
    Items.Clear();
    foreach (var item in items) {
        Items.Add(new ItemSupplier { Name = item.Name, Total = item.
Total, Date = item.Date, Id = item.Id });
    }
}
```

For the correct functioning of the component **CustomSearchControl**, the **OnSearchTextChanged** method will be created, which will be executed every time the property changes **SearchText**, executing the method **SearchAsync** and the **FillItems.** The **TapButtonCancel** command will also be implemented to clean the search engine.

```
partial void OnSearchTextChanged(string? value){
     CancelIsVisible = string.IsNullOrWhiteSpace(value) ? false :
true;
     if (!string.IsNullOrWhiteSpace(value)) {
         this.SearchAsync(value);
     } else {
         this.FillItems(_items);
     }
 }

private void SearchAsync(string query){
    var items = _items.Where(item =>
            (!string.IsNullOrEmpty(item.Name) && item.Name.
Contains(query, StringComparison.OrdinalIgnoreCase)) ||
            (!string.IsNullOrEmpty(item.Date) && item.Date.
Contains(query, StringComparison.OrdinalIgnoreCase)) ||
            (!string.IsNullOrEmpty(item.Total) && item.Total.
Contains(query, StringComparison.OrdinalIgnoreCase))
        ).ToList();
    this.FillItems(items);
}
[RelayCommand]
 public void TapButtonCancel() {
     SearchText = string.Empty;
 }
```

To complete the **ViewModel**, two command methods were added. **TapButtonAddNewRecords**, which will redirect the user to the purchase form, and **TapButtonItem**, which will be responsible for deleting and disabling the selected purchase.

```
[RelayCommand]
      public async Task TapButtonAddNewRecords() =>
      await Shell.Current.GoToAsync($"FormPage?typeForm=Purchase");
[RelayCommand]
public async Task TapButtonItem(you id){
    IsVisible = true;
    _items.RemoveAll(i => i.Id == id);
    var rm = Items.FirstOrDefault(i => i.Id == id);
    if (rm != null){
        Items.Remove(rm);
```

```
        }
        IsVisible = false;
    }
```

It is very likely that it will mark some errors; this is because we need to define the models of the **ItemSupplier**. Within the directory **Models** in the file **Item.cs**, the following data model will be added:

```
namespace ERP_APP.Models{
    public class Item    {
        public string? Id { get; set; }
        public string? Name { get; set; }
        public string? Email { get; set; }
        public string? Phone { get; set; }
    }
    public class ItemSupplier  {
        public int Id { get; set; }
        public string? Name { get; set; }
        public string? Total { get; set; }
        public string? Date { get; set; }
    }
    public class ItemSales {
        public int Id { get; set; }
        public string? Name { get; set; }
        public string? Unit { get; set; }
        public decimal Total { get; set; }
    }
}
```

The final steps are to create the route record and inject the **View** and **ViewModel** into **MauiProgram.cs** as follows:

```
Routing.RegisterRoute("PurchasePage", typeof(PurchaseView));
builder.Services.AddSingleton<PurchaseView, PurchaseViewModel>();
```

After finishing the preceding code, all that remains is to create the **BindingContext** and add the method **OnAppearing** in the code-behind of the **PurchaseViewModel**.

```
public PurchaseView(PurchaseViewModel viewmodel){
   InitializeComponent();
    this.BindingContext = viewmodel;
}
protected override void OnAppearing(){
    base.OnAppearing();
    if (this.BindingContext is PurchaseViewModel viewModel)    {
        _ = viewModel.OnAppearing();
    }
}
```

If you have made it this far, congratulations! We have completed the page for registering and managing purchases and product allocations.

WarehouseView

This page will have the function of showing the warehouse of products that were added within the purchasing module. In *Figure 9.11*, you can see the design that this View will have.

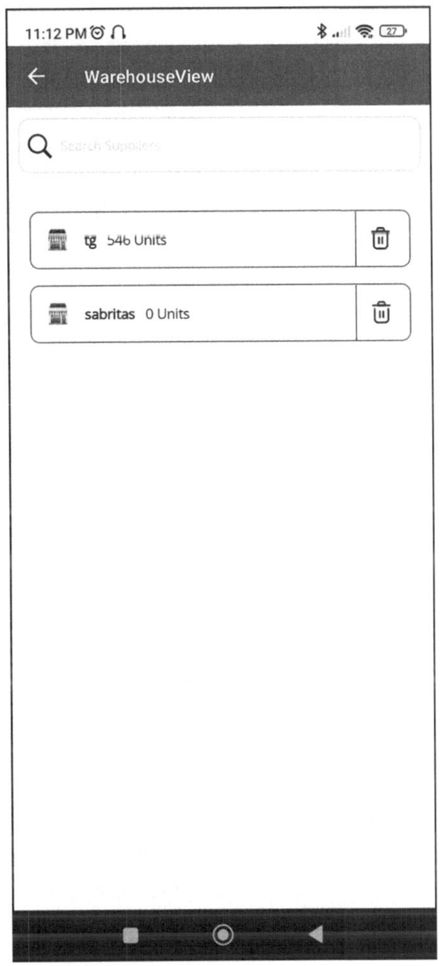

Figure 9.11: *PurchaseView page layout*

In the archive **WarehouseView.xaml**, we will create a **ContentPage** and within this, a **StackLayout** and a **Grid** to organize interface elements.

```
<Grid RowDefinitions="auto,30,*,auto" VerticalOptions="FillAnd
Expand"> </Grid>
```

In row 0 of the grid, the **CustomSearchControl** (created in the previous topics) will be added, while within row 1, **ActivityIndicator** will be defined.

```
<controls:CustomSearchControl Grid.Row="0" />
<ActivityIndicator Grid.Row="1" IsVisible="{Binding  IsVisible}"
                   IsRunning="{Binding  IsVisible}" />
```

In row 2 inside a **VerticalStackLayout**, **CollectionView** will be added, which will be responsible for showing the elements of an **ObservableCollection**, which will have the data of the registered products.

```
<VerticalStackLayout  Grid.Row="2" Margin="0" Padding="20,0,20,20">
     <CollectionView ItemsSource="{Binding Items}"
                     HorizontalOptions="FillAndExpand"
                     x:Name="CollectionItems" HeightRequest="540">
         <CollectionView.ItemTemplate>
      <DataTemplate x:DataType="models:WareHouses"> </DataTemplate>
         </CollectionView.ItemTemplate>
     </CollectionView>
 </VerticalStackLayout>
```

Let us create the card represented by the **Frame,** designed to display product data such as product name, available units, and a delete button with touch interaction. Each card will be presented within the **DataTemplate**, which will take the data from each record from an **ObservableCollection** named **Items** and use the model **WareHouses**.

```
<Frame Padding="15,0,15,0"
       Margin="0,0,0,15"
       BorderColor="{StaticResource Primary}">
     <Grid ColumnDefinitions="auto,auto,*,1,auto"
           Padding="0">
         <Image Source="store.png" Grid.Column="0"
                WidthRequest="20" Margin="0,0,15,0" />
         <Label Text="{Binding Name}" Grid.Column="1"
                VerticalTextAlignment="Center" FontSize="Subtitle"
                FontAttributes="Bold"/>
         <HorizontalStackLayout Grid.Column="2" Margin="10,0"
                                HorizontalOptions="StartAndExpand"
                                VerticalOptions="CenterAndExpand">
             <Label Text="{Binding Unit} " VerticalTextAlignment
="Center"
                    FontSize="Subtitle" />
             <Label Text=" Units"
                    VerticalTextAlignment="Center" FontSize="
Subtitle" />
         </HorizontalStackLayout>
         <BoxView WidthRequest="1" HeightRequest="50"
                  BackgroundColor="{StaticResource Primary}"
```

```
                    HorizontalOptions="Center"VerticalOptions="Center"
                    Grid.Column="3" />
            <Image Source="delete.png" Grid.Column="4" WidthRequest
="25"
                  Margin="10,0,0,0">
                <Image.GestureRecognizers>
                    <TapGestureRecognizer Command="{Binding Path =
BindingContext.TapButtonItemCommand, Source={Reference Collection-
Items}}"
                                            CommandParameter="{Binding Id}"
/>
                </Image.GestureRecognizers>
            </Image>
        </Grid>
  </Frame>
```

With this, we have finished building the page. We will continue with the implementation of the **ViewModel**. The class **WarehouseViewModel** inherits the **BaseViewModel** and will use **DatabaseContext** to access the data. Additionally, the necessary properties for interacting with the view were added.

```
public partial class WarehouseViewModel : BaseViewModel
{
    private DatabaseContext _databaseContext;
    private List<WareHouses> _items;
    [ObservableProperty] public string? searchText = string.Empty;
    [ObservableProperty] public bool cancelIsVisible = false;
    [ObservableProperty] public bool isVisible = false;
    [ObservableProperty] public ObservableCollection<WareHouses> items;
    public WarehouseViewModel(DatabaseContext databaseContext){
        _databaseContext = databaseContext;
        _items = new List<WareHouses>();
    }
  }
```

The following 3 methods will be defined: first, an **OnAppearing** method that will be executed when the page starts; this method will be responsible for calling **GetData** so that the information is consulted in the database, and the method **FillItems**, which would fill in the data from the **ObservableCollection**.

```
public async Task OnAppearing() {
     IsVisible = true;
     Items = new ObservableCollection<WareHouses>();
     await this.GetData();
     this.FillItems(_items);
     IsVisible = false;
 }
```

```
private async Task GetData() {
      try{
          _items.Clear();
          var result = (await _databaseContext.GetAllAsync
<WareHouses>());
          if(result.Any()) {
              foreach(var item in result){
                  _items.Add(new WareHouses {
                      Id = item.Id,
                      Name = item.Name,
                      Unit = item.Unit
                  });
              }
          }
      }catch (Exception ex){
          Application.Current.MainPage.DisplayAlert("WareHouses
Pages", ex.Message, "OK");
      }
 }
private void FillItems(List<WareHouses> items){
    Items.Clear();
    foreach (var item in items) {
        Items.Add(new WareHouses { Name = item.Name, Unit = item.
Unit, Id = item.Id });
    }
}
```

For the correct functioning of the component **CustomSearchControl**, the **OnSearchTextChanged** method will be created, which will be executed every time the property changes **SearchText**, executing the method **SearchAsync** and the **FillItems**. The **TapButtonCancel** command will also be implemented to clean the search engine.

```
partial void OnSearchTextChanged(string? value) {
      CancelIsVisible = string.IsNullOrWhiteSpace(value) ? false :
true;
      if (!string.IsNullOrWhiteSpace(value)) {this.SearchAsync(value);
      }else {this.FillItems(_items); }
 }
private void SearchAsync(string query){
      var items = _items.Where(item =>
              (!string.IsNullOrEmpty(item.Name) && item.Name.
Contains(query, StringComparison.OrdinalIgnoreCase))
          ).ToList();
      this.FillItems(items);
 }
[RelayCommand]
 public void TapButtonCancel(){ SearchText = string.Empty;}
```

To complete the **ViewModel**, the method **TapButtonItem** will be added, which will be responsible for removing the record.

```
[RelayCommand]
 public async Task TapButtonItem(int id){
     IsVisible = true;
     try{
          _items.RemoveAll(i => i.Id == id);
          var rm = Items.FirstOrDefault(i => i.Id == id);
          if (rm != null){
    if (await _databaseContext.DeleteItemByKeyAsync<WareHouses>
(id)){
                   Items.Remove(rm); }
          }
     } catch (Exception ex){
 Application.Current.MainPage.DisplayAlert("WareHouses Pages",
ex.Message, "OK");
     }
     IsVisible = false;
 }
```

The final steps are to create the route record and inject the **View** and **ViewModel** into **MauiProgram.cs** as follows:

```
Routing.RegisterRoute("WarehousePage", typeof(WarehouseView));
builder.Services.AddSingleton<WarehouseView, WarehouseViewModel>();
```

After finishing the preceding code, all that remains is to create the **BindingContext** and add the method **OnAppearing** in the code-behind of the **PurchaseViewModel**.

```
public partial class WarehouseView : ContentPage{
       public WarehouseView(WarehouseViewModel viewmodel){
         InitializeComponent();
        this.BindingContext = viewmodel;
    }
    protected override void OnAppearing(){
        base.OnAppearing();
        if (this.BindingContext is WarehouseViewModel viewModel){
            _ = viewModel.OnAppearing();
        }
    }
}
```

If you have made it this far, congratulations! We have completed the product warehouse page.

SaleView

This page will record sales, update the product inventory, display the list of products available for sale, include a search engine, and calculate the total sale price. *Figure* 9.12 shows the expected page layout.

Since the code for this page is extensive and may be difficult to understand if presented in full here, we have chosen not to show it in its entirety. However, do not worry: you can check out the complete, detailed code in the project repository, where you can study and reference it as needed.

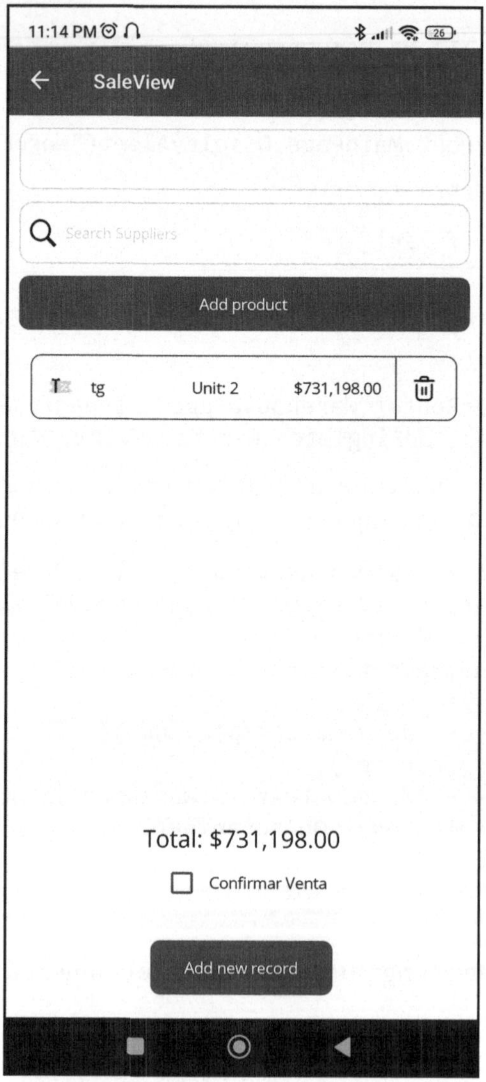

Figure 9.12: *SalesView page design*

In the archive **SaleView.xaml**, let us create a page **ContentPage** with a **ScrollView**, and **StackLayout**, and a **Grid** to organize interface elements clearly and effectively.

```
<Grid RowDefinitions="auto, auto,auto,*, auto, auto"></grid>
```

In row 0, a Frame with an elegant Picker will be added to select the client

```
<Frame Grid.Row="0"   Padding="5,2" Margin="10,10,10,0"Corner
Radius="10">
        <VerticalStackLayout>
            <Picker Title="Select an Options"
                    ItemsSource="{Binding Options}"
                    ItemDisplayBinding="{Binding Name}"
                    SelectedItem="{Binding SelectedOption,
Mode=TwoWay}"  />
        </VerticalStackLayout>
 </Frame>
```

Then, in row 1, the custom search control will be added

```
<controls:CustomSearchControl Grid.Row="1" />
```

In row 2, the "**Add Product**" button was added to add products to the list.

```
<Button Grid.Row="2" Text="Add product" FontSize="16"Padding="5"
Margin="10,10,10,0"Command="{Binding TapButtonAddProductCommand}"></
Button>
```

Next, in row 3, the **CollectionView** was defined, which is responsible for displaying the products in a dynamic list. Each product has its own card, designed with a **Frame**. This contains the product image, name, unit, and total price. It also includes a delete icon with touch-based interaction to delete the item if necessary. To view the full code and better understand its implementation, we recommend checking out the project repository.

In row 4, we display the total sale price. We also added a checkbox that allows the user to confirm the sale of the products. This is an essential detail so the customer can confirm their purchase before completing it.

```
<VerticalStackLayout Grid.Row="4">
        <Label Text="{Binding Total, StringFormat='Total: ${0:N2}'}"
           HorizontalTextAlignment="Center" FontSize="Title"/>
<HorizontalStackLayout HorizontalOptions="CenterAndExpand" Padding
="25,1,25,25">
           <CheckBox IsChecked="{Binding IsCkecked}"/>
<Label Text="Confirm Sale"HorizontalTextAlignment="Center"
               VerticalTextAlignment="Center" Margin="0"  FontSize
="Subtitle" />
    </HorizontalStackLayout>
 </VerticalStackLayout>
```

Finally, in row 5, we added a button to create a new sales record.

```
<Button Grid.Row="5" WidthRequest="150" Text="Add new record"
FontSize="16"Padding="5" Margin="0,0,0,20"
        Command="{Binding TapButtonAddNewRecordsCommand}"></Button>
```

With this, we have finished building the page. We will continue with the implementation of the **ViewModel**.

In the archive **SaleViewModel.cs**, a class has been implemented **SaleViewModel** that inherits from **BaseViewModel** and handles all the logic associated with the sales view. This class uses the library's observable properties and commands. **CommunityToolkit** to interact with the database and manage product sales. We recommend checking out the repository.

Once the necessary properties have been defined, we configure the method **ApplyQueryAttributes** to receive navigation parameters (ID, product name, unit, and purchase price). If the values are valid, the product total is calculated and added to the sales list; otherwise, the process is canceled.

Three key methods are then defined. The first is **OnAppearing**, which runs when the view is launched and is responsible for initializing collections, querying data from the database using the **GetData** method, and populating visible elements through **FillItems**.

To ensure the correct operation of the **CustomSearchControl** component, the method is implemented **OnSearchTextChanged**, which responds to changes in the search text. This method executes **SearchAsync** to filter results and update the view using **FillItems**. In addition, the command is incorporated with **TapButtonCancel**, which cleans the search engine.

The method is then implemented by **TapButtonAddNewRecords**, essential for completing the sales process. This method saves the sales data, associates the products sold, updates the inventory, and, if everything is completed correctly, displays a confirmation message.

Finally, two additional commands are added to the **ViewModel**. **TapButtonAddProduct**, which redirects to the product capture form, and **TapButtonItem**, which allows you to remove a selected product from the sales list.

The final steps are to create the route record and inject the **View** and **ViewModel** into **MauiProgram.cs** as follows:

```
Routing.RegisterRoute("SalePage", typeof(SaleView));
builder.Services.AddSingleton<SaleView, SaleViewModel>();
```

After finishing the preceding code, all that remains is to create the **BindingContext** and add the method **OnAppearing** in the **code-behind** of the **SaleView**.

```
public partial class SaleView : ContentPage{
      public SaleView(SaleViewModel viewmodel){
        InitializeComponent();
        this.BindingContext = viewmodel;
   }
    protected override void OnAppearing() {
        base.OnAppearing();
        if (this.BindingContext is SaleViewModel viewModel) {
            viewModel.OnAppearing();
        }
    }
}
```

Congratulations! You have reached the end of this project. With this, we have successfully completed the ERP implementation. Great job! All the effort invested in development, testing, and fine-tuning now results in robust and efficient functionality. Congratulations on reaching this milestone and successfully completing the project!

Conclusion

In this chapter, we developed an ERP-style application, a very common type of application in the business sector, which is essential for decision-making, inventory management, budget management, and other benefits. Throughout the chapter, we analyzed and addressed key aspects of software development, such as organization, file structure, and scalability. We implemented dependency injection and a route logging system to optimize navigation. We worked with the MVVM design pattern, managed events such as **OnAppearing**, and performed CRUD operations on our SQLite database.

In the next chapter, we delve into the development of an innovative educational application, where users can participate in interactive courses, take exams, manage their progress, and explore many other exciting features. It will be a unique experience full of new tools and opportunities to learn!

CHAPTER 10
Building a Social Media App

Introduction

In this chapter, we develop a WhatsApp-style messaging application, incorporating real-time messaging with SignalR, local storage with SQLite, and an architecture based on MVVM. We will learn to correctly structure the project, manage the life cycle of the views, and build a functional interface that allows sending and receiving messages efficiently. A solid foundation for any modern social app.

Structure

In this chapter, we will discuss the following topics:

- App Description
- SignalR API
- Application Creation
- Data Access Class
- `SignalRService`
- Controls
- `ProfilePage`
- `ChatPage`
- `ContactsPage`
- `MessagesPage`
- `FriendsPage`

App Description

In the previous chapters, we developed two types of applications: an ERP system and an online store (e-commerce). Now it is time to take it a step further and create a new category: a social networking application like **WhatsApp**.

This application will include the following screens and functionalities:

- **Chat list:** to access active conversations.
- **List of publications:** similar to states.
- **Contact list:** mobile device contact list.
- **User profile:** where you can modify the name, number, and access PIN.
- **Navigation within the chat:** to send and receive messages.
- **Pop-ups:** to manage the access PIN and add new publications.

Additionally, we will develop an API using **`SignalR`** of .NET, a library that allows incorporating real-time communication in applications, facilitating the sending of instant messages between client and server through **WebSockets** and other transportation technologies, according to availability.

The architecture of our application is shown below in *Figure* 10.1. It represents how mobile devices, with the chat interface, connect to the server using **`SignalR`** to send and receive messages in real time.

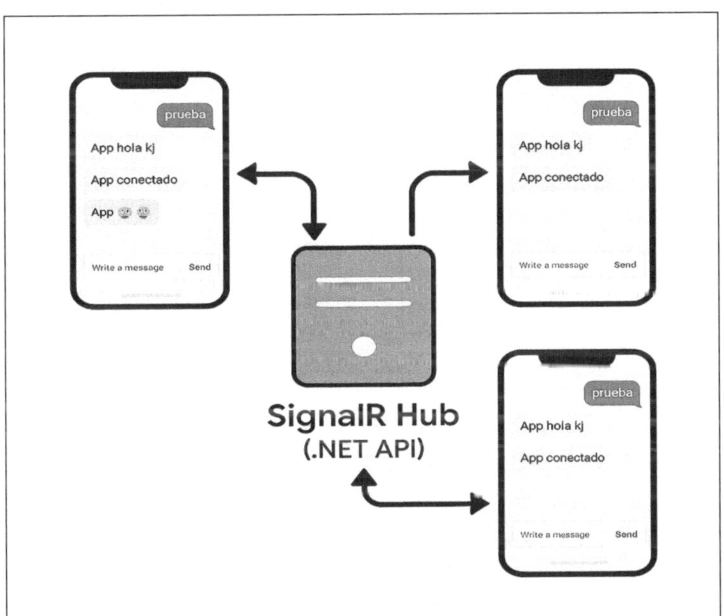

Figure 10.1: *Shows how several cell phones with the chat app connect to a SignalR server*

Now, without further ado, let us start developing our application!

In this section, we are going to start creating the server that will be responsible for sending and receiving messages between the devices.

SignalR

As we mentioned at the beginning of this chapter, we are going to create a service to send and receive messages between connected devices using the **SignalR** library, which allows us to implement real-time functionalities in a simple way.

We will not delve into the technical aspects of **SignalR** in this chapter, so we recommend checking out its official documentation for a more complete understanding.

Likewise, we will not go into detail about what an API is in .NET, so it is also advisable to review this topic separately before continuing.

First, it will be necessary to create a new project. You can do this from Visual Studio by selecting the Web API template and naming the project "**SignalRChatServer**". Alternatively, you can also create it from the terminal using the following command "**dotnet new web -n SignalRChatServer**".

Afterwards, will add the package "**Microsoft.AspNetCore.SignalR**" through NuGet; remember to select the versions compatible with your project.

In the root of the project, we will create a class called **ChatHub**, which will inherit from **Microsoft.AspNetCore.SignalR.Hub**. Within this class, we will define the method **SendMessage**, which will be responsible for sending a message to all connected clients, leaving the code as follows:

```
using Microsoft.AspNetCore.SignalR;
public class ChatHub : Hub
{
    public async Task SendMessage(string user, string message)
    {
        await Clients.All.SendAsync("ReceiveMessage", user, message);
    }
}
```

We are going to modify the **Program.cs** to register the services necessary to enable **SignalR** and define a root route, looking as follows:

```
var builder = WebApplication.CreateBuilder(args);
builder.Services.AddSignalR();
var app = builder.Build();
app.MapGet("/", () => "SignalR Server is running!");
app.MapHub<ChatHub>("/chatHub");
app.Run();
```

As a final step, we only have to run the project and verify that the service is working correctly. If everything is fine, you should see the message "**`SignalR Server is running!`**"

Congratulations! If you have made it this far, our API is completely ready. Now we can start with the development of the mobile application.

Application Creation

We will create a new project using the template **.NET MAUI App** and the framework **.NET 8** or higher. In this case, we will call the project **`MauiTalk`**, but remember that you can give it whatever name you prefer. Just be sure to stay consistent with the name throughout the development process to avoid confusion.

Once our project is created, we will proceed to install the packages that we will use in the development of this application, through NuGet:

- **`CommunityToolkit.MAUI.`**
- **`CommunityToolkit.Mvvm.`**
- **`Microsoft.AspNetCore.SignalR.Client.`**
- **`Microsoft.Data.Sqlite.`**
- **`sqlite-net-pcl.`**

Once the installation is complete, remember to register the Community Toolkit by adding "**`UseMauiCommunityToolkit()`**" in **`MauiProgram.cs`**.

We will create the following directories in the root of the project to properly organize the different components of the application. The final structure will be the following:

- **`Controls`**: Reusable user interface components.
- **`Converters`**: Value converters to transform data in the UI.
- **`Data`**: Data access layer.
- **`Models`**: Data structures used by the application.
- **`Services`**: Logic to connect with external resources.
- **`ViewModels`**: UI logic controllers.
- **`Views`**: User interface (UI).

Once we have created the directories, we will proceed to create the user interfaces (UI). Inside the directory **Views**, the following pages of type **`ContentPage`** will be created:

- **`ChatPage.xaml`**: Page that shows the list of active chats.

- **ContactsPage.xaml**: Page in charge of displaying the list of contacts added to the mobile device.
- **FriendsPage.xaml**: Page to view other users' posts.
- **MessagesPage.xaml**: Page to send and receive messages.
- **ProfilePage.xaml**: Page to create, view, and edit the user profile.

We will delete the page generated by default when creating the project, called **MainPage.xaml** and we are going to modify the file **AppShell.xaml** where we will use a design based on **TabBar** rather than **ShellContent**.

TabBar Type Menu Implementation

For the main navigation of this WhatsApp-type application, we use a **TabBar** integrated through Shell, which allows us to offer a structured and modern experience, taking advantage of the native tab capacity in .NET MAUI.

While there are several ways to implement tabbed navigation (for example, using **TabbedPage**, **Shell**, or even a custom implementation with **CollectionView** or **Grid**), in this project, we opted for configuration using **Shell**, as it simplifies the organization of paths and styles.

First, within the **AppShell.xaml** file, we define the tab bar visual styles:

```
<Shell.TabBarBackgroundColor>
    <StaticResource Key="TabBarBackgroundColor" />
</Shell.TabBarBackgroundColor>
<Shell.TabBarForegroundColor>
    <StaticResource Key="TabBarSelectedItemColor" />
</Shell.TabBarForegroundColor>
<Shell.TabBarTitleColor>
    <StaticResource Key="TabBarSelectedItemColor" />
</Shell.TabBarTitleColor>
<Shell.TabBarUnselectedColor>
    <StaticResource Key="TabBarTextColor" />
</Shell.TabBarUnselectedColor>
```

Next, we declare the four main tabs that make up the basic navigation structure of the application:

```
<TabBar>
    <ShellContent Title="Chat"
                  ContentTemplate="{DataTemplate views:ChatPage}"
                  Icon="icon_chats.png" />
    <ShellContent Title="News"
                 ContentTemplate="{DataTemplate views:FriendsPage}"
                  Icon="icon_friends.png" />
```

```
        <ShellContent Title="Contacts"
                      ContentTemplate="{DataTemplate views:ContactsPage}"
                      Icon="icon_phone.png" />
        <ShellContent Title="Profile"
                      ContentTemplate="{DataTemplate views:ProfilePage}"
                      Icon="icon_profile.png" />
    </TabBar>
```

Each tab represents a key functional section of the application: **`Chat`**, **`News`**, **`Contacts`**, and **`User Profile`**. This structure provides a solid and easily scalable base, allowing new functionalities to be added without complicating the browsing experience.

For this configuration to work correctly, it is important to ensure that the **`AppShell.xaml`** file includes the necessary namespaces. In particular:

```
xmlns:toolkit="http://schemas.microsoft.com/dotnet/2021/maui/
toolkit"
xmlns:views="clr-namespace:MauiTalk.Views"
```

These allow you to use resources from the .NET MAUI Toolkit and link the content pages (**`ChatPage`**, **`FriendsPage`**, and so on) within the project. Remember to add icons to the project that represent each page's functionality.

You can check the project repository to see the complete code for each page and how they integrate into shell navigation.

Once the above is finished, in the **`ViewModels`** directory, we will add a new class that will be called **`BaseViewModel`**, which will be used to provide common functionality to all other **`ViewModels`**. This class inherits from **`ObservableObject`**, allowing the user interface to be automatically notified of property changes, making data easier **binding** and improving the synchronization between the logic and the UI. The class **`BaseViewModel`** should be as follows:

```
using CommunityToolkit.Mvvm.ComponentModel;

namespace MauiTalk.ViewModels
{
    public partial class BaseViewModel : ObservableObject{}
}
```

The next step is to integrate the data layer, which will be responsible for managing access and storage of the information used by our application.

Data Access Class

Next, we are going to create the service layer in charge of managing all interactions with the local database using SQLite. This layer will allow us to encapsulate and reuse the CRUD operations necessary for the application to function.

Inside the directory **Data**, we will add a new class called **DatabaseContext**. It is very likely that this class is already familiar to you, since it was implemented in previous chapters, such as in *Chapter 8, Building an E-Commerce App*, and *Chapter 9, Building an ERP App*. Therefore, we will not go into detail about the implementation of each function, since the same structure and logic previously explained will be used.

If you need to review how it works, we recommend reviewing the mentioned chapters or consulting the project repository where the complete code is located.

The only thing we must take into account on this occasion is the name of the specific database for this project, which will be:

```
private const string DbName = "Chat.db3";
```

In this way, we define the name of the physical database file that will be stored on the device.

Once you finish creating the class, remember to inject it into the **MauiProgram.cs**, which will allow us to use it centrally throughout the application and access it from any part of the project

```
builder.Services.AddSingleton<DatabaseContext>();
```

Figure 10.2 represents the entity relationship model of the tables that we will use in our project.

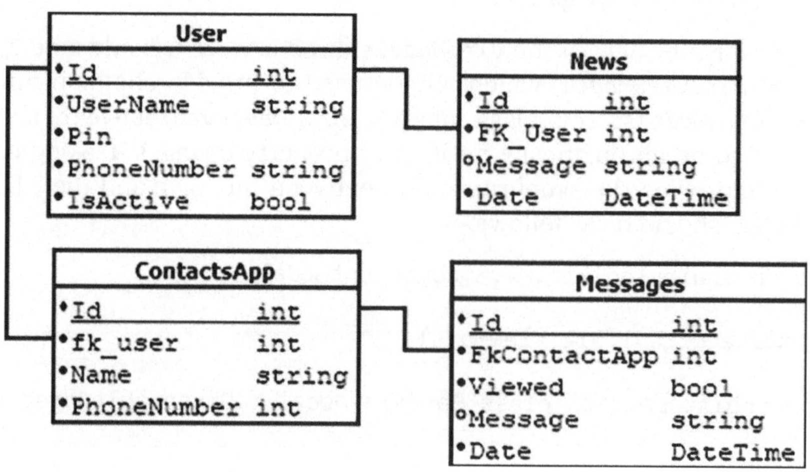

Figure 10.2: *Database schema designed for applications*

As we can see, it is a simple but functional database that will allow you to keep track of the currently logged-in user, manage your contact list, and store the history of received messages.

Based on the previous analysis, we will proceed to define the classes that will represent our data models. As is customary throughout the book, these models will be created within the directory **Models.**

We will start by defining the class **UserModel.cs**, which will be responsible for representing the data of the user who has logged in. In this class, we will store, among other attributes, a **PIN** security, which will function as an authentication mechanism every time the application is started. This will allow us to protect access to private chats and prevent third parties from impersonating our identity.

```
public class UserModel
{
    [PrimaryKey, AutoIncrement]
    public int Id { get; set; }
    public string UserName { get; set; }
    public string Pin { get; set; }
    public string PhoneNumber { get; set; }
    public bool IsActive { get; set; }
}
```

Then we will create the class **ContactsAppModel.cs**, which will be in charge of managing contacts with whom we have already started a conversation.

```
public class ContactsAppModel
{
    [PrimaryKey, AutoIncrement]
    public int Id { get; set; }
    public int FkUser { get; set; }
    public string Name { get; set; }
    public string PhoneNumber { get; set; }
}
```

We will define the class **NewsModel.cs** to manage user posts.

```
public class NewsModel
{
    [PrimaryKey, AutoIncrement]
    public int Id { get; set; }
    public int FK_User { get; set; }
    public string? Message { get; set; }
    public DateTime Date { get; set; }
}
```

Finally, we will create the class **MessagesModel.cs**, which will be in charge of managing the history of received and sent messages.

```
public class MessagesModel
{
    [PrimaryKey, AutoIncrement]
    public int Id { get; set; }
    public int FkContactApp { get; set; }
    public bool Viewed { get; set; }
```

```
        public string? Message { get; set; }
        public DateTime Date { get; set; }
    }
```

With this, we conclude the configuration of our data layer. In the next section, we will move forward with the creation of the service **SignalRService**, which will be responsible for managing real-time communication with the **SignalR** server that we implemented in the previous sections.

SignalRService

Now that we have our data layer configured, it is time to continue with one of the most interesting parts of this application: real-time communication between users. To achieve this, we are going to create a service called **SignalRService**, which will be responsible for managing all interactions with the **SignalR** server that we previously implemented.

This service will be in charge of both connecting to the server and sending and receiving messages. Thanks to the library **Microsoft.AspNetCore.SignalR.Client**, we can establish a connection with the **SignalR** server and handle events that occur during the session.

To start, inside the directory **Services**, let us create a new class called **SignalRService.cs** with the following content:

```
using Microsoft.AspNetCore.SignalR.Client;
public class SignalRService
{
    private HubConnection _connection;
    public event Action<string, string> OnMessageReceived;
    public SignalRService()
    {
        _connection = new HubConnectionBuilder()
        // usa tu IP local correcta
        .WithUrl("http://192.168.1.73:5005/chatHub")
        .WithAutomaticReconnect()
        .Build();
        // Listen to messages from the server
        _connection.On<string, string>("ReceiveMessage",
(user, message) =>
        {
            OnMessageReceived?.Invoke(user, message);
        });
    }
    public async Task ConnectAsync()
    {
```

```
            if (_connection.State != HubConnectionState.Connected)
                await _connection.StartAsync();
        }

        public async Task SendMessage(string user, string message)
        {
            if (_connection.State == HubConnectionState.Connected)
                await _connection.InvokeAsync("SendMessage", user,
    message);
        }
    }
```

As we can see, the class does the following:

- Initialize the connection using the **SignalR** server IP (make sure you enter your correct local IP).
- Listen to incoming messages through the method **On** what is subscribed to the event "**ReceiveMessage**".
- Define a public event **OnMessageReceived**, which will be used by views or **viewmodels** to react to received messages.
- Explain the methods **ConnectAsync()** and **SendMessage()** to establish the connection and send messages to the server, respectively.

This service will be the basis to allow real-time interaction between users within our WhatsApp-type app. To finish, we will have to inject this class into the **MauiProgram.cs**, which will allow us to use it centrally throughout the application and access it from any part of the project.

```
builder.Services.AddSingleton<SignalRService>();
```

Once injected, we are going to modify the file **code-behind** of the **App.xaml** to start our **ChatHub**. We will then integrate it with the rest of the system, ensuring that everything runs smoothly and without interruptions.

```
public partial class App : Application
 {
     private SignalRService _signalRService;
     public App(SignalRService signalRService){
         InitializeComponent();
         MainPage = new AppShell();
         _signalRService = signalRService;
         this.startChat();
     }
     private void startChat(){  _ = _signalRService.ConnectAsync(); }
 }
```

In the next section, we are going to create two custom Popup type controls. One of them will help us request the user's PIN when starting the application, as an authentication method. The other will be used to add new publications within the system. Both controls will be reusable and will be integrated directly into the main project pages.

Controls

Let us create some controls, specifically of type **Popup**, which will serve as a reusable component to prompt the user to write a new post or add their PIN. In .NET MAUI, controls are independent pieces of interface that encapsulate their own logic and layout and can be easily inserted into different parts of the project without repeating code. In this case, within the directory **Controls**, let us create the following controls: **`NewPostPopup.xaml`** and **`PinPopup.xaml`**.

NewPostPopup

Now we are going to create a Popup type control that will allow us to add new publications within the app. This control will be reusable and will show a small popup box in the center of the screen with an "**`Editor`**" to write the message and a button to send it. The idea is to facilitate the publication of quick messages within the interface without having to change pages.

The design is quite simple but functional. We use a **`Frame`** with rounded edges, centered on a semi-transparent background. Inside this Frame, we place a **`Label`** as a title, the **`Editor`** to capture the text, and a **`button`** to publish.

Below, I show you the XAML of this control:

```
<?xml version="1.0" encoding="utf-8" ?>
<toolkit:Popup ...
xmlns:toolkit="http://schemas.microsoft.com/dotnet/2022/maui/toolkit"
               x:Class="MauiTalk.Controls.NewPostPopup">
    <!-- Semi-transparent background using Grid -->
    <Grid BackgroundColor="#80000000" VerticalOptions="Center"
          HorizontalOptions="Center">
        <Frame Padding="20"
               BackgroundColor="White" CornerRadius="20"
               WidthRequest="300"  HasShadow="True"  Vertical
Options="Center"
               HorizontalOptions="Center">
            <VerticalStackLayout Spacing="15">
                <Label Text="Spread your message" FontSize="22"
                       FontAttributes="Bold" TextColor="#333"
                       HorizontalOptions="Center" />
                <Editor x:Name="txtMsg"
                        Placeholder="Write something..."
                        AutoSize="TextChanges"
```

```
                          HeightRequest="100"
                          BackgroundColor="#f0f0f0"
                          TextColor="#000"/>
                    <Button Text="Post" BackgroundColor="#007aff"
                          TextColor="White"  FontAttributes="Bold"
                         CornerRadius="10"  Clicked="OnCloseClicked" />
                </VerticalStackLayout>
            </Frame>
        </Grid>
    </toolkit:Popup>
```

And this is the code-behind from the popup:

```
    public partial class NewPostPopup : Popup
    {
        public MsgSavedEventHandler MsgSaved;
        public NewPostPopup()
        {
            InitializeComponent();
        }
        public delegate void MsgSavedEventHandler(string msg);
        private void OnCloseClicked(object sender, EventArgs e)
        {
            string msg = txtMsg.Text?.Trim(); // Remove extra spaces
            if (string.IsNullOrWhiteSpace(msg))
            {
    Application.Current.MainPage.DisplayAlert("Info", "The message
    cannot be empty.", "OK");
                return;
            }
            MsgSaved?.Invoke(msg);
            Close();
        }
    }
```

It is Popup. It can be used easily from any page by calling the method **ShowPopup** and then receiving the message from the delegate **MsgSaved**. In this way, we separate the publishing logic and avoid cluttering the interface.

PinPopup

We are going to create another Popup type control that we will use to request the user's PIN when logging in or unlocking the application.

The control is defined as a Popup and is displayed as a centered popup window, which cannot be closed by tapping outside of it (for added security). It includes an input field for the user to enter their 4-digit PIN and a button to validate. Its structure in XAML looks more or less like this:

```
<toolkit:Popup...
xmlns:toolkit="http://schemas.microsoft.com/dotnet/2022/maui/tool-
kit" x:Class="MauiTalk.Controls.NewPostPopup" CanBeDismissedByTap-
pingOutsideOfPopup="False">
    <Frame Padding="20" ...>
        <VerticalStackLayout Spacing="15">
            <Label Text="Enter your PIN" />
            <Entry x:Name="pinEntry"
                   Placeholder="••••"
                   IsPassword="True"
                   MaxLength="4" />
            <Button Text="Submit"
                    Clicked="OnSubmitClicked" />
        </VerticalStackLayout>
    </Frame>
</toolkit:Popup>
```

The validation logic is done within the same control, comparing the PIN entered against one that it receives as a parameter in its constructor.

```
using CommunityToolkit.Maui.Views;
namespace MauiTalk.Controls;
public partial class NewPostPopup : Popup
{
    public MsgSavedEventHandler MsgSaved;
    public NewPostPopup()    {
        InitializeComponent();
    }
    public delegate void MsgSavedEventHandler(string msg);
    private void OnCloseClicked(object sender, EventArgs e)
    {
        string msg = txtMsg.Text?.Trim(); // Remove extra spaces
        if (string.IsNullOrWhiteSpace(msg))
        {
Application.Current.MainPage.DisplayAlert("Info", "The message
cannot be empty.", "OK");
            return;
        }
        MsgSaved?.Invoke(msg);
        Close();
    }
}
```

You can easily invoke this control from any page with:

```
var popup = new PinPopup(savedPin);
popup.PinSubmitted += (pin) => { /* continue */ };
await this.ShowPopupAsync(popup);
```

Remember that you can review the full code for this control in the book's repository if you want to customize it further or use it in other projects.

Congratulations on reaching this point!

In the next section, we will start working with the application pages. The first page that we will develop will be the user profile page, where we will manage the personal information of the user who has logged in.

ProfilePage

We are going to create the page so that the user can create and modify their account. This page will be made up of a simple form where they will only request to add a username, their phone number, and a PIN to be able to access the APP. *Figure 10.3* shows the design that the page will have.

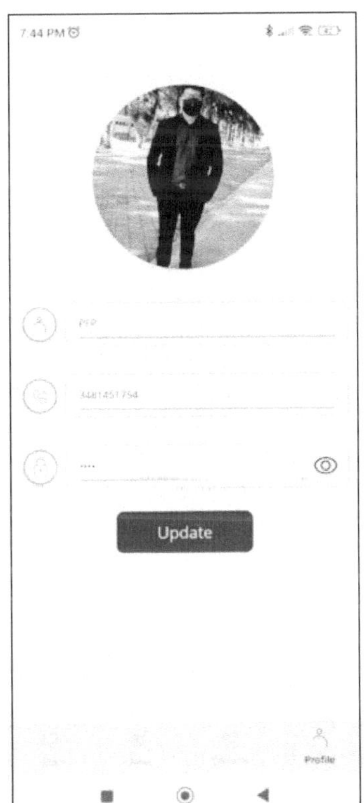

Figure 10.3: *ProfilePage page layout*

Reviewing the design of our page, we are going to break down the elements that make up this interface. We will not go into a detailed analysis of the entire UI, but we will focus on the most important aspects, both on the visual side and on its corresponding **ViewModel**. Remember that you can consult the complete code directly in the project repository.

UI

We fished for the general design. The page is built with a **VerticalStackLayout**, which contains a **Grid** with five rows, each focused on a visual component of the profile.

- **profile picture**: In the first row (**Grid.Row="0"**) we have a circular Frame that encloses the user's image. This image is fixed for now, but in the future, you could dynamically link to the data model.

```
<Frame Grid.Row="0"  CornerRadius="100"  WidthRequest="200"
       HeightRequest="200" BackgroundColor="White"
       Padding="0" BorderColor="Red"Margin="5,45,5,20"
       HasShadow="True">
    <Image Source="pedro.jpeg" WidthRequest="270"
           HeightRequest="270" Margin="0" />
</Frame>
```

- **User name:** The next row displays the user's name in an editable field (**Entry**) which is linked to **UserName** of the **ViewModel**. Accompanied by a decorative icon **(icon_profile.png)** within a small circular frame to maintain visual coherence.

```
<Grid  Grid.Row="1"  ColumnDefinitions="50,*" Margin="15">
 <Frame Grid.Column="0"  CornerRadius="50" WidthRequest="37"
        HeightRequest="37" BackgroundColor="White"
        Padding="0"  BorderColor="{StaticResource Primary}"
        Margin="0,5,5,5" HasShadow="True">
     <Image Source="icon_profile.png" WidthRequest="20"
            HeightRequest="20" Margin="0" />
 </Frame>
 <Frame Margin="0" Padding="10,0"  Grid.Column="1">
     <Entry Text="{Binding UserName}" Margin="0" />
 </Frame>
      </Grid>
```

- **Telephone number:** The same structure is repeated as in the name, but this time with the **PhoneNumber**, also linked to **ViewModel**.
- **Access PIN:** Here we have something interesting. The **Entry** is linked to a property **Pin** and can hide or show the value depending on the state of the boolean property **IcePass**. Additionally, there is an "**eye**" icon that activates

the command **TapImageEyeCommand**, allowing you to toggle between viewing and hiding the PIN.

- **Action button:** Finally, in the last row, there is a button that changes its text dynamically using **BtnText** and executes an action using the command **EditTapBtnCommand**. This can be used to save changes or trigger editing, depending on how you define it in the **ViewModel**.

```
<Button Grid.Row="4" Text="{Binding BtnText}"  FontSize="22"
        WidthRequest="150" Margin="0,10,0,0"
        Command="{Binding EditTapBtnCommand}"/>
```

Overall, this interface maintains a simple, clean, and functional design. The most important thing is that each element is bound to the **ViewModel**, which gives us flexibility to handle the screen state without complications.

ViewModel

In the directory **ViewModels**, let us create the class **ProfileViewModel.cs**. This class is responsible for managing the logic of the user's profile view. That is, it connects the interface to the data and controls the behavior of the visual elements. Here, I explain the key points:

- **BaseViewModel:** Inherits from a base class that probably already contains common logic such as change notifications (**INotifyPropertyChanged**).
- **DatabaseContext:** It is used to access the local database. All user information is saved and retrieved from here.
- **Properties with [ObservableProperty]:** Thanks to **CommunityToolkit.MVVM**, these properties automatically report changes. For example: **UserName**, **PhoneNumber**, **Pin**, **IsPass** (to show or hide the PIN), and **BtnText** (button text).
- **FillForm() method:** It is executed when creating the **ViewModel**. Loads the user's data if it already exists, and changes the button text depending on whether the user is already created or not.

```
private async Task FillForm()
 {
     var exist = (await _databaseContext.GetAllAsync<UserModel>()).
Where(x
                 => x.IsActive == true).FirstOrDefault();
     BtnText = exist == null ? "Create": "Update";
     UserName = exist?.UserName ?? string.Empty;
     PhoneNumber = exist?.PhoneNumber ?? string.Empty;
     Pin = exist?.Pin ?? string.Empty;
 }
```

- **TapImageEye command:** It is activated by touching the little eye icon and is used to show or hide the PIN.

```
[RelayCommand]
public void TapImageEye() { IcePass = IcePass ? false : true;  }
```

- **`EditTapBtn` command:** It is the heart of the form. If the number does not exist, create an account. If it already exists, update the user's data. Displays confirmation or error messages depending on the result.

```
 [RelayCommand]
 public async Task EditTapBtn(){
     try {
         var newUser = new UserModel(){
             UserName = UserName ?? string.Empty,
             PhoneNumber = PhoneNumber ?? string.Empty,
             Pin = Pin ?? string.Empty,
             IsActive = true };
         var exist = (await _databaseContext.GetAllAsync
<UserModel>())
             .Where(x => x.PhoneNumber == PhoneNumber).FirstOr
Default();
        if (exist == null){
            if (await _databaseContext.AddItemAsync(newUser)) {
              Application.Current.MainPage.DisplayAlert(
              "Account created",  "Account successfully
created!",  "OK");
                 return;  }
         } else{
             if (exist == null) return;
             newUser.Id = exist.Id;
             if (await _databaseContext.UpdateItemAsync(newUser))
{
                 Application.Current.MainPage.DisplayAlert(
       "Account updated", "The account was successfully
updated.",  "OK");
                 return;
             }
         }
Application.Current.MainPage.DisplayAlert("Warning", "invalid
operation", "OK");
     } catch(Exception ex) {
Application.Current.MainPage.DisplayAlert("Exception",
ex.Message, "OK");
     }
 }
```

In summary, this **`ViewModel`** allows you to create and edit a user's profile, connecting to the database and reacting to events that come from the graphical interface.

Next, we must inject the view (**`View`**), which we also register in the application routing.

In addition, we link it with its respective **ViewModel** inside the file **MauiProgram.cs**, leaving something like this:

```
builder.Services.AddTransient<ProfilePage>();
builder.Services.AddSingleton<ProfileViewModel>();
Routing.RegisterRoute("ProfilePage", typeof(ProfilePage));
```

To finish, in the **code-behind** of **ProfilePage**, let us set the **BindingContext**, which will allow us to connect this view with its **ViewModel** and thus handle all the logic in an organized way.

```
public ProfilePage(ProfileViewModel viewModel) {
        InitializeComponent();
        this.BindingContext = viewModel;
}
```

If you have made it this far, congratulations! We have completed the creation of our page. In the next section, we will focus on creating the page **ChatPage**, which is responsible for displaying the list of active chats.

ChatPage

Now we are going to create the page responsible for displaying the list of active chats. This view will be fed with the information stored in the table **ContactsAppModel**, which represents the contacts with whom we have started a conversation.

Additionally, we will implement a simple authentication mechanism at startup: when the user opens the application, they will be prompted for a **PIN** through a popup control called **PinPopup**. Next, *Figure* 10.4 illustrates the layout that this page will have.

Figure 10.4: *ChatPage page layout*

We are not going to delve into each XAML property, but we will explain the key elements that make it up:

- **`StatusBarBehavior`**: Here is a MAUI Toolkit behavior to customize the status bar, setting a white background and dark text for better readability.

- **Header with title:** And **Frame** reusable style displays the title of the chat (in this case, "**ChatAPP**").
- **Charging indicator:** Just below the header, we place an **ActivityIndicator** which is shown or hidden based on the property **IsVisible** of the **ViewModel**. This helps us notify the user that there are processes running (such as uploading contacts).
- **Contact List (CollectionView):** The most important part of this screen is the chat list, represented by a **CollectionView**. This binds to the **ChatsList** collection from the **ViewModel**.

```
<CollectionView ItemsSource="{Binding ChatsList}"  Grid.Row="2"
        x:Name="ChatContact" MaximumHeightRequest="650"
Margin="0,0,0,50">
<CollectionView.ItemTemplate>
<DataTemplate>
 <Frame  Style="{StaticResource ContactFrameStyle}">
    <Grid Style="{StaticResource ContactGridStyle}">
       <Frame Style="{StaticResource AvatarFrameStyle}"
 Grid.Column="0">
           <Image  Style="{StaticResource AvatarImageStyle}"-
Source="pedro.jpeg" />
       </Frame>
       <Label Grid.Column="1" Text="{Binding DisplayName}"
             Style="{StaticResource NameLabelStyle}" />
       <Label Style="{StaticResource CountLabelStyle}" Text="
{Binding numView}"
        Grid.Column="2" />
<Grid.GestureRecognizers>
       <TapGestureRecognizer
Command="{Binding Path = BindingContext.TapContactCommand,
Source={Reference ChatContact}}"
CommandParameter="{Binding}" />
       </Grid.GestureRecognizers>
   </Grid>
 </Frame>
</DataTemplate>
</CollectionView.ItemTemplate>  </CollectionView>
```

The interesting thing here is how we use **Source={Reference ChatContact}** to access the context of the **CollectionView**, making sure that each element can correctly launch the command when touched.

ViewModel

For the implementation of the **ViewModel**, we are going to create the class

ChatViewModel.cs. This class is responsible for controlling the logic related to the display of the user's chat list. Below, we explain the most important elements:

- **BaseViewModel inheritance:** This base class contains common functions such as change notification, thanks to the **INotifyPropertyChanged** interface, which allows us to keep the view in sync with the model.
- **DatabaseContext**: It is used to access the local database and retrieve user information such as contacts and messages.
- **[ObservableProperty]**: We leverage **CommunityToolkit.MVVM** to notify automatic changes. We use:
  - **ChatsList**: Observable list of type contacts **ContactData**, which contains the summary of the chats.
  - **IsVisible**: Flag to display a loading indicator while data is being processed.
- **Constructor:** By instantiating the **ViewModel**, the database context is initialized, the observable list is prepared, the loading screen is hidden, and two key methods are executed: one to show the PIN popup (**OpenPinPopup**) and another to load contacts (**LoadContacts**).

```
public ChatViewModel(DatabaseContext databaseContext)
{
   _databaseContext = databaseContext;
    ChatsList = new ObservableCollection<ContactData?>();
    IsVisible = false;
    _ = OpenPinPopup();
    _ = LoadContacts();
}
```

- **TapContact command:** This command is activated by touching a contact. Navigate to the messages page (**MessagesPage**) and pass the contact as a parameter to open the corresponding chat.

```
[RelayCommand]
public async Task TapContact(ContactData? contact)
{
    if (contact == null) return;
    var navigationParameter = new Dictionary<string, object> {
        { "Open", contact }
    };
await Shell.Current.GoToAsync("MessagesPage", navigationParame-
ter);
}
```

- **OpenPinPopup() method:** Shows a popup where the user must enter their PIN. If there is no active user, it automatically redirects to the profile page.

```
private async Task OpenPinPopup(){
    try{
        var user = (await _databaseContext.GetAllAsync<User
Model>())
            .Where(x => x.IsActive == true).FirstOrDefault();
        if (user != null){
            var pinPopup = new PinPopup(user.Pin);
            await App.Current.MainPage.ShowPopupAsync(pinPopup);
        } else {
            await Shell.Current.GoToAsync("ProfilePage");
        }
    }
    catch(Exception ex) { Console.WriteLine(ex.Message); }
}
```

- **`LoadContacts()` method:** It is the heart of this **`ViewModel`**. Loads all contacts associated with the active user and calculates how many messages have not been read by each contact. Add this information to **`ChatsList`** so that it is displayed in the interface.

```
private async Task LoadContacts() {
    IsVisible = true;
    try{
        ChatsList.Clear();
        _user = (await _databaseContext.GetAllAsync<UserModel>())
            .Where(x => x.IsActive == true).FirstOrDefault();
        if (_user?.UserName != null){
        var contacts = (await _databaseContext.GetAllAsync
<ContactsAppModel>())
            .Where(x => x.FkUser == _user.Id);
foreach(var contact in contacts) {
                if (contact != null){
var numView = (await _databaseContext.GetAllAsync<MessagesMod-
el>())
.Where(x => x.FkContactApp == contact.Id && x.Viewed == false).
Count();
 ChatsList.Add(new ContactData()
                {
                    Id = contact.Id,
                    DisplayName = contact.Name,
                    PhoneNumer = contact.PhoneNumber,
      numView = numView == 0 ? string.Empty : numView.ToString(),
                });
            }
        }
    }  else { ... }
}
catch (Exception ex)
```

```
        {
            ...
        }
        finally { IsVisible = false; }
    }
```

In summary, **ChatViewModel** allows you to control navigation to chats, shows a PIN validation popup and dynamically builds the list of contacts with their unread messages.

Next, we must inject the view (**View**) and its respective **ViewModel** inside the file **MauiProgram.cs**, leaving something like this:

```
builder.Services.AddSingleton<ChatViewModel>();
builder.Services.AddTransient<ChatPage>();
```

Finally, remember to set the **BindingContext** in its **code-behind** of **ChatPage**, which will allow us to connect this view with its **ViewModel.**

If you have made it this far, congratulations! We have completed the creation of our page. In the next section, we will focus on the creation of the **ContactsPage** page, which is responsible for displaying the list of contacts registered on the mobile device.

ContactsPage

Now we are going to create the page in charge of showing the list of all the contacts registered on the device. Before you begin, remember that you need to grant permissions to access this information. To do this, we must configure the permissions files corresponding to each platform:

- For Android, open the file **AndroidManifest.xml** and add the following inside the tag **<manifest>**:

  ```
  <uses-permission android:name="android.permission.READ_CONTACTS" />
  ```
- For iOS, open the file **Info.plist** and add the following line inside the main dictionary **(<dict>)**:

  ```
  <key>NSContactsUsageDescription</key>
  <string>This app needs to access your contacts to display the
  list of available chats.</string>
  ```

Once we have configured the necessary permissions, we can proceed with the design of the user interface. This view will be simple but efficient: it will have a **Label** that displays the title "**Contacts**", a **ActivityIndicator** linked to property **IsVisible** of the **ViewModel** to visually indicate when information is being loaded, and a **CollectionView** that connects to the collection **ChatsList**, which contains all available contacts.

Inside the **CollectionView**, each item is structured using a **Grid**, which shows the image, name, and number of the contact. Furthermore, this Grid is associated with the command **TapContactCommand**, allowing you to launch an event by tapping any contact in the list. Next, we will see the code for the **CollectionView**, which represents the visual core of this page.

```
 <CollectionView ItemsSource="{Binding ContactsList}"
                 Grid.Row="2" x:Name="CollectionContact"
                 MaximumHeightRequest="650" Margin="0,0,0,50">
     <CollectionView.ItemTemplate>
         <DataTemplate>
             <Frame Margin="10,5,10,8" CornerRadius="10"
BorderColor="#ffffff"
                     Padding="10,2,0,2" HasShadow="False">
                 <Grid ColumnDefinitions="auto,*,*" Column
Spacing="5">
                     <Frame Style="{StaticResource AvatarFrame-
Style}"
                            Grid.Column="0">
                         <Image  Style="{StaticResource Avatar
ImageStyle}"
                                 Source="user.png"  Width
Request="50"/>
                     </Frame>
                     <Label Grid.Column="1"  VerticalText
Alignment="Center"
                            FontSize="15" FontFamily="Arias"
                            Text="{Binding DisplayName}" Text
Color="Black" />
                     <Label Grid.Column="2" VerticalText
Alignment="Center"
                            HorizontalTextAlignment="Center"
                            FontSize="18"  FontFamily="Arias"
                            Text="{Binding Phones[0]}"  Text
Color="Black" />
                     <Grid.GestureRecognizers>
<TapGestureRecognizer Command="{Binding Path = BindingContext.
TapContactCommand, Source={Reference CollectionContact}}"
                       CommandParameter="{Binding}" />
                     </Grid.GestureRecognizers>
                 </Grid>
             </Frame>
         </DataTemplate>
     </CollectionView.ItemTemplate>
 </CollectionView>
```

Once the interface design is complete, the next step is to implement the logic that supports it. To do this, within the **ViewModels** directory, we will create the class **ContactsViewModel.cs,** which will inherit from **BaseViewModel**. This class will be responsible for managing the view state and coordinating the loading of contacts. Below, I detail the most relevant elements of this **ViewModel**:

- **[ObservableProperty]:** We will use the attributes of **CommunityToolkit.MVVM** to automatically generate properties with support for change notification, simplifying the code and improving its maintainability.
- **ContactsList**: It is an observable collection (**ObservableCollection <Contact?>**) that will store the contacts obtained from the device.
- **IsVisible**: Boolean flag that controls the visibility of the **ActivityIndicator**, indicating whether the data is in the process of loading.
- **ContactsViewModel**: Class constructor, in which we initialize the properties and prepare the environment for data loading.
- **OnAppearing**: Public method that can be called from the code-behind or from the view to start loading contacts when the page appears on the screen.
- **LoadContactsAsync**: Primary method that queries device contacts and adds them to **ContactsList**. It also manages the visibility of the charging indicator.

```
 public async Task LoadContactsAsync()
{
    try
    {
        if (ContactsList.Any()) return;
if (await Permissions.RequestAsync<Permissions.ContactsRead>() !=
 PermissionStatus.Granted) return;
        IsVisible = true;
        await Task.Run(async () =>
        {
var contacts = await Communication.Contacts.Default.GetAllAsync();
            if (contacts == null)  return;
            MainThread.BeginInvokeOnMainThread(() => {
                foreach (var contact in contacts)
                    ContactsList.Add(contact);      });
        });
    }
    catch (Exception ex) { Messeger = ex.Message; }
    finally { IsVisible = false; }
}
```

- **TapContact**: This command is activated by touching a contact. Navigate to the messages page (**MessagesPage**) and pass the contact as a parameter to open the corresponding chat.

```
[RelayCommand]
public async Task TapContact(Contact? contact){
      if(contact == null)  return;
      var navigationParameter = new Dictionary<string, object>
      {{ "Contact", contact }};
      await Shell.Current.GoToAsync("MessagesPage", navigation-
      Parameter);
}
```

Next, we must inject the view (**View**) and its respective **ViewModel** inside the file **MauiProgram.cs**, leaving something like this:

```
builder.Services.AddSingleton<ContactsViewModel>();
builder.Services.AddTransient<ContactsPage>();
```

Finally, it is important to establish the **BindingContext** in its code-behind of **ContactsPage** to bind the view with its corresponding **ViewModel**. Additionally, we will implement the event **OnAppearing**, which will allow us to run the contact loading logic when the page is displayed for the first time.

```
public partial class ContactsPage : ContentPage {
public ContactsPage(ContactsViewModel viewModel) {
            InitializeComponent();
            this.BindingContext = viewModel;
      }
      protected override void OnAppearing(){
            base.OnAppearing();
            if (this.BindingContext is ContactsViewModel
viewModel)
                  _ = viewModel.OnAppearing();
      }
}
```

If you have made it this far, congratulations! We have completed the creation of our page. In the next section, we will focus on creating the **MessagesPage** page, the page that is responsible for displaying received messages and sending messages to our contacts.

MessagesPage

Now we are going to create the page in charge of displaying the messages sent and received within a conversation. This view is essential, as it represents the center of the messaging experience in our app. Visually, it will have a vertical list of messages and, at the bottom, a text box along with a button to send new messages.

Before moving forward with the logic, let us focus on the visual structure. The view is divided into two areas by a **Grid**- The top part houses the message history, while the bottom part contains the input field and the submit button.

Message history is represented by a **CollectionView**, which links directly to the collection **Messages** provided by the **ViewModel**. Each message is rendered within a **Frame**, and both its background color and horizontal alignment vary depending on whether it was sent by the user or received. To achieve this dynamic behavior, we are going to use two **converters** customized: **BoolToColorConverter** and **BoolToAlignmentConverter**.

Both converters will be implemented as independent classes within the directory **Converters**, allowing us to maintain a clean and modular architecture. Next, we will show you how the class code should look. **BoolToAlignmentConverter.cs**:

```
public class BoolToAlignmentConverter : IValueConverter {
public object Convert(object value, Type targetType, object
parameter, CultureInfo culture){ return (bool)value ? LayoutOptions.
End : LayoutOptions.Start; }
public object ConvertBack(object value, Type targetType, object
parameter, CultureInfo culture) { throw new NotImplemented
Exception();  }
 }
```

Once the previous class is finished, we are going to create the class **BoolToColorConverter.cs**; we place this class inside the directory **Converters**. Its implementation is as follows:

```
public class BoolToColorConverter : IValueConverter {
      public object Convert(object value, Type targetType, object
      parameter, CultureInfo culture){ return (bool)value ? Colors.
      Blue : Colors.Gray;}
       public object ConvertBack(object value, Type targetType,
      object parameter, CultureInfo culture) { throw new NotImple-
      mented Exception(); }
}
```

Having finished creating the converters, you can see the relevant XAML code that structures the main view:

```
<ContentPage ...
             x:Class="MauiTalk.Views.MessagesPage"
             BackgroundColor="White"
             Title="{Binding DisplayName}">
    <Grid RowDefinitions="*, Auto">
        <!-- Message history -->
        <CollectionView ItemsSource="{Binding Messages}" Grid.
Row="0"
```

```
                              Margin="10" x:Name="MessagesCollectionView"
                              ItemsUpdatingScrollMode="KeepLastItemInView">
            <CollectionView.ItemsLayout> <LinearItemsLayout
Orientation="Vertical" />
            </CollectionView.ItemsLayout>
                <CollectionView.ItemTemplate>
                    <DataTemplate>
<Frame Padding="10" Margin="5" CornerRadius="15" BackgroundCol-
or="{Binding IsMine, Converter={StaticResource BoolToColorConvert-
er}}" HorizontalOptions="{Binding IsMine, Converter={StaticResource
BoolToAlignmentConverter}}">
                              <Label Text="{Binding Text}" TextColor
="White" />
                        </Frame>
                    </DataTemplate>
                </CollectionView.ItemTemplate>
            </CollectionView>
            <!-- Text box and submit button -->
            <StackLayout Grid.Row="1"  Orientation="Horizontal"
                         Padding="10" Margin="0,0,0,10"Background
Color="White">
                <Entry x:Name="MessageEntry"  Placeholder="Write a
message..."
                       HorizontalOptions="FillAndExpand" Text="{Binding
MessageText}"
                       VerticalTextAlignment="End" />
 <Button Text="Enviar" WidthRequest="80" Command="{Binding Send
MessageCommand}" />
            </StackLayout>
        </Grid>
</ContentPage>
```

With this, we now have the visual structure of the messages page ready. In the next step, we will implement the **`ViewModel`** that manages this view, including sending messages and logic to update the history dynamically.

ViewModel

Once we have designed the interface to display the messages, the next step is to implement the necessary logic for it to work correctly. In this case, within the directory **`ViewModels`**, we will create the class **`MessagesViewModel.cs`**, which will inherit from **`BaseViewModel`** and will be responsible for managing the state of the view, as well as coordinating the loading and sending of messages.

Following is a detail of the most relevant elements of this **`ViewModel`**:

We will use the **`ObservableProperty`** attribute of the **`CommunityToolkit.MVVM`** through the **[ObservableProperty]** to automatically generate properties with support for change notification. This simplifies the code and improves its maintainability, since we do not have to write boilerplate code for property change notifications.

- **MessageText**: This property stores the text of the message that the user is typing.
- **DisplayName**: It is the name that will be displayed in the view, corresponding to the name of the contact with whom we are chatting.
- **PhoneNumber**: Stores the phone number of the contact we are chatting with.
- **Messages:** It is an observable collection (**ObservableCollection <MessageModel>**) that contains all the messages in the current conversation. This allows the view to update automatically when new messages are added.

In the class constructor, **MessagesViewModel** receives as parameters the service **SignalRService** and database context **DatabaseContext**. In the constructor, we establish the connection to the server and subscribe to incoming messages using an event. Every time a message is received, it is processed and stored in the database.

```
public MessagesViewModel(SignalRService signalRService, DatabaseCon-
text databaseContext)
 {
     Messages = new ObservableCollection<MessageModel>();
     _databaseContext = databaseContext;
     MessageText = string.Empty;
     _signalRService = signalRService;
     Task.Run(async () => await _signalRService.ConnectAsync());
     _signalRService.OnMessageReceived += (user, message) => {
if (_uSer?.UserName == null || user == _uSer.UserName || user.
Contains("Post:")) return;
 var newMsg = new MessageModel { Text = $"{user}: {message}", IsMine
= false };
         string json = JsonSerializer.Serialize(newMsg);
         _ = Task.Run(async () =>{
             try { await SavedMsg(json);}
             catch (Exception ex) {
                 Console.WriteLine($"Error saving message:
{ex.Message}");
         }});
         if (user == displayName)
             MainThread.BeginInvokeOnMainThread(() => Messages.
Add(newMsg));
     };
 }
```

Then we will add the method **SendMessage**, which is executed when the user sends a message. If the contact is not registered, it shows an alert. If the message is not empty, it is sent via **SignalRService** and then added to the Messages collection locally. After that, the message is saved in the database.

```
[RelayCommand]
public async Task SendMessage(){
    try { if (_idContact == 0) {
Application.Current.MainPage.DisplayAlert("Warning", "The user is not registered", "OK"); return;}
        if (!string.IsNullOrWhiteSpace(MessageText)) {
            if (_signalRService == null)  {
             Console.WriteLine("SignalRService is not initialized.");  return;
            }
await _signalRService.SendMessage(_uSer.UserName, MessageText);
var newMsg = new MessageModel { Text = $"yo: {MessageText}", IsMine = true };
            Messages.Add(newMsg);
            string json = JsonSerializer.Serialize(newMsg);
            await SavedMsg(json);
            MessageText = string.Empty;
        }
    } catch(Exception ex){ Console.WriteLine(ex.Message); }
}
```

Then we will add the method **SavedMsg.** It is responsible for saving messages in the database, including the contact to which the message belongs and the viewing status.

```
private async Task SavedMsg(string json){  try {
        if (await _databaseContext.AddItemAsync(new MessagesModel() {
            FkContactApp = _idContact,
            Viewed = false,
            Message = json,
            Date = DateTime.Now})){
            Console.WriteLine("Msg successfully created!");
        }
    }catch(Exception ex){ Console.WriteLine(ex.Message);  }
}
```

Method **ItsContact**, which ensures that the user who is sending the message is registered in the database. If the contact does not exist, it adds it to the contact list and saves the information. If the contact is already registered, you simply get their ID.

```
private async Task ItsContact(){  try{
   _uSer = (await  databaseContext.GetAllAsync<UserModel>())
   .Where(x => x.IsActive == true).FirstOrDefault();
var contact = (await _databaseContext.GetAllAsync<ContactsAppMod-
el>()).Where(x => x.PhoneNumber == PhoneNumber?.PhoneNumber &&
x.FkUser == _uSer.Id).FirstOrDefault();
```

```
            if (contact == null){
                var newContact = new ContactsAppModel() {
                    FkUser = _uSer.Id,
                    Name = DisplayName ?? "user",
                    PhoneNumber = PhoneNumber?.PhoneNumber ?? "0"};
                if (await _databaseContext.AddItemAsync(newContact)) {
                    _idContact = newContact.Id;
                    Console.WriteLine("Contact successfully created! -");
                }else{
    Application.Current.MainPage.DisplayAlert("Warning", "invalid
    operation", "OK");
                    return;
                }
            } else{ _idContact = contact.Id;}
    int newContactId = (await _databaseContext.GetAllAsync<Contacts
    AppModel>())
    .Where(x => x.PhoneNumber == PhoneNumber?.PhoneNumber &&
    x.FkUser == _uSer.Id).Select(x => x.Id).FirstOrDefault();
            await LoadSavedMessages();
        } catch (Exception ex){
            Application.Current.MainPage.DisplayAlert("Exception",
    ex.Message, "OK");
        }
    }
```

We will define the method **LoadSavedMessages**, which loads previously saved messages from the database, marking those messages as read if necessary.

```
    private async Task LoadSavedMessages(){ try {
       var oldMsg = (await _databaseContext.GetAllAsync<MessagesModel>())
       .Where(x => x.FkContactApp == _idContact).OrderBy(m => m.Date);
            if (oldMsg == null) return;
            foreach(var msg in oldMsg)  {
                if(msg != null) {
                    if(!msg.Viewed) { msg.Viewed = true;
                        if(!await _databaseContext.UpdateItemAsync(msg))
    {
                            Console.WriteLine($"outdated message: {msg.
    Id}");
                        }
                    }
    MessageModel message = JsonSerializer.Deserialize<MessageModel>(msg.
    Message);   var newMsg = new MessageModel { Text = message.Text,
    IsMine = message.IsMine };  Messages.Add(newMsg);
                }
            }
        }catch(Exception ex) {
```

```
        Application.Current.MainPage.DisplayAlert("Exception",
ex.Message, "OK");
}}
```

Finally, you need to configure the **BindingContext** in the code-behind of the page **MessagesPage** and register the page in the router app to enable browsing.

```
builder.Services.AddSingleton<MessagesViewModel>();
builder.Services.AddTransient<MessagesPage>();
Routing.RegisterRoute("MessagesPage", typeof(MessagesPage));
```

If you have made it this far, congratulations! We have completed the creation of our page. In the next section, we will focus on creating the page **FriendsPage**, the last page of the application that is responsible for displaying user posts.

FriendsPage

Now we are going to create the page that will be responsible for displaying a list of user posts on a fictitious social network. This page will be designed using the MVVM pattern, where the view will be linked to a **ViewModel** that will manage the business logic.

The main structure of our page is a **ContentPage**, which contains a vertical layout. At the top, we will have a title with a button to add new posts, and below this, a list of posts that will be displayed using a **CollectionView**.

```
<ContentPage ...
             xmlns:toolkit="http://schemas.microsoft.com/dotnet
/2022/maui/toolkit"
             x:Class="MauiTalk.Views.FriendsPage">
    <VerticalStackLayout>
        <Grid RowDefinitions="auto,*">
            <Grid Margin="0,20,10,10" Padding="10,0"
                  ColumnDefinitions="*,50"  Grid.Row="0">
                <Label Text="Publications" Grid.Column="0"
                       TextColor="{StaticResource Primary}"
                       VerticalTextAlignment="Center"  FontSize="28"
/>
                <Button  Grid.Column="2 "Text="+" Padding="0"
                         FontSize="40"  BackgroundColor="#0CA789"
                         BorderColor="#0CA789"  WidthRequest="45"
                         HeightRequest="45"  CornerRadius="50"
                         Command="{Binding BtnAddTapCommand}"/>
            </Grid>
```

The structure is made up of a **Label** which shows the title "**Posts**", and a Button that allows adding new posts. The button is linked to a command, **BtnAddTapCommand**, to handle the action of adding content.

The list of posts is displayed using a **CollectionView**, which is linked to the property **NewsPosts** of the **ViewModel**. Each post is displayed through a template defined in a **DataTemplate**. Each cell in the list contains the user's information, such as their name and the date of the post, as well as the content of the post.

```
<CollectionView ItemsSource="{Binding NewsPosts}"
                Grid.Row="1" x:Name="NewsPost"
                MaximumHeightRequest="650" Margin="0,0,0,50">
            <CollectionView.ItemTemplate>
                <DataTemplate>
                    <Frame Margin="15,15,15,10" Padding="10">
                        <VerticalStackLayout>
                            <Grid ColumnDefinitions="auto,*,110">
                                <Frame Grid.Column="0"
CornerRadius="50"
                                       WidthRequest="37"
HeightRequest="37"
                                       BackgroundColor="White"
Padding="0"
                                       BorderColor="Red"
Margin="0,5,15,5"
                                       HasShadow="True">
 <Image Source="pedro.jpeg" WidthRequest="50" HeightRequest="50"
Margin="0" />
                                </Frame>
                                <Label Grid.Column="1"
                                       VerticalTextAlignment
="Center"
                                       FontSize="15" FontFamily
="Arias"
                                       Text="{Binding UserName}"
                                       TextColor="Black" />
                                <Label Grid.Column="2"
                                       VerticalTextAlignment
="Center"
                                       FontSize="15"  Font
Family="Arias"
 Text="{Binding Date, StringFormat='{}{0:dd MMM yyyy}'}" TextColor
="Black" />
                            </Grid>
                            <Frame Margin="0"BorderColor="White">
                                <Label TextTransform="Lowercase"
                                       Text="{Binding Post}" />
```

```
                                </Frame>
                                 <HorizontalStackLayout Margin="0">
  <Image Source="like.png" WidthRequest="22" Margin="0,0,5,0"></
Image>
  <Image Source="like.png" WidthRequest="22" Rotation="180"></Image>
                                </HorizontalStackLayout>
                            </VerticalStackLayout>
                        </Frame>
                    </DataTemplate>
                </CollectionView.ItemTemplate>
            </CollectionView>
        </Grid>
    </VerticalStackLayout>
</ContentPage>
```

In this design, the property **`NewsPosts`** is linked to the posts list, which means that the posts displayed in the **`CollectionView`** come from **`ViewModel`**. Each post has a dataset that includes the user's name, date, and message content. In the next chapter, we will make sure that the **`ViewModel`** is correctly implemented to handle posts.

The "+" button displayed at the top of the page is linked to the command **`BtnAddTapCommand`** in its **`ViewModel`**. This command is triggered when the user taps the button and executes the action of adding a new post. To do this, the command must be linked to logic that allows the user to enter the content and store it in a database or send the information through a backend service.

Once the UI is created, we will create the class **`FriendsViewModel.cs`** in the **`ViewModels`** directory, which inherits the class **`BaseViewModel.`** This is where everything related to the posts list is handled. Below, the most relevant elements of this **`ViewModel`** are detailed:

- **`[ObservableProperty]`:** We will use the attributes of **`CommunityToolkit.MVVM`** to automatically generate properties with support for change notification, simplifying the code and improving its maintainability.
- **`NewsPosts`**: Observable collection (**`ObservableCollection<NewsAppModel?>`**)
- **`FriendsViewModel`**: In the constructor, a **handler** for the event **`OnMessageReceived`** of the **`SignalRService`**. Whenever a message containing the Post: prefix arrives, it is interpreted as a post and added to the list.

  ```
  public FriendsViewModel(SignalRService signalRService, Database
  Context databaseContext){

     _signalRService = signalRService;
     _databaseContext = databaseContext;
     NewsPosts = new ObservableCollection<NewsAppModel>();
     _signalRService.OnMessageReceived += (user, message) =>{
         if (!user.Contains("Post:")) return;
  ```

```
var newMsg = new MessageModel { Text = $"{user}: {message}", IsMine
= false };
        string json = JsonSerializer.Serialize(newMsg);
        try{
            var newPost = new NewsAppModel(){
                UserName = user.Substring("Post:".Length),
                Post = message,
                Date = DateTime.Now,
            };
            NewsPosts . Add ( newPost ) ;
        } catch (Exception ex) {
            Console.WriteLine($"Error saving message: {ex.Mes-
sage}");
        }
    };
 }
```

- **BtnAddTap**: Command responsible for starting **NewPostPopup** when you tap the "**+**" button.

```
[RelayCommand]
public async Task BtnAddTap(){
    var newPost = string.Empty;
    var popup = new NewPostPopup();
    popup.MsgSaved += (msg) => { newPost += msg;};
    await App.Current.MainPage.ShowPopupAsync(popup);
    await SendMessage(newPost);
}
```

- **SendMessage**: Function responsible for sending publications.

```
private async Task SendMessage(string newPost){
    try{
        if (!string.IsNullOrWhiteSpace(newPost)){
            if (_signalRService == null){
                Console.WriteLine("SignalRService is not
initialized.");
                return;
            }
var user = (await _databaseContext.GetAllAsync<UserModel>()).
Where(x => x.IsActive == true).FirstOrDefault();
await _signalRService.SendMessage($"Post:{user?.UserName}",
newPost);
var newMsg = new MessageModel { Text = $"Post:{user?.UserName}",
IsMine = true };
        }
    } catch (Exception ex){Console.WriteLine(ex.Message); }
}
```

Next, we must inject the view (**`View`**) and the **`ViewModel`** inside the file **`MauiProgram.cs`**, leaving something like this:

```
builder.Services.AddTransient<FriendsPage>();
builder.Services.AddSingleton<FriendsViewModel>();
```

To finish, in the **code-behind** of **`ProfilePage`**, let us set the **`BindingContext`**, which will allow us to connect this view with its **`ViewModel`** and thus handle all the logic in an organized way.

```
public partial class FriendsPage : ContentPage {
      public FriendsPage(FriendsViewModel viewmodel)
      {
            InitializeComponent();
            this.BindingContext = viewmodel;
      }
}
```

Congratulations! You have reached the end of this project. With this, we have successfully completed our social networking application. Great job! All the effort invested in development, testing, and fine-tuning now results in robust and efficient functionality. Congratulations on reaching this milestone and bringing the project to successful completion!

Conclusion

In this chapter, we develop a social network-type messaging application, inspired by platforms such as WhatsApp. This type of application is essential in modern communication, as it allows users to connect in real time quickly and efficiently. Throughout the chapter, we address key development aspects such as project organization, file structure, and system scalability. We implement dependency injection, work with the MVVM design pattern, manage the lifecycle with events such as **`OnAppearing`**, and perform CRUD operations on the local database using SQLite.

Additionally, we integrated **`SignalR`** to enable real-time messaging between users, configured network services, and designed a functional interface for sending and receiving messages. With this, we took an important step towards building a complete and seamless social experience.

In the next chapter, we explore new functionalities by developing an educational application. In it, we will implement video playback and the possibility of taking structured courses. This evolution will open the door to a dynamic and enriching digital learning experience.

CHAPTER 11
Building an Education App

Introduction

In this chapter, we will develop an educational app that showcases how to build interactive learning experiences using .NET MAUI. While simplified in scope, this project demonstrates common patterns used in educational software, including user login, course listing, course registration, and favorite content. Our primary goal will be to build a clean and scalable app using MVVM, SQLite for persistence, and .NET MAUI Community Toolkit for extended capabilities. We will walk through the entire development process, from setting up the project to building user interfaces and managing data.

Structure

In this chapter, we will discuss the following topics:

- App Description
- Project Setup
- Project Structure
- SQLite Configuration
- Data Modeling
- `AppShell` Configuration
- Views and `ViewModels`
- Video Integration, Favorites, and Registration

App Description

The educational app we will build allows users to:

- Login with basic credentials.

- Browse a list of courses.
- View course details and register.
- Mark courses as favorites.

It serves as a strong foundation for more complex educational systems and can be expanded with features such as quizzes, videos, and progress tracking.

Project Setup

We begin by creating a new project using the ".NET MAUI App" template in Visual Studio, targeting .NET 8 or higher. Once created, install the following packages:

- **`CommunityToolkit.MAUI`**: For additional UI controls and helpers.
- **`CommunityToolkit.Mvvm`**: Simplifies MVVM pattern.
- **`sqlite-net-pcl`**: Lightweight ORM for SQLite.
- **`Microsoft.Data.Sqlite`**: SQLite support by Microsoft.

Enable the Community Toolkit in **`MauiProgram.cs`**:

```
builder.UseMauiCommunityToolkit();
```

Project Structure

We organize the project into these main **`folders:CommunityToolkit.MAUI:`** For additional UI controls and helpers.

- **`Data`**: SQLite context management.
- **`Models`**: Representations of data (Course, Users, and so on).
- **`ViewModels`**: Logic and interaction handlers.
- **`Views`**: User Interface pages (**`LoginView.xaml`**, **`MyCoursesView.xaml`**, and so on).

Default pages, such as **`MainPage.xaml`**, can be replaced with your own designed views.

SQLite Configuration

The educational app uses SQLite as its local database to persist in user and course data. To manage the database, we create a **`DatabaseContext.cs`** inside the Data folder.

This class is responsible for:

- Opening the connection to the SQLite database.
- Creating tables if they do not exist.
- Handling CRUD operations (Create, Read, Update, Delete).

Example setup:

```
public class DatabaseContext
{
    private readonly SQLiteAsyncConnection _database;

    public DatabaseContext(string dbPath)
    {
        _database = new SQLiteAsyncConnection(dbPath);
        _database.CreateTableAsync<Course>().Wait();
        _database.CreateTableAsync<User>().Wait();
        _database.CreateTableAsync<Favorite>().Wait();
    }

    public Task<List<Course>> GetCoursesAsync()
    {
        return _database.Table<Course>().ToListAsync();
    }
}
Register it via dependency injection in MauiProgram.cs:
builder.Services.AddSingleton<DatabaseContext>(s =>
    new DatabaseContext(Path.Combine(FileSystem.AppDataDirectory,
"educationapp.db3"))
);
```

Data Modeling

The app relies on simple but effective models to represent its core data:

Course.cs:

```
public class Course
{
    [PrimaryKey, AutoIncrement]
    public int Id { get; set; }
    public string Title { get; set; }
    public string Description { get; set; }
    public string VideoUrl { get; set; }
}
```

User.cs:

```
public class User
{
    [PrimaryKey, AutoIncrement]
    public int Id { get; set; }
    public string Username { get; set; }
    public string Password { get; set; }
}
```

```
Favorite.cs:
public class Favorite
{
    [PrimaryKey, AutoIncrement]
    public int Id { get; set; }
    public int UserId { get; set; }
    public int CourseId { get; set; }
}
```

AppShell Configuration

Navigation in our MAUI app is handled through **AppShell.xaml**. Shell provides a convenient structure for multi-page applications with Tab menus and simple routing.

Basic **AppShell** Setup:

```
<Shell
    x:Class="EducationalApp.AppShell"
    xmlns="http://schemas.microsoft.com/dotnet/2021/maui"
    xmlns:x="http://schemas.microsoft.com/winfx/2009/xaml"
    xmlns:views="clr-namespace:EducationalApp.Views"
    xmlns:toolkit="http://schemas.microsoft.com/dotnet/2022/maui/
toolkit"
    Shell.FlyoutBehavior="Disabled"
    Title="EducationalApp">
<Shell.Behaviors>
    <toolkit:StatusBarBehavior StatusBarColor="#ffffff"
                               StatusBarStyle="DarkContent" />
</Shell.Behaviors>

    <TabBar>
    <Tab Title="My Courses"
         Icon="play.png">
        <ShellContent
        ContentTemplate="{DataTemplate views:MyCoursesView}"
        Route="MyCoursesView" />
    </Tab>
    <Tab Title="Search"
         Icon="search.png">
        <ShellContent
        ContentTemplate="{DataTemplate views:SearchView}"
        Route="SearchView" />
    </Tab>
    <Tab Title="Wish List"
         Icon="heart.png">
        <ShellContent
```

```
            ContentTemplate="{DataTemplate views:WishListView}"
            Route="WishListView" />
        </Tab>
        <Tab Title="Account"
             Icon="account.png">
            <ShellContent
            ContentTemplate="{DataTemplate views:AccountView}"
            Route="AccountView" />
        </Tab>
    </TabBar>

    </Shell>
```

Each view is mapped into the **Tab** Menu automatically.

You can also define routes for manual navigation:

```
    <ShellContent
              ContentTemplate="{DataTemplate views:LoginView}"
              FlyoutItemIsVisible="False"
              Route="LoginView" />

     <ShellContent Title="Create User"
             ContentTemplate="{DataTemplate views:UserView}"
             FlyoutItemIsVisible="False"
             Route="UserView" />
```

Views and ViewModels

The application is built using the **Model-View-ViewModel (MVVM)** pattern to maintain a clean separation of concerns. Each screen (or view) is paired with a corresponding **ViewModel**. We will focus on a few important ones; we will not explain the others in depth since, in previous chapters, we have given a lot of emphasis to similar views and **viewmodels**, and we do not want to be redundant in this information.

These are the core **Views** and **ViewModels**:

- **LoginView.xaml + LoginViewModel.cs**
- **MyCoursesView.xaml + MyCoursesView ViewModel.cs**
- **CourseDescriptionView.xaml + CourseDescriptionViewModel.cs**
- **WishListView.xaml + WishListView Model.cs**

Login View

The Login screen allows users to authenticate by entering their credentials.

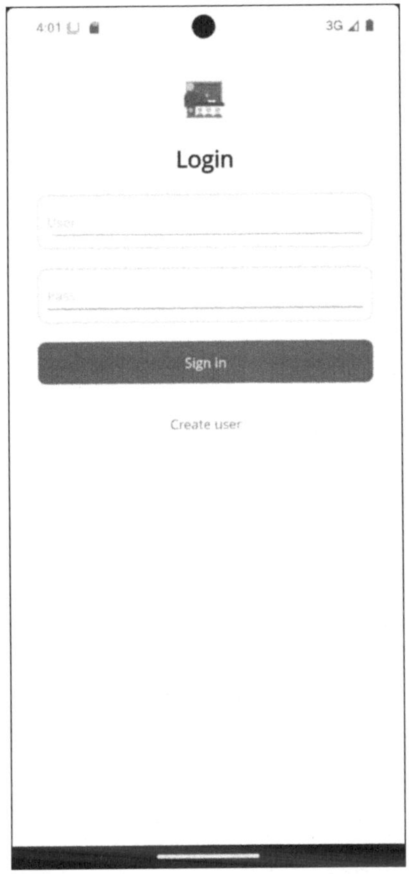

***Figure 11.1**: Representation of the login view*

- Username field
- Password field
- Login button
- Bindings to **LoginViewModel** properties: Username, Password, and **LoginCommand**.

View:

```
<?xml version="1.0" encoding="utf-8" ?>
<ContentPage xmlns="http://schemas.microsoft.com/dotnet/2021/maui"
             xmlns:x="http://schemas.microsoft.com/winfx/2009/xaml"
             x:Class="EducationalApp.Views.LoginView"
             xmlns:viewmodels="clr-namespace:EducationalApp.
ViewModels"
             x:DataType="viewmodels:LoginViewModel">
    <VerticalStackLayout Padding="30"
                         Spacing="20">
```

```
        <Image Source="course.png"
            HeightRequest="50"
            WidthRequest="50"
            HorizontalOptions="Center" />

        <Label Text="Login"
            FontSize="24"
            FontAttributes="Bold"
            HorizontalOptions="Center" />

        <Frame CornerRadius="10"
            Padding="5"
            BorderColor="#ccc">
            <Entry  Placeholder="User"
                 TextColor="Black"
                 Text="{Binding UserName}"/>
        </Frame>

        <Frame CornerRadius="10"
            Padding="5"
            BorderColor="#ccc">
            <Entry Placeholder="Pass"
            IsPassword="True"
            TextColor="Black"
                Text="{Binding PassUser}"/>
        </Frame>

        <Button Text="Sign in"
             BackgroundColor="#007AFF"
             TextColor="White"
             Command="{Binding TapButtonSignInCommand}"/>

        <Button Text="Create user"
             BackgroundColor="#ffffff"
             TextColor="#007AFF"
             Command="{Binding TapButtonCreateUserCommand}" />

    </VerticalStackLayout>
</ContentPage>
```

ViewModel:

```
[ObservableProperty]
private string username;

[ObservableProperty]
private string password;
```

```
[RelayCommand]
async Task LoginAsync()
{
    var user = await _databaseContext.GetUserByUsernameAsync
(Username);
    if (user != null && user.Password == Password)
    {
        await Shell.Current.GoToAsync("//DashboardPage");
    }
}
```

My Courses View

The My Courses View displays all available courses fetched from the database.

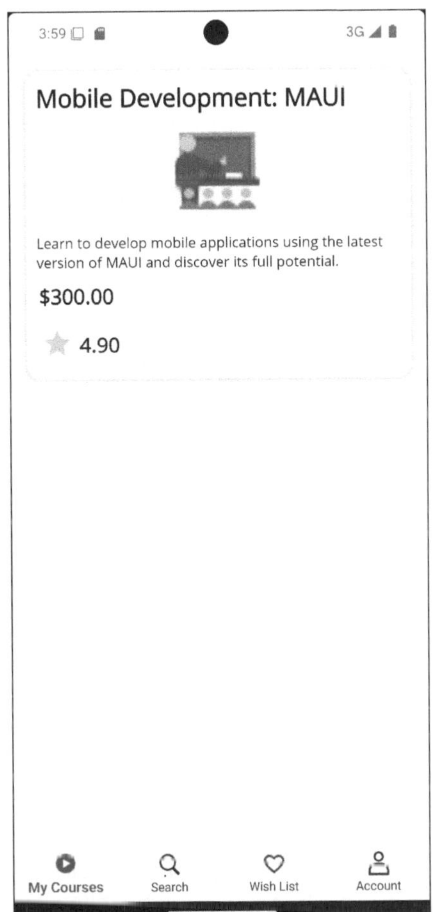

***Figure 11.2**: Representation of the screen my courses view*

- List of courses in a **CollectionView**.
- Search bar to filter courses.
- Bindings to Courses **ObservableCollection** and **LoadCoursesCommand**.

View:

```
<?xml version="1.0" encoding="utf-8" ?>
<ContentPage xmlns="http://schemas.microsoft.com/dotnet/2021/maui"
             xmlns:x="http://schemas.microsoft.com/winfx/2009/xaml"
             x:Class="EducationalApp.Views.MyCoursesView"
             xmlns:viewmodels="clr-namespace:EducationalApp.
ViewModels"
             xmlns:models="clr-namespace:EducationalApp.Models"
             x:DataType="viewmodels:MyCoursesViewModel">
    <VerticalStackLayout>
        <CollectionView ItemsSource="{Binding MyCourses}"
  VerticalOptions="Fill"
  x:Name="CollectionCourse"
  Margin="10">
            <CollectionView.ItemsLayout>
                <GridItemsLayout Orientation="Vertical"
                  Span="1"/>
            </CollectionView.ItemsLayout>
            <CollectionView.ItemTemplate>
                <DataTemplate x:DataType="models:Course">
                    <Frame CornerRadius="15"
     BackgroundColor="White"
     BorderColor="#E0E0E0"
     Padding="10"
     Margin="5"
     HasShadow="True">
                        <VerticalStackLayout>
                            <Label Text="{Binding Name}"
             FontAttributes="Bold"
             FontSize="Title"
             InputTransparent="True" />

                            <Image Source="{Binding Image}"
             WidthRequest="100"
             Margin="5,5,5,10"/>

                            <Label Text="{Binding Description}"
             HorizontalTextAlignment="Start"
             FontSize="14"
             InputTransparent="True" />
```

```
                              <Label Text="{Binding Price, String
Format='${0:N2}'}"
            FontSize="20"
            FontAttributes="Bold"
            Margin="2,10"
            InputTransparent="True" />

                              <HorizontalStackLayout>

                                 <Image Source="star.png"
WidthRequest="30"
HeightRequest="30"
Margin="5,5,5,10"/>

                                 <Label Text="{Binding Calification,
StringFormat='{0:N2}'}"
FontSize="20"
FontAttributes="Bold"
Margin="2,10"
InputTransparent="True" />
                              </HorizontalStackLayout>

                           </VerticalStackLayout>
                           <Frame.GestureRecognizers>
                              <TapGestureRecognizer Command="{Binding
Path = BindingContext.DescriptionCommand, Source={Reference
CollectionCourse}}"
                              CommandParameter="{Binding Id}"/>
                           </Frame.GestureRecognizers>
                        </Frame>
                     </DataTemplate>
                  </CollectionView.ItemTemplate>
               </CollectionView>
    </VerticalStackLayout>
</ContentPage>
```

ViewModel:

```
[ObservableProperty]
ObservableCollection<Course> courses;

[RelayCommand]
async Task LoadCoursesAsync()
{
    Courses = new ObservableCollection<Course>(await _database
Context.GetCoursesAsync());
}
```

Course Description View

The Course Description screen shows information about a specific course and allows registration or favoriting.

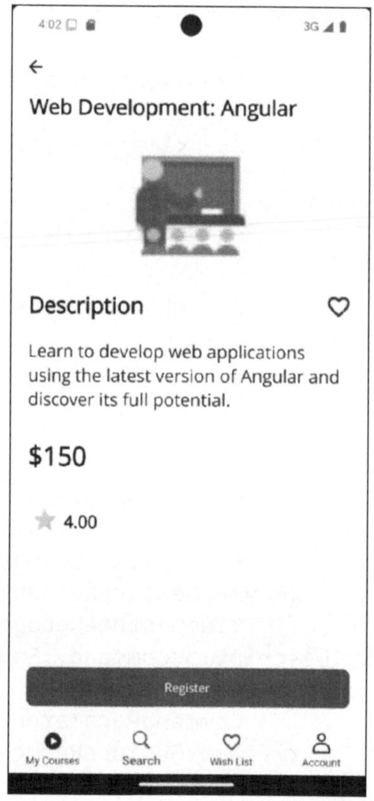

Figure 11.3: *Representation of the course description view*

- Title
- Description
- Favorite toggle button
- Register button

View:

```
<?xml version="1.0" encoding="utf-8" ?>
<ContentPage xmlns="http://schemas.microsoft.com/dotnet/2021/maui"
             xmlns:x="http://schemas.microsoft.com/winfx/2009/xaml"
             x:Class="EducationalApp.Views.CourseDescriptionView"
             xmlns:viewmodels="clr-namespace:EducationalApp.
ViewModels"
             xmlns:models="clr-namespace:EducationalApp.Models"
             x:DataType="viewmodels:CourseDescriptionViewModel">
```

```
    <ScrollView >
        <Grid RowDefinitions="10*, Auto" Padding="20, 0" >
            <VerticalStackLayout Grid.Row="0" Spacing="20">
                <Label Text="{Binding Course.Name}"
                       FontSize="Title"
                       FontAttributes="Bold"/>

                <Image Source="{Binding Course.Image}"
                       HeightRequest="150"
                       WidthRequest="150"/>

                <Grid HeightRequest="35">
                    <Label Text="Description"
                           FontSize="25"
                           FontAttributes="Bold"
                           VerticalOptions="Center"
                           HorizontalOptions="Start" />

                    <Image Source="{Binding HeartIcon}"
                           WidthRequest="30"
                           HeightRequest="30"
                           VerticalOptions="Center"
                           HorizontalOptions="End" >
                        <Image.GestureRecognizers>
                            <TapGestureRecognizer Command="{Binding
HeartIconTapCommand}"/>
                        </Image.GestureRecognizers>
                    </Image>
                </Grid>

                <Label Text="{Binding Course.Description}"
                       FontSize="20"/>

                <Label Text="{Binding Course.Price, StringFormat
='${0:0}'}"
                       FontSize="30"
                       FontAttributes="Bold"
                       Margin="0,10"/>

                <HorizontalStackLayout>

                    <Image Source="star.png"
WidthRequest="30"
HeightRequest="30"
Margin="5,5,5,10"/>

                    <Label Text="{Binding Course.Calification,
```

```
StringFormat='{0:N2}'}"
FontSize="20"
FontAttributes="Bold"
Margin="2,10"
InputTransparent="True" />
                </HorizontalStackLayout>
            </VerticalStackLayout>
            <Button Text="{Binding ButtonText}" Grid.Row="1"
                    Margin="0,20"
                    Command="{Binding TapButtonCommand}" />
        </Grid>
    </ScrollView>
</ContentPage>
```

ViewModel:

```
using CommunityToolkit.Mvvm.ComponentModel;
using CommunityToolkit.Mvvm.Input;
using EducationalApp.Data;
using EducationalApp.Models;
using EducationalApp.Services;
using System.Collections.ObjectModel;

namespace EducationalApp.ViewModels;

public partial class CourseDescriptionViewModel : BaseViewModel,
IQueryAttributable
{

    public void ApplyQueryAttributes(IDictionary<string, object>
query)
    {
        _courseId = query["courseId"] as string;
    }

    private string? _courseId { get; set; }

    [ObservableProperty]
    public string buttonText;

    [ObservableProperty]
    public Course course;

    [ObservableProperty]
    public string heartIcon;

    [ObservableProperty]
    public bool isEnabledButton = false;
```

```
    private readonly DatabaseContext _databaseContext;
    private readonly ICourseService _courseService;

    public CourseDescriptionViewModel(DatabaseContext database
Context, ICourseService courseService)
    {
        HeartIcon = "heart.png";
        ButtonText = "Register";
        _databaseContext = databaseContext;
        _courseService = courseService;
    }

    public async void ConsultCourse()
    {
        IsEnabledButton = false;
        var id = Guid.Parse(_courseId);

        Course = (await _courseService.List()).FirstOrDefault(x =>
x.Id.ToString() == _courseId);

        if (Course != null)
        {
            this.IsFavorite();
        }

        if((await _databaseContext.GetFileteredAsync<Register-
Course>(
                    x => x.Course_Id == _courseId)).FirstOrDefault()
!= null)
        {
            ButtonText = "Unregister";
        }
    }

    public async void IsFavorite()
    {
        try
        {
            var idCourse = Course.Id.ToString() ?? string.Empty;
            if (!string.IsNullOrWhiteSpace(idCourse))
            {
                var favorite = (await _databaseContext.GetFiletered
Async<Favorite>(
                    x => x.Course_Id == idCourse))
                    .Select(x => (Guid?)x.Id)
                    .FirstOrDefault()?.ToString();
```

```
                if (!string.IsNullOrWhiteSpace(favorite))
                {
                    HeartIcon = "heartselect.png";
                }
            }
        }
        catch (Exception ex)
        {
            Console.WriteLine(ex.Message);
        }
    }
```

Wish List View

The Wish List View lists all courses marked as favorites by the user.

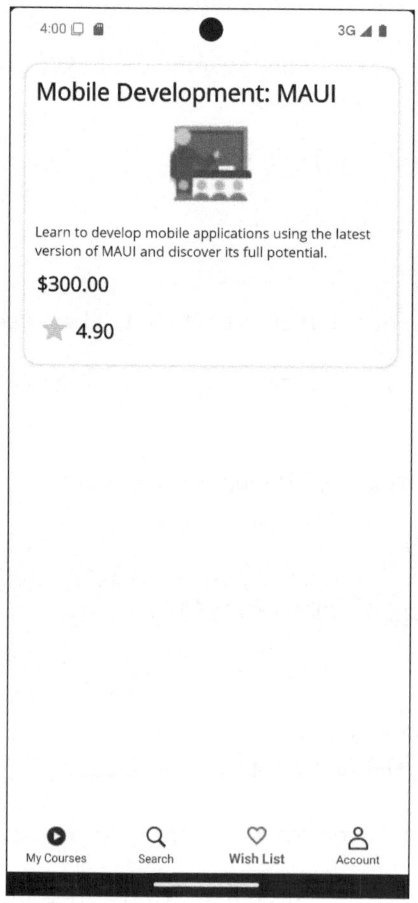

***Figure 11.4**: Representation of the wish list view*

- Courses are favorited by the user.

View:

```
<?xml version="1.0" encoding="utf-8" ?>
<ContentPage xmlns="http://schemas.microsoft.com/dotnet/2021/maui"
             xmlns:x="http://schemas.microsoft.com/winfx/2009/xaml"
             x:Class="EducationalApp.Views.WishListView"
             xmlns:viewmodels="clr-namespace:EducationalApp.
ViewModels"
             xmlns:models="clr-namespace:EducationalApp.Models"
             x:DataType="viewmodels:WishListViewModel">
    <VerticalStackLayout>
        <CollectionView ItemsSource="{Binding WishList}"
         VerticalOptions="Fill"
         x:Name="CollectionCourse"
         Margin="10">
            <CollectionView.ItemsLayout>
                <GridItemsLayout Orientation="Vertical"
                        Span="1"/>
            </CollectionView.ItemsLayout>
            <CollectionView.ItemTemplate>
                <DataTemplate x:DataType="models:Course">
                    <Frame CornerRadius="15"
            BackgroundColor="White"
            BorderColor="#E0E0E0"
            Padding="10"
            Margin="5"
            HasShadow="True">
                        <VerticalStackLayout>
                            <Label Text="{Binding Name}"
                    FontAttributes="Bold"
                    FontSize="Title"
                    InputTransparent="True" />

                            <Image Source="{Binding Image}"
                    WidthRequest="100"
                    Margin="5,5,5,10"/>

                            <Label Text="{Binding Description}"
                    HorizontalTextAlignment="Start"
                    FontSize="14"
                    InputTransparent="True" />

                            <Label Text="{Binding Price, String
Format='${0:N2}'}"
                    FontSize="20"
                    FontAttributes="Bold"
                    Margin="2,10"
```

```
                    InputTransparent="True" />

                        <HorizontalStackLayout>

                            <Image Source="star.png"
WidthRequest="30"
HeightRequest="30"
Margin="5,5,5,10"/>

                            <Label Text="{Binding Calification,
StringFormat='{0:N2}'}"
FontSize="20"
FontAttributes="Bold"
Margin="2,10"
InputTransparent="True" />
                        </HorizontalStackLayout>

                    </VerticalStackLayout>
                    <Frame.GestureRecognizers>
                        <TapGestureRecognizer Command="{Binding
Path = BindingContext.DescriptionCommand, Source={Reference
CollectionCourse}}"
                                CommandParameter="{Binding Id}"/>
                    </Frame.GestureRecognizers>
                </Frame>
            </DataTemplate>
        </CollectionView.ItemTemplate>
    </CollectionView>
    </VerticalStackLayout>
</ContentPage>
```

ViewModel:

```
[ObservableProperty]
ObservableCollection<Course> favoriteCourses;

[RelayCommand]
async Task LoadFavoritesAsync()
{
    var favorites = await _databaseContext.GetFavoritesAsync(UserId);
    FavoriteCourses = new ObservableCollection<Course>(favorites);
}
```

Account View

The Account View provides access to user profile information and account-related actions.

***Figure 11.5**: Representation of the account view*

Typically, it would show:

- Username or email display.
- Option to **Edit Profile** (optional future feature).
- **Logout button** to sign out of the application.
- Application version information (optional).

View:

```
<?xml version="1.0" encoding="utf-8" ?>
<ContentPage xmlns="http://schemas.microsoft.com/dotnet/2021/maui"
             xmlns:x="http://schemas.microsoft.com/winfx/2009/xaml"
             xmlns:viewmodels="clr-namespace:EducationalApp.
ViewModels"
             x:Class="EducationalApp.Views.AccountView"
             x:DataType="viewmodels:AccountViewModel">
    <VerticalStackLayout Margin="10" Spacing="10">

        <HorizontalStackLayout Margin="0,20,0,0">
            <Frame Style="{StaticResource AvatarFrameStyle}"
```

```
               Padding="15"
               WidthRequest="70"
               HeightRequest="70"
               BackgroundColor="#E0E0E0">
                <Image Source="account.png"
                   VerticalOptions="Center"
                   HorizontalOptions="Center"/>
            </Frame>

            <VerticalStackLayout VerticalOptions="Center">
                <Label Text="{Binding Title}"
                   FontSize="Title"
                   FontAttributes="Bold" />

                <Label Text="{Binding SubTitle}"
                   FontSize="Subtitle"
                   TextColor="Silver" />
            </VerticalStackLayout>

        </HorizontalStackLayout>

        <Button Text="Sign Out"
        BackgroundColor="{StaticResource LogOut}"
        Command="{Binding SignOutCommand}"/>

    </VerticalStackLayout>
</ContentPage>
```

ViewModel:

```
using CommunityToolkit.Mvvm.ComponentModel;
using CommunityToolkit.Mvvm.Input;
using EducationalApp.Data;
using EducationalApp.Models;

namespace EducationalApp.ViewModels;

public partial class AccountViewModel : BaseViewModel
{

    [ObservableProperty]
    public string? title;

    [ObservableProperty]
    public string? subTitle;

    private DatabaseContext _databaseContext;
```

```
    private Users? _userLogin;

    public AccountViewModel(DatabaseContext databaseContext)
    {
        _databaseContext = databaseContext;
    }

    public async Task OnAppearingAsync()
    {
        try
        {

            _userLogin = (await _databaseContext.GetAllAsync<Users>())
                .Where(x => x.ActiveSession == true).FirstOr
Default();

            if (_userLogin != null)
            {
                Title = _userLogin.Name;
                SubTitle = _userLogin.Email;
            }
        }
        catch (Exception ex)
        {
            Console.WriteLine($"Error in {nameof(OnAppearingAsync)}:
{ex}");
        }
    }

    [RelayCommand]
    public async Task SignOut()
    {
        try
        {
            if (_userLogin != null)
            {
                _userLogin.ActiveSession = false;
                if (await _databaseContext.UpdateItemAsync
(_userLogin))
                {
                    await Shell.Current.GoToAsync("//LoginView");
                }
            }
        }
        catch (Exception ex)
        {
            Console.WriteLine(ex.ToString());
```

```
            }
        }
    }
```

Video Integration, Favorites, and Registration

Three main parts will be explained, such as video integration, adding or removing from favorites, and registration.

Video Integration

In the Course Content View, you can provide users with a video preview of the course.

***Figure 11.6**: Representation of the course content view*

There are two options to show video content:

- Using a **`WebView`** to embed YouTube/Vimeo/royalty-free videos.
- Using a **`MediaElement`** for local or streaming video playback.

`WebView` Example:

```
<WebView
    Source="{Binding SelectedCourse.VideoUrl}"
    HeightRequest="300"
    WidthRequest="500" />
```

`MediaElement` Example:

```
<MediaElement
    Source="{Binding SelectedCourse.VideoUrl}"
    AutoPlay="False"
    ShowsPlaybackControls="True"
    HeightRequest="300"
    WidthRequest="500" />
```

Favorites Management

Users can **mark or unmark a course as a favorite** directly from the Course Detail screen.

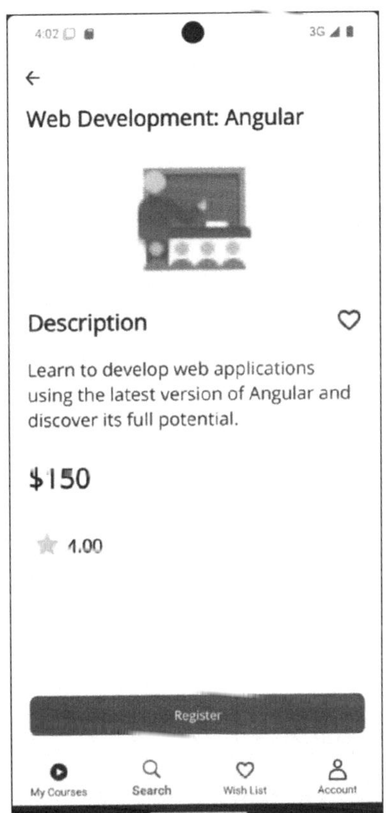

Figure 11.7: *Representation of the course description view*

In the **CourseDescriptionViewModel**:

```
[RelayCommand]
    public async Task HeartIconTap()
    {
        await this.AddOrRemoveToFavorites();
    }

    private async Task AddOrRemoveToFavorites()
    {
        try
        {
            if (HeartIcon.Equals("heart.png"))
            {
                var favorite = new Favorite()
                {
                    Id = Guid.NewGuid(),
                    Course_Id = Course.Id.ToString()
                };
                if (await _databaseContext.AddItemAsync(favorite))
                {
                    HeartIcon = "heartselect.png";
                }
            }
            else
            {
                var idCourse = Course.Id.ToString();
                var favorites = (await _databaseContext.GetFiletered
Async<Favorite>
                              (x => x.Course_Id == idCourse)).Select(x
=> x.Id).ToList();
                if (favorites is null) return;
                foreach (var item in favorites)
                {
                    if (await _databaseContext.DeleteItemByKeyAsync
<Favorite>(item))
                    {
                        HeartIcon = "heart.png";
                    }
                }
            }
        }
        catch (Exception ex)
        {
            Console.WriteLine(ex.Message);
        }
    }
```

The app updates the **Favorites** table accordingly.

Course Registration

Users can **register for a course** by clicking a Register button on the Course Description screen.

ViewModel:

```
[RelayCommand]
    public async Task TapButton()
    {
        if (!ButtonText.Equals("Unregister"))
        {
            await this.Register();
        }
        else
        {
            await this.Unregister();
        }
    }


private async Task Register()
    {
        try
        {
            var registerCourse = new RegisterCourse()
            {
                Id = Guid.NewGuid(),
                Course_Id = Course.Id.ToString()
            };
            if (await _databaseContext.AddItemAsync(registerCourse))
            {
                ButtonText = "Unregister";
            }
        }
        catch (Exception ex)
        {
            Console.WriteLine(ex.Message);
        }
    }

    private async Task Unregister()
    {
        try
        {
```

```
            var removed = false;
            var idCourse = Course.Id.ToString();
            var itemForRemove = (await _databaseContext.GetFiletered
Async<RegisterCourse>
                        (x => x.Course_Id == idCourse)).FirstOr
Default();
            if (itemForRemove is null) return;
            if (await _databaseContext.DeleteItemAsync<Register-
Course>(itemForRemove))
            {
                removed = true;
            }
            if (removed)
                ButtonText = "Register";
        }
        catch (Exception ex)
        {
            Console.WriteLine(ex.Message);
        }
    }
}
```

Search and Filter Courses

The **SearchView** allows users to **search for courses** by title or keyword.

***Figure 11.8**: Representation of the search view*

View:

```
<?xml version="1.0" encoding="utf-8" ?>
<ContentPage xmlns="http://schemas.microsoft.com/dotnet/2021/maui"
             xmlns:x="http://schemas.microsoft.com/winfx/2009/xaml"
             xmlns:viewmodels="clr-namespace:EducationalApp.
ViewModels"
             xmlns:models="clr-namespace:EducationalApp.Models"
             x:Class="EducationalApp.Views.SearchView"
             x:DataType="viewmodels:SearchViewModel">
    <VerticalStackLayout>
        <Frame CornerRadius="20"
               Padding="1,1,1,0"
               Margin="10">
            <SearchBar Placeholder="Search courses" Text="{Binding
SearchText}"/>
        </Frame>

        <ActivityIndicator IsVisible="{Binding IsLoading}"
                   IsRunning="{Binding IsLoading}"
                   VerticalOptions="Center"
                   HorizontalOptions="Center" />

        <CollectionView ItemsSource="{Binding FilteredCoursesList}"
                VerticalOptions="Fill"
                x:Name="CollectionCourse"
                Margin="10">
            <CollectionView.ItemsLayout>
                <GridItemsLayout Orientation="Vertical"
                                 Span="1"/>
            </CollectionView.ItemsLayout>
            <CollectionView.ItemTemplate>
                <DataTemplate x:DataType="models:Course">
                    <Frame CornerRadius="15"
                    BackgroundColor="White"
                    BorderColor="#E0E0E0"
                    Padding="10"
                    Margin="5"
                    HasShadow="True">
                        <VerticalStackLayout>
                            <Label Text="{Binding Name}"
                            FontAttributes="Bold"
                            FontSize="Title"
                            InputTransparent="True" />

                            <Image Source="{Binding Image}"
                            WidthRequest="100"
```

```
                                    Margin="5,5,5,10"/>

                                    <Label Text="{Binding Description}"
                                    HorizontalTextAlignment="Start"
                                    FontSize="14"
                                    InputTransparent="True" />

                                    <Label Text="{Binding Price, String
Format='${0:N2}'}"
                                    FontSize="20"
                                    FontAttributes="Bold"
                                    Margin="2,10"
                                    InputTransparent="True" />

                                    <HorizontalStackLayout>

                                        <Image Source="star.png"
WidthRequest="30"
HeightRequest="30"
Margin="5,5,5,10"/>


                                        <Label Text="{Binding Calification,
StringFormat='{0:N2}'}"
FontSize="20"
FontAttributes="Bold"
Margin="2,10"
InputTransparent="True" />
                                    </HorizontalStackLayout>

                                </VerticalStackLayout>
                                <Frame.GestureRecognizers>
                                    <TapGestureRecognizer Command="{Binding
Path = BindingContext.DescriptionCommand, Source={Reference
CollectionCourse}}"
                                                    CommandParameter="
{Binding Id}"/>
                                </Frame.GestureRecognizers>
                            </Frame>
                        </DataTemplate>
                    </CollectionView.ItemTemplate>
                </CollectionView>
            </VerticalStackLayout>
</ContentPage>
```

ViewModel:

```
    [ObservableProperty]
    private string searchTerm;

    [RelayCommand]
    async Task SearchCoursesAsync()
    {
        var allCourses = await _databaseContext.GetCoursesAsync();
        if (!string.IsNullOrEmpty(SearchTerm))
        {
            Courses = new ObservableCollection<Course>(
                allCourses.Where(c => c.Title.Contains(SearchTerm,
    StringComparison.OrdinalIgnoreCase)));
        }
        else
        {
            Courses = new ObservableCollection<Course>(allCourses);
        }
    }
```

This provides a smooth user experience for navigating through large course catalogs.

Conclusion

In this chapter, we built a complete Educational App using .NET MAUI, focusing on the MVVM architecture to ensure a clean separation of concerns, implementing an SQLite database for local data persistence, and using **AppShell** with TabBar navigation for straightforward yet scalable routing. We structured each screen according to best practices, clearly dividing responsibilities between **Views** and **ViewModels**, and integrated media capabilities for engaging video previews. Additionally, we incorporated functionality for managing favorites and registering for courses. This Educational App lays a solid foundation for more advanced projects, demonstrating clean coding standards, performance optimization, and scalability.

Future Improvements

There are several exciting directions to further enhance this app:

- **Backend Integration:** Connect the app to a remote server or cloud database for real-time synchronization of courses and user data.

- **Push Notifications:** Send course updates, reminders, or announcements to users via device notifications.
- **Quizzes and Assessments:** Add quiz modules after course completions to assess learning.
- **User Progress Tracking:** Implement dashboards showing completion rates, earned certifications, or goals.
- **In-App Purchases:** Offer paid premium courses or subscription models.
- **Multi-language Support:** Expand the app's reach by supporting multiple languages through localization.

Each of these features would take the app from a simple educational prototype to a professional e-learning platform ready for market deployment.

Final Thoughts

By completing this app, you have applied crucial skills necessary for modern cross-platform app development with **.NET MAUI**.

You now have a solid foundation for building real-world, scalable, and responsive applications.

The next steps are to **keep building**, **keep experimenting**, and **keep refining**. Every project you complete will take you one step closer to mastering mobile and desktop development.

Index

Symbols

A

H

J

L

M

N

O

P

R

S